MACHU PICCHU

RYAN DUBÉ

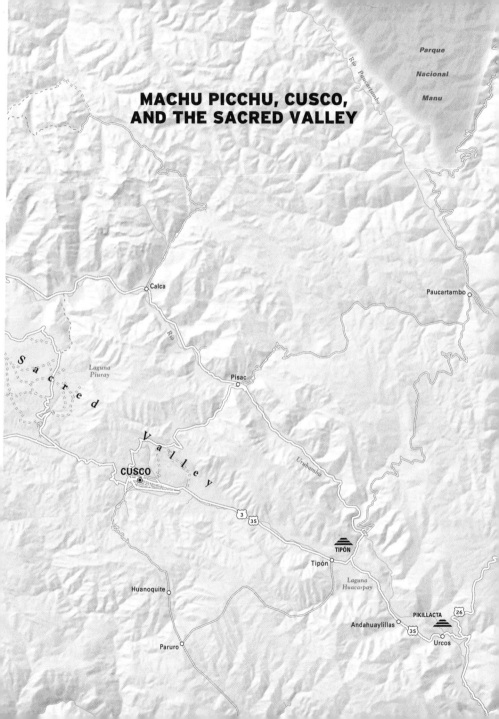

MACHU PICCHU, CUSCO, AND THE SACRED VALLEY

Parque

Nacional

Manu

Río Paucartambo

Calca

Paucartambo

Río

Sacred

Laguna
Piuray

Pisac

Valley

Urubamba

CUSCO

3 3S

TIPÓN

Tipón

Laguna
Huacarpay

Huanoquite

PIKILLACTA 26

Andahuaylillas 3S

Urcos

Paruro

Contents

DISCOVER

Machu Picchu

My first trip to Machu Picchu was over a decade ago. After an arduous trek through the Andes, I can still recall the excitement of approaching the mist-covered Inca citadel just after sunrise. As my group and I caught our breath, the clouds lifted to reveal one of the wonders of the world, with its perfect stonework backed by the towering mountain of Huayna Picchu. We had found Machu Picchu, the lost city of the Incas. It was ours to explore for one unforgettable day. A lot has changed since then, but Machu Picchu retains the memorable, mystical aura that left such an impression on me and the many other travelers who have visited the ruins.

Machu Picchu is the culmination of a once-in-a-lifetime pilgrimage. It begins in the relatively comfortable lower elevations of the Sacred Valley, where quiet Inca communities offer access to the ruins of Pisac and Ollantaytambo, and continues along one of the three major Inca Trails. Each offers a different experience, from the adrenaline-filled adventure of the jungle to the sublime mountain scenery of Salcantay. And then there

Clockwise from top left: Pisac market; an indigenous woman in Cusco; rainbow-colored flag of the Inca Empire; statue in Aguas Calientes; Catedral de Lima on Plaza de Armas in Lima; the ruins of Machu Picchu.

is the beautiful, schizophrenic city of Cusco, where the Incan and colonial cultures live in a fascinating fusion, resulting in an abundance of attractions.

Whether experienced over weeks or just a matter of days, this Peruvian region packs more punch than a pisco sour. Where else in the world can you experience a timeless but still thriving culture, and the center of a lost empire, but in this jewel in South America's crown?

Clockwise from top left: Plaza de Armas in Lima; incredible stonework at Machu Picchu; the stone streets of Cusco; terraces at Moray.

Planning Your Trip

Where to Go

The Sacred Valley

Leave the giddy heights of Cusco behind and head to the Sacred Valley, which the Inca considered paradise for its fertile earth. This charming valley has a great range of lodging, restaurants, and adventure sports, making it an ideal base for acclimatizing. The temples, fortresses, and terracing of **Pisac** and **Ollantaytambo** are second only to Machu Picchu in terms of beauty. Don't miss the concentric circles of **Moray** and the shimmering spectacle of the salt mines of **Salineras.**

Machu Picchu

Follow the rushing **Río Urubamba** down toward the cloud forests that surround the Inca's most fabled achievement: Machu Picchu. The famous lost city is a stunning example of a citadel built in perfect harmony with nature. Stay overnight nearby before and after your visit to maximize your time or, even better, hike either the **Salcantay route,** the **Inca Jungle Trail,** or the original **Inca Trail,** a paved stone path that culminates in a bird's-eye view of the ruins.

Cusco

After visiting the Sacred Valley and Machu Picchu, travelers are acclimatized to Cusco's high altitude. They are also primed for Cusco's complex culture, which remains today an antagonistic mixture of Inca and Spanish cultures. The Spanish erected more than a dozen **baroque churches** atop flawless **Inca walls.**

The rail line ends at Aguas Calientes, the town at the base of Machu Picchu.

Cusco must-visits are the artisan barrio of **San Blas**, the Inca sun temple **Coricancha**, and the fortress of **Sacsayhuamán** overlooking the city.

Stopover in Lima

Once avoided by travelers because of its gray weather and grimy downtown, Lima is making a roaring comeback. On the **Plaza de Armas** (or **Plaza Mayor**), upscale restaurants and cafés now neighbor the country's most important colonial *catedral* and the presidential and archbishop's palaces. The outlying districts of **San Isidro** and **Miraflores** offer the greatest range of lodging, bars, and Peruvian cuisine. Bohemian **Barranco** is the nightlife district and a favored backpackers' den.

When to Go

The traditional time to visit Peru is in the South American winter, **June-August,** when dry, sunny weather opens up over the Andes. Because Peru's dry months coincide perfectly with summer vacation in North America and Europe, this is also the **high season** when most travelers visit Peru. Prices for lodging tend to go up during these months, and Machu Picchu can be crowded. Especially crowded times are **Inti Raymi,** the June 24 sun festival in Cusco, and **Fiestas Patrias,** the national Peruvian holiday at the end of July.

The bulk of the **rainy season** is **December-April,** when trekking and other outdoor activities are hampered by muddy paths and soggy skies. The Inca Trail is closed in February.

To avoid crowds, travel in the **shoulder months** between rainy season and high season. **April, May, September, October,** and even **November** are excellent times to visit Peru. The weather is usually fine, and prices for lodging tend to be lower.

one of Machu Picchu's resident llamas

traditional Peruvian woven fabric

Know Before You Go

Passports and Visas

Citizens of the United States, Canada, United Kingdom, South Africa, New Zealand, and Australia and residents of any other European or Latin American country do not require visas to enter Peru as tourists. Departure taxes for international flights and domestic flights are now usually included in the ticket price. When entering the country, you can get anything from 30 to 180 days stamped into both a **passport** and an **embarkation card** that travelers must keep until they exit the country. If you require more than 30 days, be ready to support your argument by explaining your travel plans and showing your return ticket. Extensions can be arranged at Peru's immigration offices in Lima, Arequipa, Cusco, Iquitos, Puno, and Trujillo.

Transportation

Most travelers arrive to Peru by **plane,** and all international flights into Peru arrive in **Lima.** Travel to **Cusco** is an additional plane ride. Because of flight patterns, most travelers end up spending a night or a day in Lima either when coming from, or going to, Cusco. It's worth spending at least a day or two exploring Lima, preferably on the way home.

Vaccinations

Most travelers to Peru get the vaccinations recommended by the **Centers for Disease Control** (www.cdc.gov), which include **hepatitis A and B** and **typhoid** for the Cusco area.

Avoiding Altitude Sickness

Altitude sickness is a real health concern when traveling to this area. You will know if you're suffering from this illness very soon after your arrival. Symptoms include shortness of breath, quickened heartbeats, fatigue, loss of appetite, headaches, and nausea. There is no way to prevent it, but you can minimize its effects by **avoiding**

heavy exercise until you get acclimatized and by drinking plenty of water and liquids in general. Also avoid alcohol.

Many travelers carry acetazolamide, commonly known as Diamox, usually prescribed by a doctor in doses of 125-250 milligrams, taken during the morning and evening with meals. However, these medications are not for everybody and can cause drowsiness. In Cusco, coca leaf tea *(mate de coca)*, taken in plentiful amounts, is the best remedy for *soroche*, the Quechua word for altitude sickness. A 100-milligram dose of the Chinese herb ginkgo biloba, taken twice a day, seems to work efficiently too. If you feel sick, it's good to know that all hospitals and clinics in Cusco have bottled oxygen.

The best cure for altitude sickness is to ascend slowly. Flying directly to Cusco from Lima and staying overnight is best avoided; go down in altitude to the Sacred Valley, which is below 3,000 meters, and return to Cusco after a few days.

Advance Reservations

Machu Picchu, and the Inca Trail hike to get there, are among the most popular tourist attractions in South America, so you need to book months in advance before your trip. If you want to hike the Inca Trail during the high season of June to September, look at booking six months before. For the rest of the year, three to four months is recommended; however, this may change too. If you are planning a day trip, you should also book tickets once you know when you'll be visiting.

Tickets need to be purchased before arriving at Machu Picchu—not at the gate. You can purchase tickets through any travel agency that offers tours to Cusco and Machu Picchu, as well as through the Ministry of Culture's ticket page (www.machupicchu.gob.pe).

Tour Companies

Trekking in the Andes can be tenuous, especially if you're not adjusted to the altitude. If you prefer not to do one of the multiday hikes into Machu Picchu, the only other option to visit the site is by train. That can be done during a day trip or a two-day stay.

There are several tour companies from Lima, Cusco, and abroad that can organize both the day trips and the longer hikes. Organized tours from Lima or Cusco are helpful in reducing worry about logistics and other issues. But one disadvantage in Cusco is that they may not give enough time to acclimatize to the altitude. If you go with a tour company, consider arriving a day or two before to reduce chances of altitude sickness.

Reputable tour companies include the recommended Fertur Peru (www.fertur-travel.com), which has offices in central Lima at the Plaza Mayor (Junín 211, tel. 01/427-2626) and Miraflores (Schell 485, tel. 01/242-1900) as well as in Cusco (Simon Bolivar F23, tel. 084/22-1304); Condor Travel (Armando Blondet 249, San Isidro, Lima, tel. 01/615-3000; Saphy 848, Cusco, tel. 084/24-8181; www.condortravel.com); and InkaNatura (Manuel Bañón 461, San Isidro, Lima, tel. 01/203-5000; Ricardo Palma J1, Urb. Santa Monica, Cusco, tel. 084/25-5255; www.inkanatura.com). They all offer tours to Machu Picchu, Cusco, and the Sacred Valley.

Explore Machu Picchu

This classic loop starts off in the lush Sacred Valley, where you will explore ruins, experience indigenous culture, and adjust to the altitude. Then you take the train to enjoy the cloud forests and magnificent stonework of Machu Picchu.

At the end of the trip, allow at least two days to take in Cusco, the Spanish Renaissance city built atop Inca foundations.

Day 1

Begin by flying into **Lima,** the capital of Peru. Most planes arrive here at night, so you'll have the choice of either staying at a Lima hotel or hanging out at the airport for an early-morning flight to **Cusco.** Arrange with your hotel ahead of time for transport from Cusco to **Pisac,** a well-preserved Inca village in the **Sacred Valley** that is lower in elevation than Cusco, making it better for adjusting to the altitude.

Day 2

On Day 2 settle in, acclimatize, and explore your surroundings. In Pisac, see the **Inca ruins,** which include a sun temple and fortress complex. Then hike down the mountain back into town to take in the market and dine in the main square. Spend the night in Pisac. (Skip this day as necessary to save time and go to Day 4.)

Day 3

Now that you understand your immediate surroundings, head out and explore farther afield. An excellent option is to explore the weaving village of **Chinchero** before hiking or mountain biking from the enigmatic circular Inca terraces at **Moray** to the crystallized salt mines at **Salineras.** Descend to the Sacred Valley for transport to **Ollantaytambo,** which has plenty of good restaurants for dinner. Spend the night in Ollantaytambo. (Skip this day for time if necessary and go to Day 4.)

Day 4

In Ollantaytambo, explore the ruins in early

Lima's Plaza de Armas is home to the presidential palace and archbishop's residence.

morning to beat the rush. Head first to the **sun temple** above town. It's a great place to understand the layout of both Ollantaytambo and the Sacred Valley, and you can see where the Inca and Spanish battled for control. In the late afternoon, catch a train to **Aguas Calientes** and stay overnight.

Day 5

Take an early-morning shuttle bus to **Machu Picchu.** Wander around the ruins in the morning before the crowds arrive. Then head off midmorning to climb the nearby peak of **Huayna Picchu** and explore the **Temple of the Moon.** Alternatively, walk to the Inca bridge or up to Inti Punku, the Sun Gate. In the afternoon, return to Aguas Calientes for a late lunch and a mug of coca tea. Then board the train to Ollantaytambo and board a comfortable tourist bus back to **Cusco.**

Day 6

Now that you're used to Cusco's altitude, you can walk this city's cobblestoned streets all day long. Start with a morning walk through the neighborhood of **San Blas** and see the Inca sun temple

of **Coricancha.** Save the afternoon for visiting other museums and art galleries.

Day 7

Today you choose between shopping, exploring more museums and churches in Cusco, or taking a walk above town and visiting the ruins of **Q'enqo** and **Sacsayhuamán,** the Inca fortress overlooking Cusco. For more suggestions on Cusco, see page 22.

Day 8

Fly from Cusco to **Lima** early in the morning. Since most planes depart for North America around midnight, you'll have a day in Lima to explore. Start in central Lima on the Plaza de Armas to see the **Catedral de Lima, Palacio Arzobispal de Lima, Palacio del Gobierno,** and the catacombs at **Santo Domingo.** If you're hungry and want to shop, skip downtown Lima and head straight to the swanky neighborhood of **Miraflores** for a ceviche lunch overlooking the Pacific Ocean and an interesting variety of museums, shops, and art galleries. For more suggestions on Lima, see page 25. In the evening, head back to the airport for the flight home.

The Inca used terraces to maximize space for agriculture.

Machu Picchu, a former Inca citadel

Llamas, which are common in the Andes, also call Machu Picchu their home.

Trekking Guide

Most travelers to Peru think there is just one option for trekking to Machu Picchu—the four-day Inca Trail hike—but now there are at least four ways to hike to the Inca citadel. The following treks are the best ways to make a pilgrimage to the lost city of the Inca.

When to Go

The traditional **trekking season** in Peru is **May-August,** but the **best weather** is **June and July.** Avoid the last week in July, when Peru's hotels are often booked solid for the Fiestas Patrias (Independence Day) celebration around July 28. On the Inca Trail, you will encounter fewer people during the months of April, May, September, and October. These **"shoulder months"** are the **best times to trek** in Peru, as they are outside of both the **rainiest months (November-March)** and the busiest tourist months (June-August). April and May, and even March if you don't mind an occasional rainstorm,

are especially scenic because the rainy season has just ended and the highlands are lush and green.

Acclimatization

Plan for at least **3-4 days** to acclimatize before heading out on a trek anywhere in Andean Peru. The Inca Trail has two passes of approximately 4,000 meters, and you will tackle these far better if you are physically ready to do so.

Acclimatize by **sleeping low** and **hiking high.** A great way to acclimatize in the Cusco area is to spend your first few days in the Sacred Valley and then hike up out of the valley floor from places like Pisac, Urubamba, and Ollantaytambo.

Inca Trail

Peru is one of the world's top trekking destinations, and the Inca Trail is Peru's number one trek. Beginning in the high Andes with views of sparkling glaciers, the Inca Trail passes a dozen

Inca Ruins

- **Pisac Ruins:** What's unique about Pisac's ruins, apart from their extraordinary beauty, is their range. Here you will find not only religious Inca architecture, but also residential, agricultural, and military structures.

- **Ollantaytambo Temple:** Second in importance only to Machu Picchu, Ollantaytambo includes some of the Inca's best stonework, including a series of ceremonial baths, elegant trapezoidal doorways, and a sun temple that faces the rising sun. If you only have time to see one other site on the way to Machu Picchu, Ollantaytambo is a good option not only due to the ruins, but also because it is one of the last living Inca cities.

- **Sacsayhuamán:** This stone fortress of huge zigzag walls, carved from stone blocks weighing hundreds of tons, was the scene of the Inca's last stand in Cusco.

the massive stone walls of Sacsayhuamán

major Inca ruins before plunging into the cloud forest toward Machu Picchu.

PLANNING FOR THE INCA TRAIL

The Inca Trail is the only trek in Peru where all trekkers must hike with a **licensed guide** and where there is a **limit of 500 people per day.** These rules are a result of the Inca Trail's popularity and the impact that tens of thousands of trekkers have had on its stone trail and the surrounding ecosystem. For the Inca Trail, your only option is to sign up with a licensed agency—and **sign up early,** as the Inca Trail fills up **six months or more** ahead of time.

As a result of these new rules, **Inca Trail prices** have increased from as low as US$90 in 2000 to a minimum of US$500 today. Local agencies no longer offer last-minute Inca Trail trips; bookings are now done almost exclusively online because the trail's licensed operators have to confirm all reservations several months in advance. To check the official departure availability,

visit the website www.machupicchu.gob.pe. If a date you want is already booked, it's still worth checking with agencies, as they often have cancellations.

FOUR-DAY INCA TRAIL

This hike, which threads two 4,000-meter passes on the way from the high Andes to the cloud forest, has become a signature experience for arriving at Machu Picchu. The first and third days contain moderate hikes, while the second day is the toughest and the fourth day is a short hike to Machu Picchu followed by the full ruins tour.

TWO-DAY INCA TRAIL

If camping is not for you, or you are short on time, try the abbreviated version of the Inca Trail. Trekkers start farther down the trail in order to take in the final set of spectacular ruins at Wiñay Wayna and enter Machu Picchu at dawn and through the Sun Gate. You spend your first day hiking the Inca Trail and seeing ruins and your first night sleeping in a hotel in Aguas Calientes, at the base of Machu Picchu. The second day is spent exploring Machu Picchu.

Other Treks
PLANNING FOR OTHER TREKS
Any other trek in Peru, including the Salcantay alternative route to Machu Picchu, has a couple of planning options. The easiest, and most expensive, is to sign up with a reputable **agency** and let it take care of all the details. But you can also custom-design a trip and then hire an agency to take care of logistics such as transport, food, lodging, porters, cooks, and certified guides. If you can find a reliable **trekking or climbing guide,** available for US$80-110 per day, he or she can organize all these details for you for an extra fee. Or you can do it all on your own, which is complicated to negotiate properly but possible if you speak Spanish and are experienced at trekking.

FIVE-DAY SALCANTAY TREK
While the trek past sacred **Nevado Salcantay,** a 6,000-meter-plus peak, does not contain the stone paths and ruins of the Inca Trail, this five-day trek offers a wilderness experience and spectacular views of the surrounding snow-covered peaks. It's also far less expensive than the Inca Trail, and trekkers are free to travel independently (unlike on the Inca Trail, where all hikers must sign up with a licensed agency). The trek is longer and higher than the Inca Trail, but new sustainable eco-lodges have been built along the Salcantay route to allow trekkers to travel fast and light and stay in relative comfort.

INCA JUNGLE TRAIL
This multi-activity option is a good choice for backpackers on a budget. What it lacks in Inca ruins it makes up for with wonderful cloud forest scenery. The route enters Machu Picchu from the high mountains and cloud forests on its downstream side. Participants are first transported to the Abra Málaga (4,300 meters), a high pass into the jungle, for a stunning mountain bike descent from the alpine zone to lush cloud forest nearly 3,000 meters below. From here, trekkers camp and then head out the second day on a cloud forest trek to Santa Teresa, a riverside village. On the third day, hikers head up the Río Urubamba to Aguas Calientes.

on the five-day Salcantay trek

Saddle up: Horseback riding is one way to take in the beauty of the Andes.

The Sacred Valley has a rich history of conquest and exploration written across a landscape that attracts modern-day adventurers. The altiplano, or high plain, stretches in all directions with endless possibilities for mountain biking, hiking, and horseback riding. The whole area is rich with off-the-beaten-path routes that lead to seldom-visited ruins, Quechua-speaking villages, and breathtaking scenery.

MOUNTAIN BIKING

Maras and Moray

Hop on a mountain bike at the highland village of Maras and cruise across green grasslands to the concentric Inca terraces at Moray. From here, head down a technical single-track past the salt mines of Salineras and keep cruising until you get to Ollantaytambo. Travel agencies can transport your bike back when you are done.

Q'engo and Sacsayhuamán

Explore Inca ruins by mountain bike just outside Cusco. Bike from the shrine of Q'enqo to the hilltop fortress Sacsayhuamán, one kilometer apart.

HORSEBACK RIDING

Urubamba

If you've never ridden a *caballo de paso*, get ready for the unbelievably smooth gait of this world-famous horse. Head to Sol y Luna Hotel, outside Urubamba, to saddle up with a guide and head out on a ride of your choice.

RAFTING

Río Apurímac

Head out on a three-day rafting trip on the upper section of the Río Apurímac. Run Class IV rapids, float past pre-Inca ruins, and camp out on the remote banks of this wild river.

CLIMBING

Via Ferrata

Go rock climbing up the 300-meter face of the Via Ferrata, located in Pacha between Urubamba and Ollantaytambo.

Machu Picchu contrasts with the rugged surroundings.

Trekking Logistics
AGENCIES AND GUIDES
The motto **"you get what you pay for"** is especially true when it comes to hiring a trekking agency or guide. If you skimp on an agency, you can be guaranteed the agency will either skimp on you (poor food, no bathroom tent), the porters (low wages, no health care), or the environment (pit latrines, no regard for Leave No Trace principles). Go with an established, well-recommended agency. See pages 13 and 202 for more information about tour companies.

ON YOUR OWN
Because of the altitude, most groups end up hiring a **porter** (mule driver) who carries loads on donkeys or llamas. It's hard to enjoy the scenery while hiking with a full pack at Peru's altitudes, no matter how fit you are. There are other reasons to hire a porter: It is a great cultural experience, helps the local economy, and makes your trip safer—porters often know the routes as well (or better) than a mountain guide, provide evacuation support, and can serve as camp guards.

Porters will expect you to pay their wages the day that they return to the main town, usually the day after the end of your trek. This means that for a four-day trek, you will pay the porter five days of wages.

Groups usually hire a **cook,** too. Peru's cooks pack in fruit, vegetables, sacks of rice, and often a live chicken or two.

Pay the people you hire fairly and treat them with respect. You are their employer, so you are ultimately responsible for their health and safety. These are some standard **daily wages:** US$10 for a porter and US$8 for every mule, US$15 for camp guardian, US$25 for a porter, and US$25-30 for a cook. Also, you are expected to provide shelter and food for your cook and porters.

If you are on your own, you will have to negotiate the **entry and grazing fees** that Andean communities increasingly charge trekking groups that pass through their lands. The fees change rapidly and, in general, are relatively minor. Grazing fees are generally around US$2-5 per horse. Inquire with an agency about fees ahead of time.

MAPS AND GEAR
The best place to get maps is the **South**

pack horses on the Salcantay trek

American Explorers Club (www.saexplorers.org) in Cusco (Pardo 847, tel. 084/24-5484, www.saexplorers.org) or in the Miraflores neighborhood of Lima (Enrique Palacios 956, tel. 01/444-2150).

Most people who are trekking or climbing on their own bring all their own **gear,** but high-quality equipment can be rented for affordable prices in Cusco and Huaraz. Email agencies ahead of time for reservations and prices.

Peru's tropical sun is intense, so bring strong **sunscreen,** a **sun hat, sunglasses with UV protection,** and a **long-sleeved shirt.** Most trekkers use **trekking poles** for descending the scree slopes and steep trails. The weather is cold, but extreme storms are rare in the dry months from May to September. Bringing plenty of layers, including waterproof ones, is essential. On most Peru treks, **sleeping bags** rated for 0°F and thermal long underwear or fleece pants are fine.

Pretty much all supplies, with the exception of freeze-dried **food,** are available in markets in Cusco. You'll find pasta, powdered soup, cheese, powdered milk, beef jerky, dried fruit, and more. **White gas** (*bencina blanca*) is sold at hardware stores along Calle Plateros in Cusco and at numerous places in Huaraz and Caraz. Get a shop recommendation from an agency or gear store to ensure you find the highest-quality gas, and fire up your **stove** before you go to make sure everything works. Remember that airlines sometimes reject travelers with camp stoves and fuel bottles that have been previously used. It's best to travel with a new stove and bottles, if at all possible.

HAZARDS AND PRECAUTIONS

While the vast majority of trekkers to the Cusco and Huaraz areas never encounter any safety threats, the more popular trekking areas have seen an increase in **theft.** If you leave your camp for a day hike, make sure to leave behind a camp guardian, such as a porter. Minimize the impact by bringing the **minimum of valuables** and only enough **cash** for the duration of your trek.

The main hazards of trekking in Peru, however, are straightforward: **sun, altitude,** and **cold.** If you protect yourself from the sun, acclimatize properly, and have the right gear, you will have a great time.

Two Days in Cusco

For the Incas, Cusco was the center of the world from where they expanded their vast empire across western South America. While it's a gateway to Machu Picchu and other ancient ruins, the city is just as splendid in its own right. There is the history, as seen in its ornate churches and Inca walls. There is good shopping for artisan products and alpaca clothing. And increasingly, there are great restaurants and fun nightlife. Because of its altitude, we recommend visiting Cusco after Machu Picchu and the Sacred Valley to better acclimatize.

Day 1

After buying your *boleto turístico* (tourist ticket), which covers admission to 16 sites, head to the **Plaza de Armas** to start your day with a visit to Cusco's churches. First, step inside Cusco's baroque **cathedral,** famous for its gold decorations and Last Supper painting with a guinea pig served for dinner. On the right of the cathedral there is the **Iglesia de Jesús María** (1733)

and on the left there is the **Iglesia del Triunfo** (1539), the first Christian church in Cusco. The last church to visit is the 17th-century **Iglesia de la Compañía,** which was built by the Jesuits on top of the palace of Inca Huayna Cápac.

Before lunch, head up the alley to the left of the cathedral to the **Museo Inka,** a colonial home with Inca ceramics, textiles, and mummies. Farther up the alley is the **Museo de Arte Precolombino (MAP),** which has an impressive collection of ceramics, painting, and jewelry made of silver and gold.

For lunch, head over to either **Trujillo** or **Nuna Raymi** to try some Peruvian dishes. After a cup of coca tea, check out the **12-sided Inca stone** and then wander among the cobblestone streets of the **San Blas** neighborhood, where many artisan families have shops. Try **Artesanía Mendívil** for religious sculptures and **Centro de Textiles Tradicionales del Cusco** for high-quality textiles.

For dinner, relax at the **Inka Grill,** an excellent

Cusco was the capital of the Inca Empire.

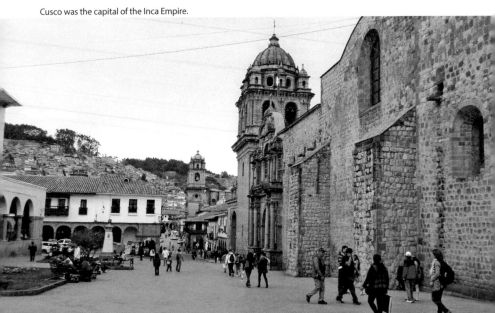

The Sacred Steps of the Inca

Step designs are found everywhere in important Inca ruins and are versions of the *chacana,* a sacred Andean symbol similar to the Christian crucifix. The *chacana* is the key to understanding the spiritual beliefs of the Inca, which are alive and well today in the syncretic Catholic belief systems of Peru's Andean people. The *chacana* is based on the Southern Cross, a constellation revered by the Inca.

The Andean Cross, or Cruz Andina, is a combination of two figures: an equal-armed cross that indicates the four corners of the Inca world (north, south, east, and west) and a superimposed square indicating the four elements of Inca cosmology (water, air, earth, and fire).

The three steps on each side of the *chacana* correspond to the three levels of the Inca universe. The bottom step is the underworld *(uku pacha),* associated with serpents, death, and the wisdom of ancestors. The middle step is the earth *(kay pacha)* and relates to everyday human life, pumas, and life energy. And the top level is the sky or heavens *(hanan pacha),* linked to condors, stars, virtuous beings, and gods.

You will see the *chacana* symbol displayed in art and jewelry everywhere in Cusco. You can see the *chacana* in different ruins in the Cusco area:

chacana steps at Machu Picchu's Royal Tomb

- **Ollantaytambo:** The famous walls of Ollantaytambo's **Temple of the Sun** are decorated with faint step patterns of the *chacana.* At the foot of the temple, the **Princess Baths** are a sequence of fountains decorated with elaborate *chacana* symbols.

- **Pisac:** There is the top half of a *chacana* symbol in front of Pisac's **Intihuatana,** the sacred stone pillar used to measure the sun's movement. Above the *chacana,* sculpted out of rock, is another stone pillar that is easy to miss if you aren't looking for it. During the June 21 winter solstice, the sun casts a shadow from this pillar that hits the *chacana.* The resulting shadow completes the bottom half of the *chacana* and marks the beginning of the harvest season.

- **Machu Picchu:** *Chacana* step patterns are found throughout the ruins, most notably at the **Funerary Rock, Intihuatana,** and **Royal Tomb.**

- **Q'enqo** and **Sacsayhuamán:** These two ruins, near each other on the outskirts of Cusco, both feature prominent rock outcroppings carved with *chacana* steps. Below Sacsayhuamán is a cave with a *chacana*-shaped entrance.

choice for Novoandino cuisine. For a drink, head to **The Muse** lounge, or if you're looking to party, try any of the bars on the Plaza de Armas.

Day 2

Get up early and grab a taxi or bus to the Inca ruins just outside of Cusco. Depending on how you're feeling, you can start at the farthest ruin, **Tambomachay,** known as the Inca's Bath, and walk eight kilometers back down into Cusco, visiting along the way **Puka Pukara,** known as the Inca's "red fort"; the shrine of **Q'engo;** and

Peruvian Cuisine

Peruvian food has won international attention for its rich diversity and flavor. Here are just a few of the Peruvian specialties. Keep in mind that some—like the raw seafood dish ceviche—are best on the coast where the fish is fresh, rather than the highlands.

These dishes are served at almost all Peruvian restaurants:

- *Causa limeña* is a creamy potato dish that often includes chicken or seafood, along with avocado and other vegetables in the middle.

- *Lomo saltado* is a beef stir-fry served with french fries and rice.

- *Ají de gallina* is a chicken stew in a hot and creamy yellow sauce, often served with potatoes and an egg.

- *Papa rellena* are stuffed potatoes with meat.

- *Tallarin verde,* a green Peruvian spaghetti pesto, is a great option for pasta.

- *Pollo a la brasa*—flavorful rotisserie chicken with a heaping side of french fries—is also a favorite among Peruvians.

Other dishes are more regional. In Cusco, many restaurants serve *cuy,* or guinea pig, as well as *alpaca* steaks. Another specialty in the highlands is *pachamanca,* where chicken, lamb, beef, and other meats and vegetables are cooked in an oven in the ground. Wait until you get back to Lima for ceviche.

pisco sour

For drinks, the most popular is the pisco sour, the cocktail made from the grape brandy pisco. Another great pisco drink is the Chilcano, a mix of pisco and ginger ale. Also worth a try is Inca Kola, a yellow, bubble gum-tasting soft drink that competes with Coca-Cola in Peru. While in Cusco, also be sure to have a hot cup of coca tea in the morning and evening to warm up and help with altitude sickness.

Sacsayhuamán, which is the must-see fortress and the best of the four ruins. A shorter walk starts at Q'engo and includes Sacsayhuaman.

After the vigorous morning, you'll be hungry. Try Incanto, which has Italian and fusion dishes. After a rest, walk over to Coricancha and Santo Domingo, where the Spaniards built a Dominican church on top of the foundations of the Inca sun temple. For a music-and-dance show, there is Centro Qosqo de Arte Nativo, and then head back to the Museo de Arte Precolombino for a late dinner at the MAP Café, where you can try traditional Andean cuisine in a gourmet setting.

Two Days in Lima

While the Peruvian capital has developed a bad reputation over the years, it is making a comeback as a modern megacity known for its colonial history, delicious cuisine, and excellent nightlife. There are endless ways to explore Lima, but here are a few suggestions.

Day 1

Head to central Lima, which is jammed full of interesting colonial houses, churches, and museums. After visiting the **Plaza de Armas**, do a tour of the **Casa de Aliaga**, a half block from the plaza. Afterward, check out the **Santo Domingo** church, and then walk upriver along Ancash to Desamparados. Peek inside Lima's old train station and then head a few doors down to the **Museo de Sitio Bodega y Quadra.** Continue down Ancash and you'll reach **San Francisco**, the 16th-century convent best known for its catacombs, or public cemetery.

After a tour of San Francisco, walk back toward the Plaza Mayor, stopping at the historic **El Cordano** for a quick drink. Back on the Plaza Mayor, walk six or so blocks to Plaza San Martín along a commercial walkway, where you'll find a statue honoring Argentine liberator José San Martín.

By this point you're probably thinking of lunch. Grab a taxi and head to Miraflores and the elegant **Huaca Pucllana** restaurant, next to the ancient adobe and clay pyramid of the same name. Or ask the driver to take you to the **Museo Larco** in Pueblo Libre. At Larco, pay your entrance fee and head to the excellent restaurant in the back. After lunch, admire the museum's collection of textiles and ceramics.

In the evening, find out what all the fuss is about Peruvian cuisine. Put on some long pants and head out to one of Lima's top restaurants, like **Astrid y Gastón, Central,** or **Rafael.** After an unforgettable meal, finish the day off with some live music. If you're in the mood for

wooden colonial balcony in Lima

Iglesia de San Francisco in Lima

mosaic benches along Miraflores's *malecón*

a show of Peruvian folkloric dance, go to **Brisas del Titicaca.** If you want jazz, try **Jazz Zone.**

Day 2

Your second day in Lima starts with a stroll along **Miraflores's** *malecón,* the elegant promenade overlooking the Pacific Ocean. Enjoy the green parks perched on top of the seaside cliffs. After, walk a few blocks to Parque Kennedy, where artists display their paintings during the weekends. Next, grab a taxi for the short ride to the **Museo de la Nación,** a large museum that provides a good layout of Peru's archaeological history.

Grab an early lunch and beat the lines. Try ceviche at **Punto Azul,** which also serves heaping plates of other seafood, or **Pescados Capitales.** After your meal, take a cab to Barranco, Lima's bohemian district. Get off at its main plaza and wander its streets lined with beautiful old mansions. Walk over to the romantic *puente de suspiros* (Bridge of Sighs). A short walk on the cobblestone pathway underneath the bridge will take you to the sea. Back on Barranco's main streets, check out one of the many shops selling sophisticated handicrafts. At night, stay in Barranco. For a rowdy night among locals, go to a *peña,* like **La Candelaría.** For some live rock, go to **La Noche.**

The Sacred Valley

Look for ★ to find recommended
sights, activities, dining, and lodging.

Highlights

★ **Pisac Ruins:** What's unique about Pisac's ruins, apart from their extraordinary beauty, is their range. Here you will find not only religious Inca architecture, but also residential, agricultural, and military structures (page 32).

★ **Moray and Salineras:** This six-hour downhill hike is a gorgeous introduction to the Sacred Valley. Start at Moray, a complex of concentric agricultural terraces, and then head downhill past Salineras, a centuries-old salt mine that is still in operation (page 46).

★ **Ollantaytambo Temple:** Second in importance only to Machu Picchu, Ollantaytambo includes some of the Inca's best stonework, including a series of ceremonial baths, elegant trapezoidal doorways, and a sun temple that faces the rising sun (page 51).

★ **Inca Granaries (Pinkuylluna):** This moderate, 1.5-hour hike offers a spectacular view of Ollantaytambo, its gleaming sun temple, and interesting grain storehouses, known in Quechua as *colcas* (page 53).

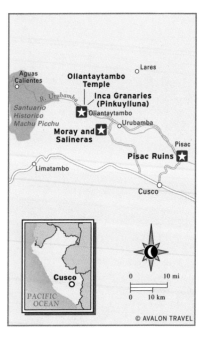

Gazing upon this astonishingly beautiful valley, it's no surprise that the Inca considered it sacred and an earthly reflection of the Milky Way galaxy.

While stargazers can debate the intricacies of Inca astronomy, what is beyond doubt is the fertility of the Sacred Valley. As Cusco was considered the navel of the world by the Inca, the Sacred Valley was the breadbasket and the Río Urubamba that flows through it the lifeblood. The valley's warm climate and sunbaked red granite hills have always been ideal for agriculture, and this region continues to keep Cusco well fed with myriad varieties of vegetables and grains.

The Sacred Valley runs roughly from Pisac to Ollantaytambo and beyond to Piscacucho before plunging toward the cloud forests around Machu Picchu and the jungle farther on. The climate is perfect: warmer than the chilly, thin air of Cusco and, crucially, below 3,000 meters, so altitude sickness is less of a factor. Inca palaces, fortresses, and sun temples dot this valley, along with charming Andean villages that produce and sell some of the country's finest handicrafts. Along with Machu Picchu and Cusco, the Sacred Valley is at the top of Peru's must-see list.

Two of the most interesting destinations in the Sacred Valley are the Inca villages of Pisac and Ollantaytambo. Pisac has always been well known for its daily handicrafts market, which gets busy on Sunday, Tuesday, and Thursday. But the market is not what it used to be, and the important Inca ruins in the hills above town are arguably a bigger draw. These ruins offer an interesting window into Inca life because they combine religious, civilian, and military architecture in a single location.

Ollantaytambo is Peru's best example of a living Inca village, where people still reside in graceful Inca homes and use the same waterways used by their ancestors 500 years ago. Ollantaytambo's sun temple towers above town and contains Inca stonework as impressive as that found in Cusco and Machu Picchu, and it is the second-most impressive Inca site in Peru.

Most Inca architecture, especially in the Sacred Valley, was built with the movements of the sun and stars in mind. The

---

Previous: storehouse at Ollantaytambo; view of the fertile Sacred Valley. **Above:** doorway at the Pisac ruins.

The Sacred Valley

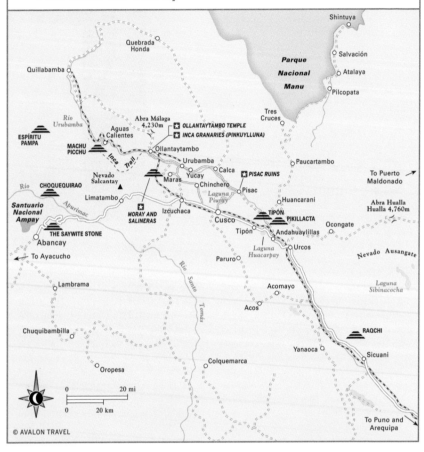

temple-fortresses of Pisac and Ollantaytambo both correspond precisely to lunar and solar events. Moray, an area of terraced natural depressions, was probably designed to use sun and shade as part of an agricultural laboratory. The Inca went to great effort to redirect the Río Urubamba into a stone channel—to maximize farming land, but also probably to reflect the shape of the Milky Way. The great care the Inca took in aligning buildings with the sun, moon, and stars reflects their vision of the Sacred Valley as a sacred, celestial landscape.

PLANNING YOUR TIME

Most travelers arrive at the giddy heights of Cusco (3,400 meters) and plan their trip from there, visiting the Sacred Valley on day trips and seeing Machu Picchu in one very long day. This is the worst way of doing it. You are far better off getting out of Cusco as soon as you arrive and staying in the warmer, lower towns of the Sacred Valley. The first reason is that altitude sickness is far less of a problem below 3,000 meters. You may experience light-headedness and breathlessness, but it will be far less severe than in Cusco.

Additionally, by staying in Pisac, Urubamba, or Ollantaytambo, you are afforded far more time to see these spectacular sets of ruins. The standard one-day Sacred Valley tour from Cusco is far from ideal; this tour whisks visitors through the Pisac ruins and market, lunch in Urubamba, and an afternoon visit to the Ollantaytambo ruins, which are very busy by lunchtime and heaving by midafternoon. By staying overnight in town, we were at Ollantaytambo ruins at 8am and were the first tourists there.

Furthermore, visiting the Sacred Valley first is infinitely preferable to seeing it after Machu Picchu, as any ruins seem modest in comparison to the region's main attraction. It's far better to build upwards in scale, seeing Pisac, Moray, and Ollantaytambo before Machu Picchu. Finish up in Cusco, which will keep you busy for several days when you are acclimatized and ready to tackle this fascinating city. The best plan is to start your Peru trip with 2-3 days in the Sacred Valley and then take a train from Ollantaytambo to Machu Picchu. Return can be from Machu Picchu directly to Cusco, or you can go back to Ollantaytambo and take a *taxi colectivo*.

Pisac and Vicinity

Pisac is an attractive Andean town with a pleasant center and the most important Inca ruins in the Sacred Valley besides Ollantaytambo. A bigger draw for tourists

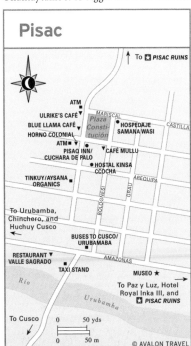

used to be the Pisac market, but its popularity has waned, not least because similar wares can be found all over the Sacred Valley. Some day tours now bypass the market altogether. The town still swells with day-trippers on Sunday, Tuesday, and Thursday mornings but is very quiet later in the day. Aside from the market, there is little to see in Pisac itself, but it is a very agreeable town in which to spend a few hours.

The Inca fortress above town contains a rare combination of residential, military, and religious construction that sheds light on the daily life of the Inca. In the high plains beyond the fortress, there are remote villages that can be reached only on foot. Several hotels lead trips into the surrounding countryside to visit these Quechuan villages, spectacular mountain lakes, and the remote ruins of Cuyo Chico and Cuyo Grande.

SIGHTS
Pisac Market
Pisac used to be one of the biggest *artesanía* markets in South America, but it is quieter than it used to be. The market begins every day at 9am when the first tour buses arrive from Cusco and winds down around 5pm

when the last tourists leave. The town's main square is filled with stalls selling the full range of Peruvian *artesanía*: carved gourds *(mates burilados)*, ceramics, felt hats, alpaca sweaters and mittens, musical instruments, paintings, antiques, a huge variety of trinkets, and, most of all, weavings and jewelry. Even if you are not buying, the café balconies overlooking the market offer superb people-watching as hundreds of camera-toting tourists haggle with Quechuan-speaking merchants. Quality tends to be in the low to middle range—the good stuff is found in the homes of the *artesanos* themselves or in upscale city galleries—but, after a bit of bargaining, prices can be very reasonable, especially if buying in quantity.

More interesting is the authentic Sunday market, when campesinos from surrounding villages set up a barter market, or *mercado de treque,* which is an ancient Peruvian custom and an interesting example of the informal economies upon which highlanders depend. Quechuan-speaking people sit behind piles of vegetables in one corner of the square. They sell these products to buy essentials (salt, sugar, kerosene, matches, and medicines) but also trade to acquire other foods, such as oranges from the Quillabamba Valley. It exists side by side with the Pisac market but ends by 3pm so that villagers can walk home before dark. Also on Sunday only, Masses in Quechua are held at 6am and 11am in **San Pedro Apóstol de Pisac,** the colonial church on the main square that was rebuilt after the 1950 earthquake. The church has Inca foundations and an interesting collection of colonial paintings.

★ Pisac Ruins

Pisac is one of the valley's few great Inca ruins that features all types of architecture—agricultural, hydraulic, military, residential, and religious. Little is known for certain about Pisac's precise function, and there is no mention of it in Spanish chronicles, perhaps because it was never used by the Inca in their battles against the invaders. However, it probably began as a military garrison to guard against incursion from the Anti people, who occupied the easternmost corner of the empire known as **Antisuyo** (present-day Paucartambo and the Manu jungle). Inca emperor Pachacútec probably built Pisac's imperial architecture and may have used it as a royal residence, while the temples indicate that Pisac also had religious status.

There are two main entrances to the ruins, where you need to present or purchase the

the Inca fortress above Pisac

boleto turístico. If taking the steep walk from town, you arrive at the terraces at **Andenes Acchapata** and can climb up toward the Intihuatana, the ceremonial center, and the agricultural and urban zones. However, most people take a taxi to enter the ruins from the parking area next to the main entrance at **Qantus Raccay,** one of three residential areas in Pisac. It is composed of rough stone buildings, walls with niches, and small squares. These were probably military garrisons and, in the style of a medieval castle, shelter for villagers in times of war. From here you can appreciate some of the best views of the terraces of Pisac—there are 500 in total. Corn was grown on the lower terraces, potatoes in the middle, and quinoa grain on the high terraces. To the right, embedded in the hillside, is a huge Inca cemetery with some 3,500 tombs, although the mummies are long gone.

An Inca trail traverses the hillside, arrives at a small pass, then heads up and over a rocky summit to the sun temple. At the pass, four purification baths flow with water brought down from a lake at 4,500 meters. On the other side of the pass to the left, a 10-minute detour around the corner reveals Inca buttresses, which were once spanned by a hanging bridge made of plant fibers.

The main path crosses through a military wall with a perfect trapezoidal door, known as the **Door of the Serpent.** Above is the second residential area, **Hanam P'isaq** (upper Pisac). The path now climbs up steep staircases and niches carved out of the rock itself, alongside a cliff and through the **Q'alla Q'asa** (Split Rock) tunnel. Faced with a vertical rock face, Inca engineers decided to enlarge a rock fissure and bore through the entire cliff—how they did this, with no iron or steel implements, remains a mystery.

The best view of the **Intihuatana,** which means "sun calendar" in Quechua, is from above. Like the sun temple at Machu Picchu, the Intihuatana is an oval building of perfect masonry encasing a votive rock. The pillar atop the rock was used to track the sun's movements, and, fascinatingly, the sun rises precisely above one peak to the east on June 21 and another on December 21. The walls of five other temples surround the temple, including one that was probably devoted to the moon. To the right is a series of restored baths that flow into an underground canal. In front of the Intihuatana is a sacred *chacana* (Inca cross).

Off the easier trail back to the main entrance of the ruins is **P'isaqa,** the third and

wide, sweeping Inca terraces near Pisac

finest residential area, with its own ritual bath. These were probably homes for the elite, as opposed to the military garrisons closer to the pass. Most people head back at this point to the main entrance, though there are two trails from here that make a pleasant two-hour walk back to Pisac. One descends directly to the Río Quitamayo, with spectacular views, while the other drops through the lookout towers of Coriwayrachina and an area of steep terracing. Both trails merge on the other side of the river for the final descent into town.

There are several ways to see the Pisac ruins (7am-3pm, admission only with *boleto turístico*), but the most popular is to take a US$8 taxi up the eight-kilometer highway to the main entrance. Allow 1.5 to 2 hours to see the ruins and another 2 hours to walk downhill all the way to town (or take a taxi back for a further US$8).

Museo Comunitario de Pisac

In 2009, **Museo Comunitario de Pisac** (Amazonas and Federico Zamalloa, 8am-5pm Sun.-Fri., free) opened southeast of Pisac's center with an exhibition of traditional textiles and a small collection of ceramics from the Pisac ruins. The highlight is the exhibition of Inca mummies.

ENTERTAINMENT AND EVENTS

There are no discos in Pisac, but the cafés around the square serve beer and cocktails.

Pisac's big festival is **Fiesta de la Virgen del Carmen**, which begins on July 15 and runs for five days. The first day includes a horse-riding contest followed by a series of religious processions and dances.

SHOPPING

Apart from the Pisac market, there are crafts shops open all week long (10am-9pm daily) on all the main streets leading from the square, especially **Mariscal Castilla, San Francisco,** and **Bolognesi.** Contemporary art is sold in the first floor of the **Café Art Gallery Mullu**

(Plaza de Armas 352, tel. 084/20-3073, www. mullu.pe).

Aysana Organics (Av. Pardo, cell tel. 984-081-970, 10am-4pm daily) is a good place to pick up healthy products. Everything from soap to chocolate, dried fruit, and coca toffee is available.

FOOD
Cafés, Bakeries, and Ice Cream

★ **Ulrike's Café** (Manuel Prado, tel. 084/20-3195, 7am-9pm daily, US$5) offers a lunch menu (US$8), vegetarian options, and pizza. Ulrike Simic, the German owner of this playful establishment, makes a delectable array of cheesecakes, including chocolate chip, coffee, and lemon. The colorful walls and laid-back atmosphere make this the perfect respite on busy market days.

★ **Café Art Gallery Mullu** (Plaza de Armas 352, tel. 084/20-3073, 9am-8pm daily, US$5) has the most diverse menu in town. Billed as an Asian fusion restaurant, it has an interesting collection of contemporary art on the first floor and a café with nice market views on the second. The menu blends Peruvian, Asian, and international dishes, including Thai curry, *tahine* lamb stew, and Kashmiri ravioli.

Blue Llama Café (Plaza de Armas, tel. 084/20-3135, 7am-8pm daily, US$5) offers good food and service. Great coffee, brownies, and pancakes go down well early in the day, and soups and mains such as teriyaki chicken, pot roast, and trout are good for dinner. It's a comfy place to hang out with a book or friends.

Tinkuy Café (Pardo, no phone, breakfast, lunch and dinner daily) is another fun place in Pisac, where owners Alfredo and Nancy offer a good range of juices, coffee, and vegetarian food. They have a daily set menu for US$5. Alfredo speaks English and can help with tours of the area.

Peruvian

The best place for trout in Pisac is **Restaurant**

Natural High: Coca Tea

The coca plant's bad reputation is rather unfair. Although its most lucrative use involves refining its alkaloids into cocaine, the most natural use of the leaves is as a refreshing and useful drink.

Mate de coca is a very popular tea in the Andes, renowned for its medicinal properties and ability to combat altitude sickness. The tea itself can be made with teabags, but it's better with fresh leaves. It looks and tastes a little like Japanese green tea but sweeter. Amusingly, just like decaffeinated coffee, de-cocainized tea does exist, although it's hard to find. Coca tea containing alkaloids remains illegal in the United States, so you are inviting trouble if you attempt to take any back with you.

Although coca tea's effectiveness in combating altitude sickness has not been scientifically proven, the stimulant seems to help oxygenate the blood and ease discomfort. The average cup contains approximately 4 milligrams of alkaloids, so it is mildly stimulating. As a guide, a line of cocaine contains 20 milligrams, so five cups of coca tea could conceivably get you a little high.

Valle Sagrado (Amazonas 116, tel. 084/43-6915, 8am-8pm daily, US$4-6). During lunch, this place is packed with locals who come not only for the trout but for chicken, soups, sandwiches, and lamb ribs.

The gourmet option in town is **Cuchara de Palo** (Plaza de Armas, tel. 084/20-3062, www.pisacinn.com, 7:30am-8:30pm daily, US$5-15), inside Pisac Inn. The atmosphere (bright green walls and tree-trunk tables) and the food are all natural. Vegetarians should try the *quinoa chaufa* (fried quinoa), and meat eaters should go for *lomo saltado*.

Markets

The best supermarket is **Sofis Market** (Bolognesi s/n, tel. 084/20-3017, 6:30am-10pm daily).

ACCOMMODATIONS
US$10-25

The best budget option is **Hostel Kinsa Ccocha** (Arequipa 307, tel. 084/20-3101, US$15 s, US$20 with private bathroom), a block from the Plaza de Armas, which has several plain, clean rooms with shared or private bath. Ask for a newer room; they have higher ceilings.

Hospedaje Samana Wasi (Plaza de Armas 509, tel. 084/20-3133, US$15 s, US$20 d with private bathroom) offers small rooms overlooking the plaza with shared or private bathrooms, and a restaurant with a great value three-course set menu for just US$5 (7am-9pm daily).

US$25-50

Pisac Inn (Plaza de Armas, tel. 084/20-3062, www.pisacinn.com, US$45 s, US$55-65 d with breakfast) is owned by Roman Vizcarra and Fielding Wood-Vizcarra, a Peruvian-American couple who founded the hotel in 1993. The adobe building, covered in bright murals, includes the highly regarded Cuchara de Palo restaurant, whose balconies overlook the market square. Additional perks include a US$35 Cusco airport pickup, laundry, and a constant supply of water from the hotel's own well. Roman speaks English, Spanish, Quechua, Italian, and German and leads tours throughout the area that combine culture with spirituality (www.peruculturaljourneys.com).

New Yorker Diane Dunn's pride and joy, ★ **Paz y Luz** (off the road to the ruins 2 km outside of town, cell tel. 984-216-293, www.pazyluzperu.com, US$45 s, US$65 d with breakfast, cash in *soles* and Mastercard only on arrival, Visa in advance) is a collection of earth-colored lodges on the edge of the Río Urubamba outside Pisac. Paz y Luz (peace and light) has become a center for spirituality in the Sacred Valley, and its focal point is the healing center, the inspiration for Diane's book *Cusco: Gateway to Inner Wisdom*. Diane is a kindhearted host, and the location is spectacular, with wonderful views of the mountains and Pisac ruins. The 24 rooms are located in three buildings, all comfortable and tastefully decorated, with new bathrooms. A central area has a woodstove, dining table, and polished wood staircase. The growing complex includes a restaurant, conference room, meditation room, massage, and rooms for long-term residents. Two-bedroom bungalows with their own living room, fireplace, kitchen, and bathroom are under construction at the back. Prices for long-term guests and descriptions of spiritual workshops and tailor-made tours are on the website.

US$50-100

On the outskirts of town, **Hotel Royal Inka III Pisac** (on road to the ruins 1 km outside of town, tel. 084/20-3064, www.royalinkahotel.pe, US$58 s, US$80 d) is located in a converted hacienda with a mid-19th-century chapel, but most of the rooms are in a cold and charmless modern addition. It offers an Olympic-size pool (available to nonguests), a private whirlpool tub, sauna, tennis court, horses, bikes, a game room, restaurant, bar, videos, and a spa. Without a discount, this hotel can seem overpriced, especially when compared to cheaper and more charming options nearby.

Also outside town is **Melissa Wasi** (on road to the ruins 1 km outside of town, tel. 084/79-7589 or 998-676-860, www.melissa-wasi.com, US$95 d, bungalow US$130), a charming hotel with eight double rooms and three separate bungalows built into the hillside. Owners Joyce and Chito have created a beautiful house with colorful gardens. Bungalows sleep up to four people, and all have WiFi and a complete kitchen.

INFORMATION AND SERVICES

Advice on Pisac and surrounding excursions is available from Tinkuy Café, Ulrike's Café, Paz y Luz, or Pisac Inn.

There is a clinic and pharmacy above the plaza near the public parking area. Other pharmacies are on Bolognesi and are generally open 8am-9pm daily, with a midday closure for lunch.

There is a **Global Net ATM** on the corner of the main square up from Blue Llama Café and a money changer on the square near the church.

A **mailbox** is on the main square inside Restaurant Samana Wasi, which also sells

The hotel and healing center Paz y Luz has a stunning location on the outskirts of Pisac.

stamps. There are **phone booths** at Sofis Market on Bolognesi and near the municipality on the main square. **Internet** is available at several sites around the Plaza de Armas. Hours are usually 9am-10pm daily.

GETTING THERE AND AROUND

Buses for Pisac leave Cusco from Avenida Pachacútec, southwest of the center toward the bus terminal, every 20 minutes and charge US$1 for the one-hour journey. For a 45-minute ride, hire a taxi in Cusco's Plaza de Armas for US$25 or prebook with a Pisac hotel for US$30. Taxis are also available at the airport but are more expensive. Buses drop passengers off at the bridge on the main highway, from which it is a three-block walk uphill to the market and main square. Return buses to Cusco leave from the same spot every 15 minutes up until 7pm. Buses heading in the opposite direction also stop here on the way to Yucay and then Urubamba (US$0.50, 30-40 minutes). Once in Pisac, taxis can be taken eight kilometers to the main Pisac ruins entrance (US$8). *Mototaxis* offer short trips around town for US$1.

SIDE TRIPS
Huchuy Cusco

After Ollantaytambo and Pisac, Huchuy Cusco is the next most important Inca ruin in the Sacred Valley, but is not included on any day-trip itineraries and remains comparatively difficult to reach. This site features a two-story *kallanka*, or Inca hall, that is nearly 40 meters long and topped off by a well-preserved third story of adobe—it is easy to imagine this adobe painted, as were the buildings in Cusco, and topped off with a pyramid of thick thatch. There are also terraces, a square, an Inca gate, and many other ruined buildings within a few hundred meters of the hall. The whole site commands a small plateau, 800 meters above the Sacred Valley, with spectacular views.

This was probably the royal estate once known as Caquia Jaquijahuana, where,

according to myth, Inca Viracocha hid when the Chancas threatened to invade Cusco in 1438. One of his sons, who later renamed himself Pachacútec ("shaker of the earth"), rose up and defeated the Chancas, thus beginning the meteoric rise of the Inca. After the conquest, the Spaniards found a mummy at this site—said to be that of Viracocha.

Reaching Huchuy Cusco is not easy. The shortest way to get there is a three-hour, uphill hike from Lamay, a village between Pisac and Urubamba. The entrance to the footbridge that crosses the Río Urubamba is marked with a large blue sign erected by the Instituto Nacional de Cultura.

Another recommended option is to approach Huchuy Cusco from the opposite direction in a two-day hike across the high plains from Cusco. The trip starts at Sacsayhuamán in Cusco and follows the original Inca Trail to Calca, heading past finely wrought canals, villages, and several 4,000-meter passes. The total trip is 27 kilometers, including the final descent to Lamay, where you can catch a bus back to Cusco via Pisac. For either route, bring plenty of water and food as there is little along the way.

Chinchero

Chinchero is a small Andean village that is about to go through major changes. The town lies along the shortest driving route between Cusco and the Sacred Valley. Chinchero is perched on the high plains at 3,800 meters above sea level and has great views over the snowcapped Urubamba range. It is nearly 400 meters above Cusco, so visitors should be aware of potential altitude sickness. Chinchero is now included on several day-trip itineraries, including the Moray and Salineras tour and some Sacred Valley tours, chiefly for demonstrations of traditional weaving techniques.

While some tourists stop by Chinchero today, almost all of them will in the future in order to visit Cusco and Machu Picchu. That is because the village has been chosen as the site for a new, and controversial, international airport that will replace the current airport in the city of Cusco. The airport isn't expected to be operational until 2020, but construction of the multimillion dollar project is already altering the quiet village.

Past Chinchero's less-than-appealing street front is the main square, where a handicrafts market is held on Tuesday, Thursday, and Sunday. Talented weavers in Chinchero exhibit their wares at this market, which is smaller and less touristy than Pisac's. The highlight of the square is an Inca wall with huge niches, which probably formed part of an Inca palace. Above the square is a 17th-century adobe church that was built on Inca foundations and has deteriorated floral designs painted on its interior. It is open for visitors on market days only.

On market days, you can also catch a weaving demonstration at one of the local workshops (these demonstrations are usually included on day tours). Starting as young as age 5, girls learn to wash wool; a couple of years later they are spinning the wool into thread, and finally by 12 or 15, they are weaving actual pieces. To understand the complexity and incredible skill that goes into creating these pieces, stop by **Exposición de Artesanías Mink'a Chinchero** (Albergue 22, tel. 084/30-6035, minka@hotmail.com, hours vary).

If you're looking for a more active day, and you can leave Chinchero by noon, there is a four-hour hike that drops along an old Inca trail into this valley and ends at Huayllabamba, where *combis* pass in the late afternoon for Urubamba or Pisac. From the church, a wide trail leads up the opposite side of the valley and then gradually descends into the Sacred Valley. Once you arrive at the Río Urubamba, the Sacred Valley's main river, head right (downstream) toward the bridge at Huayllabamba.

Accommodations in Chinchero are very basic, and the town's high altitude and bone-chilling nights make the Sacred Valley—almost 1,000 meters lower—a much better option. In Cusco, *colectivos* for Chinchero can be taken from the first block of Grau near the bridge (US$0.75, 45 minutes).

YUCAY

This quiet town, a few kilometers east of Urubamba, is centered on a large, grassy plaza where soccer games are played in the shade of two massive pisonay trees reputed to be 450 years old. On the far end of the square, near the highway, lies the adobe palace of Sayri

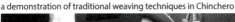
a demonstration of traditional weaving techniques in Chinchero

Túpac, who settled here after emerging from Vilcabamba in 1558. Various colonial homes, now hotels, front the square along with the restored colonial church of Santiago Apóstol. Other than that, there is little to do in the town itself, but it makes a quieter alternative accommodation base to Urubamba. There are few services outside the hotels clustered around the square.

Food

A renowned restaurant in the Sacred Valley is ★ **Huayoccari Hacienda Restaurant** (km 64 Pisac-Ollantaytambo highway, call for directions beforehand, tel. 084/22-6241 or cell 084/962-2224, reservas@huayoccari. com, US$45 pp). This elegant gourmet retreat, two kilometers up a dirt road near Yucay, is a converted country manor perched high on a ridge overlooking the Sacred Valley. Past a rustic courtyard, the restaurant's walls are lined with colonial paintings, altars, and ceramics collected by José Ignacio Lambarri, whose family has owned the land and nearby hacienda for more than three centuries. The garden terraces offer walks past roses and fuchsias to Inca terraces and fertile farmland.

The cuisine is completely organic, based on the hacienda's original recipes. Lunch begins with *sara lagua,* a cream soup made of local white corn, fresh cheese, and the herb *huacatay.* Main courses include steamed river trout with a sauce of herbs and fresh capers, or chicken rolled with fresh cheese and country bacon and covered with *sauco*-berry sauce. The desserts are made of delectable fruits found only in Peru: cheesecake with *aguaymanto* marmalade, *chirimoya* meringue, or a *sachatomate* compote. Though off the beaten path, Huayoccari is well worth the trek for the food, the country setting, and the private

collection of art. There are only a handful of tables, so make reservations well in advance. Huayoccari is between Pisac and Urubamba and can be reached via taxi from either town.

A more conventional option, but with a diverse menu and good-value buffet lunch, is **Allpa Manka** (St. Martin 300, tel. 084/20-1258, 11am-3:30pm and 6pm-9:30pm daily, US$12-15).

Accommodations

Sonesta Posadas del Inca (Plaza Manco II, Yucay 123, tel. 084/20-1107, www.sonesta. com, US$100-180 s, US$100-190 d, prices depend on season, breakfast included) has rooms spread out among plazas and gardens, courtyard fountains, a miniature crafts market, and a chapel. The hotel is built around the charming 16th-century Santa Catalina de Sena monastery, where 21 rooms are located. The colonial-style building next door has another 40 rooms with high ceilings, cable TV, and bathrooms with tubs. Amenities include a restaurant, jewelry shop, ATM, and spa. Even if you don't stay here, stop in and see the interesting museum, which has a range of ceramics, *quipus,* and weavings from most of Peru's cultures, from the Chavín to the Inca.

The well-decorated **La Casona de Yucay** (Plaza Manco II 104, tel. 084/20-1116, www. hcy.pe, US$85 s, US$105 d with breakfast) is a colonial hacienda that has been converted into a hotel with an elegant sitting room, large guest rooms, and great views.

Getting There and Around

From Cusco, buses leave for Yucay from the first block of Grau. Frequent buses pass Yucay's main square going one direction to Pisac (30 minutes) or to Urubamba (10 minutes) in the other.

Urubamba and Vicinity

Urubamba (2,863 meters) lies in the center of the Sacred Valley. It's busier and less appealing than Ollantaytambo, 20 minutes down the valley, and Pisac, 40 minutes back up the valley. Urubamba also has too much traffic, and there is a dearth of good accommodations and restaurants for budget travelers. However, the town has a growing range of high-end accommodations, including some of the best hotels in the Sacred Valley. The masses of tourists traveling through the Sacred Valley tend to stop just for lunch at the many buffet restaurants on the edge of town, but Urubamba does have a pleasant square, colonial cathedral, busy local market, and a few bars that get going on weekends.

The surroundings of Urubamba are far more spectacular than the town itself: The snow-covered Cordillera Urubamba rises over a patchwork of russet and chocolate-brown fields. In the middle is **Maras,** a dense cluster of red tile roofs, along with two startling visual anomalies. **Moray** is a set of huge natural depressions in the earth that were elaborately terraced by the Inca. **Salineras** is a blinding-white salt mine that sprawls across the mountain slope. These three attractions are combined on a half-day trip from Cusco but can easily be explored on bicycle, horseback, or foot independently, with Urubamba as a base.

ENTERTAINMENT AND EVENTS

The best way to begin an evening is with a drink at **Red Valentina** (Grau and Palacios, cell tel. 956-395-942, noon-2am Wed.-Sat.), just up from the main plaza. Around midnight, options include several places along Mariscal Castilla east of the center. The most popular is **Tequila Bar** (third block of Mariscal Castilla, tel. 084/80-1646, tequilaclub@hotmail.com, 10pm-6am Fri.-Sat.).

Urubamba erupts in bullfights, dancing, and partying during the Pentecostal celebration of **Señor Torrechayoc** in late May or early June and then once again for **Urubamba Day** on November 9. An even better party, however, is Huayllabamba's

Urubamba's main church and plaza

Urubamba

Map labels:

BOLIVAR
ZAVALA
LA POSADA DE LAS TRES MARIAS
BELEN
SAGRARIO
MARKET
HUASCAR
MARKET
MARKET
RED VALENTINA
POLICE
CAFÉ PLAZA
Plaza de Armas
PALACIO
ATM
BOTICA VALLE SAGRADO
POST OFFICE
COMERCIO
ESPINAR
MAINIQUE
SEMINARIO CERAMICS
SUCRÉ
BOLIVAR
GRAU
BOLOGNESI
DON CORLEONE
EL HUACATAY
LAUNDRY
THREE KEROS
YUPANQUI
ARICA
PIZZA WASI
CENTRO MEDICO
TEQUILA BAR
CASTILLA
9 DE NOVIEMBRE
MARISCAL CASTILLA
STADIUM
JR PADRE BARRE
FRANK'S MARKET
HOTEL TORNADO
AV
HOSTAL MAURU'S
LAUNDRY
FERROCARRIL
To Bus Terminal,
Ollantaytambo, Kuychi Rumi,
Casa Andina Sacred Valley, Sol y Luna
Hotel, and Libertador Tambo del Inka
GAS STATION/ ATM
CONNECTION
Rio Urubamba
0   100 yds
0   100 m
To Cusco, Hotel San Agustín,
Los Geranios, and Hacienda Urubamba

© AVALON TRAVEL

Virgen de la Natividad, held September 7-10.

SHOPPING

When in Urubamba, do not miss the art of **Seminario Ceramics** (Barriózabal 405, tel. 084/20-1002, www.ceramicaseminario.com, 8am-7pm daily). With Pablo Seminario focusing on form and Marilú Behar on color, this husband-and-wife team began to crank out ceramics from a small home in Urubamba in 1979. Thanks to international recognition and lucrative contracts, their original adobe workshop has blossomed into an expansive, garden-filled complex where visitors can watch an educational video and see the whole ceramics-making process. The workshop produces a range of objects, from compotes and coffee cups to sculptures and large painting frames adorned with delicate touches of silver. Everything is handmade, painted with natural mineral oxides, and kiln fired.

RECREATION
Hiking, Biking, and Horseback Riding

The Urubamba Valley is a fast-growing center of adventure sports, including horseback riding, mountain biking, rafting, trekking, and paragliding. There are some highly recommended bridle trails that can also be done on foot or mountain bike. Several operators in Cusco offer daily organized tours, as do a few operators based in the valley itself.

Note that the sun in the Sacred Valley is intensely bright, so bring a sun hat and sunscreen. It is best to get an early start to avoid the often-cloudy (sometimes rainy) afternoons.

For those who can take a full day on a horse or on a bike, there is a breathtaking circuit on the south side of the valley that traverses the high plains around Maras and Moray and then descends via the salt mines to Urubamba. The scenery is spectacular.

Wayra (part of the Sol y Luna Hotel outside Urubamba, tel. 084/20-1620, www.wayrasacredvalley.com) rents mountain bikes and has the best selection of *paso* horses in the valley. Day tours cost from US$105 per person. Another good option for *paso* horses is Perol Chico (Carretera Urubamba-Ollantaytambo, tel. 950-314-065, www.perolchico.com). These elegant animals are best for the Maras-Moray-Salinas loop or a flat loop around the valley.

Rafting

All of the Cusco rafting agencies descend the Río Urubamba, which is at its wildest during the high-water months of December-May. Day trips run US$40-55. Some trips include one night of camping near Ollantaytambo, mountain biking, and a chance to see ruins the next day. As the river drops between June and November, the agencies run the steeper, lower section that ends just past Ollantaytambo, though the rapids rarely exceed Class III. The water itself, unfortunately, is somewhat polluted, with plastic festooning the banks.

The best rafting agencies in Cusco include Amazonas Explorer (Collasuyo 910, Urb. Miravalle, Cusco, tel. 084/25-2846, www.amazonas-explorer.com), ExplorAndes (Paseo Zarzuela Q-2, Cusco tel. 084/23-8380, Lima tel. 01/200-6100, www.explorandes.com), Apumayo Expediciones (Jr. Ricardo Palma N-11, Santa Monica, tel. 084/24-6018, www.apumayo.com), Mayuc (Portal Confituras 211, Plaza de Armas, Cusco, tel. 084/24-2824, www.mayuc.com), Loreto Tours (Calle del Medio 111, Cusco, tel. 084/22-8264, www.loretotours.com), Terra Explorer Peru (Santa Ursula D-4, Huanchac, tel. 084/23-7352, www.terraexplorerperu.com), and Munaycha (based in the Sacred Valley, cell tel. 984-770-108 or 984-770-381, www.munaycha.com). Note that there are cheaper operators in Cusco, but they are generally less reliable and can be inexperienced, which is a key factor when considering the potential risks of rafting.

Climbing

A new adventure in the Sacred Valley is the Via Ferrata (tel. 084/793-019 or 951/373-240, www.naturavive.com, US$65 pp), a system of ropes and pulleys that allows you to climb a 300-meter cliff and then rappel, or descend, about 100 meters. The whole experience lasts 3-5 hours and can be done even by small children. Reservations must be made in advance.

Paragliding

The best place to get paragliding lessons in the Cusco area is Wayra (part of the Sol y Luna Hotel outside Urubamba, tel. 084/20-1620, www.wayrasacredvalley.com), where owners Marie-Hélène Miribel and Franz Schilter offer instruction. They are the only internationally certified instructors in Cusco. They charge US$150 for a tandem one-hour flight, taking off from a nearby mountain and landing in the valley itself.

FOOD

The Sacred Valley day tours use Urubamba as a lunch spot, so there are a half-dozen restaurants that offer good lunch buffets. These

Peru's Battle with the Bottle

Every time travelers buy a plastic water bottle, they are contributing to a solid-waste problem that is reaching epic proportions not only in Cusco but all over Peru. The best way to understand the problem is to raft along Cusco's Río Urubamba, where tree roots are blanketed in thick gobs of plastic bags and beaches are completely covered with plastic bottles.

What resources Peru's municipal governments have are used to fight poverty, not improve the environment. Aside from an admirable local project in Ollantaytambo, there is little organized plastic recycling program in Peru. Nearly 200 million plastic bottles are produced every month in Peru alone, and a good chunk of these are consumed by tourists—who need a few liters of purified water for each day in Peru.

A boycott campaign has been initiated by longtime Ollantaytambo resident Joaquín Randall, who manages his family's El Albergue hotel in the town.

Here's how travelers can do their part to resolve Peru's plastic addiction:

· Carry a reusable hard plastic or other water bottle and fill it with treated or boiled water.

· Buy sodas and water in refillable glass bottles.

· Demand that your hotel provide water tanks (bidones) or at the very least boiled water for refilling bottles.

· Reuse plastic bags over and over and do not accept new ones.

· Spread the word.

include **Alhambra** (km 74 Urubamba-Ollantaytambo Hwy., tel. 084/20-1200, noon-3:30pm and 7pm-close daily, US$12-14) and **Killa Wasi** (tel. 084/20-1620, www.hotelsolyluna.com, noon-7pm Tues., Thurs., and Sun., US$30), the restaurant connected to Sol y Luna Hotel, three kilometers from Urubamba's main plaza on the road toward Ollantaytambo and Machu Picchu.

For pizza try **Don Corleone** (Mainique and Urubamba, tel. 084/63-3783, lunch and dinner daily, US$7-14) or the most popular pizzeria in town, **Pizza Wasi** (Av. Castilla, tel. 084/43-4751, lunch and dinner daily, mains US$8-12). Pizza Wasi also does decent Peruvian meat, chicken, and fish dishes. **Café Plaza** (Plaza de Armas/Bolivar, tel. 084/20-1118, breakfast, lunch, and dinner daily, mains US$7-11) is a decent option on the main square with a range of breakfasts ($4-7) and interesting mains, including chicken in mango and beef in gorgonzola. Service is a little slack, though.

★ **3 Keros** (Sr. de Torrechayoc, tel. 084/20-1701, noon-3:45pm and 6:30pm-9:30pm Wed.-Mon., US$14-16) is renowned as one of the best restaurants in Urubamba. Ricardo, the owner of this laid-back restaurant, dishes up *cuy* specials, steak, lamb, trout, and chicken, all cooked to perfection in delicious sauces. Try the lamb in wild berries.

Chef Pio Vasquez, with the help of his German wife, Iris, has created an elegant restaurant and garden. Have your passion fruit pisco sour on the patio of **El Huacatay** (Arica 620, tel. 084/20-1790, www.elhuacatay.com, 1pm-9pm Mon.-Sat., US$12-16) before moving into the intimate dining room for a main course based on local produce—from arugula to fresh trout. Dessert is Pio's passion, so leave room for the chocolate mousse.

ACCOMMODATIONS

Finding accommodation in Urubamba is difficult for those on a tight budget. There are very few cheap places, and be sure to avoid the *hospedajes* in the center, as these are seedy motels for local lovers. However, if you have the resources, several of the best top-range hotels in the Sacred Valley are here.

US$10-25

One of the few decent budget options is **Hostal Mauru's – Tambo del Sol** (Convención 113, tel. 084/20-1352, www.hoteltambodelsol.com, US$20 s, US$28 d), which has pleasant rooms with private bath and cable TV.

US$25-50

A midrange hotel on the main highway south of the center is **Hotel Tornado** (Av. Cabo Conchatupa and Boliva, tel. 084/20-1120, www.hoteltornadoperu.com, US$50 s, US$70 d, including breakfast). Several double rooms have a Jacuzzi ($95).

US$100-150

The **Hotel San Agustín Monasterio de la Recoleta** (Recoleta s/n, tel. 084/20-1666, www.hotelessanagustin.com.pe, US$130 s, US$154 d) occupies a stunning 16th-century Franciscan monastery. There is a modern addition with a few spectacular rooms upstairs, outfitted with exposed beams, stone showers, and sun windows; the rest of the modern rooms are nondescript. Rooms in the old section are surrounded by a stone courtyard and are superior to the blander modern rooms.

Over US$150

Kuychi Rumi Lodging (km 74.5 Urubamba-Ollantaytambo Hwy., tel. 084/20-1169, www.urubamba.com, US$120 s, US$140 d, with breakfast) offers six fully equipped houses that each have two bedrooms, a sitting room, and a kitchenette. Tastefully designed and decorated, the houses are meant for longer stays, but even if you only have a night, they are worth it for the privacy and comfort. The grounds are filled with hummingbirds.

Sol y Luna Hotel (tel. 084/60-8930, www.hotelsolyluna.com, US$350 s/d to US$660 for a deluxe suite, with breakfast), three kilometers from Urubamba's main plaza on the road toward Ollantaytambo and Machu Picchu, was opened in 2000 by Marie-Hélène Miribel and Franz Schilter. This French-Swiss couple has carefully designed every last detail of their 43 bungalows, including terra-cotta tiles, exposed beams, marble bathrooms, and king-size beds. The deluxe bungalows include a hot tub on the patio. The poolside buffet is excellent, using local produce from the valley. Groups are often treated to *pachamanca* cooking with *marinera* dance demonstrations. The hotel has extensive gardens, a pool, a gym, and a spa with whirlpool tub and massage. There are 20 Peruvian horses *(caballos de paso)* lodged in stables in the back and available for half- and full-day rides. The hotel also rents mountain bikes, coordinates cultural trips to a local school and orphanage, and offers paragliding outings with the owners, Cusco's only internationally certified instructors. Through an associated nonprofit organization, the hotel has also created a local school.

In the Sacred Valley, the **Willka Tika** (Paradero Rumichaka, 2 kilometers north of Urubamba, tel. 707/202-5340, www.willka-tika.com) is a luxury retreat that offers ceremonial activities. It has seven relaxing gardens with winding paths, a yoga studio and meditation cottages.

The best upscale hotel in the Urubamba area is the ★ **Libertador Tambo del Inka** (Av. Ferrocarril, tel. 084/58-1777, www.luxurycollection.com/tambodelinka, US$275 s/d), designed by Bernard Fort and set on the banks of the Urubamba. It is the only hotel in Peru with a Leadership in Energy and Environmental Design (LEED) certificate, and therefore one of the most environmentally friendly hotels in the country. The elegant lobby, with 12-meter ceilings, mixes international standards with Peruvian decor. The 128 rooms and suites all have a balcony or terrace, WiFi, cable TV, and iPod docks. The buffet breakfast is a veritable feast, and a highlight is the 1,800-square-meter spa, gym, and sauna. Cool off with a dip in the pool and Jacuzzi, which command great views of the river. At night, visit the Bar Kiri, with its striking backlit onyx wall. The hotel can organize kayaking and cycling excursions.

A new option in the area is Inkaterra's **Hacienda Urubamba** (Pie del cerro

Huayllawasy, Lima tel. 01/610-0400, www.inkaterra.com, US$462 s/d, US$935 suite), which offers rooms with fireplaces and sweeping views of the green countryside. The hotel opened in 2015 with 12 luxury rooms and added 24 stand-alone casitas in 2016. The hotel offers excursions for everyone from birders to guests interested in medicinal plants and *chicha de jora,* the ancient Andean beer.

Outside Urubamba

In Yanahuara, just 15 minutes outside of Urubamba on the road to Ollantaytambo, the hotel chain **Casa Andina** has constructed one of its **Private Collection** hotels (5th Paradero, cell tel. 984-765-501, www.casa-andina.com, US$116 s/d with breakfast). The result is a labyrinth of glassed lobbies, gardens, a spa center, and a planetarium. You might just have to spend two nights to take advantage of it all. It's also very child-friendly, with a small playground, llamas, and lots of open space.

In Huayllabamba, the **Aranwa** chain of hotels has a 100-bedroom, 15-suite complex (Vía Urubamba-Huayllabamba, tel. 01/434-6199, www.aranwahotels.com, US$240 s/d) that includes one of the largest spas in the Sacred Valley as well as a business center,

three restaurants, a sushi bar, and even a cinema. The newer buildings are built around a historic hacienda.

Rio Sagrado (km 75.8 Cusco-Urubamba Hwy., tel. 084/20-1631, www.riosagrado.com, US$325 s/d) is part of the Belmond line of hotels (formerly Orient-Express) and is located on the outskirts of Urubamba. It has a mixture of high-quality rooms, suites, and two-story bungalows, plus a spa.

INFORMATION AND SERVICES

There's a **police station** on Palacio (s/n, tel. 084/20-1012). The **town clinic** is on 9 de Noviembre (s/n, tel. 084/20-1032, lab open 8am-1pm). There are now tourist clinics in Urubamba, including **SOS Urgent Medical** (Mariscal Castilla, tel. 084/20-5059), which is a modern facility that works with different insurance companies. There are pharmacies all over town, but a good option is **Botica Valle Sagrado** (Bolivar 469, tel. 084/20-1830, 8am-10pm daily).

On the highway in front of Urubamba, there is a **Banco de Crédito** ATM, and in the Pesca gas station there is a **Global Net** ATM.

The **post office** is on the main square, along with several pay phones. There are

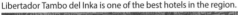
Libertador Tambo del Inka is one of the best hotels in the region.

several **Internet** locales, which are generally open 9am-10pm daily.

Do your laundry at **Clean Wash Laundry** (Mariscal Castilla 100, 8am-7pm Mon.-Sat.).

Volunteering

ProPeru (Apartado 70, tel. 084/20-1562, www.proworldsc.org) is a highly recommended organization arranging homestays for college students (and older folks, too) in Urubamba, Cusco, and other areas of Peru. Students take classes in art, history, anthropology, and Spanish, and work on service projects that range from reforestation to setting up a women's shelter. ProPeru receives very good reviews from its students and is one of the better foreign study programs in Peru. Other volunteer organizations in Urubamba include **Niños del Sol** (formerly Casa de los Milagros) (www.ninosdelsol.org), which works with children with disabilities.

GETTING THERE AND AROUND

From Cusco, *combis* for Urubamba leave from the first block of Grau near the bridge (US$2, 1 hour). Buses take longer and cost a little less. *Combis* drop passengers at Urubamba's bus station on the main drag, where frequent transport continues for the 20-minute ride to Ollantaytambo ($1.50) or up to Pisac (40 minutes, US$2). Taxis can be hired, costing less than US$10 for Ollantaytambo and US$20 for Pisac. To see Maras, Moray, and Salineras, a taxi costs about US$30 for a four-hour tour.

Mototaxis are ubiquitous in Urubamba and cost US$1-1.50 for getting around town.

★ MORAY AND SALINERAS

The high plains above Urubamba contain two very different attractions that are usually combined on a day trip.

First stop is **Maras,** a dusty town with a few colonial churches and *chicherías,* shops selling beer made from fermented corn. About seven kilometers farther, or a half hour along a good dirt road, lie the **four natural depressions of Moray** (7:30am-5:15pm daily, US$4 or included in *boleto turístico*). These sinkholes, 150 meters deep, were caused by rain eroding the calcium-rich soil. More than 20 terraces descending into concentric circles were used by the Inca to create microclimates for growing different vegetables. Gradations of sun, shade, and elevation among the terraces create dramatic differences in temperature. Irrigation canals and the discovery of

the spellbinding salt mines at Salineras

different seeds on the terraces are additional clues that Moray was once a gigantic agricultural laboratory. It was here, perhaps, that the Inca learned to grow corn and potatoes in a variety of elevations, fueling the expansion of the empire. The irrigation is so good that it never floods, even in torrential storms.

On the nearby hills that lead down to the Urubamba Valley is a very different attraction, Salineras, unique in the Sacred Valley. Here the Inca once again transformed nature: A spring of warm, salty water was diverted into thousands of pools, where sunlight evaporates the water and leaves a thin crust of salt. The salt mines (entrance US$3, not included in *boleto turístico*) continue to be worked by a collective of 260 salt miners from the nearby villages of Maras and Pichinjoto. (You may see this salt marketed overseas as "Peruvian pink salt.") Today there are 5,740 pools, or *pocitos,* each of which yields 150 kilograms of unrefined salt per month. There is a dazzling and oft-photographed contrast between the barren hillsides and the snow-white salt pools, which visitors can explore along narrow, crunchy paths. The water that flows through these mines is 60 percent salt, twice the salinity of the ocean.

Getting There and Around

To reach Moray, take a Cusco-Urubamba bus and get off at the Maras turnoff (say *"ramal a Maras, por favor"*). *Colectivos* wait here and charge US$10-12 for a half-day tour of Maras, Moray, and Salinas. A recommended company is Empresa Transporte Moray. To get from Moray to Salineras, car-bound travelers must return to Maras and then proceed another five kilometers downhill to the salt mines. Another option is to get a ride to Maras (four kilometers) and then walk the remaining seven kilometers to Moray (two hours, mostly uphill) through a patchwork of fields. From Moray, it is a two-hour walk—ask for directions along the way—to the salt mines. A steep but beautiful path continues for another kilometer or two from Salinas to the Urubamba Valley, ending five kilometers down from Urubamba and at the doorstep of the recommended Tunupa Restaurant (km 77 Pisac-Ollantaytambo Hwy., cell tel. 984-630-520, lunch daily, $15-20). This whole circuit makes for an excellent full-day tour on horse or bike, or do it yourself by electing to be dropped off at Salineras and taking the scenic, one-hour walk back to Urubamba.

Maras, Moray, Salineras, and Chinchero are combined on a half-day tour ($12) bookable with agencies in Cusco as well as with some operators in Urubamba.

Ollantaytambo and Vicinity

Ollantaytambo (2,792 meters) is the last town in the Sacred Valley before the Río Urubamba plunges through steep gorges toward Machu Picchu. It is such a shame that so many tourists rush through here on a day trip or, worse still, don't even stop on the way to Machu Picchu. More fool them, because Ollantaytambo is the best-preserved Inca village in Peru, with narrow alleys, small street canals that supply water, and trapezoidal doorways. The Inca temple and fortress above town is second in beauty only to Machu Picchu and deserves to be explored at length. In the terraced fields above town, men still use foot plows, or *chaquitacllas,* to till fields and plant potatoes. The town is overlooked by snowcapped Verónica mountain and surrounded on all sides by Inca ruins, highways, and terraces. It is well worth lingering here for a day or two.

However, Ollantaytambo also epitomizes the uneasy relationship between tradition and progress. While the town's Inca heritage stands out proudly, there are far too many pizzerias, and the streets shake under the weight of huge trucks bound for the Camisea gas pipeline in the jungle around Quillabamba.

Ollantaytambo

To Chilca

To Huilloc

HOSTAL
EL MAÍZ

To
INCA GRANARIES
(PINKUYLLUNA)

HOSTEL ISKAY

PATECALLE

CALLE CHAUPI

CALLE HORNO

★ OLLANTAYTAMBO TEMPLE

Plaza
Araccama

CONVENCIÓN

PUKA RUMI
KUSICÓYLLOR

AWAMAKI STORE

MAYUPATA

SEE DETAIL

KB TAMBO
HOTEL &
TOURS

ATOQ K'IKLLU

VENTIDERIO

PRINCIPAL

HOSTEL
EL CHASQUI

Plaza

HEART'S
CAFÉ

HOTEL
LAS ORQUIDEAS

HOTEL
PAKARITAMPU

To English Pub

AWAMAKI NGO

Río Patacancha

FERROCARRIL

0   100 yds
0   100 m

HOSTAL
SUMAC CHASKA   HOSTEL   SEÑOR
EL TAMBO   GANZO   HOSTEL
QUILLA

PATECALLE

ALCÁZAR
CAFÉ

ATOQ K'IKLLU

CALLE CHAUPI

CALLE HORNO

GRAN
TUNUPA

PANAKA
GRILL

VENTIDERIO

TRAIN TICKET OFFICE
HOSTEL KISWAR

PRINCIPAL

ATM

HOSTEL
SAUCE/ATM

CALLE

BOTICA

POLICE

Plaza

HOSTEL
OLLANTA

PACHAMAMA
GRILL

EL ALBERGUE/
CAFÉ MAYU

TRAIN TICKET
OFFICES

KB TOURS

TOURIST INFO

TRAIN STATION

INTIKILLA

LOCAL MARKET

Train to Machu Picchu

To Urubamba

Río Urubamba

© AVALON TRAVEL

But some recent changes have been positive: After a concerted campaign, the mountain of plastic bottles and trash that filled the river around town has been reduced, if not eliminated, by a new recycling program, and the town still retains its strong sense of community. Archaeologists and philanthropists further help to preserve and strengthen the town's unique heritage.

HISTORY

Ollantaytambo (population 3,000) was occupied long before the Inca by the Quillques, who built some of the rougher buildings at Pumamarca and on the ridge near the Ollantaytambo temple itself. After Inca emperor Pachacútec conquered this area around 1440, construction began on a ceremonial center and royal estate that housed an estimated

1,000 workers year-round. Even though it was never completed, the result is the most impressive Inca ruins in Peru after Machu Picchu.

Ollantaytambo is most famous for a 1537 battle that was the final time that the Inca defeated a Spanish army—and nearly massacred it altogether. The battle happened during the 1536-1537 Inca rebellion, when Manco Inca was forced to withdraw his troops to Ollantaytambo after being defeated by the Spanish at Sacsayhuamán. Hernando Pizarro arrived at Ollantaytambo one morning at dawn, his brothers Juan and Francisco and his cousin Pedro among the force's 70 cavalrymen and 30 foot soldiers. But Manco Inca's men were waiting on the terraces of the sun temple, which had been hastily converted into a fort. Pedro Pizarro wrote afterward, "We found it so well fortified that it was a thing of horror."

From high on the upper terraces, Manco Inca commanded his troops from horseback—co-opting the symbol of Spanish strength—as jungle archers shot volleys of arrows and Inca soldiers fired off slingshots and rolled boulders. Sensing defeat, the Spaniards retreated, but Manco Inca pulled a final surprise. In a brilliant move, he diverted the Río Urubamba through previously prepared channels and flooded the plains below Ollantaytambo,

causing the Spaniards' horses to get bogged down in the mud as they beat a hasty retreat. The Spanish were pursued by thousands of Inca soldiers all the way to Cusco, where Pizarro then waited for Diego de Almagro to return from his Chile campaign with reinforcements. Manco Inca, meanwhile, recognized the growing strength of the Spaniards and withdrew to Vilcabamba.

After Manco's departure, the whole valley became an *encomienda* for Hernando Pizarro, who pursued Manco deep into Vilcabamba and raided his camp in 1539. Manco narrowly escaped, but his wife and sister, Cura Ocllo, was captured and brought to Ollantaytambo. After Manco refused to surrender, Francisco Pizarro had Cura Ocllo stripped, whipped, and killed with arrows. To make sure Manco got the message, they floated her body down the Río Urubamba toward Vilcabamba, where Manco's troops found her.

About two-thirds of the inhabitants of the Sacred Valley died of diseases brought by the Spanish over the next century. The descendants of the survivors were put to work in haciendas that sprung up in the valley, often the result of Spaniards marrying Inca elite. A road down the Urubamba Valley to Quillabamba was constructed in 1895. It was this road that

a look down at the town of Ollantaytambo, from the ruins of the same name

The Brilliance of Inca Stone

The Inca's building work is their greatest legacy and the biggest draw for millions of tourists who flock to Peru to gaze upon these astounding architectural achievements.

The central theme of Inca construction is **homage to nature. Cusco** was designed in the shape of a puma with **Sacsayhuamán** as the head, the city as the body, and the **Coricancha sun temple** as the tail. Many Inca temples, including at **Machu Picchu, Ollantaytambo,** and **Pisac,** were designed specifically to catch the light of the sun on winter or summer solstice, dates that still pull in thousands of tourists to witness the spectacle every year.

The biggest stones in Sacsayhuamán are eight meters high.

On a practical level, the Inca built on **higher ground,** mindful of the destructive power of landslides, in direct contrast to modern civilizations that continue to inadvisably live at the bottom of the valley. Size mattered for the Inca, and they used huge blocks of stone rather than the small bricks common in Europe. The best examples of this are the eight-meter blocks at **Sacsayhuamán.** The human effort involved in transporting these blocks, probably using log sleds and levers, was immense, but the result was impeccable.

Just as important, the Inca used **inclines** to increase stability. Walls were slightly inclined, with corners rounded, and the trapezoidal shape for doors and windows—wider at the bottom and narrower at the top—added crucial stability.

Most famously, the Inca did not use mortar but **cut stones precisely** to fit together. Mortar erodes in time and causes walls to become unstable, while Inca walls made of stones fitted so closely together were far sturdier. One of the most famous examples of Inca craftsmanship is the **12-sided stone** in the alleyway Hatun Rumiyoc in Cusco.

Last but not least were the **Inca roads,** many of which still exist in their original form, such as the **Inca Trail,** or have become the basis for parts of the Panamerican Highway. Overcoming the inhospitable mountain terrain, the Inca found a way to carve trails and steps as well as build bridges using natural fibers.

It wasn't just the Inca's buildings that were brilliant, but also their **agricultural terracing.** This efficient use of land increased the available space for food production and created microclimates at different altitudes for various crops—corn on lower terraces, potatoes in the middle, and quinoa higher up. The best examples of terracing are at **Moray, Ollantaytambo,** and **Pisac.** Many modern engineers in North America have since copied Inca agricultural methods.

The final proof of the superiority of Inca construction is best demonstrated by its survival in a volatile geological zone. In the 1950 earthquake, while much of the colonial architecture of Cusco collapsed, the Inca walls remained unscathed, and the foundations of the sun temple Coricancha were once again revealed to the world. Pachacútec, the Inca's greatest builder (the name means "shaker of the earth"), would have surely smiled with satisfaction.

Hiram Bingham took to "discover" Machu Picchu in 1911. In the 1920s, the road was converted into the rail line that now carries travelers to Machu Picchu.

Today Ollantaytambo is a busy tourist town but still preserves its unique Inca heritage. It is probably the most attractive of all Sacred Valley towns and makes a popular base to get the early morning train to Machu Picchu.

SIGHTS
City Tour

Ask your bus driver to let you off one kilometer before Ollantaytambo at the original Inca Trail, which follows the hillside on the right (north) side of town. To the left is the plain that Manco Inca flooded in the 1537 battle against the Spanish. The path leads up to the town's restored terraces and through a massive Inca gate, through which a water channel still runs. The path then joins with the road past the Wall of 100 Niches, whose inward slant indicates this was the inside—not the outside—of a roadside building (or maybe the road went through the building).

Once in the main plaza, head a half block north to the original Inca town, named **Qozqo Ayllu,** which is laid out in the form of a trapezoid and bisected by narrow, irrigated alleys. Oversized trapezoidal doorways open in the courtyards of homes, or *kanchas,* occupied continuously since Pachacútec's time.

★ Ollantaytambo Temple

The main attractions of Ollantaytambo are the ruins towering above town. The temple was still under construction when the Spaniards arrived—and was later converted into a fortress by Manco Inca.

From a distance, the most impressive part of the ruins is the agricultural terracing. Two hundred steps lead up these terraces to a double-jamb gateway and the **Temple of Ten Niches,** a long wall with odd protuberances. Some say these bumps draw heat away from the slabs, preventing them from expanding. Others say they somehow served in the transport of the blocks. Or perhaps the Inca valued them as we do today, for the graceful shadows they cast across the stone.

Above is the unfinished **Temple of the Sun,** considered one of the masterpieces of Inca stonework. Six giant monoliths of pink rhyolite are perfectly slotted together with thin slices of stone and oriented to glow with the rising sun. Traces of the *chacana* symbols and pumas that once decorated the walls can still be seen. What is unusual about the wall is the long straight lines—and the molten bronze that was poured in the T-joints to hold the wall together. These features indicate the wall was probably the handiwork of Lake Titicaca's Colla people, who were brought to work here by Pachacútec as part of the forced labor system known as *mitimayo.* According to J. P. Protzen, the wall was probably intended to be one side of a great platform, which seems likely with the unfinished

the unfinished Temple of the Sun

blocks, rough walls, and plaza nearby. It is impressive enough now, but one cannot help but wonder what it would have become had the Inca been allowed to finish their work. It is not entirely clear why the construction stopped—perhaps it was Pachacútec's death, a rebellion of the Colla people, the smallpox epidemic of 1527, or (most likely) the arrival of the Spaniards.

To the left of the plaza, the **Cachicata quarry** appears high on the hillside. The Inca dragged boulders weighing up to 52 tons down the mountain, across the Río Urubamba and the valley floor, and then up a steep ramp. The human effort involved in doing this boggles the mind. On the ridge above the temple are rougher buildings and the **Incahuatana,** the hitching place of the Inca, where prisoners may have been lashed into the human-sized portals. There are also the ruins of a control zone above the temple, the highest point used as a lookout to the *colcas* (storehouses) where food was kept. Walk down the terraces of **Andenes Manyaraki** to the base of the ruins. Here you'll find the **Baños de la Ñusta** (Princess Baths) and the **Water Temple;** there are a half-dozen fountains adorned with *chacana* symbols. Some of the fountains are engineered in such a way as to cause a whirlpool that allows sediment to drop before the water continues over a delicately shaped spout. From here you can walk along to the right beside a stream to a small ceremonial site, **Incamisana.** Opposite the ruins, on the steep flanks of Pinculluna, the sacred hill that rises above town, are the ruins of several granaries, which glow in the afternoon sun.

ENTERTAINMENT AND EVENTS

Bars and clubs change often in Ollantaytambo. The town has a small but lively nightlife scene on weekends, due mainly to a community of expats who live in town year-round. **Señor Ganso** (Horno Calle, 1.5 blocks from the square, 9am-11pm daily) has a great second-floor lounge.

During the **Fiesta de Reyes** (Celebration of the Kings) on January 6, a revered image of Jesus is brought down to Ollantaytambo from Marcacocha, a town high up in the Patacancha Valley. The event includes a solemn procession around Ollantaytambo's main square, which involves even more images of baby Jesus.

On January 6, over 200 Wallta dancers come down from the hills of Mount Pinkuylluna. These Quechua-speaking peoples, dressed in the traditional red outfits, dance and lead processions until the following day.

During the eight-day **Carnaval** season in late January and early February, the upper Patacancha Valley explodes into a series of traditions: cow branding, offerings to mountain *apus* by local priests, *wallata* (the dance of the condor), and ritual battles between towns that are now fought with mature fruit instead of rocks.

The town's most important celebration is the **Señor de Choquequilca,** which happens during Pentecost at the end of May or early June. The festival dates back to the miraculous appearance of a wooden cross near the town's Inca bridge. A chapel dedicated to El Señor de Choquequilca was completed in the main square in 1995.

SHOPPING

To find authentic, all-natural weavings and handicrafts, head to **Awamaki** (Calle Convención s/n, across from the temple, tel. 084/43-6744, www.awamaki.org). All proceeds go to the people of the communities with which Awamaki works.

RECREATION

Several agencies operate trips, including horseback riding, rafting, and biking excursions, in this area. Prices range US$50-100 for day tours. Recommended operators include **KB Tambo Tours** (Ventiderio s/n, tel. 084/20-4091, KBperu@hotmail.com, www.kbperu.com), run by a longtime resident originally from the United States; **Sota Adventures**

(Procuradores 351, Office 120, cell tel. 984-455-841, www.sotaadventure.com), operated by two local brothers; and **KB Tours Travel** (Plaza de Armas s/n, tel. 084/23-3896, info@ kbtourstravel.com). NGO **Awamaki** (Calle Convención s/n, across from the temple, tel. 084/43-6744, www.awamaki.org) also organizes excursions to the communities outside Ollantaytambo.

Hikes

Ollantaytambo is a great base for a number of excellent hikes, treks, and community visits in the area. A detailed map of a dozen local hikes is available from the NGO **Awamaki** (Calle Convención s/n, across from the temple, tel. 084/43-6744, www.awamaki.org). Summaries of these hikes, taken from the Awamaki guide with permission, are listed here. Before setting out on these hikes, check with Awamaki for updated directions.

★ INCA GRANARIES (PINKUYLLUNA)

This moderate, 1.5-hour hike explores the Inca ruins that can be seen from town on the hillside opposite the Ollantaytambo fortress. The larger buildings were used for agricultural storehouses called *colcas*. Along with the multiple Inca sites, this steep hike offers great elevated views of Ollantaytambo and the fortress.

To reach the trailhead from the plaza, take Calle Principal toward Cusco. Take your first left after leaving the plaza completely on Calle Lares. After a few blocks, you will see a stone staircase on your right with a sign for Pinkuylluna. The stone staircase continues up the mountain for 10 to 15 minutes before the trail forks. The trail to the right (with the wooden handrail) will lead you around the corner to the first Inca ruins.

After exploring these, the best option is to descend back down to the fork in the trail and take the trail uphill in the other direction. The trail passes another Inca site and arrives at the large four-tiered storehouse in about 20-30 minutes. From here you can continue up the trail to the four towers that mark the crown of the head of the Tunupa, the god of abundance. If you continue up the mountain from here the views improve but the trail becomes unclear.

PUMAMARCA

The round-trip hike to the ruins of Pumamarca takes about 4-6 hours from Ollantaytambo on a moderate, steadily climbing trail. The ruins of Pumamarca sit on a hillside overlooking the convergence of the Río Patacancha and the Yuracmayo (White River). The well-preserved site was thought to be a checkpoint to control access to Ollantaytambo.

To reach Pumamarca, follow Patacalle out of town. Shortly after the first bridge, a large path leaves the main road to the right and follows the river. Follow this path for about 15 minutes until it rejoins the main road at the small town of Munaypata. Just up the road you will see an electrical pole on the left labeled 2224 and a path leading behind the adjacent house. Follow this path uphill for 15 more minutes to a blue archaeological marker for the Media Luna terraces in front of you. At this point, follow the switchback up the hill to your right (and not the path in front of you toward the terraces). The trail continues to climb steeply but soon becomes more gradual.

After another hour or so of hiking, the trail comes to a clearing with small waterfalls and the beginning of ancient aqueducts. The trail follows an aqueduct, and in 20-30 minutes the ruins of Pumamarca become apparent on the hillside in front of you. The trail becomes less clear at this point, but you can take multiple routes through the terraced fields up to the ruins (the main entrance is on the right side of the complex). At times there is someone working at the ruins who can provide information, but if not there is currently no entrance fee or hours when the ruins are closed. After exploring the ruins, return to Ollantaytambo by the same path or descend the hillside to the town of Pallata and take the road down from there.

INCA QUARRIES (CANTERAS)
AND INTI PUNKU (SUN GATE)

This round-trip walk, which takes 4-6 hours to the quarries and a few more to reach the Sun Gate, begins at the Inca bridge near Ollantaytambo and along the banks of the Río Urubamba. It follows a fairly well-preserved Inca trail to Cachicata, the stone quarry 700-900 meters above the valley floor that is visible from the Ollantaytambo sun temple. It was here that the great stone blocks were slid down the hillside and hauled across the river to Ollantaytambo. There are three separate stone quarries, within half a kilometer of one another, littered with massive chiseled blocks and small *chullpas*, or burial towers. The western and highest quarry contains mysterious needle-shaped blocks that are up to seven meters long.

From Cachicata, it is possible to see that the terraces below the Ollantaytambo ruins form a pyramid shape, with one 750-meter-long wall aligning with the rays of the winter solstice. New Age theorists Fernando and Edgar Elorieta believe this is the original Pakaritampu, where the four Inca brothers emerged to found Cusco. A few hours' walk above the Cachicata is a perfect Inca gate that frames a view of Salcantay. On the trail approaching the quarries, numerous *piedras cansadas* (tired stones) that never made it to their final destination can be observed. The trail climbs high on the hillside, offering great views of Ollantaytambo and the surrounding peaks. Be prepared; the majority of the hike is fully exposed to the sun, and the only available water is near the beginning of the hike.

Begin the hike by taking a right after the Inca bridge. After about 15-20 minutes take a left at the fork up the hill (a boulder at the fork is labeled "Canteras"). Continue to stay left, following the main path when other trails diverge. In about 20-30 minutes you reach agricultural terraces and stone building foundations. Follow the trail straight past the foundations, not the smaller trail uphill. You arrive at the first quarry 1.5-2 hours after starting. Look for small stone buildings

built on top of large boulders beneath you. Just after passing through the quarry, look for a smaller path to the left leading uphill from the large trail. If you choose to filter water, a small switchback to the left immediately after this turn will lead to the last water source.

Follow switchbacks up the hillside past the first quarry for one hour. As the grassy trail starts to level out, watch for a rounded stone resembling a primitive wheel off the trail to your left. As the trail plateaus you will see a much larger quarry to your left and several small fields. These flat fields are a great place to camp if you plan to spend the night. A large boulder in the middle of the quarry has "Instituto Nacional de Cultura" painted in white. Before and to the left of this boulder, a path made of smaller stones leads up though the quarry. Exploring this path, you can find a burial site with skeletons under a large boulder, along with many quarried stones that never made it to Ollantaytambo.

Looking farther ahead on the same trail, you can see Inti Punku, or the Sun Gate, on the ridge ahead. To continue to Inti Punku, pass the large boulder with "I.N.C." painted on it and head toward the largest boulder you see. Find the trail on the left side of the boulder and follow it uphill, crossing a scree field. After 30-45 minutes the trail comes to a grass field with Inca ruins (another good campsite). The trail continues just beyond and uphill from these. The trail forks once at a small ravine about 10 minutes from the Sun Gate; take a right through the ravine. About 30-45 minutes from the ruins you reach Inti Punku. From Inti Punku, return along same path to the last quarry (about 1 hour).

The return route from the *canteras* (quarries) should take 1.5-2 hours. Follow the trail down switchbacks to the first quarry. Take a left just past the first quarry on a small path and circle back under the quarry. From here you see two houses with metal roofs on the left hillside. Continue to descend along this ridge toward the houses and the trail improves. From the houses, continue along the trail downhill into the valley. The trail improves and continues downhill through more houses and finally to a bridge. Cross the bridge and follow the railroad tracks on your right. Turn left at a set of stone stairs reached after 10-15 minutes of walking on the tracks, and follow the path back to town.

FOOD

Ollantaytambo has an increasingly varied range of restaurants. You're never more than a few yards from a wood-fired pizza. One of the better places in town for pizza is Intikilla (Plaza de Armas, tel. 084/79-6062, 9am-10pm daily, US$6-12). It also does a range of meat, fish, and chicken, including trout ceviche and stroganoff. Elsewhere on the square, Pachamama Grill (Convención s/n, tel. 084/20-4168, 11:30am-10pm daily, US$7-10) has trout, pizza, and *lomo saltado*. The set menu for US$10 is good value. Panaka Grill Restaurant (Plaza de Armas s/n, 7am-10pm daily, US$11-16) is an upscale option with fine dining upstairs. They have a good-value set menu for US$14, while à la carte specialties include a range of steaks and pasta dishes.

Kusicoyllor Café-Bar (Calle Convención across from the temple, tel. 084/43-6725, 8am-10pm daily, US$5-8), located directly in front of the ruins, serves traditional dishes such as alpaca steak, as well as croissants, pancakes, espresso, and homemade ice cream. Just in front of the ruins, a favorite in town is Puka Rumi (Calle Convención near the entrance to the ruins, tel. 084/20-4091, 7:30am-8:30pm daily, US$6-12). The Chilean owner has brought over the traditions from his home country and is well known for his excellent *lomo saltado*. The menu is extremely varied and has options for all budgets. For dessert, try the brownies. Note that service is slow, but the food is worth the wait.

For the best meal in town, head down to the train station to the restaurant ★ El Albergue (Ferrocarril s/n, tel. 084/20-4077, www.elalbergue.com, 5am-9:30pm daily, US$10-20). Using organic vegetables, the menu is inventive and has great vegetarian options. Try the alpaca with *huacatay* mash

or the lamb tenderloin with chimichurri and quinoa risotto. Pasta lovers can order a plate of homemade fettuccini with their favorite sauce. Reservations are recommended. The best coffee in Ollantaytambo is also found at the El Albergue's Café Mayu (Ferrocarril s/n, tel. 084/20-4014, 4:30am-9pm daily, US$5-15).

★ Heart's Café (Plaza de Armas s/n, tel. 084/43-6726, 7am-10pm daily, US$5-18) was founded by retired Brit Sonia Newhouse, an inspirational lady who has established her own charity. This place serves home-cooked meals using organic ingredients and specializes in vegetarian fare. It has everything from soups and salads to main dishes and even afternoon tea with scones. The sandwiches are particularly imaginative. Try the veggie sausage and blue cheese or hummus and chutney. Profits go to Sonia's NGO, Living Heart (www.livingheartperu.org).

Markets

The best minimarket for snacks or a picnic is Inka Misana on the Plaza de Armas. But head to the local market for fresh fruit and produce.

ACCOMMODATIONS
Under US$10

Unlike Urubamba, Ollantaytambo has some good budget options for backpackers. Hostal El Tambo (Calle Horno, 1.5 blocks from the plaza, tel. 084/77-3262, US$9 pp, www.hostaleltambo.com) is cheap and adequate. The baths are shared and have hot water. According to the owner, Hiram Bingham stayed at this hostel back in 1911. In the old Inca town, Hostal Sumac Chaska (Calle del Medio s/n, tel. 084/43-6739, US$8 dorm, US$20 d) has several clean rooms with wooden floors arranged around a tiny courtyard. The terrace on the top of the building has good views of the Inca granaries.

US$10-50

The best value hostel on the main square is probably Hostal Kiswar (Plaza de Armas, tel. 084/436-706, www.hostalkiswarperu.com,

US$28 pp). It has comfortable rooms upstairs and a good café below with soups and snacks.

An excellent budget option is ★ **Hostal El Chasqui** (Av. Estación del Tren, cell tel. 984-995-031, US$20 pp). Rooms with private baths and WiFi are great value for the price. There is a popular restaurant downstairs with a range of national and international food ($4-12).

One of the best midrange options is **Hostal Iskay** (Patacalle s/n, tel. 084/20-4004, www. hostaliskay.com, US$34 s, US$43 d with continental breakfast), a small, homely hostel with a beautiful garden and an astounding view of the ruins. The friendly Spanish owners are longtime residents of Ollantaytambo. The rooms are clean and simple, and the common living/dining area has sofas, television, books, and board games, along with real Inca walls and an open kitchen.

Another comfortable option is **KB Tambo** (Ventiderio s/n, tel. 084/20-4091, www.kb-peru.com, US$28 s, US$35 d), which has cozy, unpretentious modern rooms with private bathrooms from singles and doubles to family suites. It has a pleasant garden and a rooftop with excellent views of the ruins, plus a Jacuzzi, full bar, and pizza oven.

US$50-100

Ollantaytambo's most charming and best-known hotel is ★ **El Albergue** (Ferrocarril s/n, tel. 084/20-4014, www.elalbergue.com, US$70-80 s/d with breakfast). The lodge was opened by Wendy Weeks, a painter from Seattle, who arrived here in 1976 after an overland journey with her husband, writer Robert Randall. After her husband's death in 1990, Wendy stayed to raise her two sons here—Joaquín, who now runs the lodge, and Ishmael, who is an internationally recognized sculptor. Wendy Weeks is a well-respected member of the community and a passionate spokeswoman for its preservation.

To reach El Albergue, head to the train station, through the gate, and down the tracks in the direction of an arrow and large sign for El Albergue painted on a wall. Or if you are arriving by train, simply disembark, and you'll be there. Compared to the mayhem of the station, El Albergue is a tranquil retreat. Blue-and-yellow tanagers flit among datura flowers and a huge Canary Island palm that was planted in the 1920s. The 16 rooms are spacious, with whitewashed walls, wood tables, and beds. The newest have floor heating and bathtubs. Decorations include local weavings and Wendy's paintings. The balconies are ideal for reading and taking in the breathtaking views of Mount Verónica. There is a wood-fired sauna for relaxing, and the hotel has its own organic farm out back, from which it sources most of the vegetables for the excellent restaurant. Pachamanca farm lunches are also available for groups. Book ahead because it fills up fast.

Hostal Sauce (Ventiderio s/n, tel. 084/20-4044, www.hostalsauce.com.pe, US$100 s, US$110 d with breakfast) is a serene, upscale establishment with eight sun-filled rooms overlooking the Ollantaytambo ruins. The restaurant, serving salads, meats, and pastas, has a cozy sitting area with a fireplace and couches. This hotel is deservedly very popular, so book in advance, particularly in high season.

INFORMATION AND SERVICES

There is a **municipal tourist office** (tel. 084/204030, 8am-5pm Mon.-Fri., 7am-4pm Sat.-Sun.) on the plaza.

KB Tambo (tel. 084/20-4091, www.kb-peru.com) and the NGO **Awamaki** (Calle Convención s/n, across from the temple, www.awamaki.org) also have good information. Also visit the website www.ollantaytambo.org.

The **police** and the **Botica Drugstore** (tel. 084/20-4015, 8am-9pm daily), which has public phones, are both located on the main square. For medical needs, **Centro de Salud** (Ferrocarril s/n, tel. 084/20-4090) is open 24 hours. **Banco de Crédito** has an **ATM** in Hotel Sauce, and there is another ATM on the Plaza de Armas.

Volunteer Opportunities and NGOs

There are several NGOs in Ollantaytambo worth contacting if you're looking for volunteer and homestay opportunities. Based in Ollantaytambo, **Awamaki** (Calle Convención s/n, across from the temple, www.awamaki.org), founded by American Kennedy Leavens, is a Peruvian NGO partnered with a U.S. NGO of the same name that administers a weaving project with Quechua women and promotes health, education, and sustainable tourism. They have been instrumental in helping weavers in Patacancha and other communities restore their ancient weaving techniques and find sustainable ways to market their products. Awamaki can arrange all kinds of volunteer experiences, Spanish-language programs, homestays, excursions to the communities outside of Ollantaytambo, and classes in ceramics, basket weaving, and cooking. A highly recommended experience is Awamaki's weaving class in Patacancha.

Another NGO is **Living Heart** (www. livingheartperu.org), founded by Sonia Newhouse, who owns **Heart's Cafe** on the Plaza de Armas. Living Heart aims to improve the quality of life for disadvantaged Andean children and has volunteering opportunities.

GETTING THERE AND AROUND

To get to Ollantaytambo from Cusco by bus, take the bus from the first block of Grau near the bridge (US$1.50, 90 minutes) to Urubamba and then hop another *combi* for the 20-minute, US$1 ride to Ollantaytambo. However, the most convenient option to get to Ollantaytambo from Cusco is to take a car or *colectivo* from the Paradero Pavitos (US$3.50, 90 minutes) to Ollantaytambo.

The station where you catch the train from Ollantaytambo to Aguas Calientes is a 10- or 15-minute walk down from the main square along the Río Patacancha. There are *moto-taxis* if you are weary. From Ollantaytambo, various trains leave for Machu Picchu with PeruRail (www.perurail.com), which has the most departures, as well as **Inca Rail** (www.inkarail.com) and **Machu Picchu Train** (www.machupicchutrain.com). Prices start at US$75 per person one-way. For up-to-date prices and times, see the websites. Note that new regulations mean that only one small piece of hand luggage weighing up to 5 kilograms is allowed on the trains. You are advised to leave the rest of your luggage at your hotel in Ollantaytambo or Cusco, or you must send it ahead on a freight train, which is inconvenient.

Reaching Cusco from Ollantaytambo is easy. *Combis* leave Ollantaytambo's main square for Urubamba, where another *combi* can be taken to Cusco. Direct buses for Cusco (US$1.75, 80 minutes) leave from Ollantaytambo when the evening trains arrive. However, the most convenient option is taking a car or *colectivo* from the train station or the main plaza ($3.50-5), but you need to wait for them to fill up (which they invariably do as soon as the train arrives).

PATACANCHA

Patacancha is a traditional Quechua community about an hour's drive above Ollantaytambo on a dirt road. People in Patacancha live much as they have for centuries, weaving, farming, and raising animals.

While in Patacancha please be aware that tourism can be harmful. Be sensitive and discreet in taking photos, avoid gaping into people's doorways, and avoid visiting the school, as this is very disruptive to classes. Be aware that you will probably be flocked by women trying to sell you things, much of it junk purchased in Cusco. Look for the naturally dyed, hand-woven textiles for which the community is known.

Patacancha is difficult to visit independently, as very little Spanish is spoken and there is no daily public transportation. *Combis* leave the plaza of Ollantaytambo Wednesday and Friday very early in the morning (around 6am). Or, just head up Patacalle. It's a four- to five-hour walk to the community, and most drivers, if you see any, are willing to pick you up for a few *soles*.

For a deeper understanding of life in Patacancha, the Ollantaytambo-based NGO Awamaki (Calle Convención s/n, across from the temple, www.awamaki.org) offers alternative community visits. The half-day tour, in English, includes transport, a visit to the Awamaki cooperative's weaving center, a demonstration of the weaving process, and the opportunity to buy top-quality, authentic weavings directly from the women. The tour also includes a visit to a Quechua house with permission, a respectful environment for photo-taking, and nutritious snacks and a small tip for the women who participate. All proceeds benefit the project. Cost is US$15-30 per person depending on group size. Awamaki can also arrange weaving lessons and home stays in Patacancha.

Machu Picchu

Highlights

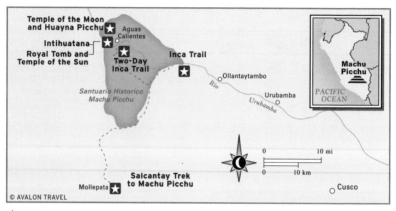

★ **Royal Tomb and Temple of the Sun:**
This semicircular temple aligns perfectly with the movement of the sun and sits on top of a cave, which may have once contained the mummy of Inca Pachacútec, the Inca's most revered ruler (page 68).

★ **Intihuatana:** Experts continue to debate the function of this carved stone. There are theories that it's a sundial, sacrificial altar, or a temple to the surrounding mountain gods. Whatever its purpose, it is profoundly beautiful and spiritual (page 70).

★ **Temple of the Moon and Huayna Picchu:** Towering above Machu Picchu is Huayna Picchu, a sacred summit reached via a two-hour hike up stairs, switchbacks, and, for the final part, a ladder. Partway up is a separate path

to the enigmatic Temple of the Moon, sculpted with curving stone walls (page 72).

★ **Inca Trail:** This sacred path is part trek, part religious pilgrimage. Winding down from the windswept mountains to lush cloud forest, it passes 30 ruins along the way, notably Wiñay Wayna (page 75).

★ **Two-Day Inca Trail:** A great option for those short on time, or not wanting to camp, this two-day hike includes some spectacular ruins and the glorious entry to Machu Picchu via the Sun Gate (page 78).

★ **Salcantay Trek to Machu Picchu:** This five-day option offers stunning views of snow-covered mountains for hard-core trekkers wanting to get a taste of the high Andes (page 79).

Many photographers claim that it is impossible to take a bad photo of Machu Picchu, but even the best camera cannot capture the magnificent panorama that fuses man-made and natural beauty at the lost city of the Inca.

Machu Picchu has to be seen to be believed, and despite the enormous flow of tourist traffic through here daily, it retains an awe-inspiring grandeur. Even if no Inca city had been built here, the horn-shaped, forested peak of Huayna Picchu swirling in the mist at dawn or gleaming in the sun at midday, along with the dramatic 300-meter drops from cloud forest to the Río Urubamba, would be breathtaking enough. Add the genius of Inca architecture, built in perfect harmony with earth and skies, and it's no surprise that Machu Picchu is among the New Seven Wonders of the World.

There is not a stone out of place at Machu Picchu. Terraces, gardens, temples, staircases, and aqueducts all have purpose and grace. Shapes mimic the silhouettes of surrounding mountains. Windows and instruments track the sun during the June and December solstices. At sunrise, rows of ruins are illuminated one by one as the sun creeps over the mountain peaks. The sun, moon, water, and earth were revered by the Inca, and they drive the city's layout.

A visit to Machu Picchu is many visitors' main motivation for coming to Peru. The place has a vibrant, spiritual feel and is probably the world's best example of architecture integrating with the landscape. It is in some respects the Inca's lesson to the Western world, teaching us how to build our world around nature, not against it. Today, some 60 percent of the site is original, while the rest has been restored or rebuilt.

Frustratingly though, many visitors get shortchanged on a visit to Machu Picchu. The worst way to do it is to get up before dawn in Cusco, take a bus and train to the site, arrive midmorning (when the site is already very busy), and then return to Cusco by midnight. Why, if you have traveled thousands of miles to see one of the world's great wonders, should you rush through it in one long, grueling day? It is far better to hike the Inca Trail

Previous: tourists exploring Machu Picchu; view of the Machu Picchu ruins. **Above:** the rugged cloud forest around Machu Picchu.

Machu Picchu

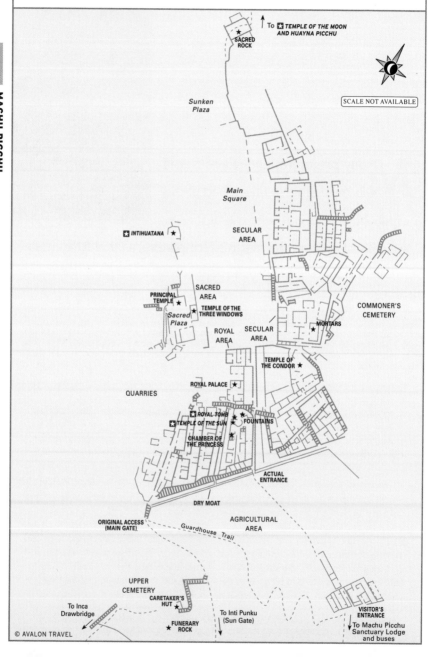

To **+** TEMPLE OF THE MOON AND HUAYNA PICCHU

SACRED ROCK

SCALE NOT AVAILABLE

Sunken Plaza

Main Square

SECULAR AREA

+ INTIHUATANA ★

SACRED AREA

PRINCIPAL TEMPLE ★

TEMPLE OF THE THREE WINDOWS ★

Sacred Plaza

ROYAL AREA

SECULAR AREA

COMMONER'S CEMETERY

MORTARS ★

TEMPLE OF THE CONDOR ★

ROYAL PALACE ★

QUARRIES

+ ROYAL TOMB ★

+ TEMPLE OF THE SUN ★

FOUNTAINS ★

CHAMBER OF THE PRINCESS ★

ACTUAL ENTRANCE

DRY MOAT

AGRICULTURAL AREA

ORIGINAL ACCESS (MAIN GATE)

Guardhouse Trail

UPPER CEMETERY

CARETAKER'S HUT ★

To Inca Drawbridge

FUNERARY ROCK ★

To Inti Punku (Sun Gate)

VISITOR'S ENTRANCE

To Machu Picchu Sanctuary Lodge and buses

© AVALON TRAVEL

a doorway at Machu Picchu

inspiration for the character Indiana Jones, came to Peru to find Vilcabamba, the legendary lost city of the Inca. This was the jungle enclave, well described by Spanish soldiers, to which Manco Inca and his followers retreated following their unsuccessful rebellion against the Spanish in 1537. Bingham began his search walking down the newly built road along the Río Urubamba (now the train line) and asking locals if they knew of any ruins along the way.

It was in this way that local resident Melchor Arteaga led Bingham to the vine-covered site, which Bingham would return to in 1912 and 1915 to excavate. He was convinced, to the end of his life, that Machu Picchu was the "lost city of the Inca." But historians are now certain he was incorrect. A wealth of supporting evidence indicates the real Vilcabamba was farther into the jungle at Espíritu Pampa, which Bingham also visited but dismissed at the time as too insignificant.

Bingham discovered more than 180 human skeletons in cemeteries around Machu Picchu, and an inexperienced scientist on his team incorrectly concluded that 80 of them belonged to women. The finding prompted the idea of Machu Picchu as a giant *acllahuasi*, or house for the Inca's chosen "virgins of the sun." Subsequent research on the skeletons proved that there were men, women, and children, with women being the majority.

The latest theory about Machu Picchu's original use, which is gaining widespread acceptance, is that it was a winter retreat built by Inca Pachacútec in the mid-15th century (around 1440). Scholars had long believed this, but concrete proof came in the form of a 16th-century suit filed by the descendants of Pachacútec, which University of California anthropologist Dr. John Rowe found while searching through archives in Cusco. Pachacútec was without doubt the greatest of Inca constructors, so it seems likely that this city was his work.

Machu Picchu's status as a sacred site is due to the quantities of *huacas* (shrines), and while Machu Picchu certainly had a religious sector, and probably an *acllahuasi* too, its primary

or stay overnight in Ollantaytambo or Aguas Calientes, get to Machu Picchu early, and linger longer, staying nearby in the evening.

HISTORY

Adding to the wonder of Machu Picchu is the mystery surrounding it. Nobody knows what the city was originally called or its precise purpose. In fact, the name *Machu Picchu*, which translates as "old peak" in Quechua, does not even refer to the city but the large mountain that overlooks it. The ruins were known to locals for generations, but they were never recorded by the Spanish, who probably did not venture this far into the cloud forest, and they had long been abandoned to be covered for centuries by dense foliage. All this changed forever when a certain young Yale archaeologist, Hiram Bingham, was brought to the site in 1911. Bingham cleared the site, recognized its importance, and announced Machu Picchu to the world.

Bingham, a 36-year-old adventurer who ended up being both a U.S. senator and the

purpose was likely to indulge the pleasures of the Inca and his family. Pachacútec could come here to escape the chill rains of Cusco, enjoy the jungle fruits of nearby Quillabamba, and hunt in the surrounding jungle.

It is not known if Pachacútec's successors ever used Machu Picchu, but many of them were likely too busy fighting wars to have time for a winter retreat. As the city had no military significance, the Spanish never discovered it and Machu Picchu remained untouched for centuries after the Inca's final defeat.

PLANNING YOUR TIME

According to an agreement reached by the Instituto Nacional de Cultura (INC) and UNESCO, only 2,500 people are allowed to visit Machu Picchu a day. The centenary celebrations of Bingham's discovery of the city saw 2011 visitor numbers top one million. Even with restrictions, that's a heck of a lot of people tramping through a relatively small site. In order for you to get the most out of your visit to Machu Picchu, here are a few tips:

- Avoid the busiest months of June-September. The "shoulder" months of April-May and September-October are usually sunny as well.

- Avoid the Peruvian holidays, July 28-August 10. The days around Cusco's Inti Raymi festival, June 24, are also busy.

- Skip solstice days (June 21 and December 21), when the ruins are full by 6am.

- Visit on a Sunday. Although Sundays are discounted for locals, Sundays tend to draw large crowds at the Pisac and Chinchero markets, thereby pulling travelers away from Machu Picchu.

- Hike one of the Inca trails. This will give you a greater sense of anticipation, and the final arrival at Machu Picchu will be more spectacular.

- If you're not hiking a trail, at least stay the night at Aguas Calientes or Ollantaytambo and take the earliest train in the morning in order to beat the train crowds, which arrive at the ruins around 10am and start departing around 2pm. Either arrive early in the morning or linger in the late afternoon. When Machu Picchu is most crowded, you can hike to Huayna Picchu, the Temple of the Moon, the Inca bridge, or the Sun Gate. Consider staying the night nearby after your visit to avoid a long trip back to Cusco.

the intricate stone work of Machu Picchu

Machu Picchu admission is expensive by Peruvian standards and only lasts one day. Foreigners pay US$40, and nationals and students under age 26 with an ISIC card pay US$20. Including the climb up Huayna Picchu costs an extra US$10 and should be reserved at least 10 days in advance. Note that there are **no ticket sales on-site** and tickets must be bought in advance in *soles* at the **INC** office in Cusco (Av. el Sol) or in Aguas Calientes at **Centro Cultura Machu Picchu** (Pachacútec s/n, tel. 084/21-1196). A passport is essential to complete the transaction, so don't leave your passport in Cusco! Tickets can also be bought online at www.machupicchu.gob.pe. The ruins are open 6am-5:30pm daily.

Shuttle

Buses to Machu Picchu leave every 5-15 minutes from just below Aguas Caliente's second bridge. **Consettur Machupicchu** (Infancia 433 – Wancha, tel. 084/22-2125, www.consettur.com) sells the tickets, US$12 one-way and US$24 round-trip, with the first bus leaving at 5:30am and the last at 5:30pm. If you want to catch the first bus up to Machu Picchu, which is a good idea, arrive at least 45 minutes early because morning lines form. The bus takes about a half hour to wind its way up the switchbacks to the ruins. It is also possible to follow the footpath to the ruins, which cuts the switchbacks. This arduous, all-uphill hike in the moist cloud forest takes about 90 minutes.

Facilities

Outside the gate of the ruins, there are bathrooms and **El Mirador Snack Bar** (US$4), which sells bottled water, sandwiches, and hamburgers that you can take away or eat at picnic tables. Note that there are no bathrooms inside the ruins (so go before you enter), although you are allowed to exit and enter as many times as you want on the same day. The gourmet **Restaurante Bufe Tinkuy** (tel. 084/21-1038, 11am-3:30pm daily, US$35) serves a huge buffet lunch open to the public that is worth the price if you have a good appetite and want to spoil yourself. There is also a separate dining room with an à la carte menu (US$40-50) serving international and Peruvian food. If you plan on eating at Machu Picchu, bring ample cash with you as prices are high. However, it is better to bring snacks and plenty of water, as it can be a long day out, and you save money by buying these in Aguas Calientes. Note: There are no ATMs at Machu Picchu, so bring cash!

Guides and Tours

During the day there are always guides, of varying quality, waiting at the entrance. A typical price is US$40 for small groups. Always check that they are registered guides with photo ID. Another option is the **Belmond Sanctuary Lodge** (tel. 084/21-1038, www.belmond.com/es/sanctuary-lodge-machu-picchu), where expensive, top-notch guides can be hired.

Ruins Tour

CARETAKER'S HUT
(LOS CUARTELES)

From the ticket booth, the path enters the south side of Machu Picchu through the Guards' Quarters, which are two-story storehouses orientated to the June solstice. There are many different ways to continue through the ruins from here—some tours begin with the agricultural area, but it's preferable to begin with the Caretaker's Hut, which commands the best views of the entire site.

The zigzag path is usually marked with white arrows on the left just after walking through the ticket area and before arriving at the Guards' Quarters. The 10-minute hike switchbacks up alongside the terraces and arrives at a lookout. This hut is one of the highest points in Machu Picchu, which allowed a caretaker to see a large stretch of the Río Urubamba in addition to the main entrance from the Inti Punku (Sun Gate). The Caretaker's House is built in the *wayrana* style, whereby one of the four walls is left completely open to promote ventilation. It opens up to the **Terrace of the Ceremonial Rock.** The significance of the rock itself is unknown. Nowadays, the terrace acts as the most popular spot to take panoramic photos of the city.

From here, it is easy to understand Machu Picchu's basic layout: A large grassy square divides the city in three areas. To the left are the **Royal and Sacred Areas,** which were probably reserved for the Inca emperor and his court. To the right is the **Secular Area,** where the workers lived, and below the lookout itself is the **Agricultural Area.** Running near the lookout area is the main Inca Trail, which comes all the way from Cusco. Looking left, you can see the trail coming down the terraced hillsides from the **Inti Punku,** or Sun Gate, the ceremonial entrance to Machu Picchu. On the other side of the Inca Trail are smaller paths that lead uphill to the Caretaker's Hut and another that leads across the terraces to the **Inca drawbridge.**

FUNERARY ROCK
(ROCA FUNERARIA)

A carved slab is situated on the left-hand side of the Caretaker's Hut. It is a large, white, granite altar with carvings of three steps and a large, flat bed on top. There is also a ring pointing in the direction of the solstice; its significance remains unknown. The Funerary Rock is surrounded by many other foreign rocks, such as limestone, which is found in Sacsayhuamán and other quarries far from Machu Picchu. These rocks are believed to have been left over from Inca offerings. Above the rock is a small, four-sided building whose function also remains unknown.

AGRICULTURAL AREA
(SECTOR AGRICOLA TERRAZAS)

Beneath the lookout and above the Guards' Quarters are more than 100 agricultural terraces that face the sun year-round and were used to grow multiple crops. These terraces used fertile dark earth brought from the valley below; the earth's porous quality drains waters efficiently, so despite the region's wet climate, Machu Picchu's terraces were not prone to flooding. In 2002, Cusqueñan archaeologist Elva Torres took samples from different terraces to determine what crops

terraces at Machu Picchu

the Inca cultivated in Machu Picchu. The results showed that they cultivated pumpkins, squash, tomatoes, peppers, and other indigenous tubers, such as *yacon,* which is used to treat diabetes.

MAIN GATE
(LA PUERTA PRINCIPAL)

Continuing from the Caretaker's Hut, follow the Inca Trail downhill to the Main Gate to Machu Picchu. A gigantic entrance door with locks on its inner part was used to close Machu Picchu. This is where the Inca rulers would have entered the city with great pomp. Looking through, there is a great photograph opportunity of Huayna Picchu framed by the gate. Passing through, continue on for about 40 meters, where, to your right, you will find a building with many doors on the first floor. The ground floor of this building was probably used as a meeting area, while the second floor was a storage room where produce was dried by ventilation. Below these storehouses, there are more than 15 constructions on different levels that were used as housing. Going back up to the main trail, continue three minutes until you arrive at an open area with numerous rocks. This area is the quarry of Machu Picchu.

QUARRIES
(LAS CANTERAS)

The main quarry of Machu Picchu lies on the hillside just past the Main Gate. However, there are two more quarries beside the **Sacred Rock** and another below the **Secular Area.**

There are some houses in the Main Gate quarry, and they probably belonged to the workers. One noteworthy highlight of the quarry is the **Serpent Rock;** if you look closely you will see it is etched with snake designs.

Returning to the main path, walk down the main stairway of the citadel, which has 16 different fountains that are all interconnected. The first fountain is on the right-hand side before arriving at the rest hut. From this first fountain, walk downhill, following the water into the **Royal Tomb** and **Temple of the Sun,** the most sacred of Machu Picchu's religious areas.

FOUNTAINS
(LOS FUENTES)

There are two different theories behind the fountains. Some say they were used to supply drinking water to the people of Machu Picchu, and others say that they were ritual baths.

The fountains have two very distinct styles.

the Main Gate with a view of Huayna Picchu

The first three fountains are constructed in fine stone, and the rest are built in a more rustic style using stone and mortar. Walk down 10 steps, where you will see a small entrance to the right that will take you to the impressive natural cave that the Inca fashioned into the Royal Tomb.

★ ROYAL TOMB AND TEMPLE OF THE SUN
(LA TUMBA REAL Y EL TEMPLO DEL SOL)

Here you will find a beautiful chamber where the mummy of Inca Pachacútec may have been stored, although no remains were ever found. The stonework and overall design of the building make it one of the Inca's most famed and elaborate constructions. The rocks are elegantly fitted into the contours of the natural cave, a perfect example of the Inca using carved stone to enhance the beauty of natural stone. The tomb contains three long niches and one smaller one, which has its own altar. At the entrance of the cave, there is bedrock with three long steps believed to have been used to give offerings to the dead. Inside the tomb is a chalk grid, which has been drawn by the government to determine any seismic movement in Machu Picchu.

Straight ahead is a wooden stairway next to an Inca stairway; both lead to the Temple of the Sun. *Please note:* It is forbidden to use the Inca stairway.

The Temple of the Sun, also called El Torreón (The Tower) in Spanish, is above the Royal Tomb and is unmistakable thanks to its perfect circular walls, which lean inwards for stability and recall the Coricancha in Cusco. The temple has two windows. One faces the sunrise at Inti Punku (the Sun Gate) on the December solstice, and the other is oriented to the June solstice. These windows created rays of light inside the temple during these sacred days. Therefore, the temple is considered a solar observatory.

The temple was excavated to strengthen

Royal Tomb

the walls. During this process, three niches were discovered, of which the middle niche has the distinctive double jamb. The authorities have covered this new discovery with glass. On the left side of the temple is a small, two-story building that is believed to have been the house of either a princess or a high priest. Near the sun temple is an exquisite fountain that unifies the sacred elements of Inca cosmology (sun, rocks, water, and wind).

ROYAL PALACE
(PALACIO REAL)

The buildings on the other side of the main staircase are known as the Royal Palace, because it is here that Inca Pachacútec and his family must have lived while visiting Machu Picchu. There are a few beautiful trapezoidal doorways and perfect Inca stonework, both telltale signs of royal architecture. Follow the doorways and staircases to a large stone patio.

On the right-hand side of the patio there is a large, fine door that is presumed to be the entrance to the Inca's bedroom. There are a few other rooms, including a bathroom with its own drainage system and a cooking area.

Climb to the top of the main staircase and turn right before the quarry. Continue about 60 meters to the botanical garden, where you may see various species of native flora. There are orchids, passion fruit trees, and a coca plant.

Beyond the garden to the left is the Sacred Plaza, containing both the Temple of the Three Windows and the Principal Temple.

SACRED PLAZA
(PLAZA SAGRADA)

This square has major buildings on three sides, making it one of the more important ceremonial areas of Machu Picchu. As you enter the plaza, the main attraction is the temple on the right, known as the Temple of the Three Windows.

Temple of the Sun

Temple of the Three Windows
(EL TEMPLO DE LAS TRES VENTANAS)

On the northern side of the plaza, this temple overlooks the main square of Machu Picchu and is built of gigantic stones like the structures in Sacsayhuamán. The three giant trapezoidal windows were perfectly fitted, and there are two additional windows, which were later filled to make niches. Although the exact purpose of this building is unknown, ritual ceramics such as *keros* (drinking cups) were found in the foundations in the 1980s. The view through the windows is impressive, taking in an expanse across the Main Plaza to the eastern urban sector.

The construction here was never completed. We know this because a marker that indicates where a rock should have been chiseled is still visible on the northwestern wall. To the west of the Sacred Plaza is a circular wall similar to Cusco's Coricancha (sun temple).

Principal Temple
(TEMPLO PRINCIPAL)

This building is on the western side of the Sacred Plaza and is composed of enormous horizontal stones hewn from bedrock. The temple faces Cerro Machu Picchu and has an enormous altar on the back wall. Some scholars believe that this temple was dedicated to Pachamama (mother earth). Above the altar are very high niches where ceremonial items were placed. The wall is collapsing on the right side; damage sustained to the stonework is due to insufficient foundations (an uncommon problem at Machu Picchu, where an estimated 80 percent of all stonework is underground and used to shore up the buildings on extremely steep and uneven ground).

The House of the Priest

On the eastern side of the plaza, directly opposite the Principal Temple, is a rustic house. It is believed to have been the house of the priest.

The Sacristy

Leaving the Sacred Plaza, going west behind the Principal Temple, you will come to a small construction on the right-hand side known as the Sacristy.

The Sacristy is the only room within the city that has the Inca imperial style but that is not a temple or a palace. If you look carefully, you may notice the anti-seismic construction using bedrock, keystones, and the famous 32-sided stone. Also note the unfinished polishing on the rocks.

Leaving the Sacristy, go to your right and climb up the impressive stairway to the top. On your right-hand side, there is a rock that represents the mountains of Putucusi and Yanantin. Continue upwards to the home of the Intihuatana.

★ INTIHUATANA

To the west of the Principal Temple, climb the staircase of the Intihuatana pyramid to the highest point in the urban area. The centerpiece is the fascinating four-sided sculpture, probably considered the most sacred in Machu Picchu. It was named by Hiram Bingham—the Quechua name translates as "place to which the sun was tied." Scholars dispute the function of this stone and have

largely dismissed the view that it was used as a sundial. More plausible theories include a solar observatory, sacrificial altar, or a temple aligned with the surrounding mountains and their resident *apus* (gods). There is no obvious logical explanation for its careful but bizarre shape, although if you stand facing Huayna Picchu, the stone's form could be a replication of the mountain's. Whatever its use or meaning, the Intihuatana is a deeply spiritual work of art, and perhaps the world's first abstract sculpture.

In front of the Intihuatana there is a stone on the ground that looks like an arrow and points directly south, similar to a stone found on Huayna Picchu. This observatory is surrounded by two three-walled constructions, one of which is completely intact. Follow the white arrows down the stairs to the bottom. Turn right and cross the plaza. To the north, two more *wayrana* buildings surround the Sacred Rock.

SACRED ROCK
(LA ROCA SAGRADA)

The form of the Sacred Rock, which is 25 feet long and flanked by sacred *wayrana* buildings, is identical to the form of the mountain Yanantin in the background. Before this rock

Intihuatana

was protected a few years ago, hundreds of Machu Picchu visitors every day would spread their arms across it to feel its energy. Behind the Sacred Rock to the left is the entrance to Huayna Picchu and the Temple of the Moon, and to the right is a short trail that heads back in the direction of the Guards' Quarters (the entrance to Machu Picchu). This trail leads past a quarry with the **Main Plaza** on the right and **Secular Area** on the left. The grass lawns of the Main Plaza are no longer accessible to visitors, but if you keep walking in the direction of the Guards' Quarters, you will have a great view of the **Artisans' Wall,** which runs along the perimeter of the Secular Area. It is one of the finest walls in the whole site.

SECULAR AREA
(SECTOR URBANO)

The Secular Area is where hundreds of workers and servants for Machu Picchu lived and worked. Many visitors miss out this area and walk straight down the stairs parallel to the outside wall. If you decide to explore, the area is divided between *kanchas* (living compounds) for the *ayllus* (clans), or Inca elite. The design is broken up and chaotic, and it's difficult to follow a set route through the area. Think of this area as the bustling, populated part of the citadel where most people lived and worked. If you lose track of the directions, head to the general areas indicated by the map.

After the narrow entrance, there is a large open area with two enormous buildings that probably functioned as *kallancas* (great halls). These buildings were used by workers for celebrations and doubled as large rain shelters.

Returning to the trail and heading in the direction of the Guards' Quarters, continue until you find a series of two-story *colcas* or storehouses. Continue along this trail for about 50 meters until you reach a corner. Head left on the steps and then head right, again in the direction of the Guards' Quarters. Continue ahead for about 60 meters until you reach an area known as the Mortars.

MORTARS
(LOS MORTEROS)

In the open space to the east, there is a large *wayrana*. Mortars that are sculpted in a circular shape with a concave base are found in the ground. While Bingham thought they were grinders, the modern-day hypothesis is that they were filled with water and used as earthquake detectors. Another theory is that they were mirrors to view constellations.

This area is also the *acllahuasi,* the "house of the chosen ones." If you explore the area, you will see that it has a large, secure doorway. Exiting the principal door, head left to the corner and go down the stairs, where you will see a tomb, known as **Intimachay** or Cave of the Sun. This was an important burial site in the citadel, and it contains a window that aligns perfectly with the first sunlight of the December solstice. Next to Intimachay is a large cave that contains a well-carved altar where many remains were found.

Back up the stairs and to your left is a large rock that has a slide on it. On top you will find an altar. From here, go down the stairs to the left, following the arrows to the Temple of the Condor.

TEMPLE OF THE CONDOR
(TEMPLO DEL CONDOR)

At the entrance, there is an open area with a sculpted rock on the ground known as the head of the condor, a bird still revered by Andean people. Directly behind are the wings of this impressive Andean bird, which in real life has a wingspan of over eight feet. Below the wings is a cave with stairs and niches on the wall believed to have been a tomb. In 1975, this cave was excavated by Alfredo Valencia, who found the bones of both llamas and guinea pigs. Experts believe the flat rock outside was used as a sacrificial table.

Above the condor, three very unusual niches have two holes on either side. While Hiram Bingham thought this was the prison, it is now believed to have been a place to worship mummies.

Temple of the Condor

To the left of the condor, there is a large two-story building. To enter the building, you must climb down the stairs, where you will find another tomb inside the house. Under the stairs, there are small holes in the base of the wall that were used to farm *cuy* or guinea pigs, a method still used in communities throughout the Andes.

If you return to the Temple of the Condor and go to the far left, there is another cave. Go inside to find yet another tomb. To exit this chamber, duck under the small door, turn left, and then go directly to the right, where there is another secular area that offers a fabulous view of the Agricultural Area and the Temple of the Sun. Climb the stairs in the direction of the Temple of the Sun, but before arriving, turn left and follow the arrows to exit back to the Guards' Quarters, from where you started your walk.

Hikes and Treks

★ TEMPLE OF THE MOON AND HUAYNA PICCHU
(EL TEMPLO DE LA LUNA Y HUAYNA PICCHU)

The hike from the Machu Picchu ruins to the summit of Huayna Picchu (elevation 2,740 meters, or 290 meters above Machu Picchu) is approximately 1.9 kilometers round-trip. It takes over an hour to get up and just under to come down again. It is not a difficult hike, but if the sun is baking down by late morning, it can be a little tough, especially if you have been trekking for several days. It starts at the Sacred Rock and passes through a gate that is open 7am-1pm. However, most people arrive before 10am with a prebooked ticket (you can pay extra for your Machu Picchu entrance ticket to include Huayna Picchu). Only 400 adults a day are allowed to do this climb (children are not allowed), 200 at 7am and 200 at 10am. If you haven't got a ticket, head there at 10am to see if there are any spaces left, but be aware that it is often completely booked, even outside high season. It makes sense to climb Huayna Picchu in the morning and then see the ruins in the afternoon to avoid missing this hike.

While it is steep, the path is in good shape, although the last 20 meters include a steep

Hikes and Treks

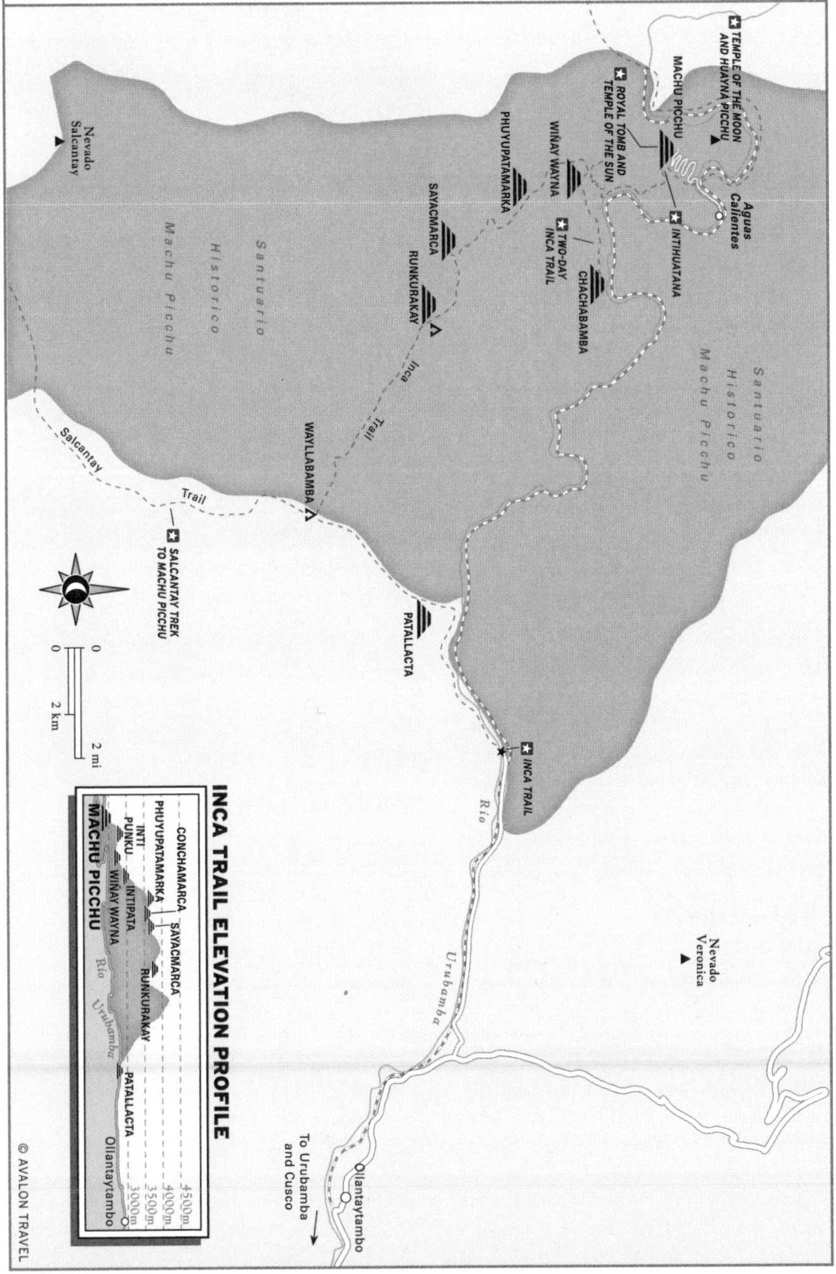

Nevado
Salcantay

TEMPLE OF THE MOON
AND HUAYNA PICCHU

MACHU PICCHU

ROYAL TOMB AND
TEMPLE OF THE SUN

PHUYUPATAMARKA

WIÑAY WAYNA

Aguas
Calientes

INTIHUATANA

SAYACMARCA

TWO-DAY
INCA TRAIL

CHACHABAMBA

RUNKURAKAY

Santuario

Historico

Machu Picchu

Santuario

Historico

Machu Picchu

WAYLLABAMBA

Inca
Trail

Salcantay

Trail

SALCANTAY TREK
TO MACHU PICCHU

N

0
0
2 km
2 mi

PATALLACTA

Rio

INCA TRAIL

Urubamba

Nevado
Veronica

INCA TRAIL ELEVATION PROFILE

CONCHAMARCA

PHUYUPATAMARKA

INTI
PUNKU

INTIPATA

SAYACMARCA

WIÑAY WAYNA

RUNKURAKAY

MACHU
PICCHU

Rio
Urubamba

PATALLACTA

4500 m
4000 m
3500 m
3000 m

Ollantaytambo

To Urubamba
and Cusco

Ollantaytambo

© AVALON TRAVEL

rock slab that must be climbed with a ladder and a rope. Take extra care in the rainy season. The Inca built retaining terraces, buildings, tunnels, staircases, and a shrine on the top of the mountain. Human remains were also found in caves. The splendor of Huayna Picchu is the breathtaking view of the entire complex, which spreads out before the summit like a map.

Farther down on the slopes of Huayna Picchu is the Temple of the Moon, a construction almost as impressive as the Temple of the Sun but with an entirely different mood. The easiest way to visit the Temple of the Moon is to retrace your steps down from Huayna Picchu and take the marked trail turnoff halfway down, which leads directly to the site. Visiting the Temple of the Moon adds about 1-2 hours onto the Huayna Picchu hike. If you visit both Huayna Picchu and the Temple of the Moon, expect to spend 3-4 hours, so take plenty of water and food.

The Temple of the Moon is a medium-sized natural cave where rocks have been fitted perfectly in flowing, gentle shapes. Instead of the tower and bright sunlight of the Temple of the Sun, everything here is recessed and dark with sinuous lines. The Temple of the Moon itself is a wall of doors and windows sculpted perfectly into the space created by a giant overhanging rock. A bit below there is a doorway that leads to other structures, including a lower cave that is near where the trail from Huayna Picchu descends.

INTI PUNKU
(SUN GATE)

For a less strenuous hike, head to the Caretaker's Hut and hike up the Inca Trail, which arcs across the mountain slope to a high pass. It is about a one-hour walk to this pass, where there is a stone construction known as the Sun Gate or Inti Punku (2,720 meters). From here you can appreciate a spectacular view of the ruins from high above. This view is the first glimpse of Machu Picchu for hikers on the classic Inca Trail. If you have enough

Hiking up Huayna Picchu offers a spectacular view of Machu Picchu.

energy you can hike a little of the Inca Trail backwards, but be aware that the checkpoint officially closes at 3pm. After visiting Inti Punku, go back down the same trail to the Caretaker's Hut.

CERRO MACHU PICCHU

Cerro Machu Picchu (3,051 meters) is the mountain above Machu Picchu in the direction of Inti Punku. This moderate three-hour hike is a good alternative to climbing Huayna Picchu, with the added bonus that you can say you've climbed the real Machu Picchu. Unknown to many visitors, this hill actually gave the city its name (Old Peak). The hike is a good way to escape the crowds, and there's a great view at the top. To get there take the Inca Trail out of the Machu Picchu ruins past the Caretaker's Hut and toward Inti Punku. About 150 meters past the Caretaker's Hut, head right up a set of stairs with a sign that says "To Machu Picchu Mountain." Follow the trail for one hour through a habitat of exotic birds, orchids, lichen, moss, and trees, until arriving at the bottom of a set of Inca stairs. From here, it is a steep, 45-minute uphill walk. This is an excellent acclimatization hike for anyone preparing for a post-Machu Picchu trek. Hiram Bingham's expedition revealed skeletons at the base of Cerro Machu Picchu. This area is therefore called **Upper Cemetery.**

INCA DRAWBRIDGE

A shorter and gentler hike than Inti Punku or Cerro Machu Picchu is along the path branching off to the right as you climb up to the Caretaker's Hut from the ruins. After you sign in at a checkpoint, the path heads into the forest before arriving at a path with sheer cliff walls. At one point, it even passes over a man-made ledge, like that found on the upper route at the Pisac ruins. The trail ends near a gap at the stone ledge, where the Inca evidently placed a drawbridge or a series of logs that could be withdrawn if necessary. It's not possible to cross the gap, and the sheer drops down to the valley far below remind you to take care on the trail. Retrace your steps back to the Caretaker's Hut.

★ INCA TRAIL

Though at times crowded, the hike to Machu Picchu is an unforgettable experience—both a backpacking trip and a religious pilgrimage. There are lots of ways to do it, with or without a pack on your back. All hikers on the actual Inca Trail must go with an agency to ensure everyone's safety and keep trash off the trail. The Inca Trail is part of the Santuario Histórico de Machu Picchu (Machu Picchu Historical Sanctuary), administered by the Instituto Nacional de Cultura (National Institute of Culture). There is a wide range in price and quality among Inca Trail agencies, and reservations should be made at least six months in advance.

The two- or even one-day option begins at kilometer 104 of the railroad line and includes a steep hike to reach the final stretch of the Inca Trail, including the ruins at Wiñay Wayna. Some agencies continue the same day to Machu Picchu and stay overnight in Aguas Calientes, while others camp near Wiñay Wayna to enter Machu Picchu the following morning.

The full four-day trip passes more than 30 Inca sites along the way and includes the most spectacular scenery, but it is arduous at times—day two especially—if you aren't a seasoned trekker. For a lighter experience, the two-day Inca Trail is also very good.

Trekking Agencies

Peruvian Andean Treks, ExplorAndes, and Tambo Tours are the longest-established trekking companies in Cusco; they pioneered the contemporary trekking culture. They are recommended, not only for their unsurpassed experience and professionalism, but also because they consistently recycle their trash, pack out all human waste, treat water carefully, and pay porters fair wages.

Among the more than 150 licensed agencies operating in Cusco, the standards of service and social and environmental responsibilities vary greatly. It is up to the client to be discerning and to research thoroughly before booking. All agencies listed here are recommended.

Peruvian Andean Treks (Pardo 705, tel. 084/22-5701, U.S. tel. 617/924-1974, www.andeantreks.com) is a long-standing company operating throughout South America.

ExplorAndes (Paseo Zarzuela Q-2 Huancaro, tel. 084/23-8380, www.explorandes.com) is Peru's most established adventure sports agency. It offers the traditional Inca Trail hike, as well as variations that combine it with treks above the Sacred Valley or around Nevado Salcantay and Nevado Ausangate. ExplorAndes was voted Peru's best overall tour operator by the Ministry of Tourism in 2005.

Tambo Tours (Casilla 912, tel. 084/23-7718, www.tambotours.com) is owned by Andreas Holland and has been operating for over 30 years. It offers diverse treks and tours with tailor-made itineraries (six people minimum) that accommodate group specifications and a wide range of special interests. The staff are very knowledgeable, and since its foundation Tambo Tours has had a profound commitment to helping local communities.

Andina Travel (Santa Catalina 219, tel. 084/25-1892, www.andinatravel.com) offers frequent departures for the Inca Trail as well as interesting sociocultural projects.

Auqui Mountain Spirit (José Gabriel 307, Urb. Magisterial, tel. 084/26-1517 or 084/25-1278, www.auqui.com.pe), run by Roger Valencia, has been operating for over 20 years. This high-end agency has a very experienced team and specializes in customized trips, especially for corporate clients.

Aventours (Saphi 456, tel. 084/22-4050, www.aventours.com) was founded by Ricky Schiller, who has been involved in the tourism industry for over 30 years. The expert staff provides excellent service.

Enigma (Fortunato L. Herrera 214, Urb. Magisterio 1a etapa, tel. 084/22-2155, www.enigmaperu.com) is one of the newer agencies. It offers Inca Trail treks combined with visits to Nevado Salcantay, Vilcabamba, and the ruins of Choquequirao. The company's treks include gourmet cooks.

Inca Explorers (Calle Peru W - 18 Urb. Ttio, tel. 084/24-1070, www.incaexplorers.com) has a range of longer trips to Vilcabamba, Choquequirao, and the Cordillera Vilcanota.

Perú Sur Nativa (Magisterio 2da etapa K-7-302, tel. 084/22-4156, www.perusurnativa.com) is owned by longtime Cusco adventurer Raúl Montes and has a wide range of trips.

Peru Treks & Adventure (Av. Pardo 540, tel. 084/222-722, www.perutreks.com) is also responsible for the very informative website Andean Travel Web (www.andeantravelweb.com).

Q'ente (Choquechaca 229, tel. 084/22-2535, www.qente.com) has been running since 1995 and provides good service and trained staff.

Quechuas Expeditions (San Juan de Dios 295, tel. 084/22-3548, www.quechuasexpeditions.com) is one of the most highly recommended trekking agencies in Cusco. It has a vast range of Andean treks.

United Mice (Av. Pachacútec 424 A-5, tel. 084/22-1139, www.unitedmice.com) is probably the most recommended backpacker's choice. It also offers a seven-day Salcantay trek, among others.

Xtreme Tourbulencia (Plateros 364, tel. 084/222-405, U.S. tel. 702/560-7220, www.x-tremetourbulencia.com) receives good reviews and offers a range of treks and tours throughout Peru.

Four-Day Inca Trail

DAY 1

This trip traditionally begins with an early-morning three-hour bus ride to **Piscacucho,** which is at kilometer 82 of the train line at 2,700 meters (some agencies use the train instead, which drops backpackers a bit farther down at kilometer 84). The trail begins in a subtropical ecosystem, with lots of agave plants and Spanish moss hanging from the trees. Many of the cacti along the trail have a parasite that turns crimson when you crush it in your fingers, a trick local woman use for lipstick. The first ruins you pass are **Patallacta,** meaning "city above terraces" in Quechua; this middle-class residential complex was used as a staging ground for Machu Picchu. There is a modest 12 kilometers of hiking this first day, making it a relatively easy day, with an elevation gain of 500 meters to **Wayllabamba,** where most groups camp the first night with stunning views of the Huayluro Valley.

DAY 2

The 12 kilometers covered on this day are much more strenuous, because you climb 1,200 meters in elevation, including two mountain passes back to back. On the first pass, at 4,200 meters, you will pass by the ruins of **Runkurakay,** a round food storehouse strategically located at a lookout point. This site has an incredible view over a valley and nearby waterfall. The second pass, at 3,950 meters, is named Dead Woman's Pass after a mummy discovered there. In the late afternoon you will see the ruins of **Sayaqmarka** (3,625 meters), where there are good views of the Vilcabamba range. Sayaqmarka was probably used as a *tambo,* or resting spot, for priests and others journeying to Machu Picchu. The complex is divided into a rough lower section and a more elaborate upper area that was probably used for ceremonial purposes. Most trekkers camp this second night at **Pacaymayo,** with views of snow-covered peaks, including Humantay (5,850 meters) and Salcantay (6,271 meters), the highest peak in the area.

DAY 3

After a very tough second day, this is a relatively easy day with plenty of time for meandering and lots of memorable sights. You enter the cloud forest, full of orchids, ferns, and bromeliads, to reach the ruins of **Phuyupatamarka,** a ceremonial site

from where you get a first glimpse of the back of Machu Picchu, marked with a flag. Look out for hummingbirds, finches, parrots, and the crimson Andean cock of the rock. Most groups rest at a halfway lookout point that is often shrouded by clouds. From here, it is a two-hour hike straight down, dropping 1,000 meters to the third campsite at 2,650 meters, where there are hot showers, cold beers, and a restaurant. There is usually plenty of time in the afternoon to see the ruins of **Wiñay Wayna,** a spectacular ceremonial and agricultural site that is about a 10-minute walk away. These are easily the most spectacular ruins on the Inca Trail. This complex is divided into two sectors, with religious temples at the top and rustic dwellings below. The hillside is carved into spectacular terraces, and the Río Urubamba flows far below.

DAY 4

Most groups rise very early in the morning in an attempt to reach the sanctuary before sunrise, and it can feel like walking in a herd of cattle. The walk is flat at the start and then inclines steeply up to **Inti Punku** (the Sun Gate), from where you

Colorful flora is part of the Machu Picchu experience.

Camisea Gas Field: The Last Place on Earth

Up until the discovery of the Camisea Gas Field, few outsiders had ever entered the lower Urubamba basin, a vast swath of rainforest downriver from Machu Picchu. A treacherous river gorge deterred boat traffic, and the sheer flanks of the **Cordillera Vilcabamba** hindered would-be colonists.

Thanks to its geographic isolation, the lower Urubamba has evolved over millions of years into one of the world's top 25 megadiversity hot spots, according to Conservation International. Biologists continue to discover an unprecedented variety of endemic plant and animal species in the area.

This swath of mountains and jungles is also home to several thousand seminomadic indigenous people. Some of these groups fled to these remote headwaters a century ago to escape the disease and slavery of the rubber boom. Their way of life was supposedly protected in the 1970s when the Peruvian government declared the area a cultural reserve for the Yine, Nahua, and Kirineri peoples.

The area has come under pressure ever since engineers discovered an estimated 11 trillion cubic feet of gas under the jungle floor, now known as the Camisea Gas Field. After more than two decades of negotiations, the Peruvian government signed an agreement to develop Camisea in early 2000. The lower Urubamba hasn't been the same since.

Dynamite explosions replace the murmur of rivers and shrieking of parrots, as engineers map the contours of the vast gas deposit along a checkerboard of paths spaced a mere 300 yards apart. Chainsaws and bulldozers clear forest to make way for unloading zones, a processing plant, and drilling platforms, several of which are inside the cultural reserve. Helicopters routinely buzz the canopy. A 25-meter-wide corridor of cleared land reaches over the Cordillera Vilcabamba and down into the jungle below.

The lead Camisea players are Texas-based **Hunt Oil** and the Argentine companies **PlusPetrol** and **Grupo Techint,** which led the US$1.6 billion effort to drill the gas and then ship it to the coast via two separate pipelines. Hunt built a US$2.1 billion liquefied natural gas plant on the coast south of Lima. Another Texas company, the KBR division of **Halliburton,** runs a Camisea gas plant next to **Paracas,** Peru's most important marine reserve. Conservationists

---

will be rewarded with a 180-degree view of **Machu Picchu.** If you're lucky, you'll witness the unforgettable sight of the sun rising at Machu Picchu, although all too often the stubborn mist can leave you frustrated. Your guide will take you through the ruins, leaving you time to wander on your own and to climb **Huayna Picchu** or **Cerro Machu Picchu** if you still have the energy after a four-day trek.

★ Two-Day Inca Trail

This two-day trip consists of one day of trekking and one day of visiting Machu Picchu. It is a fairly easy hike, and for those who like to avoid camping, there's the advantage of staying in a hotel.

DAY 1

A short train ride from Ollantaytambo brings you to kilometer 104 (altitude 2,100 meters) of the train tracks. Your trek begins across the river at the ruins of **Chachabamba,** where visits to the complex are offered by most trekking agencies. From here, an eight-kilometer ascent through orchids, waterfalls, and hummingbirds in the cloud forest brings you to the impressive site of **Wiñay Wayna.** In Quechua this means "forever young," and it is home to the beautiful bright purple Wiñay Wayna orchids. Most people stop here for lunch before continuing along the Inca trail to **Inti Punku** (the Sun Gate), after which trekkers arrive at **Machu Picchu** itself. Due to changes in

opposed the project on the grounds that a single tanker spill could wipe out Paracas's already endangered marine life. The project went ahead regardless and began operation in 2004.

During the early stages of the project, U.S. media coverage focused on the behind-the-scenes lobbying, from both the Bush administration and the Inter-American Development Bank (IDB), which helped make the project happen. For some environmentalists, the real story, however, is the destruction in the lower Urubamba. They fear the same pattern of destruction that destroyed parts of the Amazon in the 20th century.

The pipeline was built with aging pipework, and since December 2004, there have been at least five ruptures of the Camisea pipeline, which sent thousands of barrels of gas into the pristine Urubamba River and polluted local water supplies. Unchecked erosion from the pipeline has also muddied water supplies and decimated fish, a main food source. A Peruvian government report estimated that 17 indigenous people have died of diseases brought to the area by oil workers. The government has promised to build fish farms to replace the extinct river fish, but these promises have yet to be fulfilled.

The Peruvian government has defended the Camisea project for producing valuable foreign revenue and helping Lima make its transition to cleaner-burning fuels. The government has received billions of dollars in royalties from Camisea, while the cheap gas has helped fuel Peru's economic growth during the past decade, allowing millions of people to escape poverty.

At the same time, not all environmentalists are opposed. Some conservationists have pointed to Camisea as a model for hydrocarbon development in fragile ecosystems through its "offshore-inland" method, which means no roads. Instead, transportation is done by helicopter to minimize environmental damage.

The oil companies, meanwhile, have promised to minimize impact by using lateral drilling technology and oil platforms normally used for deep-sea drilling. And the IDB has also monitored the environmental impacts of Camisea as part of the bank's latest US$800 million loan.

However, Peru's politicians have focused far more on the availability of gas for local people than on environmental issues. In April 2012, President Humala announced a deal to guarantee that supplies from the largest block of the gas field would be used for domestic purposes.

regulations, everyone who does the short Inca Trail now hops on a bus and stays in a hotel in **Aguas Calientes.**

DAY 2
Return early by bus for a full day to see **Machu Picchu** and its surroundings.

★ SALCANTAY TREK TO MACHU PICCHU

This five-day trek, which includes one day in Machu Picchu, is one of the latest alternatives in the area and is becoming increasingly popular. As there are no restrictions, unlike on the Inca Trail, you can do this trek on your own or with a guide or agency. If you don't like camping, there are now high-quality lodges along the route operated by **Mountain Lodges of Peru** (Av. El Sol 948, Centro Commercial Cusco Sol Plaza, tel. 084/262-640, www.mountainlodgesofperu.com).

Day 1
Leaving Cusco, take the road heading toward Lima to the town of Limatambo and the site of **Tarawasi,** named after the berry *tara,* which grows in the area. Continue on to **Soraypampa** (3,869 meters), which is above the nearby herding village of Mollepata. At Soraypampa there is a campsite and a lodge operated by Mountain Lodges Peru. This company offers luxury high-altitude trekking, with four lodges located along the Salcantay route. Their lodges

are all designed with elements of environmental sustainability in mind. With heating, hot showers, incredibly comfortable beds, and Jacuzzis, this is a great option for trekkers who either do not want to camp or don't want to carry the gear on the way to Machu Picchu.

In Soraypampa, you have wonderful views of both **Salcantay** (6,264 meters) and **Humantay** (5,917 meters) mountains. If you are staying in the lodge, you can hike to the beautiful multicolored lake at the foot of Humantay glacier as an acclimatization tour. Some trekkers prefer to push on past Soraypampa to a campsite at **Soyroccocha** (4,206 meters). The campsite is at a very high altitude, so come acclimatized and bring plenty of warm clothing.

Day 2

This is the day of the **high pass** (4,300 meters) and possible sightings of the intriguing Andean chinchilla, a furry rodent that resembles a baby rabbit. Switchbacks take you up to the pass to spectacular snowy views of the mountain. From here, it is a steep 3.5-hour downhill walk through both barren high plains and cloud forest to the campsite of **Colpapampa** (2,682 meters).

Day 3

Colpapampa to **La Playa** is a breathtaking trek. You are now well into the cloud forest. This agricultural area is awash with coffee, avocados, citrus fruits, and wild strawberries. This day is the easiest, as it is only a slight descent to La Playa (2,042 meters).

Day 4

Today you get to **Aguas Calientes.** Follow an old trail for about two hours to the pass (2,743 meters) and down to the Inca town of **Llaqtapata.** Here there is a small archaeological site and a spectacular view of Machu Picchu. After Llaqtapata, the trail is hard, steep, downhill, and very slippery in the rainy season. The elevation decreases 914 meters over the three-hour hike to the train station at the hydroelectric plant. From here, to get to Aguas Calientes most people take the 4:30pm train (US$8); however, some people choose to walk along the train track, which takes approximately three hours and covers eight kilometers. Most tours offer a night in a hotel in Aguas Calientes before going to Machu Picchu the next day.

Day 5

Early in the morning, you take the short

a hut on the Salcantay trail

bus trip from Aguas Calientes up to Machu Picchu to spend the day.

INCA JUNGLE TRAIL

The latest route to Machu Picchu is locally known as the Inca Jungle Trail. This is a four-day trip that includes biking, hiking, and trains. The advantage of this route is the comparatively lower altitude. It is a completely different experience, with the emphasis on cloud forest scenery, plus a welcome dip in thermal baths. Unlike on the other trails, archaeology is scarcely visible before arriving at Machu Picchu.

Day 1

After 10 years, a decent road to Quillabamba has finally been constructed. A bus ride of about three hours passes Urubamba and Ollantaytambo to the new road, which leads to the Abra Málaga (4,300 meters), a high pass into the jungle. Most tours bike 80 kilometers down this road to the town of Santa María, which is a vertical drop of 3,000 meters. Be very careful since this road is very busy with speeding minibuses and trucks.

Day 2

This day is a six- to seven-hour trek through cloud forest. An old Inca trail has been discovered here and is currently being restored. The walk itself takes you through coffee plantations, coca fields, and fruit farms. This walk is a hiker's favorite because it leads directly to the Cocalmayo hot springs in Santa Teresa. Floods in January 2010 washed the baths out completely; they have since been restored, although they are more modest now.

Day 3

This is another day of trekking; the geography is very similar to that of the previous day. After a morning of trekking, you will finally arrive at the hydroelectric plant, where a train takes you to Aguas Calientes.

Day 4

Early in the morning, you head by bus to Machu Picchu to do the normal day tour.

Getting There and Around

There are various ways to reach Aguas Calientes, the town at the base of Machu Picchu. You can take the Inca Trail or the Salcantay route, ride the train from Ollantaytambo (90 minutes) or from near Cusco (2.5 hours), take the Inca Jungle Trail, or take the bus through Santa Teresa. In Aguas Calientes, there are frequent bus shuttles to Machu Picchu, though some choose the two-hour forest hike that cuts across the road's switchbacks. Once inside Machu Picchu, the only way to get around is by foot.

TRAIN

The breakup of the longtime PeruRail monopoly has so far failed to bring down prices, and there is no escaping that the train is expensive by backpacker standards. Expect to pay US$75 one-way (US$120 round-trip). Before booking train service to Machu Picchu or asking your hotel to book trains for you, check the websites of the companies.

Inca Rail (Portal de Panes St. 105, Plaza de Armas, Cusco, tel. 084/58-1860) has two trains that offer a number of daily departures from Ollantaytambo to Machu Picchu. The Machu Picchu Train leaves Ollantaytambo daily at 7:20am, arriving in Aguas Calientes 90 minutes later. It leaves for Ollantaytambo on the return trip at 4:12pm. Prices vary according to time but are approximately US$75 one-way.

The second train, Inca Train, offers three daily departures from Ollantaytambo at 6:40am, 11:15am, and 4:36pm, as well as three daily departures from Aguas Calientes at 8:30am, 2:30pm, and 7pm. The trains have an executive class (US$50 one-way) and a first class (US$75 one-way).

The traditional option is **PeruRail** (Av. Pachacútec, Cusco, tel. 084/58-1414, www.perurail.com), which offers train service from Ollantaytambo, Pachar (about an hour and a half from Cusco), and Poroy (near Cusco) to Aguas Calientes. The price varies depending on the station and train; the company offers the **Expedition** (US$140-240 round-trip, US$70 one-way), the **Vistadome** (US$160-260 round-trip, US$90 one-way), and the luxury **Hiram Bingham service** (US$588 round-trip, US$334 one-way). The Expedition train is nearly as comfortable as the Vistadome, with large, soft seats and plenty of legroom. Food for sale includes sandwiches (US$4) and candy bars (US$2). The perks of the Vistadome include large viewing windows in the ceilings, shows put on by train attendants (including fashion walks to promote alpaca clothing), luxurious seats, lights snacks and beverages, and live Andean music.

The Hiram Bingham service is in a whole different league. A full brunch is served on the ride from Poroy (15 minutes outside Cusco) to Machu Picchu, where guests are treated to a deluxe ruins tour and a full tea at the Sanctuary Lodge. On the ride home, predinner pisco sours are served in the elegant dark-wood bar, accompanied by a live band and dancing. A gourmet four-course dinner follows at your private table, accompanied by a selection of wines. Afterwards, there is live music and dancing for those with energy. Hands down, this is the most luxurious train service in Latin America. If it feels like the Orient Express, that's because it is—PeruRail has been operated by Orient-Express Ltd. since the late 1990s.

All trains depart from Ollantaytambo or Pachar except the Hiram Bingham service. The Hiram Bingham luxury train avoids the famous (or infamous) switchbacks out of Cusco by leaving from the Poroy station, which is a 15-minute drive from Cusco. Its bus departs Cusco at 8:10am. The train leaves Poroy at 9:40am and arrives in Aguas Calientes at 12:30pm. On the return, the train departs Aguas Calientes at 5:50pm and gets to Poroy at 8:50pm. The bus returns to Cusco at 10pm.

The Cusco-Machu Picchu train crosses high, desolate plains before descending to meet the Urubamba Valley. Once past Ollantaytambo, the rail enters a gorge that grows narrower and deeper as it continues its descent. Look for occasional glimpses of snow-covered Verónica

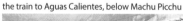
the train to Aguas Calientes, below Machu Picchu

Sinking Like Stone: The Weight of Tourism

The phenomenal beauty of Machu Picchu attracted over a million tourists in 2011, a huge increase on the previous year, and that number had increased to nearly 1.2 million in 2014. More than 3,000 tourists per day trample the grounds of the ancient Inca city, well above the limit that Peru agreed to with UNESCO. Such popularity comes at a price. Because Machu Picchu is built on a man-made mound of earth, the ground is comparatively soft and the site is actually sinking, albeit very slowly. Some of the Inca stonework already shows signs of damage, and there is evidence of soil erosion and damage to surrounding vegetation.

tourists at Machu Picchu

After pressure from UNESCO, the Peruvian government introduced the first restrictions on the Inca Trail in 2001, limiting numbers to 500 people per day, including guides and porters. At Machu Picchu, luxury helicopter rides have been banned and total visitor numbers limited to 2,500 per day. But this is still a huge number of people, and such is the value of Machu Picchu to the local economy that it seems unlikely there will be further restrictions.

In fact, the government is now looking to implement strict new measures to visit Machu Picchu that would allow for a significant increase in tourists. In 2015, Peruvian media reported the findings of a government-commissioned study that said Machu Picchu could withstand 5,940 daily visitors if managed correctly. That would be a whopping 2.2 million visitors a year.

How are they going to do it? In 2015, the government approved a US$40 million master plan for Machu Picchu that would overhaul the management of the complex and the tourist experience. The plan envisions changing the entry point to Machu Picchu and adding new routes to and around the citadel, as well as building a help center and adding toilets within the ruins.

For tourists, the biggest change would be once they are inside the complex. The plan calls for creating three marked paths, and time limits at each part of Machu Picchu to keep the flow moving. It is unclear when this could happen, but what is certain is that the old days of moving freely within Machu Picchu are likely numbered as the longstanding tension between profiteering and preservation continues.

<sidebar>

MACHU PICCHU

GETTING THERE AND AROUND
</sidebar>

(5,750 meters) to the right. At kilometer 88 there is a modern bridge built on Inca foundations. As the vegetation and the air grow thicker, the train descends into what the Peruvians call the *ceja de selva* (eyebrow of the jungle), and the Río Urubamba starts crashing over house-sized boulders. The train continues until reaching Aguas Calientes.

BUS JOURNEY FROM SANTA TERESA

The elaborate bus ride to Machu Picchu via Santa Teresa is hardly worth it unless you are really counting your pennies. From the Terminal de Santiago in Cusco, take a bus to Santa María (six hours, US$3). From Santa María, it is a two-hour bus ride to Santa Teresa. From there, shared taxis called *colectivos* will take you across the river to Oroya, where you can take a 5:30pm train to Aguas Calientes (US$8), or where you can walk three hours to the town. No matter what, if you choose this route, you will need to spend the night in Aguas Calientes, which may put another dent in your pocket.

Aguas Calientes

Ever since a landslide destroyed the railway past Machu Picchu to Quillabamba, Aguas Calientes is literally the end of the line for the Cusco-Machu Picchu train. While the Sacred Valley towns of Pisac and Ollantaytambo boast a vibrant Inca heritage, the town that is the gateway to Machu Picchu is unashamedly modern. There is nothing authentically indigenous about Aguas Calientes; it is a pure tourist town that has sprung up to accommodate the hordes of tourists—over one million per year at the last count—who flock to Machu Picchu.

That said, Aguas Calientes is not a disagreeable place. Its isolation and complete lack of cars make it relaxing to wander around, and there is an ever-increasing range of hotels and restaurants for all budgets. At 2,000 meters, it's also considerably lower and warmer than the Sacred Valley and Cusco. Few people stay here for longer than one night before or after a day at Machu Picchu, which is infinitely preferable to rushing to Machu Picchu on a day trip. But factor in the hair-raising climb up Putukusi, the Mandor waterfalls,

and the thermal baths that give the town its name (Hot Waters), and you could do worse than stay here for two nights.

SIGHTS

The town spreads uphill from the tracks alongside the Río Aguas Calientes past a square and up the main drag of Pachacútec, which is lined with hotels and restaurants. On the other side of the river, the Orquideas neighborhood is quieter, with a few new hotels, and is also home to the new stadium.

At the top of Pachacútec are the town's **thermal baths** (US$4 with towels, 5am-8pm daily). The six baths are cleanest in the morning and are usually quite grimy by evening. A dirt trail leads uphill for several hours to a string of remote but attractive waterfalls.

Follow the road toward Machu Picchu, and just before the uphill zigzag road to the ruins is **Museo del Sitio Machu Picchu** (highway to Machu Picchu at Puente Ruinas, 9am-4:30pm daily, US$8). The English-Spanish signs in this small, modern museum lead you geographically, culturally, and historically

statue of Inca emperor Pachacútec in the main square of Aguas Calientes

Aguas Calientes

© AVALON TRAVEL

0   50 yds
0   50 m

To Museo del sitio Machu Picchu,
Belmond Sanctuary
Lodge, and Machu Picchu

To Sacred Valley
and Cusco

Río Urubamba

Río Aguas Calientes

Río Alcamayo

RUPIWASI/
TREE HOUSE

THE TREE HOUSE
MACHUPICCHU HOSTAL
EL TOLDO
PACHAMAMA
APU INKA
SPA

TOTO'S HOUSE

ATM

CENTRO
MEDICO

FORTALEZA

PERU RAIL
OFFICE

ANTISUYO

SINCHI ROCA

HOSTAL LOS
CAMINANTES

TOURIST
INFORMATION

GRINGO BILL'S

CENTRO CULTURA
MACHU PICCHU

Plaza
Principal

IPERU/
INDIO FELIZ
EL MAPI

PUEBLO
VIEJO

LLOQUE UPANQUI

MAYTA CAPAC

WASICHA
INKATERRA

PIZZERIA
INKA WASI

AV. PACHACUTEC

PIZZERIA
KEROS

INCA ROCA

Artesian
Market

TRAIN
STATION

EL PUEBLO
MARKET

CANDELA'S

HOSPEDAJE
Q'ENTE

PACHAMAMA INN

MACHU PICCHU
PUEBLO HOTEL

KANTU
INN

YAHUAR HUACA

Soccer
Field

LAS ORQUIDEAS

HOSPEDAJE
INTI WASI

YAHUAR HUACA

EL KINTU
INN

INTI
INN

WIRACOCHA

CHEZ
MAGGY

HOSTAL
QUILLA

HOSTAL
PIRWA

Hospedaje
Inti Wasi

LA CABANA

BIG BROTHER

COLLASUYO

CONTISUYO

HUANACAURE

through Machu Picchu. Dioramas explain a typical Incan day in Machu Picchu, and enlarged photos explain the site's investigation. There is also an attached orchid garden, which contains some 300 species.

ENTERTAINMENT AND EVENTS

The disco **Wasicha** (Lloquey Upanqui, 6pm-late) is one of the few spots for dancing. **Big Brother** (6pm-midnight) at the top of Pachacútec has a pool table and is a good place for a drink. Most people, however, simply hang out in the town's many restaurants that stay open until midnight.

SHOPPING

Most Machu Picchu travelers pass through the Aguas Calientes **market,** which lies between the train station and the town itself. The market has touristy knickknacks for sale, as well as some good jewelry and textiles, but better quality can be found in the Sacred Valley and in Cusco.

RECREATION
Putukusi

This forested rock dome 400 meters above Aguas Calientes is a superb but spine-chilling half-day hike that offers great views of Machu Picchu and a chance to see many different cloud forest birds. However, you must negotiate 200 meters (600 feet) of wooden ladders nailed to the near-vertical cliff face. The trailhead is signed and is 150 meters past the control point on the railroad tracks. The walk is approximately three hours, allowing you to arrive in leisure and get a very different photo of Machu Picchu. Note that this hike is dangerous after heavy rains, so always check locally with the tourist office for the latest conditions.

Cataratas de Mandor

Another option for out-of-town recreation is the Mandor waterfalls. About a one-hour walk (five kilometers) along the railway track in the direction of the hydroelectric plant brings you to a small house where you pay the entrance fee ($3.50). From here, it is a 45-minute hike through a banana plantation and jungle that starts from kilometer 115 off the tracks. Make sure to take the trail on the right-hand side.

FOOD

Along the railroad tracks and up on the main street, Pachacútec, Aguas Calientes is packed with restaurants. Most have a range of Peruvian meat, chicken, and fish specialties as well as the standard pizza, pasta, steaks, and other international fare. There are so many options that it seems that you are spoiled for choice. However, be advised that hygiene in Aguas Calientes is hit-and-miss, so take care where you eat. For your Machu Picchu tour, various hotels and restaurants prepare box lunches, including Gringo Bill's, Rupa Wasi, La Cabaña, and Inkaterra Machu Picchu Pueblo Hotel.

International

For something different, try ★ **The Tree House** (Huanacaure 180, in the Rupa Wasi hotel, tel. 084/21-1101, 5:30am-3pm and 7pm-11pm daily, mains US$20-25). The ecologically minded restaurant brings a fine selection of wines and pisco to accompany its high-quality food. Try the delicious trout coated in quinoa, Thai chicken, Asian soup, or sushi. They can also provide a very good box lunch for visits to Machu Picchu.

The French-Peruvian-owned ★ **Indio Feliz** (Lloque Yupanqui 103, tel. 084/21-1090, www.indiofeliz.com, 10am-6pm Mon.-Fri., US$12) is easily the best restaurant in town, combining the best of Peruvian and French food, but served in American-sized portions. The two-story restaurant has a peaceful, homely feel, with tables in a sunny upstairs dining room. The three-course set menu is outstanding value for US$22 and includes a wide selection. Start with French onion soup and follow with salmon, trout, or chicken breast cooked in a wide range of sauces—lemon, garlic, mango, ginger, pineapple, pisco, or rum. The apple and orange pies with custard are delicious desserts. If you get a chance, talk to the French owner, Patrick, a very entertaining, friendly man who is passionate about his restaurant.

Pueblo Viejo (Pachacútec s/n, tel. 084/21-1193, 10am-11pm daily, US$5-10) is at the bottom of the restaurant row and has a cozy atmosphere with live music and a fireplace. There is a huge range of food here, from vegetarian and pizza to grilled meats. There are affordable lunchtime menus as well. Also check out **Toto's House** (tel. 084/22-4179, www.grupointi.com, 9am-11pm daily, US$18-25), a more upscale restaurant on the tracks specializing in grilled meat. It offers a US$20 lunch buffet along with river views.

Pachamama (Av. Imperio de los Incas 145, tel. 084/21-1141, 9am-9pm daily, US$8-10) has been part of Aguas Calientes for many years. It offers ceviche, deep-fried trout, and good desserts, and is a great place for groups. And yet another restaurant on the tracks, **El Kintu** (Av. Pachacútec 150, tel. 084/21-1336, 8am-10pm daily, US$7-10) is an interesting establishment with an Inca decor, open kitchen, and barbecue. It has a very relaxed atmosphere and a wide-ranging menu—trout, quinoa soup, lasagna, fajitas. There's also a small hostel attached to the restaurant. Across the tracks is **Fortaleza** (Av. Pachacútec, tel. 084/21-1119, US$14-17), a popular place for food or just an alfresco drink. Specialties include trout ceviche and *ají de gallina* (chicken in spicy sauce).

Pizza

Restaurant-Pizzeria Inka Wasi (Imperio de los Inkas 123, tel. 084/21-3322, www.inka-wasirestaurant.com, 9am-10pm Mon.-Sat., 1pm-10pm Sun., US$15) offers a US$13 buffet but also serves trout, chicken brochettes, ceviche, pastas, pizzas, and their specialty dish—guinea pig. Along Pachacútec, other recommended places include **Pizzeria Keros** (Pachacútec 116, tel. 084/21-1374, 9am-11pm daily), which also serves Peruvian dishes like guinea pig and grilled alpaca, and **Chez Maggy** (Pachacútec 156, tel. 084/21-1006, 11am-4pm and 6pm-11pm daily, US$10). Along with its sister restaurants throughout the country, Chez Maggy has an established reputation for great pastas and wood-fired pizzas.

Markets and Shops

The biggest minimarket is **El Pueblo,** next to the main market. With juices, yogurts, fresh bread, deli meats, and cheeses, it's a good place to put together a picnic.

ACCOMMODATIONS

Lodging in Aguas Calientes is expensive. The town lacks good-value budget accommodations, and those at the higher end are overpriced. However, it's possible to find some good deals. Note that the train is loud, so staying right next to the tracks is not appealing.

The biggest cluster of budget places is in the Orquideas neighborhood, across from the Río Aguas Calientes, but still choice is limited. Aguas Calientes itself is more expensive, offering plenty of midrange options, while the most upscale hotels are slightly outside of town. The Inkaterra Machu Picchu Pueblo Hotel is upstream from town, and the Machu Picchu Sanctuary Lodge is next to the ruins themselves.

US$10-25

Hospedaje Inti Wasi (Los Artesanos 102, tel. 084/21-1036, www.intiwasispiritual-center.com, US$25 pp) is a step up from some of the bare-bones options in town due to the natural surroundings. To get there, walk from the train station up the right side of the Río Aguas Calientes until it dead-ends at a point a few hundred meters below the hot baths. The main sitting area is a plant-filled courtyard. The bunk rooms are small and sparse, with foam beds, and have a tendency to heat up in the sun. Bathrooms are clean and have electric showerheads. Down by the train tracks, on the other side of town, is **Hostal Los Caminantes** (Imperio de los Incas 140, tel. 084/21-2007, US$20 pp). This old wooden building has been receiving backpackers for decades and has friendly management. The older rooms with shared bath are a little tired, while newer rooms with private baths are good value.

Hostal Pirwa (Tupac Yupanqui s/n, tel. 084/244-315, www.pirwahostelscusco.com, dorms US$13 pp, private rooms US$35 d) is part of the Pirwa chain of hostels found throughout Peru.

Off the road to Machu Picchu, just before Puente Ruinas, there is a **municipal campground** (US$10 pp). Some Inca Trail tours choose to camp here as part of the package. If you opt to camp, make sure you have plenty of bug repellent; the campground is right next to the river.

US$25-50

Hostal Quilla (Aymuraypa Tikan 109, tel. 084/21-1096, hostalquilla1@hotmail.com, US$30 s, US$45 d including breakfast) has rooms with tile floors and colorful bedspreads, and service is friendly.

Machupicchu Hostal (Imperio de los Inca 313, tel. 084/21-1034, www.hostalmachupicchu.com, US$50 s, US$65 d with breakfast) has rooms arranged around a plant-filled courtyard overlooking the river. There is a sitting area with a great river view, while the rooms themselves are plain, clean, and comfortable.

US$50-100

One of the best midrange hotels in town is ★ **Wiracocha Inn** (Calle Wiracocha 206, tel. 084/21-1088, www.wiracochainn.com, US$80 s or d), which has 25 rooms, many overlooking the river. With feather pillows, Wi-Fi, cable TV on plasma screens, walls adorned with paintings, and a decent buffet breakfast, it's a very good choice.

Next door to Machupicchu Hostal is its sister property, **Presidente Hostal** (Imperio de los Inca 135, tel. 084/21-1212, www.hostalpresidente.com, US$90 s, US$110 d), a similar production with carpeted, bigger rooms

with earth-colored walls—ask for one that overlooks the river.

The clean and modern **Pachamama Inn** (Las Orquideas Chaskatika s/n, tel. 084/21-1141, hostalpachamamainn@hotmail.com, US$80 s, US$100 d, plus US$20 for a Jacuzzi in your room) has 24-hour hot water, a money exchange, tourist information, and a restaurant. Strangely, all rooms are equipped with mirrors on the bathroom ceiling.

Even though the gringo owner is long gone, the charming ★ **Gringo Bill's** (signed well off one corner of the main square, tel. 084/21-1046, www.gringobills.com, US$98-190 d with breakfast) continues to be one of the best hotels in the center of town. It is also one of the oldest hotels in Aguas Calientes, with large rooms, balconies, a roof terrace, and great views over the town and surrounding hills. The newer suites on the top floors are the best.

US$100-150

Rupa Wasi (Huanacaure 180, tel. 084/21-1101, www.rupawasi.net, US$110 s/d, suites US$190) has great views of town, a stringent ecological policy, and nice though overpriced rooms. However, the attached restaurant, The Tree House, is one of the best in town.

La Cabaña (Pachacútec 805, tel. 084/21-1048, www.lacabanamachupicchu.com, US$140 s/d with breakfast) is a friendly place at the top of the main street. Rooms have tile floors, textured walls, and wood ceilings. The owners, Beto and Marta, take an eco-friendly approach. Additional services include guides for walks, security boxes, laundry, and a DVD player. They also offer better rates in the restaurant for guests of the hotel.

Over US$150

A formerly state-owned hotel has been taken over by the Inkaterra Group to create **El Mapi** (Pachacútec 109, tel. 084/21-1011, www.inkaterra.com, US$220 s/d with breakfast buffet). This hotel is by far the most modern looking of the Inkaterra Group, with a beautiful bar, restaurant, and wooden fencing along the windows. To get there from the main square take the main road, Pachacútec; the hotel is on the right-hand side.

★ **Inkaterra Machu Picchu Pueblo Hotel** (railroad km 110, tel. 084/21-1132, www.inkaterra.com, US$433 s, US$547 d) is one of Peru's best hotels. It has a tranquil, natural setting in the cloud forest teeming with birdlife, and it contains top-notch facilities. Stone paths wind through the forest past fountains and pools and up to secluded bungalows with colonial-style furniture, spacious bathrooms, outdoor hot tubs, and couches on your own private patio. The hotel has an eco-friendly philosophy that includes building all of its furniture on-site; it has received the Sustainable Travel award from *National Geographic Traveler*.

This is also the only Machu Picchu hotel that gives visitors a taste of the jungle. The biologist guides lead early-morning bird-watching walks and nature walks that include the biggest orchid collection in Peru (372 species), a butterfly house, and a miniature tea plantation. The hotel has reintroduced the *Oso anteojos* (Andean spectacled bear) to the area; three bears now live in the grounds of the hotel, and you can also take a tour to visit them. Facilities include an excellent restaurant and bar, as well as a spa, sauna, springwater swimming pool, and hot tub.

The latest five-star hotel in Machu Picchu, which took two years to build, is **Sumaq** (Av. Hermanos Ayar s/n, tel. 084/21-1059, www.sumaqhotelperu.com, US$480 s, US$600 d). The hotel has spacious rooms, each with its own range of amenities, beautiful king-size beds, and bathtubs. The hotel offers cooking classes, bird-watching tours, and access to a spa equipped with a sauna, massage service, and Jacuzzi. Dinner is also included.

If you have deep pockets and want to stay within a stone's throw of the lost Inca city, check out the **Belmond Sanctuary Lodge** (next to the entrance to the ruins, tel.

084/21-1038, www.belmond.com, US$1,025 s/d with full board). The lodge is owned by Belmond (formerly Orient-Express Hotels), which also operates Cusco's finest hotel, Hotel Monasterio. Belmond is not allowed to make any additions to the building, so it remains a small, modest hotel on the outside with an elegant interior. The 31 rooms have been outfitted with antiques, king-size beds, and cable TV, and the slightly more expensive rooms have views over the ruins. One advantage of staying here is a night excursion to the ruins, hosted by a local shaman, which is difficult to do from Aguas Calientes. There are two restaurants, one serving gourmet à la carte items (US$40-50) and the other offering an extraordinary buffet. The hotel also offers trekking, river rafting, and mountain-biking trips; walking paths behind the hotel lead through an orchid garden. In high season, this hotel is booked solid, so make reservations at least three months in advance.

INFORMATION AND SERVICES

There is a helpful **Iperú** office (Pachacútec s/n, tel. 084/21-1104), which hands out free maps (just up the main street from the square). If you haven't bought your Machu Picchu entrance ticket, you can do it at **Centro Cultura Machu Picchu** (Pachacútec s/n, tel. 084/21-1196, US$37). Tickets *must* be purchased before heading to the ruins. They can also be bought online in advance at www.machupicchu.gob.pe.

Where the tracks cross the Río Aguas Calientes is an **EsSalud** clinic (tel. 084/21-1037) with emergency 24-hour service, and on the other side is the **Ministerio de Salud clinic. Señor de Huanca drugstore** (8am-10pm daily) is on the tracks across from the Hostal Presidente. If they don't have what you need, the **Pharmacy Popular** (Puputi s/n, tel. 084/22-8787, 8am-10pm daily) is just off the plaza.

Banco de Crédito has an **ATM** on Imperio de los Incas near Toto's House.

The **post office** (10am-2pm and 4pm-8pm Mon.-Sat.) is on the Plaza de Armas.

There are **Internet** places around the main square.

Laundry Angela (Pachacútec 150, tel. 084/21-2205, US$2/kg) washes clothes the same day.

GETTING THERE AND AROUND

The only way to reach Aguas Calientes is by trekking or taking the train from Ollantaytambo. There are few vehicles and taxis in Aguas Calientes; the place is small enough that most visitors walk everywhere.

Cusco

Look for ★ to find recommended
sights, activities, dining, and lodging.

Highlights

★ **Catedral de Cusco:** Cusco's baroque cathedral, built atop a former Inca palace, dominates the town's Plaza de Armas and is filled with paintings from the Cusco School, elegant carved choir stalls, and a gold-covered Renaissance altar (page 99).

★ **San Blas:** This charming neighborhood is quieter and quainter than the city center. Escape the urban bustle in its narrow cobblestone streets, lined with stunning colonial architecture (page 102).

★ **Coricancha and Santo Domingo:** Nowhere is the uneasy fusion of Inca and Spanish architecture more evident than at Coricancha. The foundations of the Inca sun temple, once covered with thick plates of solid gold, are topped by a Dominican church (page 104).

★ **Sacsayhuamán:** This stone fortress of huge zigzag walls, carved from stone blocks weighing hundreds of tons, was the scene of the Inca's last stand in Cusco (page 107).

★ **Centro de Textiles Tradicionales del Cusco:** This pioneering center not only sells Cusco's finest textiles but also supports local weavers, helping them recover their ancient techniques in the process (page 112).

Cusco more than lives up to its Inca name, which translates as "navel of the world." No visit to Peru is complete without a stay in this fascinating city.

This ancient capital of the Inca culture remains the center of backpacker trails. Whichever direction you arrive from—Bolivia and Lake Titicaca to the south, Lima to the west, or the jungle to the east—all roads lead to Cusco.

Cusco stands today as one of the most beautifully schizophrenic cities in the world—a devoutly Catholic community that is extremely proud of its Inca heritage. Hispanic and Inca architecture and traditions live side by side in an alluring cultural mix. While Cusco is filled with well-preserved architecture, one can only wonder at what it must have looked like in 1533 when Spanish conquistadores arrived. As Francisco Pizarro marched wide-eyed through the Inca empire, Cusco became the holy grail of his conquest. Two scouts sent ahead told him the city was as elegant as a European city and literally covered in gold. Before the scouts left Cusco, they used crowbars to pry 700 plates of gold off the walls of Coricancha, the sun temple.

During four centuries of domination, the Spanish tried their best to subjugate the Inca legacy, but even they could not deny the brilliance of Inca construction, leaving the perfect stonework to serve as foundations for churches and to line Cusco's cobblestone alleys. In a way, it was poetic justice that when the great earthquake shook the city in 1950, the Inca structures stood firm, including the foundations of Coricancha, while more than a third of the colonial buildings were destroyed, including many Spanish churches.

Cusco is seen as the gateway to exploring Machu Picchu and the Sacred Valley, and there are more hotels, restaurants, and tour operators in the city than anywhere else in the region. However, Cusco's altitude at 3,400 meters (11,150 feet) is a major obstacle to overcome. At the airport, vendors even sell oxygen canisters and masks, and *soroche* (altitude sickness) is not to be taken lightly—it can range from a headache and lethargy to dizziness and disorientation. The last thing most travelers want to do when they finally make a Mecca-style entrance to Cusco is to leave, but

Previous: the ruins of Sacsayhuamán; the Inca sun temple of Coricancha and the colonial church and convent of Santo Domingo. **Above:** indigenous women in colorful clothing in Cusco.

Cusco

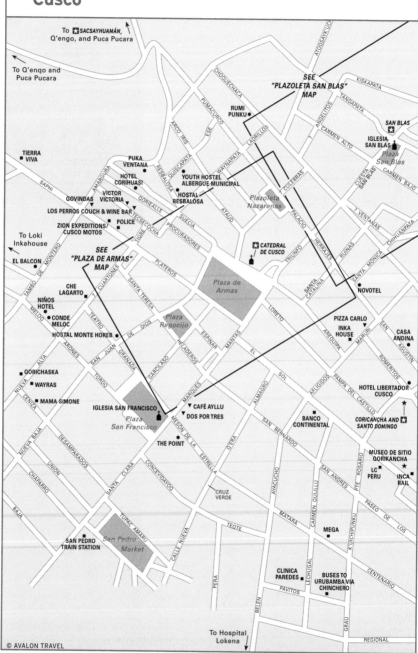

To ⊠ SACSAYHUAMÁN,
Q'engo, and Puca Pucara

To Q'enqo and
Puca Pucara

SEE
"PLAZOLETA SAN BLAS"
MAP

ATOQSAYLUCA

CHOQUECHACA

KISKAPATA

PUMACURCO

RUMI
PUNKU ●

YANDAPATA

SAN BLAS
⊞

ANGELITOS

ARCO IRIS

ESE

CARMEN ALTO

IGLESIA
SAN BLAS ⛪

TIERRA
■ VIVA

LADRILLOS

Plaza
San Blas

PUKA
VENTANA

QUISCAPATA

WAYNAPATA

CARMEN BAJO

AMARGURA

HOTEL
CORIHUASI ●

HESBALOSA

YOUTH HOSTEL
ALBERGUE MUNICIPAL

CULEBRAS

CUESTA
SAN BLAS

SAPHI

VICTOR
VICTORIA ▼

GOVINDAS ▼

HOSTAL
RESBALOSA

OORIEALLE

Plazoleta
Nazarenas

PALACIO

7 VENTANAS

CHIHUAMPATA

LOS PERROS COUCH & WINE BAR ▼

TECSECOCHA

SUECIA

ATAUD

ZION EXPEDITIONS/
CUSCO MOTOS ■

POLICE ●

TIGRE

PROCURADORES

RUINAS

To Loki
Inkahouse

DE MONTERO

TAMBO

SEE
"PLAZA DE ARMAS"
MAP

PLATEROS

CATEDRAL
DE CUSCO

⛪

TRIUNFO

HEBRAJES

SANTA MÓNICA

EL BALCON ■

CUARTONES

Plaza de
Armas

SANTA
CATALINA

NOVOTEL

CHE
LAGARTO ■

SANTA TERESA

PIZZA CARLO ▼

MELOC

NIÑOS
HOTEL

TEATRO

Plaza
Regocijo

ESPINAR

LORETO

INKA
HOUSE

MARURI

CASA
ANDINA ■

● CONDE
MELOC

DE DIOS

MANTAS

AREQUIPA

SAN AGUSTIN

HOSTAL MONTE HOREB ●

SAN JUAN

GRANADA

HELADEROS

EL SOL

ROMERITOS

ALTA

ARONES

GARCILASO

AFLIGIDOS

PAMPA DEL CASTILLO

HOTEL LIBERTADOR
CUSCO

QORICHASKA ■

NUEVA

TORDO

MARQUES

ALMAGRO

★

■ WAYRAS

CENIZA

■ MAMA SIMONE

CAFÉ AYLLU ▼

SAN BERNARDO

CORICANCHA AND ⊞
SANTO DOMINGO

IGLESIA SAN FRANCISCO ■

Plaza
San Francisco

DOS POR TRES

MESON DE LA ESTRELLA

BANCO
CONTINENTAL ■

PTE ROSARIO

MUSEO DE SITIO
QORIKANCHA ■

NUEVA BAJA

DESAMPARADOS

THE POINT ●

QERA

SAN ANDRES

LC
PERU ■

★

INCA
RAIL ■

UNION

SANTA CLARA

CONCEVIDAYOQ

AYACUCHO

CARMEN QUIJLLU

PASEO DE LOS

CHAPARRO

CRUZ
VERDE

BAJA

TUPAC AMARU

MATARA

KUICHIPUNKU

SAN PEDRO
TRAIN STATION ■

San Pedro
Market

TEQTE

MEGA ■

CALLE NUEVA

CENTENARIO

PERA

CLINICA
PAREDES ■

LECHUGAL

BUSES TO
URUBAMBA VIA
CHINCHERO ■

BELEN

PAVITOS

GRAU

REGIONAL

To Hospital
Lokena ↓

© AVALON TRAVEL

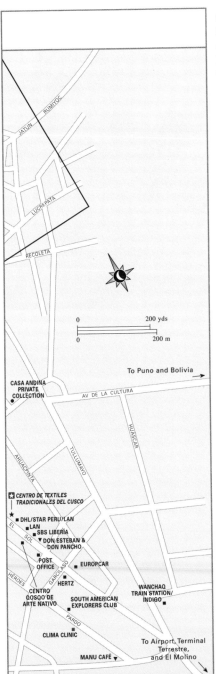

CASA ANDINA
PRIVATE
COLLECTION

To Puno and Bolivia

AV DE LA CULTURA

CENTRO DE TEXTILES
TRADICIONALES DEL CUSCO

DHL/STAR PERU/LAN
LAN
SBS LIBERÍA
DON ESTEBAN &
DON PANCHO

POST
OFFICE   EUROPCAR

HERTZ

CENTRO
QOSQO DE
ARTE NATIVO

SOUTH AMERICAN
EXPLORERS CLUB

WANCHAQ
TRAIN STATION/
INDIGO

CLIMA CLINIC

MANU CAFÉ

To Airport, Terminal
Terrestre,
and El Molino

that's exactly what you should do, unless you have arrived from a high-altitude destination such as La Paz, Puno, or possibly Arequipa. Instead of suffering for a couple of days, head to the Sacred Valley and Machu Picchu first, and return to Cusco after getting accustomed to the altitude.

The heart of Cusco is its **Plaza de Armas,** which stands out for its huge 16th-century cathedral. Beyond the Plaza de Armas, and opposite the cathedral, are two charming squares, **Plaza Regocijo** and **Plaza San Francisco.** Farther along in this direction lies the market of San Pedro. To the side of the cathedral, a narrow pedestrian street named **Procuradores** is nicknamed Gringo Alley. Behind the cathedral, steep alleys lead up to the bohemian neighborhood of **San Blas.**

Cusco's people are very welcoming, but bear in mind that the hassle level in the center is quite high. It's not for nothing that a local Irish bar sells T-shirts with the simple words "No gracias" on the front. This is exactly what you should say, firmly if necessary, if you aren't buying. Understand, though, that vendors are just trying to make a living, and don't let them get in the way of enjoying the many delights of this elegant Andean city.

HISTORY

As with most empires, the foundation of the Inca empire is shrouded in myth, and there is a tendency to romanticize what was a brutal period in history. The story of its beginning famously tells that around AD 1100, Manco Cápac and Mama Oclla, children of the sun and the moon, arose from the waters of Lake Titicaca and searched the land for a place to found their kingdom. The first place that Manco Cápac was able to plunge his golden staff into the ground was this fertile valley, and the newly founded city was christened Q'osqo, or "navel of the world."

The seeds of truth in this legend are that the **Tiwanaku** people (AD 200-1000), from the south shores of Lake Titicaca, were the first advanced culture to reach the Cusco area. Around AD 700 an even more potent culture, the Huari (AD 700-1100) from Ayacucho, spread here and built aqueducts, the large city of Pikillacta, and probably the first water temple at Pisac. The Inca, sandwiched between these two advanced cultures, rose out of the vacuum created when both collapsed. The Inca combined the Tiwanaku stonework and farming techniques with the Huari highway system; the result was the greatest empire South America had ever seen.

Because the Inca had no written language, little is known about Inca history, though it is believed Manco Cápac existed and was indeed the first Inca. There were probably 13 Inca emperors, but the first of great significance was Inca Yupanqui, the ninth Inca leader and one of the younger sons of Inca Viracocha. Around 1440, the Chancas, the tribe that toppled the Huari, had amassed a large army that was poised to overrun Cusco. Inca Viracocha fled, probably to his estate at Huchuy Cusco in the Sacred Valley, but Inca Yupanqui stayed on to defend Cusco. Of the ensuing battle, mestizo chronicler Inca Garcilaso de la Vega reports that even the stones of Cusco rose up and became soldiers. Against overwhelming odds, Inca Yupanqui and a team of seasoned generals beat back the Chancas.

After the battle, Inca Yupanqui changed his name to Pachacútec ("shaker of the earth" in Quechua), took over Cusco from his disgraced father, and launched the Inca's unprecedented period of expansion. Pachacútec created a vision of the Inca people as a people of power, ruled over by a class of elites. He used a carrot-and-stick strategy, learned from the Huari, of conquering territories peacefully by bearing down on them with overwhelmingly large armies but offering the rich benefits of being integrated into a well-functioning web of commerce in return for loyalty. Wellbehaved tribes were rewarded and resistance crushed with devastating force. Pachacútec also pioneered the *mita* system, whereby troublesome tribes were exiled to far-flung parts of the empire.

Pachacútec was an even greater builder

statue of Pachacútec in Cusco's Plaza de Armas

than he was a soldier. He fashioned the city of Cusco into the shape of a puma, a sacred animal admired for its grace and strength, with Sacsayhuamán as the head, the city as the body, and the Coricancha sun temple as the tail. He built a huge central plaza, which included both today's Plaza de Armas and the Plaza Regocijo, and also somehow devised a way to move the giant stones to begin construction of Sacsayhuamán. He is credited with building nearly all of the other major Inca monuments in the area, including Pisac, Ollantaytambo, and probably even Machu Picchu. Pachacútec's armies conquered the entire area between Cusco and Lake Titicaca and also spread north through the central highlands. He died in about 1472 and remains perhaps the most respected figure in Inca history. A statue of him was unveiled, despite objections from the government in Lima, in the center of Cusco's Plaza de Armas.

Pachacútec's son, Túpac Yupanqui, was less of a builder and even more of a warrior. He spent most of his life away from Cusco in long, brutal campaigns in northern Peru against the stubborn Chachapoyans. He dominated the entire coastline, including the Chimú empire based at Chan Chan, and pushed all the way to Quito, in present-day Ecuador.

His son, **Huayna Cápac,** the last Inca to rule over a unified empire, seemed to be ruling over a territory that had extended itself almost to the breaking point. Nevertheless, he continued the campaign in the north, fathering a son named **Atahualpa** in Quito, and pushed the Inca empire to its last limits, up against what is now the Ecuador-Colombia border.

Huayna Cápac's death in 1525 was the turning point. The empire had grown rapidly in less than a century from the Cusco area to cover most of modern-day Peru, Ecuador, Bolivia, and parts of northern Chile and Argentina—but it then began to tear itself apart. The strong-willed Atahualpa challenged his half-brother **Huáscar,** the legitimate heir in Cusco, and a disastrous civil

war broke out, killing thousands of Inca and badly damaging the empire's infrastructure.

In the end, Atahualpa was victorious. He might even have been able to unify the empire again if it were not for the fact that **Francisco Pizarro** and a small Spanish army had begun their march across Peru. Pizarro and his men took Atahualpa hostage in November 1532 as he was making his way slowly south and held him until an entire room was filled with gold, much of which was taken from Cusco and carried by llama trains to Cajamarca. Then the Spaniards murdered Atahualpa anyway and continued their march to Cusco.

To maintain stability, Pizarro needed to find a new Inca ruler, and he befriended **Manco Inca,** another son of Huayna Cápac in Cusco, who was grateful to Pizarro for having routed Atahualpa's army of Quito-based Inca. Under the guise of liberators and with Manco Inca's blessing, Pizarro and his men entered Cusco and took full and peaceful possession of the city in November 1533.

It didn't take long, however, for Manco Inca to grow resentful. The Spaniards had sacked Cusco for all of its gold and silver in the first month, picking clean the gold-filled sun temple and even the sacred Inca mummies. They melted everything into bars for shipping to Spain, lived in the palaces of the former Inca emperors, and forced Inca nobles to hand over their wives.

Manco Inca escaped from Cusco and by May 1536 had amassed an army estimated at 100,000-200,000 soldiers, who used slingshots to throw red-hot coals onto Cusco's thatched roofs, burning their beloved city to the ground. Trapped, the Spaniards made a last-ditch effort against the Inca, who had occupied the fortress of Sacsayhuamán. During a battle that raged for more than a week, the Spaniards prevailed against overwhelming odds, causing Manco Inca to retreat to Ollantaytambo, where he won the last important victory for his people before retreating to the jungle enclave of Vilcabamba. The Inca resisted for more than three decades until their last leader, Inca **Túpac Amaru,** was captured

exploring side streets in Cusco

The Right Attitude Toward Altitude

The last thing you want when arriving in Cusco, the cradle of Inca civilization and archaeological capital of the Americas, is to feel lousy, but if you're arriving from sea level or an altitude lower than 2,000 meters, that is exactly what can happen. The percentage of oxygen in the air remains roughly the same until about 2,400 meters, but at heights above that, oxygen levels decrease and fail to sustain the body's normal function.

Cusco sits at nearly 3,400 meters, and the altitude will hit you within hours of arriving. The most common symptoms are headache, nausea, dizziness, fatigue, insomnia, and loss of appetite. It can be dangerous, though, so you need to be prepared and take care of yourself, otherwise the first few days of your Peruvian adventure could be ruined. Here are some tips:

- **Leave Cusco as soon as you arrive.** Go to the Sacred Valley, where most towns are below 3,000 meters, and return to Cusco after a few days.

- **Take it easy.** Your body is starved of oxygen, so don't put it under further strain. All those hikes and adventure sports can wait a few days.

- **Drink lots of water.** Altitude sickness is usually accompanied by dehydration. Water oxygenates the blood.

- **Drink coca tea.** The locals swear by it and they should know.

- **Eat light food and plenty of carbohydrates.** Heavy foods, especially meat, make you more lethargic, while carbs give you more energy.

- **Avoid alcohol and smoking.**

- **Pack the medication acetazolamide** (Diamox) to alleviate symptoms. Take the first pill on the plane. Aspirin is a milder alternative.

in the Amazon and executed in Cusco's main square in 1573.

By this time, Cusco had already faded from prominence. After its gold was gone, Francisco Pizarro left for the coast and made Lima the capital of the new viceroyalty. More than two centuries later, a leader who claimed Inca descent and called himself Túpac Amaru II would rally Inca fervor once again and launch another siege of Cusco. But the Spaniards quickly captured him and hanged him in Cusco's main square. His body was quartered, and pieces of it were left in the squares of surrounding Inca villages as a warning.

Cusco would have ended up another quiet Andean city like Cajamarca and Ayacucho were it not for Hiram Bingham's discovery of Machu Picchu in 1911. That discovery sparked international interest in Cusco, which flourished in the 1920s with a glittering café society and a generation of intellectuals that included

photographer Martín Chambi. During the 1920s a train line was built past Machu Picchu that still carries travelers today.

A **1950 earthquake,** the most severe in three centuries, destroyed the homes of 35,000 people in Cusco but had the unexpected benefit of clearing away colonial facades that had covered up Inca stonework for centuries. Much of the Inca stonework visible today around Cusco, including the long wall at Coricancha, was discovered thanks to the earthquake. Based on these ruins, and the city's colonial architecture, Cusco was declared a **UNESCO World Heritage Site** in 1983.

PLANNING YOUR TIME

Because of its altitude and complexity, Cusco is best experienced after having visited the Sacred Valley and Machu Picchu. Most of the city can be seen in two days, though many travelers stay here for a week or two, using Cusco as a base for trekking, adventure sports, and jungle trips. Cusco's *boleto turístico* gets you into many of the major sites in and around Cusco and the Sacred Valley for US$45.

Most city attractions are clustered close to the Plaza de Armas and nearby squares Plaza Regocijo and Plaza San Francisco. There are plenty of tourist services along Avenida del Sol, which heads down toward the bus terminal and airport. For a quieter experience, head uphill on the narrow cobbled streets to San Blas, a neighborhood blissfully removed from the noise and traffic of the center. Even though cars still try to squeeze along San Blas's narrow streets, it's comparatively quiet in this area. Getting around town on your own two feet is easy enough for the majority of the city sights, but outlying sights such as Sacsayhuamán and other ruins outside the city require a taxi, bus, or guided tour, though hiking back downhill into Cusco is an enjoyable way to return.

The most popular time to visit Cusco is during the driest and sunniest season May-August, and the best weather is in June and July. Avoid the last week in July when Peru's hotels are often booked solid for Peru's Fiestas Patrias celebration around July 28. An increasing number of visitors are enjoying the solitude of Cusco during the rainy season November-March, but it can get very wet, particularly at lower-altitude sights such as Machu Picchu, and the Inca Trail closes completely during February. The "shoulder months" of April, May, September, and October are in between the dry and rainy seasons. You'll find generally good weather during these months and few crowds.

Cusco is not a particularly dangerous city, but you should still keep your wits about you. Be careful in the area around San Pedro market and, in particular, around the bus terminal. Avoid wandering into any of the poor neighborhoods on the hills. Assaults have occasionally been reported in San Blas at night, so avoid walking alone in deserted side streets. Taxi hijackings, where taxi drivers kidnap and rob their unsuspecting clients, also happen from time to time in Cusco. Never take an unmarked cab; it's preferable to ask your hotel or restaurant to call a taxi rather than hailing one on the street.

Sights

PLAZA DE ARMAS

Cusco's Plaza de Armas is the heart of the city in terms of both architecture and tourism. It is framed by elegant colonial stone arcades and dominated by not one but two stunning churches, the Catedral de Cusco and the Jesuit Iglesia de la Compañía. A statue of Pachacútec has been unveiled in the center, gesturing in the direction of the old Inca fortress Sacsayhuamán. The central government has requested its removal because it was added without permission. The square is a lively place—there are plenty of locals sitting together, attending church and regular religious and patriotic celebrations. Note that the level of vendors in the plaza is high—everything from paintings and ornaments to tours and massages. Politely decline if you're not interested.

★ Catedral de Cusco

Cusco's baroque **cathedral** (Plaza de Armas, 10am-6pm daily, US$8.50 or *boleto religioso*) sits between the more recent **Iglesia de Jesús María** (1733) on its right and, on its left, **Iglesia del Triunfo** (1539), the first Christian church in Cusco. El Triunfo was built to celebrate the victory over Manco Inca. The cathedral was built on top of Inca Viracocha's palace using blocks of red granite taken from Sacsayhuamán and took more than a century to construct, from 1560

Plaza de Armas

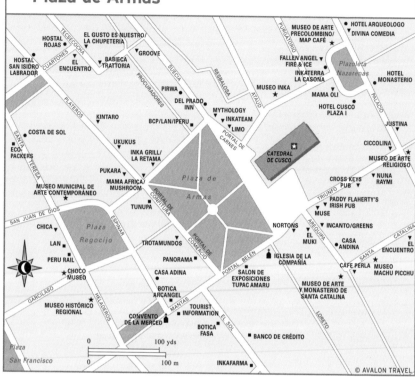

HOTEL ARQUEOLOGO
MUSEO DE ARTE PRECOLOMBINO/ MAP CAFÉ
DIVINA COMEDIA
HOSTAL ROJAS
EL GUSTO ES NUESTRO/ LA CHUPETERIA
GROOVE
PURGATORIO
HOSTAL SAN ISIDRO LABRADOR
EL ENCUENTRO
BABIECA TRATTORIA
FALLEN ANGEL FIRE & ICE
Plazoleta Nazarenas
TECSECOCHA
CUARTONES
SUECIA
RESBALOSA
INKATERRA LA CASONA
HOTEL MONASTERIO
PROCURADORES
PIRWA
MUSEO INKA
MAMA OLI
PLATEROS
DEL PRADO INN
ATAÚD
HOTEL CUSCO PLAZA I
PALACIO
KINTARO
MYTHOLOGY
INKATEAM
JUSTINA
COSTA DE SOL
BCP/LAN/IPERU
LIMO
PORTAL DE CARNES
SANTA TERESA
ECO- PACKERS
UKUKUS
CATEDRAL DE CUSCO
CICCOLINA
MUSEO DE ARTE RELIGIOSO
INKA GRILL/ LA RETAMA
PUKARA
CROSS KEYS PUB
NUNA RAYMI
MUSEO MUNICIPAL DE ARTE CONTEMPORÁNEO
MAMA AFRICA/ MUSHROOM
Plaza de
TRIUNFO
PADDY FLAHERTY'S IRISH PUB
SAN JUAN DE DIOS
TUNUPA
PORTAL DE CONFITURA
Armas
MUSE
CHICA
Plaza Regocijo
ESPINAR
NORTONS
AREQUIPA
INCANTO/GREENS
LAN
TROTAMUNDOS
PORTAL DE COMERCIO
EL MUKI
CASA ANDINA
CATALINA
EL ENCUENTRO
PERU RAIL
PANORAMA
SANTA
GARCILASO
CHOCO MUSEO
CASA ADINA
PORTAL BELÉN
IGLESIA DE LA COMPAÑÍA
CAFÉ PERLA
MUSEO MACHU PICCHU
BOTICA ARCANGEL
SALON DE EXPOSICIONES TUPAC AMARU
MUSEO DE ARTE Y MONASTERIO DE SANTA CATALINA
HELADEROS
MUSEO HISTÓRICO REGIONAL
MANTAS
TOURIST INFORMATION
LONETO
CONVENTO DE LA MERCED
EL SOL
BOTICA FASA
BANCO DE CRÉDITO
Plaza San Francisco
0   100 yds
0   100 m
INKAFARMA
© AVALON TRAVEL

onwards. At least four earthquakes from 1650 to 1986, along with damp and neglect, had taken a serious toll on the building. Fortunately, Cusco's archbishop organized a complete renovation 1997-2002, which removed much of the grime that had covered chapels and paintings over time. For the first time in a century, it is possible to make out the unique **Cusco School** paintings, including unique works such as Christ eating a guinea pig at the Last Supper and the Virgin Mary wearing a mountain-shaped skirt, thus identifying her with the Inca Pachamama (mother earth). There is also an interesting painting, reported to be the oldest in Cusco, showing the city during the 1650 earthquake; the townspeople are praying in the Plaza de Armas with a crucifix named El Señor de Los Temblores (Lord of Earthquakes). Locals still parade this crucifix every year on Holy Monday. The church also contains considerable gold and silver, a 17th-century carved pulpit, choir stalls, and an original gold-covered Renaissance altar. In the bell tower is the huge **María Angola bell,** one of the largest bells in the world, over two meters high, made with 27 kilograms of gold and reportedly audible from a distance of 30 kilometers. If you don't want to pay the entrance fee for a full tour, you may be able to sneak in discreetly to see the cathedral's interior during morning Mass if you are Catholic, but put the camera away.

Iglesia de la Compañía

Around the corner from the cathedral is the 17th-century **Iglesia de la Compañía** (9am-11:30am and 1pm-5:30pm daily, US$3.50 or *boleto religioso*), which was built on top of the palace of Inca Huayna Cápac. This church was built by the Jesuits, who were expelled from Latin America in 1767, but not before they built a series of churches in Peru's principal cities as well as in Ecuador's capital, Quito. This graceful, ornate facade has a spectacular baroque altar, although the interior is considerably darker than that of the cathedral. Near the main door is a 17th-century painting depicting the wedding of Inca princess Beatriz Clara Coya to Spanish *capitín* Martín García de Loyola, grandnephew of San Ignacio de Loyola.

NORTHEAST OF THE PLAZA DE ARMAS
Museo Inka

Head up the alley to the left of the cathedral to reach **Museo Inka** (corner of Ataúd and Túcuman, tel. 084/23-7380, www.museoinka. unsaac.edu.pe, 8am-7pm Mon.-Fri., 9am-4pm Sat., US$4). This ornate colonial home contains an interesting collection of Inca objects, including jewelry, ceramics, textiles, mummies, and a variety of metal and gold artifacts. It also has the world's largest collection of *qeros*, wooden cups the Inca used for drinking.

Museo de Arte Precolombino (MAP)

Farther up the alley to the left of the cathedral, on the Plaza de las Nazarenas, is the impressive **Museo de Arte Precolombino** (MAP, Plaza de las Nazarenas 231, tel. 084/23-3210, www.map.museolarco.org, 9am-10pm daily, US$8, US$4 students). The Museum of Pre-Columbian Art contains an array of ceramics, painting, jewelry, and objects made of silver and gold. The museum has an elegant layout designed by Fernando de Szyszlo, one of Peru's most respected contemporary painters, and in the courtyard is a glass box containing the MAP Café, one of Cusco's best gourmet restaurants. Near the end of the plaza is the 400-year-old **Seminario San Antonio Abad,** which has been converted into the Hotel Monasterio, Cusco's first five-star hotel. Even if you are not a guest, you can sneak a peek at the courtyard and the 17th-century **Iglesia San Antonio Abad.**

Museo de Arte Religioso

Just one block downhill from MAP along Palacio, the Museum of Religious Art, also known as the **Palacio Arzobispal** (Archbishop's Palace, Palacio and Hatun

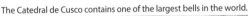

The Catedral de Cusco contains one of the largest bells in the world.

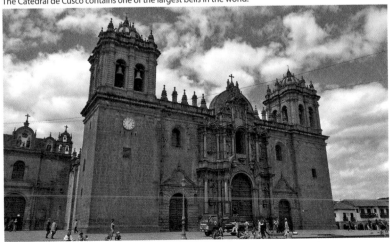

Cusco's Tourist Ticket

Cusco's *boleto turístico* covers admission to 16 sites. At first glance, it seems overpriced at US$40 (US$20 for students under age 26 with ISIC card), but when you consider the total number of sites, it is worth it. More importantly, rules have changed, and individual entrance fees are no longer possible at most of the included sites, so you cannot get into must-see ruins such as Sacsayhuamán, Pisac, and Ollantaytambo without this ticket.

The ticket can be bought at the entrances to most major sites or at COSITUC (Av. El Sol 103, #102, www. cosituc.gob.pe, 8am-6pm Mon.-Sun. tel. 084/22-7037). Unfortunately, the pass only lasts 10 days and this is strictly enforced. If you are doing the Inca Trail first, buy the ticket afterwards.

The ticket covers these 16 sites: Museo Municipal de Arte Contemporáneo, Museo Histórico Regional, Museo de Arte Popular, Museo de Sitio Qorikancha, Centro Qosqo de Arte Nativo, Monumento a Pachacútec, Sacsayhuamán, Q'enqo, Puca Pucara, Tambomachay, Pisac, Ollantaytambo, Moray, Chinchero, Tipon, Pikillacta.

Tambomachay is one of 16 sites accessible with a tourist ticket.

If you don't plan on visiting both Cusco and the Sacred Valley, consider purchasing a lower-priced circuit ticket (US$27). There are three circuits to choose from: the Sacred Valley (over two days), Cusco Inca sites, and Cusco museums (one day only).

Notable sites that are, rather frustratingly, not included in the ticket are the unmissable Coricancha temple (US$3.50) and the interesting Museo de Arte y Monasterio de Santa Catalina (US$2.50), but if you go to both you only pay US$5. The Catedral de Cusco (US$8.50), Iglesia de la Compañía (US$3.50), Iglesia San Blas (US$6), and the Museo de Arte Religioso (US$6) are not covered either, but if you plan to go to all four you can buy the *boleto religioso* at the entrance of any of these sites for US$15 (US$6 for students under age 26 with ISIC card). Other interesting sites not included are the Iglesia de la Merced (US$2.50), Museo Inka (US$4), and the Museo de Arte Precolombino (US$8).

Rumiyoc, 8am-6pm daily, US$6 or *boleto religioso*) resides in a colonial building built by the Marquis of Buenavista and later occupied by Cusco's archbishop. Its handsome salons showcase religious paintings from the 17th and 18th centuries. Walk up the alleyway Hatun Rumiyoc toward San Blas and you will see that the entire museum is built upon a foundation of Inca stones that fit perfectly into one another. Near the end of the street is the famous 12-sided stone, whose sides conform perfectly to the neighboring stones. If you can't locate it, street vendors will be happy to point it out and take your photograph for a small tip.

★ San Blas

Walk away from the Plaza de Armas up along Hatun Rumiyoc to reach Cuesta San Blas, which leads to Cusco's San Blas neighborhood. The square, known as Plazoleta San Blas, is home to several artisan families who have been operating here for decades. San Blas is a great neighborhood to find accommodations and restaurants, or just to wander around the steep cobblestone alleys and take in the excellent views over Cusco.

Iglesia San Blas (Plazoleta San Blas, 8am-6pm daily, US$6 or *boleto religioso*) is a small, whitewashed adobe church built in 1563. One

Plazoleta San Blas

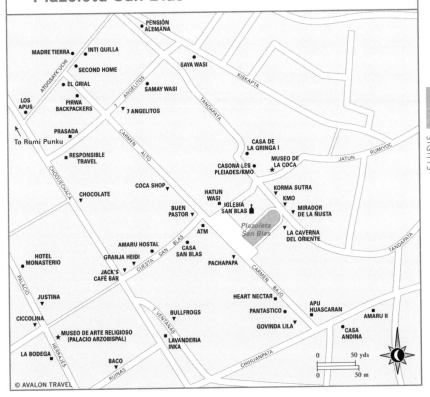

of the New World's most famous works of art is found here, a carved pulpit made from the trunk of a single tree. There is also a gold-covered baroque altar.

Another interesting place to visit is **Museo de la Coca** (Palacio 122, tel. 084/50-1020, www.museodelacoca.com, 9am-7pm daily, US$3.50, free Sun.). This interesting exhibition demonstrates the history of the coca leaf from its ancient use through to the modern production of refined cocaine. Highlights include ceramics of ancient tribesmen chewing coca leaves and an exhibition on celebrities who have fallen victim to the perils of addiction. It also has a boutique filled with a large selection of coca products—from wine and tea to candy.

EAST OF THE PLAZA DE ARMAS
Museo de Arte y Monasterio de Santa Catalina

From the Plaza de Armas, head down Arequipa to the **Santa Catalina Convent and Art Museum** (Arequipa, 8:30am-5:30pm Mon.-Sat., 2pm-5pm Sun., US$3 or US$6 with entry to Coricancha), built on top of the enclosure where the chosen virgins of the Inca lived, known as the *acllahuasi*, or "house of the chosen ones." In a strange historical twist, the Spaniards converted the building into a convent, where 30 nuns remain cloistered to this day. Holy women have thus lived in this building for at least five centuries. The museum has a good collection of Cusco School paintings and an impressive Renaissance altar. A highlight is a trunk, used by Catholic missionaries, that contains miniature figurines depicting the life of Christ.

Museo Machu Picchu (Santa Catalina, tel. 084/25-5535, 9am-5pm daily, US$8, US$4 student) proudly displays hundreds of artifacts returned to Peru from Yale University. They include metallurgy, ceramics, and several Inca skeletons and deformed skulls.

★ Coricancha and Santo Domingo

Nowhere is the delicate cultural and architectural balance between the Inca and Spanish colonial eras more evident than at the sun temple of **Coricancha** (Plazoleta Santo Domingo, 8:30am-5:30pm Mon.-Sat., US$3.50 or US$6 with entry to Museo de Arte y Monasterio de Santa Catalina). As you approach the temple, its most striking aspect is the contrast between the brooding gray-brown Inca foundations and the lighter, beige colonial walls of **Santo Domingo,** topped by an elegant dome. The building symbolizes the Spanish subjugation of Inca culture—a convent built bang on top of the Inca's most important Cusco temple. This was the greatest

prize in the Spaniards' 1533 sacking of Cusco, and for centuries, most of Coricancha's walls were hidden beneath a convent. But the superiority of Inca architecture could not be hidden forever, and in 1950 an earthquake caused large sections of the convent to crumble, exposing Inca walls of the highest quality.

For the Inca, the building, which translates from Quechua as "gold enclosure," had many functions. It was foremost a place where offerings were burned to give thanks to the sun, though there were also rooms devoted to the moon, stars, lightning, thunder, and rainbows. Like so much Inca ceremonial architecture, the building also served as a solar observatory and mummy storehouse.

The south-facing walls of the temple were covered with gold to reflect the light of the sun and illuminate the temple. Inside was the **Punchaco,** a solid-gold disk inlaid with precious stones, which represented the sun and was probably the most sacred object in the Inca empire. Pizarro's scouts had already produced approximately a ton and a half of gold by stripping the inner walls of Coricancha. When the main Spanish force gained Cusco, they gathered hundreds of gold sculptures and objects from the temple, including an altar big enough to hold two men and an

the famous 12-sided stone, part of the exterior wall of the Museo de Arte Religioso

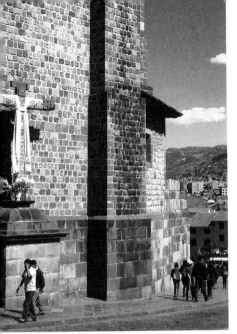

The church and convent of Santo Domingo was built on Inca stonework.

extraordinary artificial garden made of gold, including cornstalks with silver stems and ears of gold. It must have been a wonder to behold, but we will never know, because tragically, everything was melted down within a month—except for the Punchaco, which disappeared from the temple. Its whereabouts are unknown to this day. The Dominicans took over Coricancha and dismantled most of it, using the polished ashlar to build their church and convent of Santa Domingo on top of the sun temple's walls.

It requires considerable imagination today to picture how the Inca's most important temple must have once looked. The eight-sided sacrificial font, stripped of the 55 kilograms of gold that once covered it, stands in the middle of the Coricancha's main square. The rooms that surround it may once have been covered with silver and dedicated to the moon, stars, and thunder. The wall running along the temple's eastern side is 60 meters long and 5 meters high, and each block is perfectly interlocked with its neighbor. But the highlight is the curved retaining wall beneath the facade of the church, which has not budged an inch in all of Cusco's earthquakes.

Many tourists see Coricancha as part of the Cusco city tour, but this is far from ideal because you get rushed through in the early afternoon when all the day tours converge at once between 2pm and 3pm. Even on a day tour, you have to pay separately for Coricancha, so it's preferable to visit independently in the morning when it is quieter.

Museo de Sitio Qorikancha

Reached through an underground entrance across the garden from the Coricancha is the modest **Museo de Sitio Qorikancha** (Av. El Sol, 9am-6pm Mon.-Sat., 8am-1pm Sun., entry with *boleto turístico*), which exhibits a few artifacts from the excavation of Coricancha, a model of the sun temple, and blueprints of its floor plans. Of particular interest are the mummies in fetal positions and deformed skulls. There are no guides available here, and explanations are in Spanish only.

On your way back to the Plaza de Armas, walk down the narrow alley of **Loreto.** To your right are the Inca walls of the *acllahuasi,* now the Santa Catalina convent. To the left are the walls of the palace of Huayna Cápac, now the Iglesia de la Compañía.

SOUTHWEST OF THE PLAZA DE ARMAS

From the Plaza de Armas, walk up Mantas one block to the **Iglesia de la Merced** (tel. 084/23-1821, 8am-12:30pm and 2pm-5:30pm Mon.-Sat., US$2.50), which was completely rebuilt following the 1650 earthquake. Inside the church lie two conquistadores, a father and a son who were executed by the Spanish shortly after the conquest. Diego de Almagro the Elder was hanged after he rebelled against Francisco Pizarro's authority, and his son, Diego de Almagro the Younger, was executed four years later for murdering Francisco Pizarro in revenge. Hanging on the walls nearby the tombs are paintings by the 16th-century master Bernardo Bitti. The church's

Colonial Painting: The Cusco School

The religious paintings that cover the walls of Peru's colonial churches are more than decoration. For centuries after the conquest, painting was the Catholic church's main tool for converting Peru's native peoples, who for the most part did not read or speak Spanish. The church's religious campaign produced thousands of now-priceless works and renowned schools of painting in Cusco and Quito, in present-day Ecuador.

Shortly after the conquest, the different orders of the Catholic church began importing paintings into Lima from well-known painters of the ongoing European Renaissance. The museum at Iglesia de San Francisco in Lima contains works by European painters who influenced the American schools of painting, collectively known as the Spanish American baroque. These 16th-century European masters included the Spanish painters Francisco de Zurbarán and Bartolomé Esteban Murillo and Flemish master Peter Paul Rubens.

By 1580, demand for European paintings had so outstripped supply that European painters began arriving to Lima in search of lucrative commissions. One of these was Italian Jesuit **Bernardo Bitti** (1548-1610), who was a disciple of Caravaggio and the brightly colored, emotional works of the Italian baroque. He was probably the single most influential European painter to work in Peru, and his paintings can be seen at Iglesia de la Merced in Cusco, Iglesia de la Compañía in Arequipa, and Lima's Museo San Francisco. With the guidance of Bitti and other European masters, the church orders set up convent studios around Peru where indigenous and mestizo artisans cranked out a staggering quantity of paintings in serial fashion—one painter would specialize in clothing, another in landscape, and still another in face and hands.

Right from the start, the workshops in Cusco began developing a unique style that blended the European baroque with images from Peru, including local trees, plants, animals, and foods. Cusco's cathedral, for instance, contains a painting that shows the Last Supper served with roasted guinea pig and *chicha,* the local corn beer. In another painting nearby, there is a pregnant Virgin Mary with the lustrous, smooth hair of Andean women. Often the dress of the Virgin Mary has a triangular shape, which art scholars believe is a transformation of the ancient Andean practice of worshipping *apus,* or sacred mountains.

The painters of the Cusco School also used a lot of gold to highlight their paintings and create a richly decorated surface. Most paintings pictured the Virgin Mary, scenes from the life of a saint, or panoramas of devils and angels. A unique invention of Cusco's painters was the archangels, flying through the air wearing ornate Spanish clothing and armed with muskets. Far from the tranquil realism of the Flemish baroque, these paintings portrayed a dazzling otherworld, filled with powerful spiritual beings, which were meant to awe, stun, and frighten indigenous viewers into accepting Catholicism. The most famous painters of the Cusco School were Diego Quispe Tito, Juan Espinosa de los Monteros, and Antonio Sinchi Roca, though it is difficult to decipher who did what because paintings were rarely signed.

In Quito, new-world painters embarked on a different course. The founder of the Quito School was **Father Bedón,** who studied with Bitti in Lima but quickly dropped the Italian mannerist style upon returning to Quito. Instead he ushered in a type of religious painting that combined the gold decorations of the Cusco School with the colder colors and shadowy depths favored by Peter Paul Rubens and other Flemish painters. The cathedrals in northern Peru, including Cajamarca and Trujillo, often feature paintings from both schools side by side.

elegant cloisters contain a small museum, which showcases a magnificent monstrance made of gold, silver, and precious stones.

From the Iglesia de la Merced, head down Heladeros to the **Plaza Regocijo,** where there are three museums. **Museo Histórico Regional** (Heladeros, tel. 084/22-5211, 8am-5pm Tues.-Sun., entry with *boleto turístico* only) was once the home of one of colonial Peru's most famous and eloquent writers, mestizo Inca Garcilaso de la Vega, the first Peruvian to publish a book in Spain. The museum charts the history of his life and work and also provides a fine survey of Peru's pre-Inca cultures, starting with preceramic arrowheads and continuing with artifacts from the Chavín, Moche, Chimú, Chancay, and Inca cultures. The holdings include a Nasca mummy and, on the second floor, colonial furniture and paintings from the Cusco School.

A museum that will give a different taste of Peruvian history is the **ChocoMuseo** (Calle Garcilaso 210, tel. 084/24-4765, 10:30am-6:30pm daily, free). Here you can learn about the history of the cocoa bean, from its medicinal Mayan origins to current mass production. Interestingly, 40 percent of the world's organic chocolate comes from Peru. There are classes on how to make chocolate (two hours, US$25) and a well-stocked shop to satisfy the appetite.

Across the Plaza Regocijo in the municipality is the **Museo Municipal de Arte Contemporáneo** (Plaza Regocijo, 9am-6pm Mon.-Sat., entry with *boleto turístico*), which contains a less-than-impressive exhibition of contemporary art of varying quality.

From Plaza Regocijo, walk down Garcilaso to **Iglesia San Francisco** (8am-noon and 3pm-5pm daily), a convent and church that stands above the plaza of the same name. This church, with three naves and in the shape of a Latin cross, was built in 1572 and is one of the few churches in Cusco to survive the 1650 earthquake. As a result, its convent is one of the few remaining examples of the ornate 16th-century plateresque style, complemented here by *azulejo* tiles imported from Seville.

OUTSIDE CUSCO

There are four highly recommended Inca ruins outside of Cusco, which most Cusco agencies offer as part of a rushed half-day tour that also takes in Coricancha ($6-8, not including entrance to Coricancha). These ruins accept only the *boleto turístico* for admission and are open 7am-6pm daily.

All the ruins lie close to the road that runs between Cusco and Pisac. An enjoyable way to see them is to take a Pisac bus or taxi to the farthest ruins, Tambomachay, and walk the eight kilometers back to Cusco, visiting all the ruins along the way (this walk can be shortened considerably by starting at Q'enqo and Sacsayhuamán, which are only one kilometer apart). Robberies are occasionally reported in this area, so it is better to walk in a group of two or more during the early part of the day.

★ Sacsayhuamán

Looming over the city to the north are the most impressive ruins in the Cusco area: **Sacsayhuamán** (7am-6pm daily), a hilltop fortress with three ramparts of zigzag walls that run for nearly 300 meters on the complex's north side. The Quechua name means "satisfied falcon," although most guides can't resist drawing attention to its similarity in sound to "sexy woman." Most striking about the site are the enormous stones—the largest are nearly 8.5 meters high, weighing 361 tons, placed at the apex of the walls to strengthen them. Every Inca citizen had to spend a few months of the year on public works, and the Inca used this tremendous reserve of labor to move the stones, using log sleds and levers. But even engineers have a hard time understanding how the Inca fitted these huge stones so perfectly together.

Only the largest stones of Sacsayhuamán remain. Up until the 1930s, builders arrived at Sacsayhuamán to cart away the precut stone of this apparently limitless quarry, so it is difficult to appreciate how impregnable Sacsayhuamán must have been. Three towers once crowned the top of Sacsayhuamán, and the foundations of two of them are visible. During Manco Inca's great rebellion in 1536, the Spaniards managed to establish a base on the opposing hill and spent two days charging across the plain on horseback and attempting to scale the defensive walls. On the first day, one of the stones fired by the Inca slingshots struck Juan Pizarro, Francisco's younger brother, who died that night. On the evening of the second day, the Spaniards launched a surprise attack with ladders and successfully forced the Inca into the three stone towers. As the Spaniards massacred the estimated 1,500 soldiers trapped inside, many Inca preferred to leap to their deaths from the high tower. The next morning, condors feasted on the dead bodies, and this grisly image is emblazoned on Cusco's coat-of-arms. Manco Inca himself escaped to Ollantaytambo, where he later recorded a famous victory over the Spanish before retreating into the jungle. However, as far as Cusco was concerned, the battle at Sacsayhuamán was the Inca's last stand at the former seat of their power; it was a crushing defeat in the supposedly impregnable fortress.

These days the flat fields outside of Sacsayhuamán, where the Inti Raymi culminates each June, make for a peaceful stroll. In the mornings, Cusco residents come here to jog or do yoga on the grassy lawn, which is considerably larger than a soccer field. A huge trapezoidal door leads up a walkway to the top of the ruins, which commands marvelous views over Cusco. Because many tourists come here in the evening, guards are posted to put visitors at ease as dusk falls. If you have time, visit the top of Rodadero hill, where the Spaniards based themselves during their assault on Sacsayhuamán (guides will point it out). There is a rock outcrop on top, beautifully carved with sacred steps.

Sacsayhuamán is a steep, two-kilometer walk from Cusco or a 10-minute taxi ride (US$3). Taxis wait in the parking lot for the return trip to Cusco.

Q'enqo
One kilometer past Sacsayhuamán is the shrine of **Q'enqo** (7am-6pm daily), which means "zigzag" in Quechua. It is a large limestone outcrop carved with enigmatic steps leading nowhere, a sacred motif that is found on nearly every *huaca*, the sacred stone revered by the Inca. On the top of the rock are faint carvings of a puma and a condor. Carved into the rock are perfect zigzag channels, which probably flowed with *chicha* or llama blood during ceremonial rituals, much like the Sayhuite Stone between Cusco and Abancay. Below the rock are caves carved with niches where mummies of lesser nobility may once have been kept. Nearby is an amphitheater with niches framing an upright stone, which was probably defaced long ago by Spanish extirpators of idolatry. Q'enqo is about four kilometers northeast of Cusco.

Puka Pukara
The least significant of the ruins outside Cusco, **Puka Pukara** (7am-6pm daily),

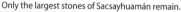
Only the largest stones of Sacsayhuamán remain.

meaning "red fort" in Quechua, was probably not a fort at all but rather a storage facility or an Inca *tambo,* or lodge. Perhaps when the Inca emperor came to visit the baths of Tambomachay, his court waited here. There are several chambers below and a platform on top with excellent views. The distance between Puka Pukara and Q'enqo is six kilometers along the road.

Tambomachay

Known as the Inca's Bath, **Tambomachay** (7am-6pm daily) lies about 300 meters off the Pisac road and is the farthest of the Inca ruins on the outskirts of Cusco, although it is well marked with a sign. It is a well-preserved example of the sacred water fountains found at nearly every important Inca temple, including Pisac, Ollantaytambo, and Machu Picchu. The Inca took a natural spring and painstakingly channeled the water through three waterfalls, which continue to work perfectly today. There is a fine Inca wall above with ceremonial niches. The Inca worshipped water as a vital life element, and this site no doubt formed part of a water cult. From here you can see Puka Pukara, which is on the other side of the road.

Entertainment and Events

FOLKLORIC MUSIC AND DANCE

The **Centro Qosqo de Arte Nativo** (El Sol 604, tel. 084/22-7901, included in *boleto turístico* or US$8 separately), founded in 1924, has a highly recommended music and dance show 6pm-8pm on most evenings. It was founded in 1924 as the first organized music and dance center in Cusco. In addition to the offerings here, most of the Peruvian restaurants in the Plaza de Armas have live Andean music during dinner.

BARS, PUBS, AND LIVE MUSIC

Cusco's steady stream of backpackers and robust student population means it has a lively nightlife scene, although it's far more low-key than Lima. During the week, most tourists frequent one of the many pleasant bars on or near Plaza de Armas. Many of them have draft beers, including Old Speckled Hen and Abbot Ale for a taste of home. Many restaurants have live Andean music, and the venues listed here get busy later in the evening.

At present the best expat pub, hands down, has to be **Paddy Flaherty's Irish Pub** (Triunfo 124, tel. 084/24-7719, 11am-2am daily), which claims to be the highest-elevation 100 percent Irish-owned pub in the world. Draft beer and canned Guinness, as well as Irish and British pub food such as shepherd's pie and stuffed potato skins, go down well. There's the obligatory happy hour 7pm-8pm, and it's a good place to meet other travelers over a drink. The T-shirts emblazoned with "No gracias" are popular for fending off street vendors.

There are a few other decent pubs close to Paddy's, notably American-owned **Nortons** (Santa Catalina Angosta 116, 7am-2am daily), with an impressive selection of imported beers, a classic English breakfast, darts, and, best of all, balconies overlooking the plaza.

The English **Cross Keys Pub** (Triunfo 350, 2nd Fl., tel. 084/22-9227, 10am-2am daily), owned by Barry Walker, British owner of Manu Expeditions, is good for a quiet drink, but it has seen better days and is waning in popularity. However, the dartboards, typical pub fare, and English beer on tap mean it remains an authentic pub experience.

Up Procuradores (Gringo Alley), there are a few bars in the quiet cobbled street of Tecsecocha. One of these is **Los Perros Couch & Wine Bar** (Tecsecocha 436, tel.

084/24-1447, 11am-midnight daily, US$5). The relaxed atmosphere and comfy couches make an inviting backdrop for a glass of red.

Plenty of places offer live music, and a popular spot is **Ukukus** (Plateros 316, tel. 084/25-4911, www.ukukusbar.com, 8pm-late daily, sometimes a small cover on weekends), a live music venue and bar that has been a classic of Cusco's nightlife scene since it opened in 1993. Shows range from Afro-Peruvian to rock, with affordable drinks. **The Muse** (Triunfo, 084/242-031, www.themusecusco.com, 8am-late Wed.-Sat.) is a lounge bar with eclectic decor, couches, a varied menu in the restaurant, and regular live music.

In San Blas, a local expat favorite and a good live music spot that has been around for years is **7 Angelitos** (Siete Angelitos 638, tel. 084/23-6373, 3pm-late daily). There are two-for-one happy hours (7:30pm-9:30pm and 11pm-11:30pm); the mojitos are excellent and there are regular live bands.

Another popular spot is **Frogs** (Warankallki 185, tel. 084/22-1762, 3pm-late daily), a large, gay-friendly bar with stone walls and colorful beanbags. It has good cocktails, a pool table, foosball, movies during the day, and regular live music.

Above the Plazoleta San Blas, **KMO** (Tandapata 100, tel. 084/23-6009, 3pm-2am daily) is small but a good spot for live music.

DISCOTHEQUES

For most travelers in Cusco, the altitude and long days of sightseeing and trekking mean that there is little energy left after a few drinks at the pub. However, there are many places to dance until dawn on weekends. The Cusco nightclub scene is constantly changing; clubs open and close monthly, and the popular places change regularly. The local government has been threatening to move discos out of the historic center due to noise levels, but amid substantial opposition, it is unclear if this will happen. A good local website to check out for nightlife is www.keytocusco.com.

One of the most frequented dance spots and therefore extremely crowded is

Inkateam (Portal de Carnes 298, 9pm-5am daily). Tourists and locals dance to the blasting sounds of techno, reggae, and electro. Happy hour is 9pm-midnight, and there are free salsa classes every night 9pm-11pm. It's officially for over-23-year-olds only. Next door, **Mythology** (Portal de Carnes 298, 9pm-5am daily) has a similar offering but is not quite as busy.

Mama África (Portal de Panes 109, 3rd Fl., 9pm-6am daily) has been around since the mid-1990s but is constantly moving and has at various times been the place to go. It still fills up, and every Wednesday at 2am they have electronic sessions. Upstairs, **Mushroom** (6:30pm-late daily) is a very popular bar with locals, has happy hour until 11pm, and offers a pool table and a wide selection of music.

FESTIVALS

Celebrated continuously since the devastating quake of 1650, Cusco's procession of the **Señor de los Temblores** (Lord of the Earthquakes) traditionally begins at Cusco's cathedral on the Monday before Easter.

One of Peru's most enigmatic festivals is **Qoyllur Ritt'i,** which takes place in May or June before Corpus Christi on the slopes of the Nevado Ausangate at 4,800 meters. During the three-day festival, elaborately costumed men climb in the middle of the night to hew huge blocks of ice, which they carry on their backs down the mountain at dawn. Thousands of campesinos from neighboring communities come to this spot to bring ice down from the mountain or participate in the colorful masked dances. This festival, Christian only on the surface, grew out of the Andean tradition of worshipping mountains, or *apus*, to ensure rains and good harvests. The pilgrims trek toward the mountain from the town of Tinki, which is several hours away from Cusco on the rough road to Puerto Maldonado. If you are in Cusco during this time, you can find agencies along Plateros in Cusco that sell transport-and-camping packages.

During Cusco's **Corpus Christi,** which

usually happens in early June, elaborate processions fill the streets of Cusco as all the bells in the city ring. Each procession carries a different saint, which is treated as if it were a living person, in the same way the Inca paraded their ancestors' mummies around these same streets five centuries ago.

A country festival that is straightforward for travelers to attend is the June 15-17 festival of the **Virgen del Carmen** in Paucartambo, a pleasant colonial town that is a four-hour bus ride from Cusco on the way to the Manu. The festival includes an extraordinary range of dances and costumes. Many Cusco agencies offer inexpensive lodge-and-transport packages to the festival, which include a dawn trip to Tres Cruces, a fabulous place to watch the sun rise over the Amazon basin.

Cusco's biggest festival is **Inti Raymi**, the Inca celebration of the June 21 winter solstice. Because Peru is in the Southern Hemisphere, some chroniclers, including Garcilaso de la Vega, have claimed that it is akin to the Incan New Year. The festival is celebrated throughout the Peruvian and Ecuadorian Andes, and lasts 10 days on either side of the solstice. It was banned by the Spaniards in 1535, but in 1944, a group of Cusco intellectuals re-created

the sacred ceremony by studying chronicles and historical documents. Each year, hundreds dress up as Inca priests, nobles, and chosen women, and one man, chosen by audition, gets to be Inca Pachacútec. The main day, June 24, begins at 10am at the Coricancha (the sun temple) and ends around 2pm at Sacsayhuamán, where thousands of tourists sit on the fort's walls for a good view as a man dressed as Pachacútec speaks with a sun god through a microphone. It is a highly staged, touristy production, completely unlike the more down-to-earth countryside festivals.

Fiestas Patrias, the national Peruvian holiday at the end of July, is one of Peru's most important holidays. The festival honors Peru's independence on July 28 and Peru's armed forces on July 29. A large number of Peruvians travel in the week that falls around these dates, and it is usually the busiest week of the year in Cusco. Hotels, transport, and other services are often booked during this time.

Santuranticuy, on December 24, is one of the largest arts-and-crafts fairs in Peru. Nativity figures, miniature altars, and ceramics are laid out on stalls in the Plaza de Armas by hundreds of artists.

festival in the Plaza de Armas in Cusco

Shopping

Crafts shops are wall-to-wall along Triunfo, which leads from the Plaza de Armas and becomes Rumiyoc and Cuesta San Blas before reaching Plazoleta San Blas, the center of Cusco's bohemian/art district. Several families who have been producing crafts for decades have their workshops here and can often be seen at work.

CERAMICS AND WEAVINGS

The family workshop **Artesanía Mendívil** (Plazoleta San Blas 634, 9am-6pm Mon.-Sat.) is known worldwide for its religious sculptures made of plaster cloth, rice paste, and wood. The figures have long, mannerist necks. Hilario Mendívil began working as a craftsman at the age of 10 in 1939; though he has passed away, his sons continue the tradition.

World-acclaimed ceramicist Pablo Seminario, whose studio is in Urubamba, has a showroom on the Plaza de Armas.

A great association run by the altruistic Franco Negri is **Casa Ecológica** (Portal de Carnes 236, interior 2, cell tel. 984-117-962, www.casaecologicacusco.com, 9am-9:30pm daily), which was created to promote sustainable development in rural communities. The shop sells traditional handicrafts produced with natural fibers, as well as organic cosmetics and food products.

For mainstream touristy products, there are crafts markets in Cusco where bargaining is standard procedure. **Salón de Exposiciones Tupac Amaru** is right on the Plaza de Armas next to Iglesia de la Compañía (10:30am-1pm and 3:30pm-9pm Mon.-Sat., 4pm-9pm Sun.). A 10-minute walk down Avenida El Sol takes you past many more markets, but the biggest is **Centro Artesanal Cusco** (El Sol and Tullumayo, 8am-10pm daily).

★ Centro de Textiles Tradicionales del Cusco

The highest-quality textiles for sale in all of Cusco are at the **Centro de Textiles Tradicionales del Cusco** (Av. El Sol 603, tel. 084/22-8117, www.textilescusco.org, 7:30am-8:30pm Mon.-Sat., 8:30am-8:30pm Sun.). Nilda Callañaupa, a weaver and scholar from

traditional weaving

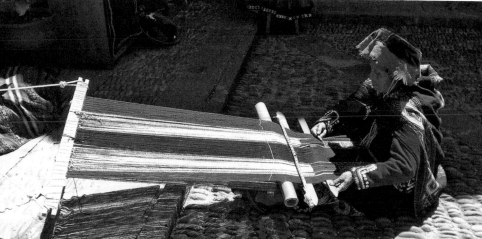

Chinchero, set up the center with the admirable goal of recovering ancient technologies, showcasing high-quality weavings, and sending revenue straight back to the remote, neglected villages that produce them. Local weavers give daily demonstrations, and there are displays that explain all the plants, minerals, and berries used for natural dyes. The textiles here are far better than those found elsewhere in Cusco and only slightly more expensive.

ALPACA PRODUCTS, CLOTHING, AND JEWELRY

For the finest alpaca clothing, head to **Kuna,** which has shops all over Cusco. The most central is on the Plaza de Armas (Portal de Panes 127, tel. 084/24-3191, www.kuna.com. pe, 9am-10pm daily). Another reliable option is **Sol Alpaca** (Plazoleta Nazarenas 167, tel. 084/23-2687, www.solalpaca.com, 9am-9pm Mon.-Sat.).

Werner & Ana (Plaza San Francisco 295-A, tel. 084/23-1076, 9:30am-9pm Mon.-Sat.) is a clothing boutique with styles in alpaca and other fine materials.

Hilo (Carmen Alto 260, tel. 084/25-4536, 10am-1pm and 2pm-6pm Mon.-Sat.) is a funky little shop with original clothes handmade by self-taught Irish designer Eibhlin Cassidy. Browse through her unique collection of dresses, blouses, and belts while sipping on a cup of tea.

There are exclusive jewelry shops all around the Plaza de Armas and up Cuesta San Blas; they mostly sell works of silver. The most well-known and ubiquitous is **Ilaria** (Portal Carrizos 258, tel. 084/24-6253, www.ilariainternational.com, 8am-9:45pm daily).

CONTEMPORARY ART AND HANDICRAFTS

Contemporary art can be found in several shops along Triunfo, between the Plaza de Armas and San Blas. **Primitiva** (Hatun Rumiyoc 495, tel. 084/26-0152, www. coscio.com, 10am-9pm Mon.-Sat.) features the art of Argentine painter Federico Coscio, who captures the landscapes and people around Cusco.

If you are looking for something a little different, **Indigo** (Plazoleta de Limacpampa chico 473 www.galeriaindigo.com.pe, 9am-10pm daily) has modern housewares and handicrafts inspired by traditional Andean designs.

BOOKSTORES

SBS Bookshop (Av. El Sol 864, tel. 084/24-8106, www.sbs.com.pe, 9am-8:30pm Mon.-Fri., 9:30am-1:30pm and 4pm-8pm Sat.) is Peru's foremost importer of English-language books and has a good collection at its small Cusco shop.

With choices in English, French, German, Portuguese, Spanish, and Quechua, you'd be hard pressed not to find a book at **CBC La Familia** (Tullumayo 465, tel. 084/23-4073, 10am-2pm and 4pm-8pm Mon.-Sat.). Genres include novels, cookbooks, art, and even photography.

The largest book exchange in Cusco can be found at **Libreria Puro Peru** (Heladeros 167, tel. 084/22-1753, librarypuroperu@hotmail. com, 9am-10pm daily).

MUSIC STORES

Director Kike Pinto has collected more than 400 instruments for the **Taki Andean Music Museum (Museo Taki Musica Andina)** (Pumakurku 519, tel. 084/226-897, www.institutotaki.blogspot.com, pinto.kike@gmail. com, 10am-8pm Mon.-Sat.), some of which are for sale, along with CDs, books, and music lessons.

OUTDOOR AND TRAVEL GEAR

The best shops for getting high-end outdoor apparel and equipment, although expensive, are **Tatoo** (Triunfo 346, tel. 084/22-4797, 10am-9pm Mon.-Sat., 2pm-9pm Sun.), **Cordillera** (Garcilaso 210, shop 102, tel. 084/24-4133, 9am-9:30pm daily), and **The North Face** (Portal Comercio 195, Plaza de Armas, tel. 084/22-7789, 9am-9pm Mon.-Fri., 9:30am-9pm Sat., 10am-9pm Sun.).

Recreation

Along with Huaraz in the Cordillera Blanca, Cusco is Peru's main adventure travel center. The variety of intriguing options and high-quality agencies are heaven for adrenaline-seekers. Options include rafting down rapids, climbing Andean peaks, biking, horseback riding, paragliding, and trekking in the nearby Amazon jungle.

Among the more than 150 licensed agencies operating in Cusco, the standard of service and handling of social and environmental responsibilities vary greatly. It is up to the client to be discerning and to research thoroughly before booking. The agencies listed here are all recommended.

For your safety, and for the environment, choose your agency carefully. If you choose to raft a serious river, like the Class IV Río Apurímac, go with accredited agencies, and before you depart check the equipment. An average of two tourists a year die on the Apurímac alone, and though not even the best agency can take away all the risk, a new raft, full safety equipment, and, most importantly, an experienced guide will make a big difference.

Fly-by-night agencies, with which Cusco is crawling, offer incredibly cheap prices but usually at the expense of your comfort and safety—and at the expense of the environment. This is especially true on the Inca Trail, where trash and human waste is becoming a serious problem. These low-budget agencies do not tend to follow the principles of sustainable adventure travel, nor do they treat their staff fairly. The porters and cooks are not paid enough, they are not provided with acceptable standards of food and camp accommodation, and they do not receive proper training. Most agencies' websites claim to practice responsible tourism, but these claims are probably unfounded if their prices are bargain-basement.

Dozens of these agencies are closed down each year once the rangers in the Machu Picchu sanctuary catch on. However, the same agency can open again under a new name, which often mimics the high-quality leaders in the field. The excellent Trek Peru, for instance, is often confused with Peru Trek, Peruvian Trek, Trekking Peru, etc. The courts

The hills near Cusco are ideal for exploring on foot.

are so backlogged with copyright cases that rarely do agencies defend their name. So the confusion lingers. Travelers who spend a bit more money to go with reputable agencies are helping to raise the bar of quality for all of Cusco's agencies.

Most of the agencies offer a variety of activities, but they are organized here according to their main focus.

TREKKING

The Inca Trail is by far the most popular trekking route in the Cusco area because of its spectacular route of ruins and varied ecosystems, but there are other excellent treks worth considering. Though they do not have the Inca Trail's variety of ruins or the unbeatable culmination at Machu Picchu, they are less crowded and plunge into remote areas of Andean villages, tumbling jungle, and out-of-the-way archaeological sites. While all hikers on the Inca Trail must go with a licensed agency, the other routes described here can be done independently by those with enough Spanish to ask directions, although most travelers tend to go with an agency. The best time to trek in the Cusco area is during the dry winter months April-November; the most crowded months on the Inca Trail are June-August.

Make sure your agency is one of those licensed by INRENA, the government conservation agency. A list of approved agencies can be obtained through Iperú (www.peru.info). Before scheduling your trip, ask your chosen agency pertinent questions: What is included in the price (e.g., train fares and entry fees), what type of tents and general equipment do they provide, what is the maximum number of trekkers in a group? Also very important is to confirm that your operator is bringing a bathroom tent. The most reputable and responsible agencies do not use the public bathrooms but instead carry PETT toilets, which use organic compounds to break down human waste so that it can be packed out of the trail and disposed of properly. Groups are accompanied by porters, and there is a legal limit of 20 kilograms (44 pounds) for group gear and 5 kilograms (11 pounds) for personal gear, per porter, which is checked at the beginning of the trail.

Nevado Salcantay, at 6,271 meters, is the sacred mountain that towers above the Inca Trail and eventually drops to Machu Picchu itself. Many agencies offer a four- to five-day trek starting from Mollepata, a town 3.5 hours from Cusco in the Limatambo Valley. If you are trekking on your own it can be reached by any bus heading from Cusco to Abancay. In Mollepata, you can hire mules and local guides. The route traverses part of the Cordillera Vilcabamba, including spectacular views of several snow-covered peaks. It crests the 4,700-meter Salcantayccasa Pass before descending between the stunning glaciers of Humantay and Salcantay. The trek then goes through the lovely Huyracmachaypampa and down through forested slopes to the hot springs at Colpapampa. From here the trail follows the Santa Teresa River to the humid lowlands with the option to trek a little farther to the Inca ruins of Patallacta. From here you descend to the hydroelectric station at Intihuatana to board a train for the short journey to Machu Picchu. The alternative is to walk 2-3 hours along the train track to Aguas Calientes.

Choquequirao is a huge Inca complex perched on a ridge in the Vilcabamba area that includes many fine Inca walls and double-recessed doorways. It was probably built as a winter palace by Inca Túpac Yupanqui, in the same way that his father, Pachacútec, probably built Machu Picchu. It was discovered by Hiram Bingham in 1911, though it was lost again until the 1980s when a series of explorers trudged through this rugged territory to find this and other ruins in the area. The Peruvian government (INC), backed by UNESCO, launched a campaign to restore the ruins, and much of the work has been completed to a very high standard. It is worth spending a full day exploring this site as it has some unique features, such as the wonderful stylized white stone llamas.

The most common approach is from Cachora, where guides and mules can be rented, reached by taking a bus to Abancay and getting off at a road past the Sayhuite Stone. The first day is spent hiking down to the Río Apurímac, and the second continues straight up the other side, a long six-hour slog uphill onto the cloud forest ridge. Some agencies offer a combined 10-day trek that leads from Choquequirao all the way to Machu Picchu. Another option is to reach Choquequirao from Huancacalle, near the Inca ruins of Vitcos, a spectacular eight-day traverse of the Cordillera Vilcabamba.

There are various trekking routes through the **Cordillera Vilcanota,** the range to the east of Cusco that is dominated by the sacred **Nevado Ausangate** (6,384 meters). Trekking guides say that this is one of the more untouched and spectacular areas of Peru.

The classic route is a seven-day loop around the peak of Ausangate, which begins at the town of Tinqui in the high puna grasslands and crosses four passes between 4,300 and 5,500 meters. The views include the fluted faces and rolling glaciers of all the mountains of the range, including Colquecruz and Jampa, and the route passes through remote hamlets of llama herders and weavers. This area is famous for its **Qoyllur R'itti** movable festival in May or June, when thousands of campesinos converge on the slopes of Ausangate.

The truly adventurous and fit may want to try reaching **Espíritu Pampa,** the actual "Lost City of the Inca" that served as the base for the Inca's 35-year rebellion against the Spanish. Gene Savoy's discovery of the ruins in 1964 made world news, and several subsequent expeditions have tried, in vain, to keep the jungle from growing over the immense site.

The trip starts from the village of Huancacalle, which can be reached by taking a truck or bus from Cusco over the Abra Málaga to Quillabamba and hopping off at the Huancacalle turnoff. The Cobos family, which has guided all the Vilcabamba explorers since Gene Savoy, operates a small hostel in Huancacalle and rents mules for US$7 a day. From Huancacalle, a path leads to the Inca ruler's original exile at Vitcos, where Manco Inca was murdered by the Spanish, and the exquisite sacred rock of Chuquipalta (the subject, among others, of Hugh Thomson's book *White Rock*). The path heads to **New Vilcabamba,** a colonial-era mining town, and then ascends a 3,800-meter pass before plunging into the jungle below. The path includes sections of fine Inca staircases along a steep and tortuous valley to the ruins, which are in mosquito-ridden rainforest at 1,000 meters. Instead of walking back all the way to Huancacalle, it is possible to walk for a day or two alongside the river on good paths until you reach the town of Kiteni on the Río Urubamba. From here, a bus goes back to Quillabamba. This trip takes 7-10 days.

Trekking Agencies

Peruvian Andean Treks, ExplorAndes, and Tambo Tours are the longest-established trekking companies in Cusco; they pioneered the contemporary trekking culture. They are recommended, not only for their unsurpassed experience and professionalism, but also because they consistently recycle their trash, pack out all human waste, treat water carefully, and pay porters fair wages. Over the last three decades, these operators have developed ties with a number of Quechua communities in the Cusco area, where they are embarking on a new brand of participatory cultural activities, such as harvesting potatoes, building adobe homes, and even herding llamas.

Trekking prices vary greatly based on the season, the number of people in the group, the length of the trek, the trek itself, and other factors. Because of licensing requirements, the four-night Machu Picchu trek now costs US$1,500, though most agencies charge US$500-650 for group bookings. The shorter two-day Inca Trail is around

US$250-300 for group bookings. The alternative five-day Salcantay trek to Machu Picchu is in the US$300-850 range, though most operators offer group Salcantay treks for around US$500. Other treks in the Cusco area, such as in the Lares Valley, generally run about US$100 per day. Be careful to ask your agency whether the price includes all entry fees (an important consideration for Salcantay in particular).

Peruvian Andean Treks (Pardo 705, tel. 084/22-5701, U.S. tel. 617/924-1974, www.andeantreks.com) is owned by American and longtime Cusco resident Tom Hendrickson. It operates on the Inca Trail and runs treks through jungle areas and the Lares Valley in the Cordillera. It is also the best option for climbing expeditions in the snow-covered peaks around Cusco.

ExplorAndes (Paseo Zarzuela Q-2 Huancaro, tel. 084/23-8380, www.explorandes.com) is Peru's most established adventure sports agency. It offers the traditional Inca Trail hike, as well as variations that combine it with treks above the Sacred Valley or around Nevado Salcantay and Nevado Ausangate. Kayaking on Lake Titicaca, rafting down the Tambopata or Apurímac, and llama-supported treks around the Cordillera Blanca and Huayhuash near Huaraz are also offered. It also operates special-interest tours around Peru, focusing on orchids, potatoes and maize, camelids, ceramics, cacti, textiles, and coca and other medicinal plants.

Tambo Tours (Casilla 912, tel. 084/23-7718, www.tambotours.com) is owned by Andreas Holland and has been operating for over 30 years. It offers diverse treks and tours with tailor-made itineraries (six people minimum), which accommodate group specifications and a wide range of special interests. The staff are very knowledgeable, and since its foundation Tambo Tours has had a profound commitment to helping local communities. Most importantly, however, the welfare of all their staff has always been a priority, as has working in an ecologically sustainable and responsible manner. Tambo Tours' sister company, Tambo Film (www.tambofilm.com), specializes in outfitting film and television productions throughout Peru.

Andina Travel (Santa Catalina 219, tel. 084/25-1892, www.andinatravel.com) offers frequent departures for the Inca Trail and interesting sociocultural projects.

Auqui Mountain Spirit (José Gabriel 307, Urb. Magisterial, tel. 084/26-1517 or 084/25-1278, www.auqui.com.pe), run by Roger Valencia, has been operating since 1992. This high-end agency has a very experienced team and specializes in customized trips, especially for corporate clients.

Aventours (Saphi 456, tel. 084/22-4050, www.aventours.com) was founded by Ricky Schiller, who has been involved in the tourism industry for over 30 years. The expert staff provides excellent service.

Enigma (Fortunato L. Herrera 214, Urb. Magisterio 1a etapa, tel. 084/22-2155, www.enigmaperu.com) employs gourmet cooks. It offers Inca Trail treks combined with visits to Nevado Salcantay, Vilcabamba, and the ruins of Choquequirao. Alternative adventures include horseback riding, ayahuasca therapy, and bird-watching.

Inca Explorers (Calle Peru W - 18 Urb. Ttio, tel. 084/24-1070, www.incaexplorers.com) has a range of longer trips to Vilcabamba, Choquequirao, and the Cordillera Vilcanota, as well as participative tourism such as weaving, farming, and traditional healing.

Perú Sur Nativa (Magisterio 2da etapa K-7-302, tel. 084/22-4156, www.perusurnativa.com) is owned by longtime Cusco adventurer extraordinaire Raúl Montes. Montes has a real eye for adventure and an unflappable sense of humor (we confirmed this after spending two weeks with him on a balsa raft in the Manu jungle eating only green bananas and red-bellied piraña!). Perú Sur Nativa also runs trips in other parts of South America as well as nearby Choquequirao, Carabaya, and Vilcabamba, and to the Manu rainforest.

Peru Treks & Adventure (Av. Pardo 540,

tel. 084/22-2722, www.perutreks.com) is also responsible for the very informative website Andean Travel Web (www.andeantravelweb.com).

Q'ente (Choquechaca 229, tel. 084/22-2535, www.qente.com) has been running since 1995 and provides good service and trained staff.

Quechuas Expeditions (San Juan de Dios 295, tel. 084/22-3548, www.quechuas-expeditions.com) is one of the most highly recommended trekking agencies in Cusco, with a vast range of Andean treks as well as jungle tours.

Trek Peru (Republica de Chile B-15, tel. 084/26-1501 or 800/566-1305, www.trekperu.com) has been leading high-quality tours since the mid-1990s. It offers a wide range of Inca Trail options, as well as treks to Lares, Salcantay, and Ausangate. Treks start at $460.

United Mice (Av. Pachacútec 424, tel. 084/22-1139, www.unitedmice.com) is a recommended backpacker's choice. It also offers a seven-day Salcantay trek.

Xtreme Tourbulencia (Plateros 364, tel. 084/22-2405, U.S. tel. 702/560-7220, www.x-tremetourbulencia.com) receives good reviews and offers a range of treks and tours throughout Peru.

RAFTING AND KAYAKING

There are many excellent rafting and kayaking options around Cusco. The easiest, and most common, are day trips along the Class III rapids of the **Río Urubamba** in the Sacred Valley (US$50-70). They often include one night of camping near Ollantaytambo, mountain biking, and a chance to see ruins the next day. December-May, when the river is swollen, agencies tend to raft the upper section above Pisac. When the water drops after June, they run the section of the river lower down between Ollantaytambo and Chilca. Farther downstream, the water rushes onward to Machu Picchu in great cataracts of unnavigable Class VI water.

Another day option is the easier stretch of the **Río Apurímac** below the Cusco-Abancay highway, a gentle stretch that passes the foundations of an Inca hanging bridge made famous by Thornton Wilder in his classic *The Bridge of San Luis Rey*. The Apurímac here is generally sunny and subtropical, so bring sunscreen, a hat, mosquito repellent, and swimwear, because a quick dip in local hot springs is often included.

A popular three-day rafting trip is on the upper Apurímac (US$400-650), which can

Río Urubamba offers great white-water rafting.

only be run between June and October. The Apurímac plunges through a steep and wild gorge and an endless series of Class III-V rapids. Agencies that operate this section of the river usually also offer trips on Río Cotahuasi (US$1,950 approximately), a similar though more exacting canyon near Arequipa that takes 10 days to navigate in a full-scale, supported expedition.

The most spectacular rafting expedition is the Río Tambopata (US$1,500-2,500), which is a great way to combine a mountain rafting adventure with world-class Amazon biodiversity. This 10- to 12-day trip begins in cloud forest north of Lake Titicaca with a few days of Class III-V rapids and ends floating on torpid jungle waters through the pristine Parque Nacional Bahuajua Sonene. Participants usually stay at the Tambopata Research Center, a rustic lodge operated by Rainforest Expeditions that is minutes from the world's largest macaw clay lick. Floating silently through this untouched rainforest provides a good opportunity to spot a jaguar or tapir and a huge range of birds and more common animals, such as capybara, turtles, and giant otters. The trip includes a flight back to Cusco from the jungle city of Puerto Maldonado.

If you want to go kayaking instead of rafting, agencies will often loan you a kayak on the easier rivers such as the Urubamba and lower Apurímac.

Rafting and Kayaking Agencies

Like trekking prices, rafting rates vary greatly based on the season, the number of people in the group, the difficulty of the rapids, and the section of the river. Prices for a daylong rafting trip on the Urubamba River are typically US$35-100 per person per day, including lunch. For the four-day Río Apurímac trip, which includes Class III-IV rapids, prices are typically US$300-1,100. Most operators, however, charge US$500-600.

One of the most professional rafting companies in Peru is **Amazonas Explorer** (Collasuyo 910, Urb. Miravalle, tel. 084/25-2846, www.amazonas-explorer.com). It runs a variety of innovative trips in Peru, Chile, and Bolivia, including canoeing, mountain biking, trekking, and rafting. One of the best trips is a 16-day expedition that begins with sightseeing in Cusco and Lake Titicaca and ends in rafting down the Río Tambopata and two nights at the Tambopata Research Center.

ExplorAndes (Paseo Zarzuela Q-2 Huancaro, tel. 084/23-8380, www.explorandes.com) also offers high-end rafting trips.

The following are less expensive but also experienced agencies. They are recommended for easier trips.

Apumayo Expediciones (Jr. Ricardo Palma N-5, Santa Monica, tel. 084/24-6018, www.apumayo.com) is run by Pepe López, a kayaker with a lot of experience on Peru's rivers. He built an adventure center on the banks of the Río Urubamba, downstream of Ollantaytambo. The center, which shares profits with the nearby community of Cachiccata, offers hikes and mountain biking for the rafters who arrive here after descending the Río Urubamba. Apumayo runs trips down the Apurímac, Tambopata, and Cotahuasi and offers reforestation cultural treks and the classic Inca Trail.

Loreto Tours (Calle del Medio 111, Cusco, tel. 084/22-8264, www.loretotours.com) provides varied rafting itineraries and good-quality equipment.

Mayuc (Portal Confituras 211, Plaza de Armas, tel. 084/24-2824, www.mayuc.com) is one of the pioneering rafting companies and operates an excellent day trip on Río Urubamba. It also does rafting trips on the Apurímac and in Tambopata.

Terra Explorer Peru (Santa Ursula D-4, Huanchac, tel. 084/23-7352, www.terraexplorerperu.com) is owned by Piero, the youngest of the Vellutino brothers, all dedicated and well-knit adventure sportsmen and white-water rafters. Terra Explorer offers all kinds of rafting trips, including Cotahuasi and Tambopata, mountain treks,

CUSCO
RECREATION

and mountain biking. **Munaycha** (based in the Sacred Valley, cell tel. 984-770-381, www.munaycha.com) belongs to Duilio, the oldest Vellutino brother, and also offers rafting on Peru's best-known rivers as well as sea kayaking trips off the coast of Arequipa and on Lake Huyñaymarca, a rarely visited part of the Titicaca.

MOUNTAIN CLIMBING

Cusco is surrounded by majestic snow-covered peaks that offer outstanding mountaineering possibilities, though none should be tried by people without mountaineering experience—even with a good guide. Unlike many of the mountains in the Cordillera Blanca, these Andean routes are steep, icy, and complicated. Avalanches are common, especially on Salcantay. Several international climbing agencies operate in Peru.

Mountain Climbing Agencies

Licensed mountain guides in Peru, working on an independent basis, will charge US$100-150 per day. An agency that arranges a technical climb will generally charge twice or three times that rate on a daily basis. For climbing in Cusco, it's a good idea to inquire with agencies in Huaraz, Peru's climbing headquarters. Huaraz agencies are often able to lead climbing trips all over the country.

The best local mountaineering agency is **Peruvian Andean Treks** (Pardo 705, tel. 084/22-5701, www.andeantreks.com), owned by climber Tom Hendrickson.

The best way to contact internationally certified guides is through **Camp Expedition** (Triunfo 392, office 202, tel. 084/43-9859), which leads rappelling, climbing, and canyoneering adventures in the Cusco area.

BIKING

Nearly all of the rafting and kayaking agencies do bike tours and rent bikes. A highly recommended company is **Loreto Tours** (Calle del Medio 111, Cusco, tel. 084/22-8264, www.loretotours.com, US$100 per day for guided tours). Peru's best-known mountain biker,

Omar Zarzar Casis (omarzarzar@aventurarse.com), has written a book describing routes in Cusco and across the country. He is a good English-speaking contact for those planning a major ride in the area. **Gravity Assisted Mountain Biking** (Santa Catalina Ancha 398, tel. 084/22-8032, www.gravityperu.com, US$100 per day for guided tours) has great equipment and experienced guides for adventure mountain biking tours.

Many of the Manu tour operators give clients the option to bike partway down the magnificent dirt-road descent from Acanaju Pass, at 3,800 meters, into the jungle. This route, which also passes through Pisac and Paucartambo, provides a stunning glimpse of more than a dozen ecosystems.

Many agencies also offer mountain biking in the Sacred Valley, especially on the Chinchero plateau around Moray and Maras, with a final descent past the salt mines (Salineras) to Urubamba. The Abra Málaga (4,300 meters), which lies along the highway between Ollantaytambo and Quillabamba, is another of Peru's spectacular mountain-to-jungle descents. This trip is now part of a bus/biking/walking alternative to the Inca Trail, called the Inca Jungle Trail, which takes you past the pristine Colcamayo hot springs in Santa Teresa, from where you can either walk or catch the train to Machu Picchu.

BIRD-WATCHING

The Cusco area has one of the world's highest areas of bird biodiversity, particularly where the high Andes meet the Amazon rainforest. Particularly rich environments are the Abra Málaga (4,300 meters) area, en route to Quillabamba, and the Acanaju Pass (3,800 meters), en route to Parque Nacional Manu. Barry Walker, owner of Manu Expeditions and author of *A Field Guide to the Birds of Machu Picchu, Peru,* leads excellent birding. Barry can be reached through **Manu Expeditions** (Pardo 895, tel. 084/22-6671, birding@manuexpeditions.com, www.birdinginperu.com, US$250 per day for guided tours with more than six people).

The high-quality **InkaNatura** (Ricardo Palma J1, Urb. Santa Monica, tel. 084/25-5255, www.inkanatura.com, US$275 per day for guided tours with more than six people) and **Gran Peru** (www.granperu.com.pe, US$175 per day for guided tours with more than six people) also run birding trips throughout the country. Leo Oblitas is an excellent birding guide and works for some of the leading bird-watching agencies.

HORSEBACK RIDING

Adventure Specialists (U.S. tel. 719/783-2076, www.adventurespecialists.org, prices vary, call ahead) leads highly recommended, custom horse-packing trips all over Peru and especially in the Cusco area. Founder and co-owner Gary Ziegler is a true adventurer, ar-chaeologist, and noted Inca expert.

Manu Expeditions (Los Geranios 2-G Urbanizacion Mariscal Gamarra 1ro etapa, tel. 084/22-5990, www.manuexpeditions. com, prices vary, call ahead) offers a range of horse-riding expeditions that explore areas of the Vilcabamba and Choquequirao (17 days), as well as Machu Picchu and the surround-ing cloud forest (15 days). Another of its itin-eraries is from the Andes to the Amazon (14 days). One- and two-day rides around Cusco are also offered.

The best options for riding Peruvian *paso* horses are **Wayra** (part of the Sol y Luna Hotel outside Urubamba, tel. 084/20-1620, www.wayrasacredvalley.com, US$210 per day) and **Perol Chico** (Carretera Urubamba-Ollantaytambo, cell tel. 950-314-065, www. perolchico.com, prices vary, call ahead).

EXTREME SPORTS

A wacky adventure opportunity is **Action Valley** (Santa Teresa 352, tel. 084/24-0835, www.actionvalley.com, US$75 bungee jump, US$22 paintball). This park, 11 kilometers from Cusco on the road to Chinchero, has a 107-meter bungee drop, a catapult that throws people 120 meters into the air with 3.2 G's of force, a 36-meter climbing pole, a 124-meter rappel wall, and a 10-meter climbing wall.

There are some beautiful paragliding spots in the Cusco area. **Leo Paragliding School** (UV Santiago 302-2B, tel. 084/23-9476, www. flyingexpedition-org, US$75 pp) offers tan-dem flights as well as paragliding training courses. Another recommendable option for tandem paragliding flights over the Sacred Valley is **Viento Sur,** run by the European owners of Sol y Luna Hotel in Urubamba (tel. 084/20-1620, www.hotelsolyluna.com, US$195 pp).

Via Ferrata (tel. 084/79-3019, www. naturavive.com, US$55 pp, family rates avail-able) is a 300-meter rock face located in Pacha between Urubamba and Ollantaytambo. It is equipped with wire cables and footholds to allow people with no previous experience to enjoy the adrenaline rush of rock with all the necessary safety equipment.

ESOTERIC EXPERIENCES

Cusco is a center for a range of spiritual and esoteric activities, though the main opera-tors seem to change constantly. Tourists are shown traditional practices by native heal-ers with **Back2Nature** (Alto Los Incas Calle Arequipa J-3, tel. 084/24-4454, back2nature. com.pe, prices vary, call ahead), owned by Norwegian Irene Kingswick and Peruvian Dennis Alejo.

Leslie Myburgh at **Another Planet** (Triunfo 120, tel. 084/24-1168, www.an-otherplanetperu.net, prices vary, call ahead) and Diane Dunn at **Paz y Luz** (tel. 984/216-293, www.pazyluzperu.com, prices vary, call ahead) in Pisac are other good contacts for ayahuasca and San Pedro ceremonies. In the Sacred Valley, the **Willka Tika** (Paradero Rumichaka, 2 kilometers north of Urubamba, tel. 707/202-5340, www.willkatika.com) is a luxury retreat that offers ceremonial activi-ties. It has seven relaxing gardens with wind-ing paths, a yoga studio, and meditation cottages.

MASSAGES AND SPAS

Plaza de Armas and the streets close by are filled with so-called massage therapists.

Quality is variable, and most are unqualified, but for US$8 per hour, you can't really complain. For a higher level of service, try Olga Huaman and her team at **Yin Yang** (El Sol 106, Galerias La Merced, Office 302, 3rd Fl., tel. 084/25-8201, cell 084/984-765-390, yinyang_masajes@hotmail.com, 9am-10pm daily), who give very professional massages as well as reiki; they offer room service or sessions at their premises. **Angel Hands** (Heladeros 157, tel. 084/22-5159, 6am-10pm) offers similar services. The **Siluet Sauna and Spa** (Quera 253, Interior 4, tel. 084/23-1504, 10am-10pm daily) offers massages along with a whirlpool tub and hot and dry saunas.

If you really want to treat yourself to a day of luxurious pampering, try **Samana Spa** (Tecsecocha 536, tel. 084/23-3721, cell 084/984-389-332, www.samana-spa.com), located in a nicely renovated colonial house. They offer professional massages, steam and dry saunas, Jacuzzis in the lovely stone patio, and all sorts of beauty treatments, including facials and manicures. In addition to the providers listed here, most top-class hotels in Cusco offer massage services.

The leading chiropractor in Cusco is Canadian expat Howard Levine at **Heart Nectar** (Carmen Bajo 184-F, San Blas, cell tel. 984-791-288, heartnectarperu@hotmail.com). He offers consultations and treatment for US$40, and offers a range of natural therapies, including crystal healing and energy work. Massages are also available for US$25-30, and Howard leads shamanic workshops using ayahuasca and San Pedro cactus.

SIGHTSEEING TOURS

There is fierce competition, along with frequent price wars, between Cusco's agencies for general sightseeing tours. Most of the agencies are clustered around the Plaza de Armas and offer competitive prices. There are also luxury tours.

The most popular tours include the full-day tour of the Sacred Valley (US$14), which includes Pisac, lunch in Urubamba, Ollantaytambo, and sometimes Chinchero as well, but this is a very rushed way to see the valley. A half-day tour is also offered to Maras, Moray, and Salineras (US$12, US$4 entrance to Salineras not included). The half-day city tour (US$8) takes in the ruins outside Cusco, including Sacsayhuamán, Q'enqo, Puca Pucara, and Tambomachay as well as Coricancha in Cusco itself ($3.50 entrance not included in tour). For all of these tours you will need the *boleto turístico* to gain entry to various ruins that do not offer separate entrance fees. Another half-day tour explores the ruins heading toward Puno, including the magnificent church in Andahuaylillas, along with Pikillacta and Tipón. Or take the full-day bus tour taking in the ruins along the way and finish in Puno.

Several agencies in Cusco cater to groups and also reserve tickets and provide tours for independent travelers. The highly recommended **Fertur** (Simon Bolivar F23, tel. 084/22-1304, www.fertur-travel.com) has friendly, knowledgeable staff that offers private day tours, with a long list of additional cultural and adventure options.

Condor Travel (Saphy 848, tel. 084/24-8181, www.condortravel.com, US$35 daylong group tour) is one of the most established and professional operators of traditional tourism.

Orellana Tours (Garcilaso 206, tel. 084/22-1544, www.viaorellanatours.com, US$20 daylong group tour) is an inexpensive agency with a good reputation. **Milla Turismo** (Urb lucrepata E-16, tel. 084/23-1710, www.millaturismo.com, US$32 daylong group tour) is well established and very professional.

JUNGLE TRIPS

Many people who visit Cusco do not realize how close they are to the Amazon jungle. There are two options within easy reach. The most popular is a trip via Puerto Maldonado to **Tambopata Reserve**. This can be reached by a half-hour plane ride or a whole day on the bus now that the highway has improved markedly. A few hours more in a boat take you to a jungle lodge with outstanding opportunities to see birds, mammals, and insects. Recommended lodges include **Explorer's Inn** (Circunvalación Mz: L, Lote 1 – Terminal Terrestre 2nd Fl., Office 111, Puerto Maldonado, tel. 082/57-3029, www.explorersinn.com) and **Libertador Tambopata Eco Lodge** (Nueva Baja 432, Cusco, tel. 084/24-5695, www.tambopatalodge.com), both of which have offices in Cusco.

A longer trip to **Parque Nacional Manu** offers a chance to see a greater variety of animals, especially predators such as the black caiman as well as parrots drinking at clay licks. However, beware of Cusco operators selling Manu packages for around US$300, because these short tours only go to the edge of the park, even though they claim it's still a Manu tour. To go deep inside and get the best experience, you need at least five to seven days. Recommended Cusco-based agencies include **Manu Nature Tours** (Pardo 1046, Cusco, tel. 084/25-2721, www.manuperu.com), **Manu Expeditions** (Los Geranios 2-G Urbanización Mariscal Gamarra 1ro Etapa Cusco, tel. 084/22-5990, www.manuexpeditions.com), **Pantiacolla Tours** (Garcilaso 265, interior, 2nd Fl., Office 12, Cusco, tel. 084/23-8323, www.pantiacolla.com), and **Caiman Tours** (Garcilaso 210, Office 207, Cusco, tel. 084/25-4041, www.manucaiman.com). See *Moon Peru* for more information on trips to the Amazon.

Food

CENTRAL CUSCO
Cafés, Bakeries, and Ice Cream

For a light lunch on Plaza de las Nazarenas, head to **Mama Oli** (Plaza Nazarenas 199, no phone, 9am-8pm Mon.-Fri. and 9am-5pm Sat.-Sun., US$4). This Peruvian-French-owned café has great juices, fresh soups, quiches, and desserts.

The classic Cusqueño **Café Ayllu** (Almagro 133, tel. 084/25-5078, 6:30am-10:30pm Mon.-Sat., 6:30am-1:30pm Sun., US$4) opened in the 1970s, and its glass cases still display pastries made from the age-old recipes. Be sure to try the *ponche de leche,* a pisco-and-milk cocktail, or a sliced roast suckling pig sandwich. **Dos Por Tres** (Marquez 271, tel. 084/23-2661, 9am-9pm daily, US$2.50) is another Cusco classic and artist hangout, good for drinks, cakes, and ice cream. The coffee, usually made by the owner, is cheap and delicious.

Directly across from the post office, **Don Esteban & Don Pancho** (Av. El Sol 765-A, tel. 084/25-2526, 8am-10pm Mon.-Sat., 8am-7pm Sun., US$5) has a varied menu of sandwiches, empanadas, desserts, and bread made on the premises.

Dolce Vita (Santa Catalina Ancha 366, tel. 084/63-9334, 10am-9pm daily, US$3) is the best place for homemade ice cream. Your only trouble will be deciding on a flavor: *chicha, pisco sour, lúcuma,* and coca are just a few of the exotic creations. It also has a new store at Maruri 276.

A good place for coffee, cakes, pancakes, and empanadas is the ideally located **Café Perla** (Plazoleta Santa Catalina 215, no phone, 7am-11pm daily, US$3-8). Peruvian main courses are available too.

Peruvian

On the ground floor of Portal de Panes is the hugely popular ★ **Inka Grill** (Portal de Panes 115, tel. 084/26-2992, www.inkagrill-cusco.com, 11am-11pm daily, US$10-16), the first restaurant to bring Novoandino cuisine to Cusco and one of passionate restaurateur Rafael Casabonne's six restaurants (www.cuscorestaurants.com). Try the trout *tiradito* to start, followed by chicken Milanese with gnocchi. Alpaca medallions and roasted guinea pig are for the more adventurous. There is regular live Andean music.

Pucara (Plateros 309, tel. 084/22-2027, lunch and dinner daily, US$8-12) has a decent lunch menu for US$6 and offers local dishes such as *chicharron* (fried pork) and *seco de pollo* (chicken stew). **Café Restaurant Victor Victoria** (Tecsecocha 474, tel. 084/25-2854, 7:30am-10pm daily) has a reasonable lunch menu for US$5. The food is homey and there is an ample salad bar.

A recommended, unpretentious restaurant that serves fantastic Peruvian food is **Trujillo** (Tullumayo 543, tel. 084/23-3465, 9am-8pm Mon.-Sat. and 9am-5pm Sun., US$10-15). The menu is vast and servings are generous. It is particularly famous for its *ají de gallina* and the meat of the *asado a la olla.*

Nuna Raymi is another good place to eat local specialties (Triunfo 356, tel. 084/22-4644, www.nunaraymicusco.com, 9am-10:30pm daily, delivery 11am-10:30pm, US$10-15), including *ají de gallina, lomo saltado,* and trout in a variety of delicious sauces. Set menu is US$6.

For Andean music accompanying dinner, head to **Tunupa** (Plaza de Armas, tel. 084/25-2936, noon-10:30pm daily, US$15-20), right on the plaza. It specializes in fish and seafood. Try the candied trout. Prices are a little steep, but it has a great atmosphere.

International

An excellent Italian restaurant with a varied fusion menu is ★ **Incanto** (Santa Catalina Angosta 135, tel. 084/25-4753, www.cuscorestaurants.com, 11:30am-11pm daily, US$11-17). The minimalist decor shows off the original Inca walls, and the food is delicious. Choose from inventive Peruvian-Italian dishes, such as smoked trout fettuccine, ravioli *de ají de gallina,* and vegetable cannelloni. The *lúcuma* bar crunch is a delicious dessert. Above Incanto and belonging to the same owner is ★ **Greens** (Santa Catalina Angosta 135, 2nd Fl., tel. 084/24-3379, www.cuscorestaurants.com, 11am-11pm daily, US$13), the best

organic restaurant in town. All dishes are a minimum of 90 percent organic. Choose from a wide variety of fresh vegetable and fruit juices from produce taken from the restaurant's own organic gardens in the Sacred Valley. The trout is delicious, and you should round off your meal with a dish invented by the chef: mango ravioli.

Peruvian cuisine is full of sushi-influenced dishes, but for real Japanese-style sushi, head to ★ **Kintaro** (334 Plateros, tel. 084/26-0638, www.cuscokintaro.com, noon-3pm, 6pm-10pm Mon.-Sat., US$6-15). The US$6 lunch menu is an excellent value, or try the range of rolls. Tea, extra bowls of rice, and Wi-Fi are all free.

Fine Dining

Fallen Angel Fire & Ice (Plazoleta Nazarenas 221, tel. 084/25-8184, www.fallenangelincusco.com, 11am-11pm daily, US$15-20) is a fascinating artistic creation. Decor includes glass-covered bathtub fish tanks instead of tables and a feast of artwork on the walls in a rotating exhibition. The atmosphere is set by techno music and multicolored daiquiris. The steaks are the specialty of the creative dinner menu.

At ★ **MAP Café** (Plaza Nazarenas 231, tel. 084/24-2476, www.cuscorestaurants.com, 11am-10pm daily, US$20-30), one of Cusco's best gourmet restaurants, dinner guests sit in a perfectly proportioned glass box in the stone courtyard of the Museo de Arte Precolombino. The food is a gourmet interpretation of traditional Andean cuisine. The glazed and deep-fried *cuy* legs on a *choclo* foam with *tarwi* salad is a tasty and less confrontational way to try guinea pig. A favorite dish on the menu is *capchi de setas,* a mouthwatering creamy mushroom, potato, and broad bean casserole topped with a buttery pastry. Other specialties include the *tiradito* of sea bass in chili and *tumbo* sauce, and the roast lamb and quinoa cannelloni with truffles. The desserts are some of the most creative and delectable in Cusco. The specialty is hot truffle balls with *aguaymanto* and pisco, served with vanilla ice cream and a surprise shot.

Cicciolina (Triunfo 393, 2nd Fl., tel. 084/23-9510, www.cicciolinacuzco.com, 8am-11am, noon-3pm, and 6pm-10pm daily, US$15-20) is one of the most happening restaurants in town, popular with tourists and locals alike. A casual lunch here might be a sandwich, salad, and smoothie or their daily set menu. For dinner, try the cracked black pepper tagliatelle, grilled scallops in an Asian sauce, barbecued trout in coconut milk, or beetroot ravioli, accompanied by a glass of wine. For dessert try the strawberries and port. If you leave satisfied, come back the following morning for breakfast and delicious croissants at the Cicciolina bakery. They also provide a picnic catering service.

For an evening meal with an entertaining and operatic twist, **Divina Comedia** (Pumacurco 408, tel. 084/43-7640, www.restaurantcusco.com, 11:30am-3pm and 6:30pm-11pm Wed.-Mon., US$12-16) is a lot of fun. The Divine Comedy theme, medieval-influenced decor, and waiters dressed in period clothing are a fitting backdrop to the talented opera singers who entertain you while you dine. The menu ranges from tapas and ceviche to pasta and steak.

For an all-around great dining experience, easily the best fusion restaurant in Cusco is ★ **Limo** (Portal de Carnes 236, 2nd Fl., tel. 084/24-0668, www.cuscorestaurants.com, 11am-3pm and 6pm-midnight daily, US$15-18). Rafael Casabonne's latest project is a tastefully decorated restaurant with a great view over the Plaza de Armas. The service is excellent, but most importantly the food is superb. Start the evening with a plate of exquisite sushi rolls. The *tiraditos* and ceviches, especially the *ceviche oriental,* are delicious. As a main, try the crab meat and breaded shrimp bathed in *leche de tigre* or the trout in passion fruit-infused white wine. For dessert, you can't go wrong with the *lasaña de*

suspiro (wonton filled with fruit and strawberry coulis).

Peru's most famous chef and the man responsible for introducing the country's cuisine to the world is Gaston Acurio. His best-known, world-class restaurants are in Lima, but in Cusco he also has the recommended **Chicha** (Plaza Regocijo 261, 2nd Fl., tel. 084/24-0520, noon-10:30pm daily, US$15). The menu here is as diverse as Peru's geography, offering local favorites and international dishes with a twist. Try the alpaca tartare, pachamanca (meat dish), and rocoto relleno (stuffed peppers) for a flavor of Cusco. For international dishes, there is duck pizza, lamb ravioli and a loin rump with carmelized onions in red wine sauce.

Pizza

Pizza Carlo (Maruri 381, tel. 084/24-7777, noon-3pm and 5pm-11pm Mon.-Sat., 5:30pm-11pm Sun., US$10) has traditional Italian wood-fired pizzas with thin, smoky crusts. Those meat lovers who like a bit of spice should try the Diablo.

Babieca Trattoría (Tecsecocha 418-A, tel. 084/50-6940, 11am-midnight, US$12) has excellent dough, gourmet toppings such as alpaca and trout, and a gigantic pizza called the Kilometriza for US$20.

Vegetarian

Although most restaurants in Cusco have vegetarian options, there are few places dedicated exclusively to vegetarian cuisine. A popular option is **Govinda** (Saphy 584, tel. 084/79-0687, 8am-10pm daily, US$3-5), a few blocks up from the Plaza de Armas. This small Indian-inspired restaurant has flavorful dishes, including curry, paella, pasta, and wonton with tofu. The US$4 lunch menu is a very good value.

A worthwhile and economical option is **El Encuentro** (Santa Catalina Ancha 384, tel. 084/24-7977, 9am-3pm and 6pm-9pm Mon.-Sat., US$3-6). It has a salad bar, soups, sandwiches, falafel, and pasta.

SAN BLAS
Cafés, Bakeries, and Ice Cream

The most popular café in Cusco is Irish/Australian-owned ★ **Jack's Café Bar** (Choquechaca 509/Cuesta San Blas, tel. 084/25-4606, www.jackscafecusco.com, 7:30am-11:30pm daily, US$6-10), and with good reason. It is famous for big breakfasts, such as El Gordo: a huge pile of eggs, homemade baked beans, fried potatoes, bacon, and sausages. For lunch there are great soups, salads, and sandwiches made with homemade bread. Don't miss the Tuscan veggie soup. There is a fully stocked bar, as well as milk shakes, fruit juices, and coffees. At peak periods, you have to wait to be seated, an indication of how good this place is.

Along Cuesta San Blas, you'll eventually walk into the warm baking aromas of **Buen Pastor** (Cuesta San Blas 575, tel. 084/24-0586, 7am-8pm Mon.-Sat., US$2-4). This bakery run by nuns has warm empanadas and sweet pastries at very affordable prices.

To satisfy a chocolate craving, stop in the tiny ★ **Chocolate** (Choquechaca 162, tel. 084/25-8073, 7am-11pm daily), a shop serving steaming mugs of hot chocolate and chocolates by the piece. If you fancy sampling some creative coca-flavored chocolate and baked goods, head to the **Coca Shop** (Carmen Alto 115, 9am-8pm Mon.-Fri.).

If you are after a hefty sandwich, try **Juanito's** (7 Angelitos 638, tel. 084/25-5343, 11am-10pm Mon.-Sat., US$5). There is a selection of 30 fillings both meaty and vegetarian, including alpaca and *lechón*.

Peruvian

Pacha Papa (Plazoleta San Blas 120, tel. 084/24-1318, www.cuscorestaurants.com, 9am-10pm daily, US$7-12) occupies a sunny courtyard across the street from the Iglesia San Blas. It's a good place for breakfast, with everything from Peruvian specialties (such as tamales, *chicharron,* and beef stew) to French toast and granola. For dinner, specialties range from oven-baked trout to a whole roasted *cuy.* Note that service can be slow.

International

If you are after Indian food, British-run **Korma Sutra** (Tandapata 909, tel. 084/23-3023, 6pm-10pm Mon.-Sat., US$8-12) is a good option. The curries are a little overpriced but very tasty, especially the onion *bhaji* and the *tikka masala.*

The German-owned **Granja Heidi** (Cuesta San Blas 525, tel. 084/23-8383, 8:30am-9:30pm Mon.-Sat., US$6-10) has farm-fresh produce, including delicious natural yogurt, homemade granola, and a light and tasty midday lunch menu. Prices are a little steep.

Australian Tammy Gordon's **Baco Wine Bar and Restaurant** (Ruinas 465, tel. 084/24-2808, bacorestaurante@yahoo.com, 3:30pm-10:30pm Mon.-Sat., US$10-15) has a relaxing atmosphere. There are thin-crust pizzas topped with such options as duck prosciutto and mushrooms or blue cheese, marinated figs, and basil. The organic salads and grilled meats are also delicious accompanied by a great wine from an extensive list.

A very cozy and affordable pizzeria in San Blas is **Justina's** (Palacio 100, interior, tel. 084/25-5475, 5pm-11pm daily, US$9-13). Or go to the extremely popular **La Bodega 138** (Herrajes 138, tel. 084/26-0272, noon-10:30pm daily, US$8-14), which has a great atmosphere and is renowned as the best pizzeria in town.

Markets

The **Mercado San Pedro** (Túpac Amaru, 6am-7pm), near the San Pedro train station, has a wide selection of fruit and vegetables. Come here to try the unique and delicious *granadilla* and *chirimoya* and cheap juices, but keep your eyes out for pickpockets and those who silently slice backpacks with razors to steal the goodies within.

Several blocks past Mercado San Pedro toward Avenida Ejercito is the black market **El**

Baratillo, which on Saturday morning is full of the most fascinating secondhand wares. If you have time to browse properly you can find some real treasures, but be careful with your valuables.

The largest supermarket is **Mega** (Plaza Túpac Amaru and Matara); **Market** (Portal Mantas 120) is on the Plaza de Armas. They're small and pricey but stock some hard-to-find imported products.

Accommodations

Cusco is awash in tourist accommodations, and there is huge variation, from bare-bones dorms to some of the best hotels in Peru. There is a sufficient range of hotels and hostels in the tourist center, so there is no need to stay outside this zone. Your biggest decision is between staying close to Plaza de Armas, which is busy and noisier, or heading up the hills north, south, or west of the main plazas to seek out quieter lodgings, many of which have great views. The most pleasant of these outlying areas is the bohemian neighborhood of San Blas, which has a relaxing, artsy vibe. Its narrow streets keep out the traffic and smog of central Cusco.

Traffic has made parts of Cusco unpleasant. These areas include the extension of Plateros and Avenida El Sol, where even the back rooms of hotels hum with the noise of taxis and amplified advertisements. Outside of San Blas, Cusco's nicest lodging is along out-of-the-way streets like Suecia, Choquechaca, or Siete Cuartones/Nueva Alta, where classy bed-and-breakfasts line charming cobblestone streets. Try to make a reservation ahead of time in Cusco, and ask for the kind of room you want (e.g., with a view or with a double bed). Quality is variable, so try to check the room before paying. Despite a steady increase in the number of Cusco hotels, the best ones are increasingly booked solid May-November. If you arrive and don't like your room, you can usually wriggle out of your reservation after your first night and head elsewhere—there are lots of good options, especially among the newer, lesser-known hostels.

CENTRAL CUSCO
Under US$10
For budget accommodations, backpacker hostels are a good option, and there are now quite a few in Cusco. Bear in mind that these places tend to be noisier with regular parties, which may or may not suit you. The most popular are **The Point** (Meson de la Estrella 172, tel. 084/25-2266, www.thepointhostels. com, US$8-13 dorms) and **LOKI Inkahouse** (Cuesta Santa Ana 601, tel. 084/24-3705, www. lokihostel.com, US$9-13 dorm, US$33 d private bath). Both have locations in Lima and Máncora and include dorm rooms (and a few private rooms) that open onto TV rooms, Internet stations, shared kitchens, and bars. They have a reputation for their parties, and you are bound to meet other travelers.

Youth Hostal Albergue Municipal (Quiscapata 240, San Cristóbal, tel. 084/25-2506, albergue@municusco.gob. pe, US$6 dorm, US$8 d), part of Hostelling International, has great views from the balcony, clean bunk rooms, and a shared kitchen. A discount is given to Hostelling International members.

US$10-25
The name of ★ **Hostal Resbalosa** (Resbalosa 494, tel. 084/22-4839, www.hostalresbalosa.com, US$20 s shared bath, US$30 d private bath) translates as "slippery hostel," which might not seem immediately inviting. But it is appropriate for the steep walk up here. The hostel itself is one of the best budget options in town. Service is friendly, and rooms are well-equipped with orthopedic mattresses,

hot water, and cable TV—but the highlight is the sweeping view over Cusco from the terrace. The rooms at the top are better.

Pirwa Backpackers (Portal de Panes 151, tel. 084/24-4315, www.pirwahostelscusco.com, US$12 dorm, US$35 d) has four central locations: the Plaza de Armas, Suecia, San Blas, and San Francisco. They all have a variety of dorms and private rooms, most with shared kitchen, common rooms, and a travel desk.

A great backpacker option is ★ **Ecopackers** (Santa Teresa 375, tel. 084/23-1800, www.ecopackersperu.com, US$12-15 dorms, US$40-55 d), set in a beautiful colonial home. It offers a courtyard with games, a travel agency, Wi-Fi, and a decent, well-priced restaurant. Dorms and showers are well equipped. The private rooms are overpriced, but for backpacker groups, the dorms are a very good deal.

Mama Simona (Ceniza 364, tel. 084/26-0408, www.mamasimona.com, US$10-15 pp) has a selection of dorms and private rooms, plus a colorful sitting room. **Che Lagarto** (Siete Cuartones 284, tel. 084/23-3251, US$12 dorms, US$45 d) is another hostel. The dorms are a good value but private rooms are overpriced.

The charming **Sihuar** (Tandapata 351, tel. 084/22-7435, www.sihuar.galeon.com, US$25 d) is a two-level building that looks out over a patio and garden. The good-value rooms are pleasant and tastefully decorated, with wooden floors, woven rugs, and hot water.

US$25-50

A very good value hotel is **Conde Meloc** (Meloq 420, tel. 084/22-1117, www.hostalcondemeloc.com, US$26 s, US$39 d), which has elegant rooms and a cozy atmosphere.

Niños Hotel (Meloq 442, tel. 084/23-1424, www.ninoshotel.com, US$50 s or d) is a remarkable place with a cause: Its Dutch owner uses hotel revenue to feed, clothe, and provide medical assistance to street children. Just four blocks from the Plaza de Armas, this restored colonial home is a very attractive setting. With

large, stylish rooms, hardwood floors, and a pleasant courtyard for taking breakfast, it's easy to make yourself at home. There is a second location at Fierro 476 (tel. 084/25-4611) and a Niños Hotel Hacienda in Huasao.

US$50-100

A lovely place in Tandapata is **Casona les Pleiades** (Tandapata 116, tel. 084/50-6430, www.casona-pleiades.com, US$77 s/d). Whether it be Melanie or Philip who opens the door for you, the welcome is bound to be warm and friendly. This young French couple has made their seven-room home into a guesthouse, and their aim is to make you feel right at home. There are down comforters on the beds and eggs made to order for breakfast.

The good-value European/Peruvian hotel **Madre Tierra** (Atocsaycuchi 647-A, tel. 084/24-8452, www.hostalmadretierra.com, US$49 s, US$58 d) has seven comfortable carpeted rooms. Cozy and inviting communal areas have white sofas, exposed beams, and open fireplaces.

★ **Hostal El Balcon** (Tambo de Montero 222, tel. 084/23-6738, www.balconcusco.com, US$60 s, US$75-125 d) is a restored colonial house with rustic charm and a pretty, flower-filled garden. This 16-room hostel is quaint and homely, and rooms are decorated simply with weavings on the beds.

The unpretentious **Hostal Corihuasi** (Suecia 561, tel. 084/23-2233, www.corihuasi.com, US$45 s, US$55 d) is a quick, steep walk up from the Plaza de Armas and has an old-world charm that befits Cusco. The rooms of this rambling, eclectic colonial house are connected by verandas and walkways. Some of the rooms are nicer with views over the city; others are dark, with porthole windows, so make sure you check your room before paying.

MamaSara Hotel (Saphy 875, tel. 084/24-5409, www.mamasarahotel.com.pe, US$90 s, US$110 d), a short walk from the plaza up Saphy, is very pleasant and comfortable. The rooms are heated and spacious, and they come with flat-screen TVs, good showers, and oxygen on request. Another good option right off the plaza is **Del Prado Inn** (Suecia 310, 084/224-442, www.delpradoinn.com, US$65 s, US$95 d), with stylish, warm rooms and an ideal location.

For a location one block from the Plaza de Armas, look no further than **Hostal Rojas** (Tigre 129, tel. 084/22-8184, www.hotelrojascusco.com, US$60 s, US$85 d with private bath), with clean, carpeted rooms around a sunny courtyard inhabited by an entertaining parrot.

An impressive original Inca doorway, once the entrance to a sacred place, is now the way into the hotel **Rumi Punku** (Choquechaca 339, tel. 084/22-1102, www.rumipunku.com, US$80 s, US$100 d). Light-filled terraces, a garden with an original Inca wall, and a gym and spa make this a pleasant place to stay.

Another midrange hotel with an excellent location is **Cusco Plaza** (Plazoleta Nazarenas 181, tel. 084/24-6161, www.cuscoplazahotels.com, US$55 s, US$65 d). The rooms are relatively simple, but the views are great and it's perfect to be on the quiet square.

US$100-150

The well-known national hotel chain ★ **Casa Andina** (www.casa-andina.com) has four of its Classic Collection hotels at ideal locations in the center of Cusco. Two are within one block of the Plaza de Armas (Santa Catalina Angosta 149, tel. 084/23-3661, and Portal Espinar 142, tel. 084/23-1733), one is near Coricancha (San Agustín 371, tel. 084/25-2633), and the fourth in San Blas (Chihuampata 278, tel. 084/26-3694). These well-designed, comfortable hotels provide excellent service, and all have the same prices (US$140 s/d). The aim of the hotels is to reflect the local character of a place and give a genuine experience using local ideology and local products where possible, without sacrificing comfort and convenience. All rooms have down comforters, heating, and cable TV, and a generous breakfast buffet is included. Prices may be cheaper booking online.

A good option in this range is **Tierra Viva** (Saphi 766, tel. 084/24-1414, and Suecia 345, tel. 084/24-5848, www.tierravivahoteles.com, US$129 s, US$141 d), which has two hotels near the center with impeccable rooms and a buffet breakfast.

The **Hotel Arqueologo** (Pumacurco 408, tel. 084/23-2569, www.hotelarqueologo.com, US$120 d standard, US$140 d superior) occupies an old colonial building. Rooms with high ceilings wrap around a rustic stone courtyard or overlook a grassy garden. The hotel tries to maintain an eco-friendly philosophy by having its own bio-veggie garden, recycling rubbish, providing a fountain with drinking water to refill bottles, and only providing TVs in rooms upon request. The first-floor café, **Song Thé**, has comfortable sofas, a fireplace, and French pastries.

US$150-250

The **Novotel** (San Agustín 239, tel. 084/58-1030, www.novotel.com, US$240 d modern room, US$320 d colonial room) is in a restored colonial manor that has a patio lined with stone arches and decorated with lamps and wicker furniture in which guests can enjoy evening drinks. Undoubtedly the best rooms are those on the second floor around the stone courtyard, with wood floors, high ceilings, king-size beds, sitting areas, and all creature comforts (security box, minibar, cable TV, heating). The other 82 rooms are comfortable but bland, small, and sterile, housed in an unfortunate five-story modern addition.

Equal in elegance and similar in layout, but cheaper and better value is **Costa del Sol Ramada** (Santa Teresa 344, tel. 084/25-2330, www.costadelsolperu.com, US$140 d modern room, US$159 d colonial), which has an ideal location one block from Plaza Regocijo and a two-minute walk from the Plaza de Armas. This 17th-century colonial mansion, which once belonged to the Spanish noble Marquis de Picoaga, has been well restored with stone archways and columns wrapping around a classic colonial patio. Costa del Sol, the Peruvian hotel chain, recently acquired it.

Over US$250

The five-star ★ **Hotel Libertador Palacio del Inka** (Plazoleta Santo Domingo 259, tel. 084/23-1961, www.libertador.com.pe, US$305 d) has a great location next to Coricancha, the Inca sun temple. It occupies the Casa de los Cuatro Bustos, Francisco Pizarro's last home. It is built on the foundation of the *acllahuasi,* "the house of the chosen ones," where virgins picked by the Inca lived in seclusion from society. The entrance to the Hotel Libertador is spectacular. A stone portal leads into a glass-roofed lobby, lined on one side by Spanish stone arches and on the other by exposed portions of stone Inca walls. There is an excellent buffet breakfast served alongside another large square, ringed with two stories of stone arcades. Throughout the hotel are examples of original colonial furniture, artifacts, and paintings. Ask for rooms in the colonial section, with views of the sun temple. The suites are larger and have sitting areas and marble bathrooms, and are probably worth paying extra for.

The new exclusive hotel in town is none other than the **Hilton Garden Inn** (Santa Ana, Avenida Apurimac 207, tel. 084/ 58-0130, call for rates), located on a hill overlooking Cusco and about a kilometer from the main plaza. The rooms have all of the comforts of Hiltons around the globe: 47-inch TVs, comfy beds with crisp sheets. There is excellent Wi-Fi and a good restaurant.

★ **Casa Andina Private Collection** (Plazoleta Limacpampa Chico 473, www.casa-andina.com, tel. 084/23-2610, US$320 s/d) is the best of Casa Andina's hotels in town. This beautifully renovated 18th-century manor house is just three blocks from Cusco's Plaza de Armas, and it offers the intimacy of a boutique hotel but the comforts and services of a much larger property. The hotel has three interior patios with wooden balconies and a stone fountain. In the hotel's cozy lounge and reading room is a massive stone fireplace that's always crackling, while the gourmet restaurant offers candlelit dinners in one of four connected salons richly decorated with 18th-century Cusco School paintings. Several rooms in the original structure of the hotel feature surviving colonial frescoes unearthed during renovation.

One of the more memorable places to stay in Cusco is ★ **Hotel Monasterio** (Palacio 136, Plazoleta Nazarenas, tel. 084/60-4000, www.belmond.com, US$634 basic d or US$806-2,232 suites), a 415-year-old monastery that has been converted into an elegant

Hotel Libertador Palacio del Inka occupies the former home of Francisco Pizarro.

five-star hotel. The stone lobby leads to a dramatic stone courtyard, graced with an ancient cedar tree and lined with two stories of stone archways. Colonial paintings line long hallways, which wrap around two other stone patios. The rooms are decked out in old-world Spanish decor, including carved wooden headboards and colonial paintings, and include all the plush five-star comforts. They can even be pumped with oxygen, simulating an altitude 900 meters lower and allowing guests to sleep more soundly.

The hotel occupies the former Seminario San Antonio Abad, which was built in 1595 on top of the Inca Amaru Qhala Palace but was badly damaged in the 1650 earthquake. During the restoration, a colonial baroque chapel was added, which remains open to guests and has one of the most ornate altars in Cusco. After yet another damaging earthquake in 1950, the building was condemned and auctioned by the Peruvian government in 1995. It eventually landed in the hands of Orient-Express Hotels, which carefully restored the stonework, planted fabulous gardens, and converted the former cells into 126 plush rooms. These days, guests take lunch in the main square, which is shaded by a giant cedar, scented by a rose garden, and filled with the gurgling of a 17th-century stone fountain. The hotel hosts one of Cusco's three gourmet restaurants, and also includes a small massage room. It's a few minutes' walk from the Plaza de Armas.

Diagonally opposite the Monasterio on Plaza de las Nazarenas is **Inkaterra La Casona** (Plaza de las Nazarenas 113, tel. 084/23-4010, www.inkaterra.com, US$720 patio suite, US$924 balcony suite, US$1,128 plaza suite). Literally named "the big house," it offers a homely but luxurious atmosphere. This beautiful colonial mansion was built in 1585. Following the Spanish conquest it was possessed by Francisco Barrientos, lieutenant to Diego de Almagro. It has now been officially named a historic monument by the Instituto Nacional de Cultura, and has been exquisitely restored into 11 luxurious suites with original caoba doors. The doors to La Casona are closed to the outside world, ensuring the utmost privacy. The philosophy of the hotel is to provide a personalized service; you'll struggle to find the front door, and there is no reception, just a butler and concierge who prioritize individuals' needs. Rooms are decorated with faded frescoes, colonial tapestries, Persian rugs, and antiques, ensuring the original feel of the home without sacrificing modern comfort and luxury. Every suite has thermostat-controlled heated floors, a flat-screen TV with DVD player, iPod speakers, Wi-Fi, and a minibar. There is also a private spa and massage room. La Casona also prides itself on being one of Peru's first carbon-neutral hotels.

SAN BLAS
US$10-25

Samay Wasi (Atocsaycuhi 416, tel. 084/25-3108, www.samaywasiperu.com, US$10-11 dorm, US$26-34 d) is about a 10-minute walk from Cusco's Plaza de Armas in San Blas. It offers shared and double rooms and has nice gardens.

Mirador de la Ñusta (Plazoleta San Blas, tel. 084/24-8039, US$15 pp) is a budget hotel on the main plaza of San Blas. It's very basic, and hot water is available only in the mornings, but it's a great price for the location.

US$25-50

Probably the best value for money is **Inti Quilla** (Atocsaycuhi 281, tel. 084/25-2659, www.intiquilla.8m.com, US$14-20 s, US$25-30 d). This very basic but clean hostel has two triple rooms and five double rooms arranged around a colorful lounge area. Some rooms have private bathrooms, and there is 24-hour hot water.

In the center of San Blas is **Casa de la Gringa** (Tandapata 148, tel. 084/24-1168, www.casadelagringa.com, US$24-30 s, US$30-40 d), owned by Lesley Myburgh. It is recommended for its colorful rooms, friendly staff, and small gardens. There is a New Age, spiritual air about the place.

A very popular hotel right on the square is **Hatun Wasi** (Plazoleta San Blas, tel. 084/25-3585, www.hotelhatunwasi.com, US$50 s, US$76 d), with comfortable rooms and an ideal location.

In lower San Blas, one of the nicer hotels in Cusco is ★ **Amaru Hostal** (Cuesta San Blas 541, tel. 084/22-5933, www.amaruhostal.com, US$50 s, US$60 d with private bath). The 27 rooms, with balconies, are spread around two sun-filled patios overflowing with geraniums and roses. The rooms have comfy beds and wood floors, and are small but generally pleasant. However, note that rooms vary widely—ask for the corner rooms with sun porches, wicker furniture, and vistas on both sides. For those on a budget there are cheaper rooms with shared bathrooms. The hostel has two more locations in San Blas: **Amaru Hostal Colonial** (Chihuampata 642, tel. 084/22-3521) and the private **Hostería de Anita** (Alavado 525, tel. 084/22-5499).

US$50-100

Charming, German-owned **Pensión Alemana Bed and Breakfast** (Tandapata 260, tel. 084/22-6861, www.cuzco-stay.de, US$63-68 s, US$70-75 d with breakfast) is the closest thing to a European pensione in Cusco. There are 12 light and airy rooms (many with incredible views over the city) with comfortable beds and hot showers. A pleasant garden looks out over the red-tiled roofs of the city, and a nightly fire crackles in the dining room.

Apu Huascaran (Carmen Bajo, tel. 084/23-5825, www.apuhuascaranperu.com, US$65 s, US$75 d) is a midrange hotel in San Blas with decent rooms with cable TV and private baths, a small courtyard, and a rooftop terrace with great views.

Encantada (Tandapata 354, tel. 084/24-2206, www.encantadaperu.com, US$90 s, US$115 d) is a pleasant hotel in a modern building with great views and minimalist decor. The hotel also doubles as a massage and spa center.

US$100-150

As the name suggests, **Second Home Cusco** (Atocsaycuchi 616, tel. 084/23-5873, www.secondhomecusco.com, US$110 s, 120 d) in San Blas really is a home away from home. This highly recommended bed-and-breakfast, owned by artist Carlos Delfin, son of the famous sculptor Victor Delfin, has three very simple but nicely decorated, light-filled junior suites: the skylight suite, the patio suite, and the balcony suite. Each has its own special charm. There is another Second Home located in Lima.

At the Swiss-managed **Los Apus** (Atocsaycuchi 515, tel. 084/26-4243, www.losapushotel.com, US$100 s, US$120 d), the rooms have wood floors, heating, comfortable beds, and cable TV. Breakfast is served in a glass-roofed courtyard.

The attractive boutique hotel **Casa San Blas** (Tocuyeros 566, tel. 084/23-7900, www.casasanblas.com, US$136 d, US$198 suite) prides itself on providing personalized service. The hotel is ideally located, set back off the Cuesta San Blas, and has great views of the city from its sunny roof terrace. Its eighteen rooms are comfortable, have all the necessary amenities, and are decorated simply with traditional weavings on the walls. There are also self-catering suite apartments with kitchenettes. Sustainability issues are addressed by giving guests the option to reuse bedding and towels and refill water bottles. Light bulbs are energy-saving, and there are double curtains to reduce the need for heating.

The finest of the Casa Andina Classic Collection hotels is the ★ **Casa Andina San Blas** (Chihuampata 278, tel. 084/26-3694, www.casa-andina.com, US$140 s/d), built around a colonial stone courtyard with great views of Cusco. The cozy sitting areas with wood-burning fires, a rustic bar, and a terrace make this a great place to relax.

Information and Services

TOURIST INFORMATION

The **South American Explorers Club (SAE)** (Pardo 847, tel. 084/24-5484, www.saexplorers. org, 9:30am-5pm Mon.-Fri., 9:30am-1pm Sat.) is a gold mine of information. It costs US$60 to join as an individual for a year, US$90 for a couple, though nonmembers are allowed to look around as well. This is definitely worth the cost if you will be in Peru for any length of time, and is a recommended first stop in Cusco. No matter how much research you have done, you will always learn something here and, at the very least, meet some interesting people. Club members can peruse trip reports for all over the Cusco area, use the well-stocked library, make free calls to the United States and Canada, and receive discounts at a wide range of restaurants, language schools, hotels, and agencies. It is also the only place in Cusco that sells topographical maps ($25). There are trekking sheets available (members US$2, nonmembers US$4), and the clubhouse can advise you on the best local tour operators. The club hosts weekly events, and there is a new volunteer room that helps travelers become involved in children's, women's, and environmental projects.

If all you need is some basic tourist information and a map, services are free at the friendly **Iperú** (Portal Harinas 177, Plaza de Armas, tel. 084/25-2974, www.peru.travel/iperu.aspxwww.promperu.gob.pe, 9am-6:50pm Mon.-Fri., 9am-12:50pm Sat.-Sun. or at the airport (tel. 084/237-364, 6am-5pm daily). You can also try the city tourist office, **Dircetur** (Plaza Tupac Amaru Mz. Lote 2, Wanchaq, tel. 084/22-3701, www.dircetur-cusco.gob.pe, 8am-8pm Mon.-Sat., 8am-2pm Sun.).

POLICE

Travelers can contact the tourist police through the Iperú office, but a larger, **24-hour tourist police office** is at Saphi 510 (tel. 084/24-9659), where officers speak some English.

IMMIGRATION

Tourist visa inquiries can be made at the **Oficina de Migración (Immigration Office)** (Av. El Sol 612, tel. 084/22-2741, 8am-4:15pm Mon.-Fri., 8am-noon Sat.).

HEALTH CARE

One of the major hospitals of Cusco is **Hospital Lorena** (Plazoleta Belén 1358, in the Santiago neighborhood, tel. 084/22-1581 or 084/22-6511, www.hospitalantoniolorena. com). Another is the **Regional Hospital** (Av. de la Cultura, tel. 084/22-3691).

One recommended clinic is **Cima Clinic** (Pardo 978, tel. 084/25-5550 or cell tel. 984-651-085, www.cima-clinic.com), which specializes in altitude problems.

The best pharmacies are **InkaFarma** (Av. El Sol 210, tel. 084/24-2631, www.inka-farma.com.pe, 24 hours), **Boticas Arcangel** (Mantas 132, tel. 084/22-1421, 7am-11pm daily), and **Boticas Fasa** (Av. El Sol 130, tel. 084/24-4528, www.boticasfasa.com.pe, 7am-11pm Mon.-Sat., 8am-9pm Sun.).

A recommended dental clinic is **Vivadent Clínica Odontológica** (El Sol 627-B, 2nd Fl., tel. 084/23-1558 or cell tel. 984-746-581, www.vivadentcusco.com). Dr. Virginia Valcarcel Velarde is expensive but very professional and experienced.

BANKS AND MONEY EXCHANGE

Getting money out of an ATM usually means a stroll down the first few blocks of Avenida El Sol, where **Banco de Crédito** is on the first block and **Banco Continental** and **Interbank** are on the third. The Banco de Crédito and Interbank are open all day 9am-6:30pm (the others usually close 1pm-3pm), with Saturday hours 9am-1pm. All the banks

City Safety

It is a common misconception that traveling through Peru's remote countryside is risky while spending time in a tourist town like Cusco is safe. In fact, the exact opposite is true. Taxi assaults, where cab drivers rob their passengers, are on the rise in Cusco. Most of these are simple robberies, though some have involved violence. Here are some tips for staying out of trouble:

- Take only authorized taxis; these can be easily recognized by a hexagonal yellow sticker on the windshield. Even better, go with a radio taxi company—these have advertising and phone numbers on their roofs.

- Look at the taxi driver and decide whether you feel comfortable. If you feel nervous, wave the taxi on and choose another.

- Always take a taxi late at night, especially after drinking. Night taxis anywhere in town cost about US$2.

- Walk in a group at night. Women should never walk alone.

- Carry your wallet in your front pocket and keep your backpack in front of you in a market or other crowded area. In markets, it is often better to leave most of your money and your passport at home.

- Walk with purpose and confidence.

- Stay in the main tourist areas. Avoid lesser-known suburbs and take care in the areas around San Pedro market and the bus terminal.

- When riding on a bus, store your luggage below or keep it on your lap. Do not put it on the racks above you where others can reach it as you sleep.

- Be wary of new friends at bars and on the street—many scams involve misplaced trust or the lure of drugs and sex and are hatched over the space of hours. Think twice before you go somewhere out of the way with someone you just met.

are closed on Sunday. For wire transfers, there is a **Western Union** (Av. El Sol 627-A, tel. 084/24-4167, 8:30am-7:30pm Mon.-Fri., 8:30am-1:30pm Sat.).

There is an overwhelming number of money exchange places, especially along the Avenida El Sol, and they are all much the same. A reliable option is **Panorama** (Portal de Comercio 149, 9am-10pm daily). The rate is always fair, and the bills are brand new because they come directly from the bank.

COMMUNICATIONS

Cusco's main **post office** is the Serpost (Av. El Sol 800, tel. 084/22-5232, www.serpost. com.pe, 7:30am-8pm Mon.-Sat. and 9am-2pm Sun).

The city has plenty of Internet places, all of which have cable connections and are generally good, although the availability of Wi-Fi in hotels and hostels makes them less and less important. Most are open 9am-9pm daily. Long-distance and international calls can be made at many Internet places, which are all similar in price.

LANGUAGE SCHOOLS

Cusco has more Spanish schools than any other city in Peru, though it is hard to be truly immersed in Spanish unless you can somehow isolate yourself from English speakers. Considering what they include, the school packages are inexpensive: prearranged hostel accommodations or homestay with local family, breakfast, airline reservations, volunteer work options, city tours, dance and cooking classes, lectures, and movies. An intensive group class with all these perks runs around

US$200-300 per week with 20 hours of classes, while a private package is around US$300-400 for the same schedule. A private teacher, without lodging or food, is US$10-13 per hour.

Academia Latinoamericana de Español (Plaza Limacpampa Grande 565, tel. 084/24-3364, www.latinoschools. com, US$300 private classes, US$185 group classes) is a professional, family-run business with schools in Peru, Ecuador, and Bolivia. They have great host families in Cusco and offer volunteer programs as well as university credits through New Mexico State University. **Amigos Spanish School** (Zaguan del Cielo B-23, tel. 084/24-2292, www.spanishcusco. com, US$150 group) gives half of its income to children with disabilities and has highly recommended teachers.

Centro Tinku (Nueva Baja 560, tel. 084/24-9737, www.centrotinku.com, US$165 group) is a cultural institution that offers standard and custom-made Spanish and Quechua classes. All the teachers are fully certified. Off the Plazoleta San Blas is the affordable and quaint yet professional **Mundo Antiguo Spanish School** (Tandapata 649, tel. 084/22-5974, www.learnspanishinperu. net, US$70-120 group, US$90-175 private), run by a friendly Peruvian-Dutch couple; the school keeps its programs intimate, personal, and welcoming. **Maximo Nivel** (El Sol 612, tel. 084/25-7200, www.maximonivel.com) has schools all over North and South America.

LAUNDRY

Most Cusco hostels offer laundry service for the going rate of US$2 per kilogram. Otherwise the best place for washing clothes (although a little more expensive) and especially for dry cleaning is **Lavandería Inka** (Ruinas 493, tel. 084/22-3421, 8am-1pm and 3pm-8pm Mon.-Sat.). For just regular washing, **Lavandería Louis** (Choquechaca 264-A, tel. 084/24-3485, 8am-8pm Mon.-Sat.) is a reliable and cheaper option.

PHOTOGRAPHY

It's a good idea to download your photos, particularly after visiting Machu Picchu, just to be safe. Digital photographers can download their full media cards to a CD in 20 minutes at many camera shops in Cusco. Sometimes you need the USB cord that works with your camera. An exception is **Foto Panorama** (Portal Comercio 149, in front of the cathedral, tel. 084/23-9800, 8:30am-10pm), which accepts most different media cards. Another highly recommended place for developing or digital services and products is **Foto Nishiyama** (Triunfo 346, tel. 084/24-2922). It has other locations around town, including on Avenida El Sol.

Getting There and Around

AIR

Cusco's airport, **Aeropuerto Internacional Alejandro Velasco Astete** (tel. 084/22-2611), is 10 minutes south of town, and the taxi ride costs about US$4.50.

All Cusco-bound travelers must first arrive in Lima and then board another plane in Cusco, for which there are currently three main operators. To approach Cusco's airport, planes must fly at considerable altitude and down a narrow valley, passing ice-covered Nevado Salcantay en route. Because of the tricky approach and winds, afternoon flights are frequently canceled. If possible, fly in and out of Cusco in the morning.

LAN (Av. El Sol 627-B, tel. 084/25-5552, Lima tel. 01/21-38200, www.lan.com) is the most reliable airline but also the most expensive, and has more than 10 Cusco-bound flights a day. Published fares are as high as US$400 return, but it often has special offers if you book ahead of time, plus it works out cheaper to book the international flight and internal flight to Cusco together. **Star Perú**

(Av. El Sol 627, tel. 084/25-3791 or 084/23-4060, www.starperu.com) and **Avianca** (Av. El Sol 602-B, tel. 084/24-9921 or 084/24-9922, Lima tel. 01/21-37000, www.taca.com) are also reliable and usually have cheaper flights, starting from US$200 return. **LCPeru** (Av. El Sol 520, tel. 084/23-5584, www.lcperu.pe) is a small Peruvian airline, but a reliable and economical option. It offers round-trip flights between Lima and Cusco starting at about US$130.

In addition, LAN has daily flights from Cusco to Puerto Maldonado and Arequipa, as well as various other destinations around Peru from Lima. Star Perú and Taca also fly from Lima or Cusco to Puerto Maldonado and from Lima to other Peruvian destinations.

BUS
Long-Distance Buses
The long-distance bus terminal, the **Terminal Terrestre,** is on the way to the airport (Vía de Evitamiento 429, tel. 084/22-4471). This huge building is busy, safe, and crammed with all of the long-distance bus companies, along with bathrooms and a few stores selling snacks. Companies generally are open 6am-9pm and accept reservations over the phone, with payment on the day of departure (you have to speak Spanish, though). Note that the area around the bus terminal is not particularly safe, so take a taxi directly to and from the terminal. When you have the option, traveling in the highlands is best done during the day.

A recommended way to get to **Puno** is with one of the tourist buses that visit the ruins on the way. These buses include a buffet lunch and an English-speaking guide, and they stop at most of the major ruins along the route. **Inka Express** (Plateros 320, tel. 084/24-7887, www.inkaexpress.com, US$50) makes stops at the exquisite colonial church of Andahuaylillas and the Inca ruins of Raqchi, and includes a buffet lunch stop in Sicuani. In the afternoon the bus stops at La Raya pass and the ruins of Pukará before arriving in Puno. The buses generally leave Cusco at

8am and arrive at 5pm in Puno, including hotel pickup and drop-off. There is usually a 10 percent discount for groups of more than four people.

For direct services to Puno, **Ormeño** (tel. 084/22-7501) has a daily bus leaving at 9am, which arrives in Juliaca at 1:30pm and Puno at 2pm (US$14 for Royal Class, which has on-board food service and plusher seats than even the Imperial buses). **Turismo Puma** offers a similar service. **Imexso** (tel. 084/22-9126, imexso@terra.com.pe), for the most part, has good service and new buses, with English-language videos.

Many of these companies offer transfer buses leaving for **Bolivia,** though some go through Desaguadero and others through Copacabana (launching point for Isla del Sol). **Ormeño** (tel. 084/22-7501) has a direct business-class bus (no meals) through Desaguadero to La Paz, leaving daily at 9pm. To head through Copacabana, try **Tour Peru,** which leaves at 10pm daily (US$28). Another recommended company for getting to Bolivia is **Litoral,** though there are many more options in Puno's excellent Terminal Terrestre. The border crossing, which is open between 8am and 3pm, is quick and easy: Passengers need only get off the bus for a few minutes on each side of the border to have their passports stamped. Remember to ask for the maximum number of days (usually 90).

Buses for the 20-hour haul to **Lima** now head to Abancay before crossing the mountains to the coast at Nasca and then heading north for Lima. Ormeño offers the extra-plush Royal Class service, which leaves at 10am and arrives in Lima the following day at 6am for US$50. There are also plain, one-story buses with a stop in Abancay. Another recommended company is **Expreso Wari** (tel. 084/24-7217), which has buses with seats that recline into beds. Trips including meals leave at 12:30pm and 8pm for US$52. They also have a less luxurious service leaving at 2pm and 4pm for US$28. **Cruz del Sur** (tel. 084/24-8255) has a good Imperial service leaving at 3:30pm and 6:30pm. **Tepsa** (tel.

084/22-4534, www.tepsa.com.pe) is also a reliable option for Lima. The only company with transfer service through Abancay on to **Ayacucho** is **Expreso Los Chankas** (tel. 084/24-2249).

The journey between Cusco and Nasca takes 13 hours along some pretty dicey roads. It costs US$35 during the day and a little more at night. Turismo Internacional and all companies listed above for Lima go to Nasca.

The journey to **Arequipa** via Juliaca takes 9.5 hours ($12). **Cruz del Sur** (tel. 084/24-8255) has Imperial buses that include dinner leaving at 2pm for US$34, and Ormeño offers a similar-quality service. **Enlaces** (tel. 084/25-5333) and **Cial** (tel. 804/22-1201) also have Imperial buses leaving daily.

The only direct option for Tacna, the border town for Chile, is **Cruz del Sur** (tel. 084/24-8255), which leaves at 4:30pm and arrives at 8:30am the following day.

The trip to **Puerto Maldonado** used to take two days, but with the construction of the Lima-to-Sao Paolo highway, known as the Inter-Oceanic Highway, it now only takes 10 hours ($25-30). **Transzela** (Terminal Terrestre, 084/238-223, www.transzela. com.pe) is a good company in the terminal. Atalaya, the gateway to the Parque Nacional Manu, is hard to reach, but the journey can generally be made in a long day. Travelers must first head to Paucartambo. For Quillabamba, **Ampay** (tel. 084/24-9977) has buses leaving for the 8.5-hour journey for US$7 from the Terminal Terrestre.

Regional Buses

For destinations in the Cusco region, find the informal *terminales,* where buses, *combis,* and *colectivos* leave when full. These are often located in places that are unsafe at night or early in the morning. They generally operate from 5am until as late as 7pm Most taxi drivers know where these *terminales* are.

For **Quillabamba,** there is a roadside pickup spot, called a *terminal de paso,* at the last block of Avenida Antoñia Lorena, the principal exit road for the route that goes through the Sacred Valley before heading over Abra Málaga into the jungle (7 hours, US$6).

For **Urubamba,** there are two options. Buses for the shorter, 1.5-hour route, through Chinchero, leave from the first block of Grau near the bridge (45 minutes, US$1 for Chinchero; 1.25 hours, US$2 for Urubamba). Collective taxis at Pavitos do the same route but go all the way to **Ollantaytambo** (1.5 hours, US$3.50 pp).

Collective taxis and buses for **Pisac** and **Calca** via Urubamba leave from Avenida Pachacútec on the way to the airport (one hour, US$1.50 for Pisac; 1.5 hours, US$2 for Urubamba).

For **Andahuaylillas** and **Urcos,** on the way to Puno, buses leave from Avenida de la Cultura in front of the regional hospital (1.5 hours, US$1).

Note that pickup points for some of these services change, and there are new collectives offered regularly, so it's always a good idea to ask in your hotel for the latest recommendations.

TRAINS

The train service between Cusco and Machu Picchu, while overpriced, is a spectacular route. The **PeruRail** monopoly has been consigned to the past with the emergence of a new train company: **Inca Rail.** However, prices remain high—US$75 one-way, US$120 return. Trains back from Aguas Calientes can be a little cheaper ($50) due to the volume of travelers returning from the Inca Trail.

If you're not hiking the Inca Trail, then the train is the only way to get to Machu Picchu, although most people don't take it all the way from Cusco. A major problem with trains from Cusco, especially during high season, is availability. The easiest way to get tickets is through a hotel or a travel agent. Otherwise visitors should make reservations online. The third, and least desirable option, is to head down to the Cusco train station, a process that, especially during high season, can take an hour or two.

PeruRail still operates trains from Cusco,

but most Machu Picchu travelers now depart farther down the line at Ollantaytambo in the Sacred Valley. From Ollantaytambo the train enters the narrow Urubamba gorge, which offers spectacular views of snowcapped Verónica peak (5,710 meters or 18,865 feet) on the right (eastern) side of the train as the landscape transforms into the lush and humid *ceja de selva*, or "eyebrow of the jungle." By the time the train reaches Aguas Calientes, the town closest to Machu Picchu, the scenery has changed remarkably from high Andean plains to verdant cloud forest.

The other major train service is the Cusco-to-Puno service. It is a spectacular route up through the high plains of southern Peru above 4,000 meters. However, prices are very steep—$150-220 one-way. Compare this with only US$50 for the bus and it's obvious why most backpackers now take that option instead.

PeruRail

PeruRail (www.perurail.com), a division of Belmond, offers many train services to Machu Picchu: the **Expedition** (US$70 one-way, leaves Ollantaytambo six times daily, first at 5:05 am, leaves Aguas Calientes six times daily, first at 5:35 am), the **Vistadome** (US$85 one-way, leaves Ollantaytambo six times daily, first at 7:05am, leaves Aguas Calientes six times daily, first at 10:55am), and the luxury **Hiram Bingham service** (US$380 one-way, leaves Poroy 9:40am, leaves Aguas Calientes 8:50pm). The Expedition and Vistadome can also be caught from Pichar

For trains to Puno, the PeruRail deluxe **Andean Explorer** (US$306 one-way) departs on Monday, Wednesday, and Saturday (and Friday April-October) from Wanchaq Station (Av. El Sol s/n, tel. 084/23-3592) at 8am and arrives at 6:30pm in Puno. This spectacular 10-hour trip winds through the vast altiplano past snowcapped mountains.

Inca Rail

Inca Rail (Portal de Panes St. 105, Plaza de Armas, tel. 084/23-3030, Lima tel. 01/61-35288, www.incarail.com) offers three daily departures from Ollantaytambo (6:40am, 11:15am, and 4:36pm) and three daily departures from Aguas Calientes (8:30am, 2:30pm, and 7pm) on its Inca Train. The trains have an Executive Class (US$75 one-way) and a First Class (US$135 one-way). Inca Rail has ticket offices in Ollantaytambo and Aguas Calientes next to the train line.

Inca Rail's Machu Picchu Train leaves daily from Ollantaytambo for Aguas Calientes at 7:20am, and from Aguas Calientes for Ollantaytambo at 4:12pm. Prices are also about US$75 one-way.

CAR AND MOTORCYCLE RENTAL

Through its Cusco operator, at **Hertz** (Av. El Sol 808, tel. 084/24-8800, www.inkasrac.com) you can rent a Toyota, be it a Corolla or a Land Cruiser. Rental rates include insurance, taxes, and 250 free kilometers per day. **Europcar** (Saphy 639, tel. 084/26-2655, www.europcarperu.com) also operates in Cusco. Motorcycles can be rented at **Cusco Moto** (Saphi 592, tel. 084/22-7025, www.cuscomototourperu.com). The rental includes helmet, gloves, goggles, jacket, and medical and legal insurance. It also offers tours of the Sacred Valley, Maras and Moray, and even Colca Canyon.

LOCAL TRANSPORTATION

A taxi anywhere in Cusco's center costs US$2-3 at night. Always be careful with taxis, especially at night. Never take unmarked cabs, and be sure to check the taxi's credentials. It's preferable to ask your hotel or restaurant to call a taxi from a reputable company. The extra dollar is worth it for guaranteed security. Because Cusco's center is so compact (and congested), few travelers find the need to take buses or *combis*—though the ones that head down Avenida El Sol toward the Terminal Terrestre and airport are useful.

Vicinity of Cusco

There are very interesting ruins along the road that heads south from Cusco to Lake Titicaca. These cultural sites, from pre-Inca, Inca, and colonial times, form an interesting day tour from Cusco that an increasing number of agencies are offering. These landmarks can also be visited on the highly recommended special tourist buses between Cusco and Puno, which hit all the sights described, head over La Raya Pass, and then keep going to Puno and Lake Titicaca.

Tourist bus services that travel the route and visit the sites for about US$60 one-way include **Inka Express Bus** (tel. 084/43-1398 or 084/23-3498, www.inkaexpressbus.com, Mon.-Sat. 9am-1pm and 3pm-6pm) and **Peru Bus Tickets** (Triunfo 392, Office 212, Cusco, cell tel. 974-334-261, www.cuscopunobus.com, Mon.-Sat. 9am-8pm).

Or, ask any number of travel agencies in Cusco, including **Inkas Destination** (Urb. Zaguan del Cielo F-13, Cusco, tel. 084/50-5819, www.inkasdestination.com, US$20 day tour) and **Machu Picchu Travel** (Tomasa Tito C. Av. 1430, B-601, tel. 084/26-4242, www.machupicchuviajes.com, US$32 day tour).

Alternatively, you can also rent a car and visit the sites on your own. Major rental companies include **Hertz** (tel. 084/24-8800, www.inkasrac.com), **Avis** (tel. 01/207-6000, www.avisperu.com), and **Budget** (tel. 01/444-4546, www.budgetperu.com).

Tipón

One of the most elaborate and well-preserved examples of Inca agricultural terracing is **Tipón** (7am-5pm, US$4 or included in *boleto turístico*), which lies 22 kilometers south of Cusco and then another 4 kilometers up a valley via a switchbacking gravel road. The terraces, finely fitted and incredibly tall, run in straight lines to the head of a narrow valley. They are irrigated by an elaborate aqueduct that still runs from Pachatusan, the sacred mountain that looms over the site, whose name in Quechua means "cross beam of the universe." There are remains of a two-story house on the site and other ruins, possibly a fort, near the top of the aqueduct.

Rumicolca and Pikillacta

Though the Inca refused to admit it, much of their highway network and organizational know-how was based on the **Huari empire,** which spread across Peru AD 500-1000. An example of Huari engineering is **Rumicolca,** a huge aqueduct that sits on a valley pass on the side of the highway about 32 kilometers from Cusco. The Inca altered the construction, added a few stones, and converted it into a giant gateway to Cusco, though the remains of the old water channels can still be seen.

Nearby is **Pikillacta** (6am-6pm, US$4 or included in *boleto turístico*), the largest provincial outpost ever built by the Ayacucho-based Huari. This curious walled compound, with nearly 47 hectares (116 acres) of repetitive two-story square buildings, sprawls across the rolling grasslands with little regard to topography. The floors and walls, which are made of mud and stacked stone, were plastered with white gypsum and must have gleamed in the sun. But the Inca so thoroughly erased evidence of the Huari that little about their empire is known today. For many years Pikillacta was thought to be a huge granary, like the Inca site of Raqchi. But excavations have revealed evidence of a large population that left behind refuse layers as deep as three meters. Part of the city caught fire between AD 850 and 900, and the Huari withdrew from the city around the same time, bricking up the doors as they went. Whether they abandoned the city because of the fire or burned it as they left is unclear. Some historical information is available at the museum at the entrance. In the valley below is Lago Sucre and, even farther on, Lago Huacarpay. On the far shores of this lake are the ruins of **Inca Huáscar's summer palace,** much of which continues to be enjoyed today by locals as the Centro Recreacional Urpicanca, the local country club. From the shoulder of the highway, it is possible to see ceremonial staircases the Inca built into the landscape above the lake.

Andahuaylillas

The colonial village of Andahuaylillas, 37 kilometers south of Cusco, has a charming plaza shaded with red-flowered pisonay trees and an adobe church, **San Pedro** (8:30am-noon and 2pm-5pm Mon.-Sat., 8am-10am and 3pm-5pm Sun., free), which is built on the foundations from the early Inca empire. Though it's unremarkable on the outside, the doors open to a dazzling painted ceiling, frescoes, and wall-to-wall colonial paintings. This is the most finely decorated church in all of Cusco, probably in all of Peru, though its nickname, "Sistine Chapel of the Americas," is going a bit far. One highlight is a mural by Luis de Riaño depicting the road to heaven and the road to hell, with a full-blown display of all the respective rewards and punishments.

There is a well-known natural healing center just off the square, **Centro de Medicina Integral** (Garcilaso 514, tel. 084/25-1999, 9am-7pm daily, medintegral@hotmail.com), with a charming stone courtyard with gardens and plain rooms for US$8 per person. The center attracts a considerable number of overseas visitors for massage, meditation, harmonizing energy therapy, and other treatments.

Urcos

Driving through the main square of this small village, 47 kilometers south of Cusco, it is hard not to notice Urcos's tidy colonial church with a public balcony on the second floor and stone steps in front. On the outskirts of town, there is the beautifully decorated chapel at Huaro, which is on a hilltop overlooking a small lake. According to legend, Inca Huáscar threw a huge gold necklace into these waters to protect the treasure from the Spaniards. The story seemed probable enough that *National Geographic* funded an exploration of the lake's bottom by scuba divers—though thick mud prevented them from finding anything.

Raqchi

Raqchi (119 kilometers south of Cusco, 8am-6pm, US$3) is a ceremonial center built by Inca Pachacútec that offers a fascinating glimpse into the ambition and organizational skills of his budding empire. Rising above the humble village of Raqchi, a wall of adobe nearly 15 meters high and 90 meters long sits on a carved Inca wall. This was once the center of a huge hall, the roof of which was supported by adobe columns—one of which has been restored—on either side. On the side are six identical squares, each with six stone buildings, which probably served as a soldiers' barracks. But the most impressive part of Raqchi is line after line of round stone houses—200 in all—that once were filled with a gargantuan amount of quinoa, freeze-dried potatoes, and corn.

Sicuani

There are several nice lunch spots in Sicuani, 138 kilometers south of Cusco. At the **Casa Hacienda Las Tunas** (J. C. Tello 100, tel. 084/35-2480, US$4), there is a huge, scrumptious buffet of Peruvian food from 11:30am onward, when the Inka Express bus pulls in. There are good trout and meat dishes at the **Cebichería Acuarios** (Garcilazo de la Vega 141, 2nd Fl., tel. 084/80-9531, US$3) on the plaza.

Stopover in Lima

Look for ★ to find recommended sights, activities, dining, and lodging.

Highlights

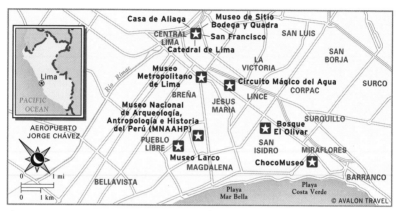

★ **Catedral de Lima:** After two decades of turbulence, Lima is roaring back, and at the center of it all is a refurbished main square and the 16th-century cathedral, with elegantly carved choir stalls and a huge gallery of paintings (page 152).

★ **Casa de Aliaga:** This colonial mansion in the heart of Lima's old town is in pristine condition and offers a fascinating glimpse into domestic life during the opulent days of the viceroyalty (page 153).

★ **Museo de Sitio Bodega y Quadra:** This museum, the former home of Spanish naval officer Juan Francisco de la Bodega y Quadra, is an example of the transition from colonial to republican life in Lima (page 154).

★ **San Francisco:** This 16th-century convent has a brightly decorated patio and art gallery upstairs, and labyrinthine catacombs downstairs (page 154).

★ **Museo Metropolitano de Lima:** Travel through Lima's history via 3D movies and an earthquake simulator (page 155).

★ **Circuito Mágico del Agua:** The biggest water fountain complex in the world has 13 interactive fountains and a laser-light show (page 155).

★ **Museo Larco:** With a huge collection of gold, textiles, and more than 40,000 ceramics, this museum offers a complete survey of Peru's archaeological treasures (page 155).

★ **Museo Nacional de Arqueología, Antropología e Historia del Perú (MNAAHP):** The best way to wrap your mind around Peru's complex succession of ancient cultures is by visiting this compact and concise museum (page 155).

★ **ChocoMuseo:** This unique museum offers chocolate lovers workshops on how to make chocolate while learning about the cacao tree (page 157).

★ **Bosque El Olivar:** Stroll among more than 1,500 olive trees in this 450-year-old park (page 157).

It's worth lingering a day or two in Lima to take in the colonial churches and palaces of the historic center. The city also boasts delicious food at some of Peru's best restaurants and great weekend nightlife.

Peru's biggest city is certainly not the biggest attraction for most foreign tourists, who often pass through without even stopping. Lima's drawbacks are clear to see—there is too much traffic, as expected in a city of nine million people, almost a third of Peru's population. Furthermore, overcast, foggy days all too often give the city a gray, depressing appearance. However, scratch the surface and Lima has plenty to offer. As the former seat of the Spanish viceroyalty, its historic center is filled with colonial churches, ancestral homes, and museums—more than enough to keep you busy for a day at least. And the sightseeing will help you work up an appetite for some of the best cuisine in South America—from mouthwatering ceviche and breaded shrimp in Miraflores and Barranco to spicy noodles in Barrio Chino (Chinatown) or a cup of purple pudding (mazamorra morada) along the riverside promenade of the historic center.

At night, Lima really comes into its own.

As well as a huge selection of restaurants, the nightlife is the best in Peru, and a pisco sour (or two) is obligatory. Bars, clubs, and local music venues, called peñas, explode most nights with dance and the rhythms of cumbia, salsa, Afro-Peruvian pop, and a dozen forms of creole music. Limeños themselves are what make the city so diverse—an exotic cocktail blending coast, sierra, and jungle with African, Asian, and European.

Lima's oceanside location is another plus. Although it's often too cool for sunbathing, it's easy to escape the city smog by wandering down to the fashionable districts of Miraflores and Barranco for some fresh air, and there are good beaches just half an hour south of the city.

To sum it up, Lima is an extraordinary city, but it takes a little getting used to. It is the maximum expression of Peru's cultural diversity (and chaos). Whether you like it or not, you will come to Lima, because nearly all

Previous: view of Miraflores; Plaza de Armas, also known as Plaza Mayor. **Above:** Peruvian chef Gaston Acurio's famous Astrid y Gaston Casa Moreyra restaurant in San Isidro.

Lima

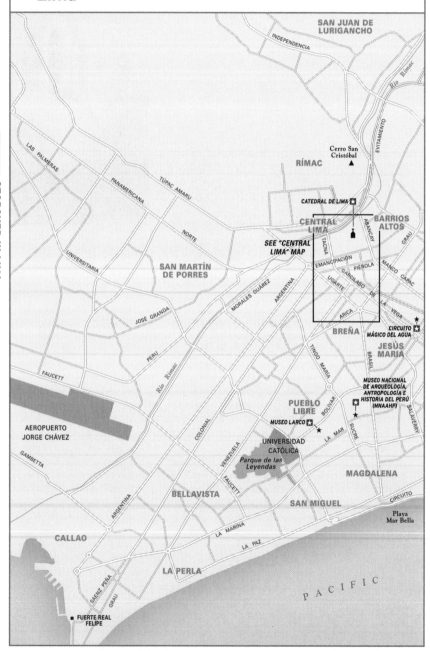

SAN JUAN DE LURIGANCHO

INDEPENDENCIA

Río Rímac

LAS PALMERAS

PANAMERICANA

TÚPAC AMARU

NORTE

RÍMAC

Cerro San Cristóbal ▲

CATEDRAL DE LIMA ⭐

CENTRAL LIMA

BARRIOS ALTOS

SEE "CENTRAL LIMA" MAP

TACNA

ABANCAY

GRAU

UNIVERSITARIA

SAN MARTÍN DE PORRES

EMANCIPACIÓN

PIÉROLA

MANCO CAPAC

UGARTE

GARCILASO DE LA VEGA

JOSÉ GRANDA

MORALES DUAREZ

ARGENTINA

ARICA

PERU

FAUCETT

Río Rímac

TINGO MARIA

BREÑA

CIRCUITO MÁGICO DEL AGUA ⭐

JESÙS MARIA

BRASIL

MUSEO NACIONAL DE ARQUEOLOGÍA, ANTROPOLOGÍA E HISTORIA DEL PERÚ (MNAAHP) ★

SALAVERRY

AEROPUERTO JORGE CHÁVEZ

GAMBETTA

COLONIAL

VENEZUELA

PUEBLO LIBRE

MUSEO LARCO ⭐

BOLIVAR

UNIVERSIDAD CATÓLICA

Parque de las Leyendas

LA MAR

SUCRE

MAGDALENA

FAUCETT

BELLAVISTA

SAN MIGUEL

CIRCUITO

Playa Mar Bella

ARGENTINA

LA MARINA

LA PAZ

CALLAO

SAENZ PEÑA

GRAU

LA PERLA

PACIFIC

■ FUERTE REAL FELIPE

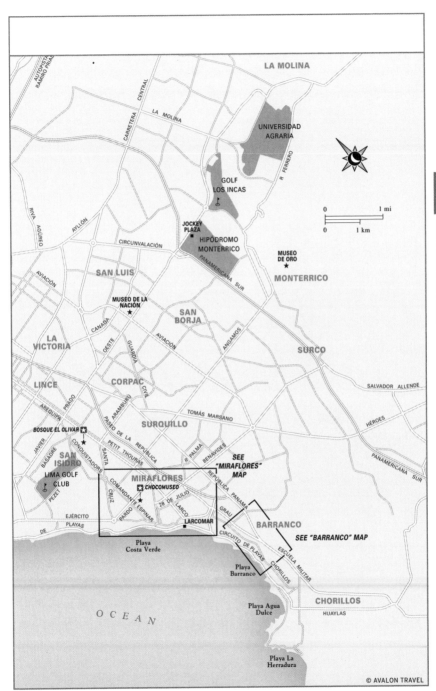

© AVALON TRAVEL

Central Lima

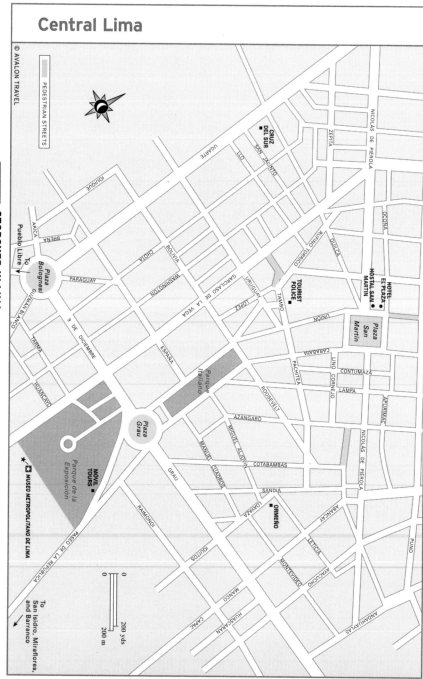

© AVALON TRAVEL

PEDESTRIAN STREETS

CRUZ DEL SUR

HOTEL EL PLAZA
HOSTAL SAN MARTÍN

TOURIST POLICE

Plaza San Martín

Plaza Bolognesi

Plaza Grau

Parque Italiano

Parque de la Exposición

MOVIL TOURS

★ MUSEO METROPOLITANO DE LIMA

ORMEÑO

To Pueblo Libre

To San Isidro, Miraflores, and Barranco

0   200 yds
0   200 m

UGARTE
SAN JACINTO
LLO
NICOLÁS DE PIÉROLA
ZEPITA
OCOÑA
QUILCA
RUFINO TORRICO
IQUIQUE
BREÑA
ARICA
GUZMÁN BLANCO
TARMA
HUANCAYO
9 DE DICIEMBRE
PARAGUAY
BOLIVIA
CHOTA
WASHINGTON
GARCILASO DE LA VEGA
LÓPEZ
URUGUAY
TAMBO
UNIÓN
CARABAYA
PACHITEA
CONTUMAZA
LINO CORNEJO
LAMPA
APURÍMAC
ROOSEVELT
AZÁNGARO
NICOLÁS DE PIÉROLA
MIGUEL ALJOVÍN
MANUEL CUADROS
COTABAMBAS
SANDIA
TAYACAJA
ABANCAY
PUNO
ESPAÑA
PARQUE ITALIANO
GRAU
RAIMONDI
IQUITOS
MANCO
HUÁSCAR
CÁPAC
MONTEVIDEO
AYACUCHO
LETICIA
ANDAHUAYLAS
PASEO DE LA REPÚBLICA

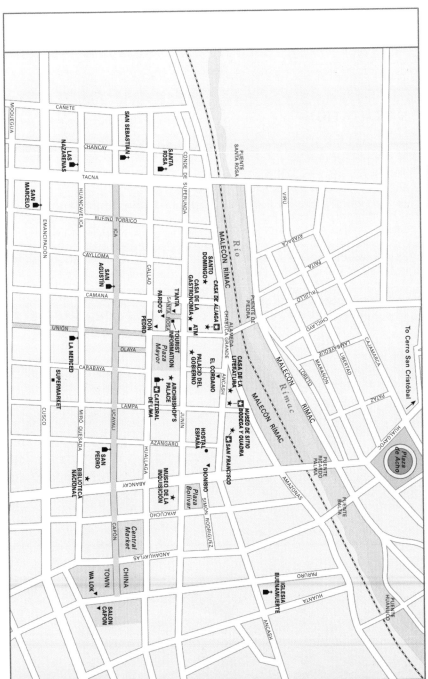

international flights land at this gateway. But do yourself a favor and see Lima at the end of your trip, not at the beginning. That way you have a better chance of understanding what you see and won't become overwhelmed in the process.

ORIENTATION

Lima can be thought of as a triangle, with the city center at the apex. The base begins with the port of **Callao** and the nearby airport and runs along the coast through the neighborhoods of **Miraflores, Barranco,** and **Chorillos.** Other neighborhoods, such as **Pueblo Libre** and **San Isidro,** are in the middle of the triangle.

Lima's best museums are spread out, set in neighborhoods that are sandwiched between the coast and the center. Excellent collections of pre-Columbian gold, textiles, and ceramics can be found at the Museo Larco in Pueblo Libre, Museo de la Nación in San Borja, and Museo de Oro in Monterrico. English-speaking and sometimes French-speaking guides are usually available at these museums.

Most Lima visitors stay in San Isidro, Miraflores, and Barranco, neighborhoods near the coast with the best selection of hotels, restaurants, and nightlife. There is little

to see here, however, except for giant adobe platforms that were built by the Lima culture (AD 200-700) and now rise above the upscale neighborhoods.

The **old town** is bordered by the Río Rímac to the north, Avenida Tacna to the west, and Avenida Abancay to the east. The center of Lima is safe during the day, but it is a good idea not to stray too far outside these main streets, except for a lunchtime foray to Chinatown.

HISTORY

Present-day Lima was never the center of any great empire but rather a verdant valley where a series of cultures flourished alongside the shrine of **Pachacámac,** which by the Inca's time housed one of the most respected, and feared, oracles in the Andes. Huaca Pucllana, in Lima's upscale Miraflores neighborhood, was a ceremonial center built out of adobe bricks by the seafaring **Lima culture** from around AD 200 onward. The valley later fell under the influence of the Ayacucho-based **Huari culture** and was integrated by 1300 into the **Ychma kingdom,** which built most of the monumental architecture at Pachacámac. The Inca **Túpac Yupanqui** conquered the area in the mid-15th century

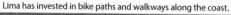

Lima has invested in bike paths and walkways along the coast.

Miraflores

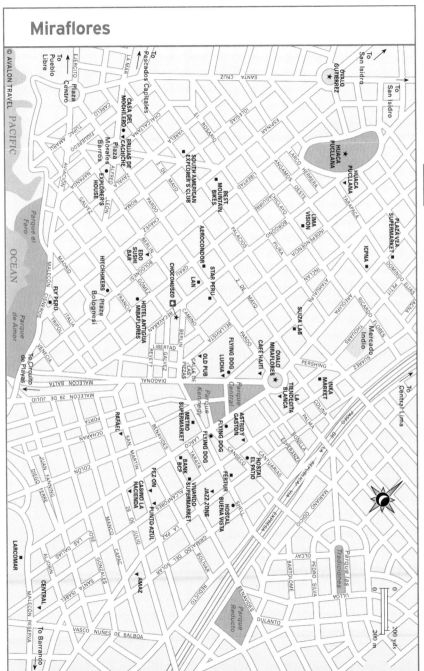

© AVALON TRAVEL

Barranco

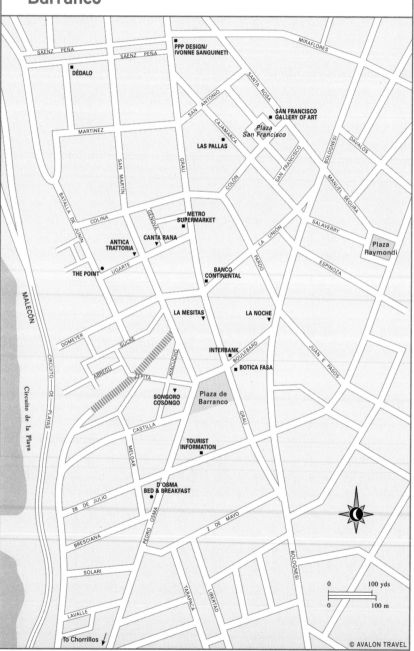

SAENZ PEÑA

SAENZ PEÑA

■ PPP DESIGN/
IVONNE SANGUINETI

MIRAFLORES

■ DÉDALO

SANTA ROSA

SAN ANTONIO

■ SAN FRANCISCO
GALLERY OF ART

CAJAMARCA

Plaza
San Francisco

MARTINEZ

SAN FRANCISCO

BOLOGNESI

DAVALOS

■ LAS PALLAS

GRAU

COLON

MANUEL SEGURA

SAN MARTIN

GENOVA

■ METRO
SUPERMARKET

LA UNIÓN

SALAVERRY

Plaza
Raymondi

BATALLA DE JUNÍN

COLINA

■ ANTICA
TRATTORIA ▼

▼ CANTA RANA

PARDO

ESPINOZA

● THE POINT

UGARTE

■ BANCO
CONTINENTAL

MALECÓN

CIRCUITO — DE — PLAYAS

Circuito de la Playa

DOMEYER

SUCRE

▼ LA MESITAS

■ LA NOCHE

JUAN F. PASOS

ABREGU

ZEPITA

AYACUCHO

■ INTERBANK

BOULEVARD

■ BOTICA FASA

▼ SONGORO
COSONGO

Plaza de
Barranco

GRAU

CASTILLA

MELGAR

■ TOURIST
INFORMATION

● D'OSMA
BED & BREAKFAST

28 DE JULIO

PEDRO OSMA

2 DE MAYO

BOLOGNESI

BRESCIANA

SOLARI

TARAPACA

LIBERTAD

| 0 | | 100 yds |
| 0 | | 100 m |

LAVALLE

To Chorrillos ↓

© AVALON TRAVEL

and built an enclosure for holy women alongside Pachacámac's stepped pyramid.

The first Spaniard to arrive in the area was **Hernando Pizarro,** who rode with a group of soldiers from Cajamarca in 1533 to investigate reports of gold at Pachacámac. They found nothing, but his brother, Francisco, returned two years later to move the capital here from Cusco. **Francisco Pizarro** was drawn to the spot because of its fertile plains and the natural port of Callao. (Both Pizarros had come here in January, in the middle of Lima's brief summer, and must have thought it was a sunny place.)

Pizarro laid the city out in typical checkerboard pattern, with the main square butting up against the **Río Rímac** ("talking river" in Quechua), a natural defensive line. He christened Lima **Ciudad de Los Reyes** (City of the Kings), and a decade later it was designated the capital of the Spanish viceroyalty in South America and eventually seat of the continent's archbishop. **Universidad San Marcos,** America's first university, was founded here in 1511, and the city was completely walled by the 17th century.

Most of the Roman Catholic orders established themselves in Lima and built more than a dozen baroque churches and convents. Even the Spanish Inquisition for South America was based here (its headquarters is now an interesting museum). By royal decree, all the commerce of the entire viceroyalty—essentially the entire west side of South America—had to pass through Lima, fueling a construction boom of elegant homes and promenades, such as the Paseo de Aguas on the far side of the Río Rímac (these days a downtrodden neighborhood).

The city was quickly rebuilt after a devastating 1746 earthquake that destroyed 80 percent of its structures and slammed the port of **Callao** with a 12-meter tsunami. Lima's prominence began to fade after the independence wars of the 1820s, when it lost its monopoly over South American commerce.

Even in the early days of Lima, neighborhoods of black, indigenous, and mixed-race workers began to crop up around the city, and the expansion continued after the city's walls were torn down by **President José Balta** (in office 1868-1872). During the **War of the Pacific** (1879-1883), Lima was sacked by an invading Chilean army, which carted off church gold and most of the national library's books to Santiago de Chile.

There had always been a main avenue leading through the countryside to the port of Callao, but as the city expanded, other principal avenues were built outside the center, and the city's first electric train was inaugurated in 1906. For four centuries Lima had been a small city, and even in 1919 had only 173,000 inhabitants. Over the rest of the 20th century, Lima's population would swell to its current size of nine million.

As in other South American capitals, Lima's population exploded as the country transitioned from a rural economy to one based on large industry. Impoverished campesinos migrated here from the countryside and built ramshackle slums, called *pueblos jóvenes*. Since the mid-1990s, these slums have turned into full-fledged neighborhoods, some of which are now working class, with Internet access and big grocery stores and malls. Others are still very poor, lacking running water and sewer services.

Lima's poverty became intense during the 1980s and 1990s, when a series of countryside massacres committed by both the **Shining Path** and the Peruvian army sparked a crushing migration to Lima. The new immigrants worked at whatever they could find, and many ended up becoming street vendors (*ambulantes*), causing the center's main streets to become completely congested. After being elected in 1990, **President Alberto Fujimori** put an end—albeit through corrupt techniques and human rights violations that landed him in prison with a 25-year sentence—to the rampant inflation, rolling blackouts, and car bombings that were terrorizing Lima residents. In 1992, he captured **Abimael Guzmán,** the former philosophy professor who founded and led the Shining

Path. **Movimiento Revolucionario Túpac Amaru (MRTA),** the country's other main guerilla group, staged a final stand in Lima in 1996 by taking 490 hostages during a gala at the Japanese ambassador's residence. The standoff ended four months later after a Peruvian special forces team freed the hostages, killing the 14 guerillas in the process (only one hostage died—of a heart attack, which occurred after being shot).

Even before the terrorism years, much of the commerce and most of the wealthy families had abandoned the center of Lima and established the upscale neighborhoods and corporate centers of Monterrico, Miraflores, and San Isidro, where nearly all of the city's best hotels and restaurants are now located.

Though still a bit grimy and unsafe to walk around in at night, the center of Lima is making a comeback. Street vendors were banned in the mid-1990s, and now the Plaza de Armas has been renovated with new riverside promenades and a spate of nice restaurants. Businesses like *Caretas,* the country's leading newsmagazine, have moved back to the center. Compared to the mid-1990s, the center of Lima feels pleasant and safe.

PLANNING YOUR TIME

Depending on your interests, Lima can be seen in a day's dash or over several days, which allows you to take in most of the museums, churches, and surrounding sights. Travelers tend to enjoy Lima more at the end of a trip than at the beginning. After visiting Cusco, travelers are more prepared to deal with the logistics of getting around this huge city. They have also seen enough of the country to make better sense of the vast, and often poorly explained, collections in Peru's museums. Things start making sense.

If you are short on time, one headache-free option is to fly from Cusco to Lima early in the morning and spend the day touring Lima on an organized tour (if you are planning on seeing Lima on your own, plan on one day for just acclimatizing). Various good day tours include lunch at one of the better restaurants in the city. You can head to the airport for your flight home in the evening, or early the following morning.

Sights

Lima is jam-packed with sights, but most interesting are either the colonial churches, convents, and homes in Lima's center or the restaurants and shops of Miraflores, Lima's upscale coastal neighborhood.

There are so many sights in downtown Lima that you would need a few days to see them all. Lima's center continues to be blighted by traffic problems, but the local government is doing its best to improve this. A long pedestrian walkway on Unión extending from Plaza San Martín all the way to Plaza de Armas will soon be joined by a horizontal walkway bisecting it, running from Barrio Chino in the east along Capon, Ucayali, and Ica to Tacna in the west. Add to these pedestrian zones the huge project to build a tunnel under the Río Rimac, and hopefully central Lima will soon be a far more pleasant place for tourists to stroll.

CENTRAL LIMA AND PUEBLO LIBRE
★ Catedral de Lima

Start on the **Plaza de Armas** (or **Plaza Mayor**), one of Latin America's most beautiful squares, graced with a bronze fountain from 1650 and flanked on the north side by the government palace and the east side by the **Catedral de Lima** (9am-5pm Mon.-Fri., 10am-1pm Sat., US$3.50 cathedral only, US$12 cathedral and Palacio Arzobispal de Lima combined), built in the late 16th century. It contains the carved wooden sepulchre of Francisco Pizarro, who was murdered in 1541 by a mob of Almagristas, a rival political faction. But the highlights of the cathedral are the choir stalls, carved in the early 17th century by Pedro Noguera, and the museum. Paintings here include a 1724 work by Alonso de la Cueva that includes the faces of the 13 Inca rulers alongside a lineup of Spanish kings from Carlos V to Felipe V.

Next door to the *catedral* on the northeastern corner of the square is the magnificent **Palacio Arzobispal de Lima** (9am-5pm Mon.-Fri., 10am-1pm Sat., 1pm-5pm Sun. US$8 palace only, US$12 cathedral and palace combined), the archbishop's palace, now open to the public. The original palace was constructed in the 16th century but demolished three hundred years later. The palace as it stands today was opened in 1924 and is a prime example of neocolonial architecture. It contains an impressive museum of religious art and rooms decorated with colonial ornaments and furniture.

Also on the main square is the **Palacio del Gobierno,** the president's palace, which forms the other side of the Plaza Mayor and was built by the Spanish on top of the home of Taulichusco, the ruler of the Rímac Valley at that time. It was at this spot that liberator José de San Martín proclaimed the symbolic independence of Peru on July 28, 1821. There is an interesting changing of the guard at noon, accompanied by traditional music, and a changing of the flag at 5:45pm Monday-Saturday.

★ Casa de Aliaga

A half block from the Plaza Mayor down Unión is **Casa de Aliaga** (Unión 224, tel. 01/427-7736, 9:30am-5pm daily, by reservation, US$10), which was built in 1535 and is the oldest home on the continent still family owned after 17 generations. It is one of the best-preserved colonial homes in Peru, with a series of salons representing decor from the 16th, 17th, and 18th centuries. The land for the home was first deeded to Jerónimo de Aliaga, one of the 13 men who remained with Francisco Pizarro during his grueling

exploration of Peru's coast in 1527. You can visit on your own, but in-house guides speak Spanish only. For English-speaking tours, try **Lima Tours** (tel. 01/619-6900).

Santo Domingo and Lima Riverfront

Near the Plaza Mayor is **Santo Domingo,** which is on the corner of Camaná and Conde de Superunda. This church was built in 1537 by the Dominicans and was remodeled in neoclassical style in the 19th century. At the end of the right nave is the Retablo de las Reliquias (Altar of the Relics), with the skulls of the three Peruvian Dominicans to have reached sainthood. Next door is the attached convent (8:30am-5:30pm daily, US$2.50), with carved balconies around a patio, fountains covered with Seville tiles, and a library with colossal 17th-century choir books.

To the west of the presidential palace is the new **Casa de la Gastronomía** (176 Conde de Superunda, tel. 01/426-7264, US$1), which celebrates Peru's varied and delicious cuisine.

Alameda Chabuca Grande on the Malecón Rímac is a new riverfront public space, within a block of the Plaza Mayor. This used to be the sprawling Polvos Azules market, which was shut down by the government in 2000 and moved to its present location along the Vía Expresa. The space is now used by musicians and artists. In the afternoon and early evening, dozens of vendors sell traditional Limeño treats, such as creamed rice and *mazamorra morada,* a delicious warm purple pudding. It is generally safe to walk here around until 10pm, when the security guards go home.

Behind the Palacio del Gobierno is the old train station, **Desamparados.** Today trains only run to Huancayo twice monthly, and the building has been regenerated into a museum, **Casa de la Literatura** (Ancash 207, tel. 01/426-2573, www.casadelaliteratura. gob.pe, 10:30am-7pm Tues.-Sun., free), which charts the history of Peruvian literature in a series of well-organized rooms. There is also a small library.

★ Museo de Sitio Bodega y Quadra

A couple doors down from the Casa de la Literatura is the small but recommended **Museo de Sitio Bodega y Quadra** (Ancash 213, tel. 01/738-2163 or 01/428-1644, 9am-5pm Tues.-Sun., US$3), a relatively new museum that shows the restored home of the Bodega y Quadra family, featuring contrasting architecture from the colonial and republican eras and illustrating what life was like during these periods. The city spent years excavating and restoring the lower portion of the house, which highlights colonial-era floors and structures. The 18th-century house was the home of Juan Francisco de la Bodega y Quadra, a Spanish naval officer who explored Canada's Pacific coast.

★ San Francisco

Farther along to the east of Museo de Sitio Bodega y Quadra, **Museo San Francisco** (Ancash and Lampa, 9:30am-5:30pm daily, US$2.50, US$1.50 students) is a 16th-century convent featuring a patio lined with centuries-old *azulejos* (Seville tiles) and roofed with *machimbrado,* perfectly fitted puzzle pieces of Nicaraguan mahogany. There are frescoes from the life of Saint Francis of Assisi, a 1656 painting of the Last Supper with the disciples eating guinea pig and drinking from gold Inca cups *(qeros),* and a series of paintings from Peter Paul Rubens's workshop depicting the passion of Christ. But the highlight is the catacombs, or public cemetery, where slaves, servants, and others without money were buried until 1821 (rich citizens were usually buried in their home chapels). The underground labyrinth is a series of wells, some 20 meters deep, where bodies were stacked and covered with lime to reduce odor and disease. After the flesh decomposed, the bones were stacked elsewhere.

The **Iglesia de San Francisco** (free) next to the convent is also highly impressive. It has yellow baroque twin towers and gilded side altars.

Museo de la Inquisición

Walking east of the Iglesia de San Francisco, you'll reach the impressive **Plaza Bolívar,** graced with a bronze statue in honor of liberator Simón Bolívar and flanked by Peru's

Iglesia de San Francisco is just one of Lima's impressive churches.

grand congress building. On the far side of the plaza is the interesting **Museo de la Inquisición** (Plaza Bolívar, tel. 01/311-7777, www.congreso.gob.pe/museo.htm, 9am-5pm daily, free), which served as the headquarters of the Spanish Inquisition from 1570 until it was abolished in 1820. The museum explains the harsh and bizarre punishments that the church doled out for crimes ranging from heresy and blasphemy to seduction and reading banned books.

★ Museo Metropolitano de Lima

Located in the Parque de la Exposición, which was built in the 19th century and is still thriving today, is the new **Museo Metropolitano de Lima** (tel. 01/433-7122, 9:30am-5pm Tues.-Sun., US$2), which provides a virtual tour of Lima's history, complete with 3-D movies and an earthquake simulator. After seeing several museums and churches, this is a good way to bring all that history together. If you don't speak Spanish, it is best to bring a translator.

★ Circuito Mágico del Agua

The **Circuito Mágico del Agua** (Petit Thouars Esquina with Jr. Madre de Dios, tel. 01/330-3052, www.parquedelareserva.com.pe, 3pm-10:30pm Wed.-Sun., US$2, free under age 5) is popular among locals. It has 13 interactive fountains and a light and laser show. The place is said to be the biggest fountain complex in the world. The fountains are within the 8-hectare **Parque de la Reserva,** which was built in 1929 to honor reservists that defended Lima from Chilean armies during the 19th century War of the Pacific. The park was recently restored after years of neglect and is now in pretty good shape. Among its gardens you'll find Italian-inspired archways and a statue to honor independence fighter Antonio José de Sucre. The yellow house in the middle of the park was designed by José Sabogal, the father of Peru's indigenist art movement.

★ Museo Larco

The charming neighborhood of **Pueblo Libre** is just south of central Lima and has a more relaxed, small-town vibe. Its best-known sight is the **Museo Larco** (Bolívar 1515, tel. 01/461-1312, www.museolarco.org, 9am-10pm daily, US$11), which rivals the Museo de Oro in terms of gold pieces and has far more ceramics and textiles. Founded in 1926 in an 18th-century mansion built atop a pre-Hispanic ruin, this museum has more than 40,000 ceramics and 5,000 pieces of gold and textiles. There are huge Mochica earrings and funerary masks, a Paracas textile with a world-record 398 threads per inch, and a jewelry vault filled with gold and silver objects. A back storage room holds thousands of pre-Hispanic ceramic vessels, including a Moche erotic collection that will cause even the most liberated to blush. There is an excellent on-site restaurant, and it is easy to reach by bus from Miraflores. Catch a bus at Arequipa Avenue that says "Todo Bolívar" and get off at the 15th block.

★ Museo Nacional de Arqueología, Antropología e Historia del Perú (MNAAHP)

A 15-minute walk away from Museo Larco is Pueblo Libre's laid-back Plaza Bolívar and the **Museo Nacional de Arqueología, Antropología e Historia del Perú (MNAAHP)** (Plaza Bolívar s/n, Pueblo Libre, tel. 01/463-5070, http://mnaahp.cultura. pe, 9:30am-5pm Tues.-Sat., US$5 includes tour). Although smaller than the Museo de la Nación, this museum presents a clearer, certainly more condensed, view of Peruvian history, and linked with the Museo Larco, it makes for a complete day in central Lima. Exhibits include Moche ceramics, Paracas tapestries, Chimú gold, and scale models for understanding the hard-to-see Chavín and Huari sites.

The museum's most important piece is the Estela Raimondi, a giant stone obelisk that once graced one of Peru's first ceremonial centers, Chavín de Huantár (1300-200 BC), near present-day Huaraz. It is carved with snakes, pumas, and the first appearance of the Dios de los Báculos (Staff-Bearing God), which would reappear, in different incarnations, throughout Peru's ancient history. The tour includes a walk through the adjacent colonial home where independence leaders José de San Martín and Simón Bolívar stayed.

Around the corner is the 16th-century **Iglesia Magdalena** (San Martín and Vivanco), which has attractive carved altars and a gold painting of Señor de los Tremblores (Lord of the Earthquakes). An excellent restaurant, café, and pisco-tasting bodega, all steeped in tradition, are down the street.

SAN ISIDRO AND MIRAFLORES

Lima's coast offers great views of the Pacific, and the best place to visit the parks on top of the cliffs overlooking the blue ocean is along **Miraflores's** *malecón.* A recommended walk is to start at the Parque Maria Reiche, near the border with San Isidro to the north of Miraflores. From there, follow the path south back into Miraflores. There are beautiful parks that offer excellent views, a small restaurant that is good for a drink, and a lighthouse. There are also playgrounds for children. If you go far enough, you'll eventually hit the Larcomar shopping center before reaching Barranco.

Pyramids

What appears to be a clay hill plunked down in the middle of Miraflores is actually a huge adobe pyramid from the Lima culture, which built a dozen major structures in and around what is now Lima between AD 200 and 700. **Huaca Pucllana** (General Bolognesi 800, Miraflores, tel. 01/617-7148, www.huacapucllanamiraflores.pe, 9am-5pm Wed.-Mon., US$4) has a small but excellent museum that includes ceramics, textiles, reconstructed tombs, and artifacts from this culture that depended almost entirely on the sea for survival. A recently discovered pot shows a man carrying a shark on his back—proof that this culture somehow hunted 450-kilogram sharks. No free wandering is allowed, but guides lead tours every 30 minutes around the ceremonial plazas and a few inner rooms. There is an upscale and delicious restaurant on-site that serves Peruvian cuisine with a modern twist.

A similar, though completely restored, stepped pyramid in San Isidro is **Huaca Huallamarca** (Nicólas de Piérola 201, tel. 01/222-4124, 9am-5pm Tues.-Sun., US$3.50), which offers a chance to understand what

Museo Nacional Arqueología, Antropología e Historia del Perú in Pueblo Libre

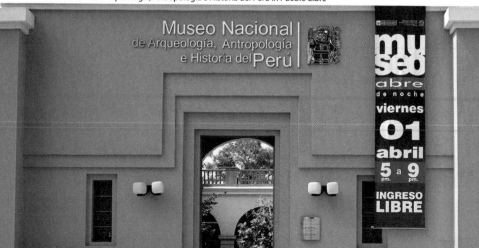

these temples once looked like. From the top, there is an interesting view over Lima's most upscale district.

★ ChocoMuseo

Chocolate lovers rejoice. The **ChocoMuseo** (Berlin 375, tel. 01/445-9708, www.choco-museo.com, 11am-7pm daily), in Miraflores only three blocks from Parque Kennedy, has hands-on workshops on how chocolate is made. Participants in the Beans to Bar class will get some theory about the cacao tree and harvesting before getting their hands dirty by roasting cacao beans and molding their own chocolate bars. There is also a workshop where you can make truffles. A two-hour workshop costs US$27.50 for adults and US$19.50 for children.

★ Bosque El Olivar

Tucked away in a residential area of San Isidro is **Bosque El Olivar,** one of the city's nicest green spaces with a history dating back more than 450 years. The 23-hectare park is home to some 1,500 olive trees that can be traced to saplings first brought to Lima by Spaniards in 1560. This is a good spot to go to take a break from the city's modern rush. San Isidro's **municipal library** (República 420, tel. 01/513-9000) is located in the park.

EASTERN LIMA
Museo de Oro

Monterrico, an upscale suburb in eastern Lima that is often sunny when the rest of the city is covered in fog, is known for its **Museo de Oro** (Molina 1110, Monterrico, tel. 01/345-1271, www.museoroperu.com.pe, 10:30am-6pm daily, US$12). This fabulous collection of gold pieces was one of Lima's must-see attractions until 2001, when a scandal broke alleging that many of the prize pieces were fakes. Newspapers pointed the finger at the sons of museum founder Miguel Mujica Gallo, whom the newspapers accused of selling the originals and replacing them with imitations. The family countered, saying that false pieces were bought by mistake and that Mujica Gallo

died of sadness in the process. Only true gold pieces are on display now at the museum, but the facility continues to suffer from a credibility problem. Gold pieces include spectacular funerary masks, ceremonial knives (*tumis*), a huge set of golden arms, exquisite figurines, and crowns studded with turquoise. It is a huge potpourri of gold, with little explanation in English, bought over decades from tomb raiders who work over Moche, Nasca, Sicán, and Chimú sites. Other objects of interest include a Nasca poncho made of parrot feathers and a Moche skull that was fitted, postmortem, with purple quartz teeth. Almost as impressive is the **Arms Museum** upstairs, which is a terrifying assemblage of thousands of weapons, ranging from samurai swords and harquebuses to Hitler paraphernalia.

Museo de la Nación

Peru's largest museum, and cheaper to see than the private collections, is **Museo de la Nación** (Javier Prado Este 2465, tel. 01/476-9873, 9am-6pm Tues.-Sun., US$4, US$3 students), in the east Lima suburb of San Borja. Though criticized for its rambling organization, this museum, which is located in the same building as the Ministry of Culture, has a great chronological layout, making it perhaps Lima's most understandable and educational museum. There are three levels of exhibits showcasing Peru's entire archaeological history, from Chavín stone carvings and Paracas weavings all the way to the Inca. There are good models of Machu Picchu, the Nasca Lines, and the Lords of Sipán tomb excavated near Chiclayo in 1987, one of the great finds of Latin American archaeology. On the sixth floor is a chilling photo exhibit called *Yuyanapaq,* which means "to remember" in Quechua. The exhibit documents Peru's internal conflict between Shining Path rebels and state security forces that claimed almost 70,000 lives in the 1980s and 1990s. A permanent home for the exhibit will be the **Lugar de la Memoria** museum, which is currently under construction on a lot donated by Miraflores and overlooking the Pacific.

Tour Agencies and Guides

A favorite travel agency in Lima is **Fertur Peru** (www.fertur-travel.com), run by the enterprising Siduith Ferrer, with offices in central Lima at the Plaza Mayor (Junín 211, tel. 01/427-2626, 9am-7pm Mon.-Fri., 9am-4pm Sat.) and Miraflores (Schell 485, tel. 01/242-1900, 9am-7pm Mon.-Fri., 9am-4pm Sat.). Fertur can buy a variety of bus and plane tickets for you and set up tours around Lima and trips to all of Peru's other attractions, including Cusco, Machu Picchu, and the Nasca Lines.

Peru's most reputable agency, in business for decades, is **Lima Tours** (Jirón de la Unión 1040, tel. 01/619-6900, www.limatours. com.pe), with offices in central Lima. Its city tours provide access to some of Lima's colonial mansions, including the pristine 17th-century mansion Casa de Aliaga. Because the company works with large international groups, it is best to make contact before arriving in Lima.

Run by an American-Peruvian couple, **Magical Cuzco Tours** (tel. 866/411-4622, www.magicalcuzcotours.com) offers several expeditions in Lima, including a half-day culinary tour and full-day visit to the nearby Caral and Pachacámac ruins. It can also help organize specialty tours to other parts of Peru.

Condor Travel (Armando Blondet 249, San Isidro, tel. 01/615-3000, www.condor-travel.com) offers a day tour of colonial and contemporary Lima, as well as visits to other attractions like Machu Picchu, Cusco, the Sacred Valley, and the Nasca Lines. **InkaNatura** (Manuel Bañón 461, San Isidro, tel. 01/203-5000, www.inkanatura.com) also offers tours to Machu Picchu, Cusco, and the Sacred Valley.

A good agency for booking flights and other logistics is **Nuevo Mundo** (28 de Julio 1120, tel. 01/626-9393), with its office in Miraflores. Another reputable agency in Miraflores is **Wagonlit Travel** (Ricardo Palma 355, tel. 01/610-1600, www.cwtvaca-ciones.com.pe). An option for day tours in Lima is **Peru Smile** (28 de Julio 399 Office 203, Miraflores, tel. 01/243-2152, perusmile@ yahoo.com), which is run by Jorge Fernández and has tours and prices similar to Lima Vision but without the large groups.

Many of the recommended agencies sell tours run by **Lima Vision** (Chiclayo 444, Miraflores, tel. 01/447-7710, www.limavision. com, 24 hours daily), the city's standard pool service, which offers three- to four-hour daily tours of Lima's center (US$30), Museo Larco (US$40), Pachacámac (US$40), and Museo de Oro (US$50). Whether you buy from Lima Vision or from an agency, the cost is the same.

Entertainment and Events

In the city center is one of the largest and best *peñas* (live *criollo* music clubs) in Lima, **Brisas del Titicaca** (Heroes de Talapaca and Wakulski 168, tel. 01/715-6960, www.brisas-deltiticaca.com, Tues.-Sat., 10pm-4am, US$18 cover). Foreigners can enjoy exhibitions of dance and music during the week, and it's busiest on weekends when locals come to party.

The nightlife in Miraflores is more spread out and harder to find than in the neighboring district of Barranco. Many travelers end up at **Calle de las Pizzas** (Street of the Pizzas), a row of seedy pizza-and-sangria joints right in front of Parque Kennedy. But there are many other better options. For a traditional English atmosphere with draft beer and fish-and-chips, head to **The Old Pub** (Calle de las Pizzas, tel. 01/242-8155, www.oldpub.com.pe, noon-late daily, US$8-14). If you want a more classic evening head across Parque Kennedy to Jazz Zone (La Paz 656, tel. 01/241-8139, http://jazzzoneperu.com, 10pm-2am Mon.-Sat., free Mon.-Wed., US$7 Thurs., US$11 Fri.-Sat.).

In Barranco, La Noche (Bolognesi 307, tel. 01/477-4154, www.lanoche.com.pe, 7pm-3am daily, US$6-9) is the best live music bar, with tables set on different levels to look down on a range of (mostly jazz) performances. Another good option is a *peña* that makes for a rowdy night out among locals; a good choice is La Candelaría (Bolognesi 292, tel. 01/247-2941, www.lacandelariaperu.com, 9:30pm-2am Fri.-Sat., US$10).

Food

One of the highlights of Lima is the wonderful food. If you have time, sample some local specialties at one of the restaurants listed here.

CENTRAL LIMA AND PUEBLO LIBRE

In the historic center, the pedestrian zone on Pasaje Santa Rosa is the most pleasant area to dine. Pardo's (Pasaje Santa Rosa 153, tel. 01/427-2301, www.pardoschicken.com.pe, noon-11pm daily, US$10-12) still serves the best spit-roasted chicken, with affordable lunch menus and open-air tables right off the Plaza Mayor. In the same pedestrian walkway, Gaston Acurio's ★ T'anta (Pasaje Nicolas de Rivera el Viejo 142, tel. 01/428-3115, 9am-10pm Mon.-Sat., 9am-6pm Sun., www.tanta-peru.com, US$10-15) serves up refined plates of Peruvian favorites *lomo saltado* and *recoto relleno*. Another option is El Cordano (Ancash 202, tel. 01/427-0181, 8am-8pm daily, www.restaurantecordano.com, US$6-12), a century-old establishment that was a favored haunt of writers and intellectuals. Try specialties such as fish in asparagus or beef stew. Right on Plaza de Armas, Don Pedro (Unión and Callao, tel. 01/713-9292, 8am-11pm Mon.-Fri., 8am-6pm Sun., US$8-14) is part of the age-old Union Club. It has a very good-value set menu and an elegant atmosphere. It specializes in a fusion of Peruvian and international styles with a wide of range of steak, chicken, and fish.

Near Iglesia de San Francisco is Dionisio (Ancash 454, tel. 01/427-5681, US$6-12). With the cozy atmosphere of a cellar, it is first and foremost a wine bar, but it also serves a wide range of traditional Peruvian dishes, such as *chuleta, bistec*, and ceviche.

When in central Lima, do not miss the opportunity to sample *chifa* (Chinese-Peruvian cuisine) at one of the largest Chinatowns in South America. There are at least a dozen places spread along Barrio Chino's two main streets, Capón and Paruro. The best known is Wa Lok (Paruro 878, tel. 01/427-2750, 9am-11pm daily, www.walok.com.pe, US$12-24), serving more than 20 types of dim sum, but prices are a little steep. A good, less expensive alternative to Wa Lok is Salon Capon (Paruro 819, tel. 01/426-9286, 9am-11pm Mon.-Sat., 9am-8pm Sun., www.saloncapon.com, US$8-16), serving Peking duck, *langostinos Szechuan* (sautéed shrimps with *ají*), and *chuleta kin tou* (grilled sweet pork).

If staying in Pueblo Libre or visiting one of its museums, there are many good options for lunch. Antigua Taberna Quierolo (San Martin 1090, tel. 01/460-0441, www.antiguatabernaquierolo.com, 10am-10pm daily, US$8) is one of Lima's oldest cafés, open since 1880. At night, it is bustling with locals sipping pisco and wine. Around the corner is El Bolivariano (Pasaje Santa Rosa 291, tel. 01/261-9565, www.elbolivariano.com, 10am-10pm daily, US$12), a time-honored Lima restaurant in an elegant republican-style home. Like Quierolo, it also becomes a popular nightspot with Peruvians. Opening onto the lawns of the Museo Larco is the tasteful ★ Café del Museo (Bolivar 1515, tel. 01/462-4757, US$20). It serves tender lamb, sea bass, and shrimp *causa*.

MIRAFLORES AND SAN ISIDRO

In Miraflores, lunch and dinner options are endless and include everything from quick-stop sandwich spots to world-class restaurants. A Lima classic right on Parque Kennedy is Haiti (Diagonal 160, tel. 01/445-0539, 7am-2am Sun.-Thurs., 7am-3am Fri.-Sat., US$10), where the indoor and sidewalk cafes are overflowing with Peruvians day and night. It is better known for its good coffee and pisco sours than its food. Across the street is La Tiendecita Blanca (Larco 111, tel. 01/445-9797, 7am-midnight daily, US$15-20), an elegant Swiss-style café and deli. Anything you eat here is good. For a quick sandwich on Parque Kennedy, try La Lucha (Benavides 308, tel. 01/241-5953, www.lalucha.com.pe, 6am-1am Sun.-Thurs., 6am-3am Fri.-Sat., US$4). A recommended sandwich is the *chicharron* (fried pork with sweet potato and red onions). Calle de las Pizzas (Street of the Pizzas), a row of pizza-and-sangria joints, is hard to miss on Parque Kennedy. There are plenty of options here for dinner and drinks afterwards, but the quality isn't always the best.

For ceviche and other seafood, there is Pescados Capitales (La Mar 1337, tel. 01/421-8808, 12:30pm-5pm Tues.-Sun., www.pescadoscapitales.com, US$15-20), which serves up plates like ceviche of tuna and *conchas negras* and ceviche of shrimps with curry and mango chutney. A popular and more affordable place is Punto Azul (San Martin 395, tel. 01/445-8078, 11am-4pm Sun.-Wed., 11am-4pm and 7pm-midnight Thurs.-Sat., US$10-12). In addition to ceviche, it serves other dishes from the sea, like *arroz con mariscos* (rice with seafood). A great option down the road is El Pez On (San Martin 537, tel. 01/713-0860, noon-11pm Mon.-Sat., noon-5pm Sun., US$10-12). Try the ceviche *clasico* with a cold Pilsen beer. Segundo Muelle

(Conquistadores 490, San Isidro, tel. 01/717-9998, www.segundomuelle.com, noon-11pm daily, US$10-15) successfully combines pastas with seafood and tasty ceviche.

For something different, there is Amaz (La Paz 1079, tel. 01/221-9393, 12:30pm-11:30pm Mon.-Thurs., 12:30pm-midnight Fri.-Sat., 12:30pm-4:30pm Sun., US$30), where chef Pedro Miguel Schiaffino serves up a variety of flavors and plates inspired by Peru's Amazon rainforest. The menu includes Amazon staples like *tacacho con cecina* (roasted green plantains with dried pork) and smoked *paiche*, the giant jungle fish.

Pampa de Amancaes (Armendariz 546, tel. 01/445-5099, www.pampadeamancaes.com, 12:30pm-4pm and 6pm-11pm daily, US$15) has an excellent menu that offers Peruvian classics like ceviche, the creamy *aji de gallina*, and *lomo saltado*. For buffet of *comida criolla*, try Brujas de Cachiche (Bolognesi 472, tel. 01/447-1133, www.brujasdecachiche.com.pe, noon-midnight Mon.-Sat., noon-4pm Sun., US$25-40). The buffet (Tues.-Sun) includes a tour de force of centuries of indigenous Peruvian cooking.

Sushi has become increasingly popular in Lima in recent years. Good places include Makoto (Malecon de la Reserva 610, tel. 01/444-5030, 12:30pm-1am, Fri.-Sat., US$20), located at Larcomar mall and Edo Sushi (Berlin 601, tel. 01/434-4545, 12:30pm-3:30pm and 7pm-11pm Mon.-Sat., 1pm-4pm Sun., US$15), near the Canadian embassy.

Lima's top restaurants are among the best in the world. Leading the scene is Virgilio Martinez's ★ Central (Santa Isabel 376, tel. 01/242-8515, www.centralrestaurante.com.pe, 1:30pm-3:30pm and 8pm-11:30pm Mon.-Wed., 1:30pm-3:30pm and 8pm-midnight Thurs.-Fri, 8pm-midnight Sat., US$30-40), ranked the fourth-best restaurant in the world by San Pellegrino's closely watched list. Martinez is known for traveling Peru's high Andes and swampy Amazon rainforest in search of rare ingredients. Like many of Peru's top chefs, Martinez got his start and inspiration from Gaston Acurio, who dropped out of law school in Europe to become a chef in the 1990s, transforming Peruvian cuisine. Acurio's flagship restaurant is ★ **Astrid y Gaston Casa Moreyra** (Av. Paz Soldan 290, Casa Hacienda Moreyra, San Isidro, tel. 01/242-5387, www.astridygaston.com, 12:30pm-3pm and 7pm-11pm Mon.-Sat., US$35-40). This adventurous gourmet restaurant is the labor of love of Acurio and his wife, Astrid Gutsche, who met at the Cordon Bleu in Paris. For a starter, try the Peking guinea pig with an *aguaymanto* sour, made with pisco and the tangy juice of *aguaymanto* fruit.

Another top contender is ★ **Rafael** (San Martin 300, tel. 01/242-4149, www.rafaelosterling.com, 1pm-3:30pm and 8pm-midnight Mon.-Fri., 8pm-midnight Sat., US$30), the creation of Rafael Osterling, located in a turn-of-the-20th-century house. Rafael cites his mother's home-cooked meals and his globe-trotting experiences for his fusion of Peruvian and international dishes. Try the *arroz con pato* (rice with duck slowly cooked in dark beer and onion relish) or the *aji de camarones* (a river shrimp stew). Osterling's other top-rated restaurant is ★ **El Mercado** (Hipolito Unanue 203, San Isidro, tel. 01/221-1322, noon-5pm Tues.-Sun., US$30), a great place for ceviche and other seafood.

The elegant **Huaca Pucllana** (General Borgono block 8, tel. 01/445-4042, www.resthuacapucllana.com, noon-4pm and 7pm-midnight daily, US$25) has a magical feel when the pre-Inca ruins of the same name, only six meters away, are lit up at night. Guests sit at linen-covered tables on an open-air patio next to the ruins and enjoy dishes like grilled portobello mushroom salad with goat cheese, rabbit stewed in red wine, and grilled lamb chops.

BARRANCO

Slow-paced, bohemian Barranco has a number of romantic eateries and cafes, and on the weekend, outdoor food stalls fill a walkway near the central plaza leading to the waterfront. At the top of the steps, **Songoro Cosongo** (Ayacucho 281, tel. 01/247-4730, www.songorocosongo.com, 12:30pm-close daily, US$10-12) has been serving up Peruvian specialties for three generations. Dishes include *ají de gallina, anticuchos, sudado de pescado,* and *chicharron de pescado.*

For a steak-and-red wine fix, **Parrillados El Hornero** (Malecon Grau 983, tel. 01/251-8109, noon-midnight Mon.-Sat., US$12-15) in Chorrillos is a must. The second-floor tables have impressive ocean views, and the grilled provolone and Argentine baby beef will do for your palate what it won't do for your cholesterol.

With bow tie-clad waiters and an old piano, **Las Mesitas** (Grau 341, tel. 01/477-4199, noon-11pm daily, US$5-7) has an old-time feel. For those on a budget, this is a great place to sample Peruvian food, including tamales and humitas. The best pizzas are at **Antica Trattoria** (San Martin 201, tel. 01/247-3443, noon-midnight daily, US$10-15), a charming Italian eatery with stucco walls, exposed beams, and rustic furniture.

Accommodations

If you want or need to stay the night in Lima, you have two options: Either pay for the new four-star hotel inside the airport, or take a 30-40-minute cab ride (depending on the time of the day) into Miraflores, San Isidro, Barranco, or central Lima. There are a few midrange options near the airport, but the area is unappealing and unsafe.

Inside the airport is the **Costa del Sol-Ramada** (Av. Elmer Faucett s/n, Aeropuerto Internacional Jorge Chávez, tel. 01/711-2000, www.costadelsolperu.com, US$275 s/d with buffet breakfast included), which has a good restaurant, a sushi bar, and plenty of facilities. The hotel is in the airport compound, right across the taxi lanes from baggage claim.

The best budget option in downtown Lima is **Hostal España** (Azángaro 105, tel. 01/428-5546, www.hotelespanaperu.com, US$10 dorm, US$18-21 s, US$22-25 d). In terms of location, character, and price, this backpacker classic is unbeatable—a labyrinth of tight halls and patios, decorated with hanging ivy, marble busts, and reproductions of colonial paintings. The rooms are weathered but that's part of the charm. A pair of parrots and a peacock patrol the rooftop terrace, where breakfast is served. Despite its location, the hostel manages to disconnect itself from the hustle and be a peaceful escape. There is also a neighboring Internet café.

Right on Plaza San Martín are two of the best-value midrange hotels in the center. **Hotel El Plaza** (Av. Nicolas de Pierola, tel. 01/424-5860, US$38 s, US$43 d) has well-appointed rooms with cable TV, fans, private bath, and breakfast included. **Hostal San Martin** (Av. Nicolas de Pierola, tel. 01/431-2729, www.hostalsanmartin.pe, US$36 s, US$45 d) nearby offers much the same deal. Be aware that, at such good prices, both fill up fast.

In Miraflores there are plenty of cheap backpacker options offering inexpensive dorms and a few private rooms. These include: **Explorer's House** (Alfredo León 158, tel. 01/241-5002, US$8 dorm, US$14 s, US$24 d with breakfast), **Casa del Mochilero** (Cesareo Chacaltana 130A, 2nd Fl., tel. 01/444-9089, juan_kalua@hotmail.com, US$6 pp dorm with shared bath, US$16 d), **Hitchhikers** (Bolognesi 400, tel. 01/242-3008, www.hhikersperu.com, US$10 dorm, US$25-35 s/d with breakfast), and **Flying Dog Hostels** (www.flyingdogperu.com, US$12 dorm, US$30-40 d with breakfast), which have three Lima locations (Diez Canseco 117, tel. 01/445-0940; Lima 457, tel. 01/444-5753; Martir Olaya 280, tel. 01/447-0673).

A great midrange option in Miraflores is **Hostal Buena Vista** (tel. 01/447-3178, Schell and Grimaldo de Solar, www.hostal-buenavista.com, US$45 s US$55 d), a beautiful house with elegantly furnished rooms set in a small garden. Or try the charming **Hostal El Patio** (Diez Canseco 341, tel. 01/444-2107, www.hostalelpatio.net, US$40 s, US$50 d with breakfast), a memorable colonial home overflowing with plants and flowers and cheerfully painted walls.

A very good upscale hotel is the charming **Hotel Antigua Miraflores** (Grau 350, tel. 01/241-6166, www.peru-hotels-inns.com, US$83 s, US$99 d with breakfast). This turn-of-the-20th-century mansion has all the comforts of a fine hotel and the warmth of a bed-and-breakfast. The rooms are large, cozy, and handsomely decorated with hand-carved furniture, local art, and warm colors. Plus, the remodeled bathrooms have big tubs.

In Barranco, a good backpacker option is **The Point** (Malecón Junín 300, tel. 01/247-7997, www.thepointhostels.com, US$10-12 dorm, US$28 s/d with breakfast). For a more comfortable atmosphere, try **D'Osma Bed & Breakfast** (Pedro de Osma 240, tel. 01/251-4178, www.deosma.com, US$29-46 s, US$36-50 d with breakfast), which has upgraded its services and is a great option if you are looking for a tranquil, family-oriented environment. It has only five rooms, which adds to the intimate vibe, but be sure to book ahead.

Information and Services

Free maps and tourist information are available at **Iperú** (Aeropuerto Internacional Jorge Chávez, main hall, tel. 01/574-8000, www.peru.info, 24 hours daily). There are other branches in San Isidro (Jorge Basadre 610, tel. 01/421-1627, 9am-6pm Mon.-Fri.) and Miraflores (Larcomar, tel. 01/234-0340, 11am-9pm daily).

The best source of travel information in Peru, along with maps, advice, trip reports, restaurant and hotel discounts, and friendly people, is the Miraflores-based

tourist information at the Kennedy Park in the district of Miraflores

South American Explorers Club (Enrique Palacios 956, Miraflores, tel. 01/445-3306, www.saexplorers.org, 9:30am-5pm Mon.-Fri., 9:30am-1pm Sat.).

Through **Iperú**'s 24-hour stand (tel. 01/574-8000) in the main hall of the airport, you can report tourist-related crimes. The tourist police have an office in Miraflores (General Vidal 230, tel. 01/445-7943). The central emergency phone number is 105.

Lima's **Migraciones** (immigrations office) is near the center (España 734, Breña, tel. 01/330-4111, 8am-1pm Mon.-Fri.).

Clínica Anglo-Americana (Alfredo Salazar, block 3 s/n, tel. 01/616-8900, www.angloamericana.com.pe, 8am-8pm Mon.-Fri., 9am-noon Sat.) is one of the best hospitals in the city. In **Miraflores,** a high-quality option is **Clínica Good Hope** (Malecón Balta 956, tel. 01/610-7300, www.goodhope.org.pe, 9am-midnight).

For money exchange, there are exchange houses inside the Lima airport, but the best place to cash travelers checks is at any Banco de Crédito. Money-change houses *(casas de cambio)* offer slightly better rates for cash than banks and are less busy. There are a few change houses on Larco in Miraflores and on Ocoña in central Lima. ATMs are now ubiquitous across Lima (and most of Peru). Almost all work with Visa, MasterCard, and Cirrus, and Interbank's Global Net and Banco de Crédito even handle American Express. Take care when getting money at night; it's a good idea to have a taxi waiting.

Getting There and Around

AIRPORT

All overseas flights from Europe and North America arrive in Lima at **Aeropuerto Internacional Jorge Chávez** (Jorge Chávez International Airport, tel. 01/517-3500 24-hour flight info, www.lap.com.pe). From here flights continue on to Cusco and other cities. Most planes from overseas arrive in the middle of the night, and flights to Cusco begin from about 5am onwards. Some travelers wait in the airport for connecting flights, while the majority head to Miraflores, San

Isidro, Barranco, or Lima's historic center, where there is a good selection of hotels. On the return, most flights from Cusco arrive here in the midday and leave for the United States at night—so many visitors have at least a half day in Lima.

Jorge Chávez has come a long way and is a pretty modern airport. It has a range of services, including banks, money-exchange booths, ATMs, a post office, stores, a café, two food courts, duty-free shops, a rent-a-cell service, and a recommended Quattro D ice cream shop with playground, among other services. There is even the **Sumaq VIP Lounge.** If you want to store your luggage, go to **Left Luggage** (tel. 01/517-3217, at the side of Domestic Arrivals, US$1.50 per piece of luggage per hour, or US$9 per piece of luggage per 24 hours).

There is a US$9 tax on all domestic flights leaving Lima and a US$31 tax on all departing international flights, but these are usually included in the price of your tickets. On your way home, arrive at the airport 2-3 hours in advance for international flights and 1-2 hours for domestic flights.

TAXIS

Pushy taxi drivers will be waiting for you outside the airport. The best thing to do is contract a taxi through **Taxi Green** (tel. 01/484-4001, www.taxigreen.com.pe), a private company that has stands just outside baggage claim. Have your destination address written down. Taxi prices from the airport to the city are about US$15-US$20. You may be able to get a slightly cheaper taxi if you negotiate with a driver in the airport parking lot, but be sure to know where you are going and ask for credentials. If you are arriving or leaving in a small group, you can save money by advance booking an airport transfer service through your hotel in Lima. Ask at your hotel

when making a reservation. Taxis between the historic center and Miraflores/Barranco cost about US$5, depending on the time of day.

PUBLIC TRANSPORTATION

For public transportation, there are a couple of options, with the best choice being the **Metropolitano,** the rapid bus system. Its buses run straight from Barranco through Miraflores and to the downtown center and back. There are several stations in Miraflores located on the Vía Expresa (15-20 minutes, www.metropolitano.com.pe, 6am-11pm daily, US$1). The Metropolitano, like other buses, can get quite full during rush hour. The other option is to head to Arequipa Avenue and catch a *Todo Arequipa* bus that runs within walking distance of the center (30-50 minutes, US$0.50). Arequipa Avenue is one of the main streets in Lima connecting the center to Miraflores. These buses run the entire avenue.

DAY TOURS

It's quite easy to get around Lima yourself using taxis, and the center is very compact, but if you are rushed and want to see some of the sights (which are spread across the city), it's a good idea to take a tour. **Fertur Peru** (www.fertur-travel.com), run by the enterprising Siduith Ferrer, has offices in central Lima at the Plaza Mayor (Junin 211, tel. 01/427-2626, 9am-7pm Mon.-Fri., 9am-4pm Sat.) and Miraflores (Schell 485, tel. 01/242-1900, 9am-7pm Mon.-Fri., 9am-4pm Sat.). This agency can arrange to pick you up at the airport for a day tour of Lima.

Taxi drivers can also be hired for the hour, day, or for a trip such as to the Nasca Lines. Recommended companies include **Lima Cabs** (www.limacabs.com) and **Taxi Lima Peru** (www.taxilimaperu.com).

Background

The Landscape

Almost any type of terrain imaginable is found in Peru: sandy beaches, mangroves, rolling hills, valleys, snowcapped mountains, glaciers, desert, canyons, cloud forest, and tropical jungle.

The snow-covered **Cordillera de los Andes** is the spine of the country, with rivers tumbling down either side to fertile plains where fruits, vegetables, and grains grow. Once ancient Peruvians developed irrigation technologies, early cultures began converting Peru's valleys into rich farming areas.

Altitude in Peru is key to understanding the lay of the land. It is only 800 kilometers from the coast to the jungle border with Brazil, but the terrain rises steeply from sea level to mountain peaks over 6,000 meters and back down again to the vast areas of **Amazon jungle.**

GEOGRAPHY

Peru's total land area is 1.29 million square kilometers, about three times the size of California. The Andes rise so abruptly from the coast that they can be seen from the ocean on a clear day. They represent the highest mountain chain on earth after the Himalayas, and Peru has 37 peaks over 6,000 meters. **Huascarán,** Peru's highest peak at 6,768 meters, is the world's highest tropical mountain. The Andes are divided into different ranges (called *cordilleras* in Spanish), which often run parallel to each other. North of Cusco is the Cordillera Vilcabamba, with peaks ranging between 4,000 and 6,000 meters, the highest of which is Nevado Salcantay (6,271 meters), less than 65 kilometers northwest of Cusco. Salcantay is the dramatic backdrop to the more mountainous version of the Inca Trail.

Cusco, the Sacred Valley, and Machu Picchu lie to the east of the main Andean mountain chain, and the terrain drops gradually at first between Cusco and the Sacred Valley and more dramatically down to Machu Picchu and the Amazon jungle to the northeast.

Cusco itself stands at a giddy 3,400 meters above sea level, surrounded by steep, sun-tanned hills, and you will certainly feel the altitude if arriving from sea level. If you are arriving from Puno and Lake Titicaca, though, it will seem relatively comfortable, since it is 500 meters lower than the plains to the south.

From Cusco the terrain drops gradually through the Sacred Valley to Pisac (2,900 meters), Urubamba (2,800 meters), and Ollantaytambo (2,600 meters). Here the terrain is noticeably greener; the fertile valley and *páramo* grasslands are the breadbasket of the region, where the majority of its indigenous highlanders live and produce about half the country's food supply. The Inca and other cultures terraced and irrigated this landscape to grow a range of crops, including maize, hardy grains such as *kiwicha* and quinoa, and indigenous tubers such as potatoes, *olluco,* and oca. It was its capacity to produce food that led the Inca to consider the valley sacred.

The valley is carved by the Río Urubamba, which winds through it and then at Ollantaytambo begins its steep drop toward the jungle. On the train down to Aguas Calientes (2,000 meters) the geography changes from Andean grasslands to cloud forest. Thickly forested rocks rising dramatically from the valley dominate the landscape around Machu Picchu and give the

---

Previous: the Peruvian flag in Lima; purple corn and limes, used to make a drink called *chicha morada.*

Ecotourism: Leave No Trace

Travelers to Peru can either help or hurt the country's long-term survival depending on how they plan their trip and how they behave. A good ecotourism reference in the United States is **The International Ecotourism Society** (TIES, tel. 202/347-9203, www.ecotourism.org), which defines ecotourism as "responsible travel to natural areas that conserves the environment and improves the well-being of local people." A handful of Peru's jungle operators belong to this association. Find out whether the lodge or agency you have chosen lives up to these basic principles set forth by TIES:

· Minimize impact.

· Build environmental and cultural awareness and respect.

· Provide positive experiences for both visitors and hosts.

· Provide direct financial benefits for conservation.

· Provide financial benefits and empowerment for local people.

· Raise sensitivity to host countries' political, environmental, and social climate.

· Support international human rights and labor agreements.

A huge concern in Peru's main trekking areas, such as the Inca Trail and the Cordillera Blanca, is environmental degradation as a result of sloppy camping. A wonderful resource for traveling lightly through wilderness is **Leave No Trace** (www.lnt.org), which has pioneered a set of principles that are slowly being adopted by protected areas around the world. More information on these principles can be found on the LNT website:

· Plan ahead and prepare.

· Travel and camp on durable surfaces.

· Dispose of waste properly.

· Leave what you find.

· Minimize campfire impacts.

· Respect wildlife.

· Be considerate of others.

Great pains have been made throughout this guide to recommend only agencies and lodges that have a solid ethic of ecotourism. But the only way to truly evaluate a company's environmental and cultural practices is by experiencing them firsthand. Your feedback is tremendously valuable to us as we consider which businesses to recommend in the future.

Please send your experiences—both positive and negative—to us at feedback@moon.com (www.moon.com).

city a magical setting. The montane cloud forest is one of Peru's most biodiverse habitats. Here live 90 varieties of hummingbirds and more than 2,000 types of orchids and butterflies. Mountain streams cascade down these slopes, eventually merging to form the broad, muddy, and winding rivers of the lowland rainforest.

CLIMATE

Peru's weather is as diverse as its landscapes: from bone-dry desert to rain-soaked jungle, and from sweltering northern beaches to freezing-cold mountain passes.

In the Andean region, average temperatures range 10-20° C but frequently dip below zero at higher altitudes. The rainy season throughout the highlands is strongest January to March, a time that Peruvians refer to as the *época de lluvia* (the rainy season), while May to August are the driest months before rains begin to return in September/October. The climate is colder and drier in Cusco and far warmer and wetter in the Machu Picchu region—hence the closure of the Inca Trail in February.

At high altitude, cloud cover and time of day have a dramatic effect on temperatures. Very cold mornings quickly give way to sweltering midday temperatures before plunging again to near freezing at night. It's essential to be prepared for these changes with plenty of layers of clothing. The sun burns quickly in Peru, and especially in the highlands. Bring a hat, shades, and plenty of sunscreen.

ENVIRONMENTAL ISSUES

Peru suffers from a range of environmental problems that are caused in large part by the abuses of mines, fish meal factories, oil and natural gas wells and pipelines and processing centers, illegal lumber operations, and other extractive industries. These industries have operated with little oversight in Peru for decades as a result of a weak political system that is cash-starved and corrupt. Legislation governing extractive industries, along with regulatory agencies, is improving in Peru but lags well behind other more developed nations.

Peru's zinc, copper, mercury, silver, and gold mines continue to pollute water supplies with mine tailings. Over the last three decades, gas and oil exploration in the Amazon has caused water pollution and deforestation and had a huge impact on native cultures. The most controversial recent project is the Camisea Gas Field, which in 2004 began exporting 13 trillion cubic feet of natural gas from the lower Urubamba basin, one of the most remote and pristine areas of the Peruvian Amazon. The project also includes a pipeline over the biodiverse Cordillera Vilcabamba and a natural-gas processing plant next to Paracas, the country's only marine reserve. The pipeline was built with aging pipework, and there have been several spills in recent years.

Population growth is also exerting tremendous pressure on Peru's resources, especially in the highlands. Overgrazing and deforestation for firewood have caused the area's thin soils to wash away in many areas. The loss of vegetation combines with heavy rains to cause mudslides, known locally as *huaycos*. The Inca were well aware of the dangers caused by landslides and therefore built their settlements on hillsides rather than at the bottoms of valleys, but modern settlements have taken little care.

A series of floods and mudslides in the Cusco area in January 2010 swept away bridges, roads, and the railway that leads to Machu Picchu. The weeks of continuous rains also flooded large areas of fields of the Sacred Valley. As a result, 3,000 tourists were stranded for almost a week in Aguas Calientes, the town near Machu Picchu, and were finally evacuated with helicopters. Worse, thousands of peasants lost their crops and homes.

Plants and Animals

> If in case of a planet catastrophe we would have the choice to choose from one country to save and rebuild the planet from, undoubtedly I would choose Peru.
>
> English scientist David Bellamy

Peru is located in the heart of the richest and most diverse region in the world. Eleven ecoregions with a unique combination of climate and geography contain a sixth of all plant life in only 1 percent of the planet's land area. The country has 84 of the 114 Holdridge life zones. Few countries can rival Peru's biodiversity, which holds world records for highest diversity of birds (more than 1,800 species), butterflies (more than 3,500), and orchids (3,500). There are at least 6,300 species of endemic plants and animals, along with an estimated 30 million insects. Most of this diversity is found in the cloud forests and Amazon jungle; the Andes have relatively low biodiversity but a high rate of endemic species.

ANDEAN FLORA

The high grasslands region or **puna** is home to a collection of unusual plants with endless adaptations for coping with the harsh climate. Many of them have thick, waxy leaves for surviving high levels of ultraviolet radiation and fine insulating hairs in order to cope with frequent frosts. They grow close to the ground for protection from wind and temperature variations. In Peru's north, wet grasslands known as *páramo* stretch along the northwestern edge of the Andes into Ecuador. The *páramo* has a soggy, springy feeling underfoot and serves as a sponge to absorb and slowly release the tremendous amounts of rain that fall in the area.

Peru's most famous highland plant, the *Puya raimondii*—baptized after Antonio Raimondi, the Italian naturalist who studied it—grows in the puna, from Huaraz all the way south to Bolivia between 3,200 meters and 4,800 meters. It is also known as Queen of the Andes, and the rosette of spiky, waxy leaves grows to three meters in diameter. The *puya* lives for a century and, before it dies, sends a giant spike three stories into the air that eventually erupts into 20,000 blooms. Once pollinated, the plant's towering spike allows it to broadcast its seeds widely in the wind. It is the largest of the *Puya* species and the largest bromeliad.

The spiky tussocks of grass known as *íchu* are the most ubiquitous feature of Peru's high plains. Highlanders use this hardy grass to thatch their roofs, start their fires, and feed their llamas and alpacas. Cattle, which were imported from Europe in the 16th century by the Spanish, are unable to digest it. Cows can only eat the *íchu* when it sprouts anew as a tender green shoot. Hence, highlanders burn

Puya raimondii

Sacred Leaf, White Gold

The world's cocaine is produced in the Andes, and the best way to understand the shifts in production is through what experts call the "Balloon Effect": If you cut production in one country or area, it will increase in another, much like how if you squeeze a balloon on one side, it rises on the other side. That is exactly what has happened in Peru for decades.

In the early 2000s, Peru was second in cocaine production after Colombia. As the United States pumped billions of dollars into Colombia to curb production, output declined there and began rising in Peru. In 2012, Peru displaced Colombia as the largest producer of cocaine worldwide, churning out more than 350 tons annually. However, that changed again in 2014 when Peruvian president Ollanta Humala expanded forced eradication of coca crops, leading to declines in production. Colombia, on the other hand, saw its coca output surge 44 percent after years of steady declines, with critics citing a shift in the government's antidrug policy.

Whether Peru is first or second, the broader picture is that the country's cocaine industry continues to undermine institutions and fuel corruption. It isn't going anywhere for the foreseeable future. In Peru, cocaine trafficking rakes in anywhere between US$300 million and US$600 million per year in under-the-table money and employs an estimated 200,000 Peruvians, mainly in remote jungle areas of the country, especially in the Apurímac Valley area in southern Peru.

The truth is, coca—scientifically known as *Erythroxylum coca*—has not always been a curse for Peruvians. Probably best known in the world through cocaine, its most popular derived product, the plant has been used for thousands of years in the Andean world, mainly for its medicinal properties and religious significance. Archaeologists have found supplies of coca leaves in mummies 3,000 years old. The Moche might have been the first to chew the leaves, a custom spread widely afterwards by the Inca, who decided that planting coca should be a state monopoly, limiting the use of it to nobles. During the colonial period, Philip II of Spain recognized the drug as an essential product for the well-being of the Andean inhabitants but urged missionaries to end its religious use.

Viewed as having a divine origin, coca has been an extremely important part of the religious cosmogony in the Andean world—from southern Colombia all the way down to northern Argentina and Chile—since pre-Hispanic times. Coca leaves play a crucial part in offerings made by shamans to the *apus* (mountain spirits), Inti (the sun god), and the Pachamama (mother earth). Leaves are also often read in a form of divination by *curanderos*, similar to the reading of tea leaves in other cultures. They are also placed inside coffins at burials.

But coca is also used in various everyday activities. Men chew leaves as they work in the fields, and women use it to ease the pain while giving birth. When a young man is about to ask a woman to marry him, he first must present a bag of leaves to his future father-in-law. Coca leaves have been used for thousands of years as a stimulant to overcome fatigue, hunger, and thirst. Once you arrive at Cusco's airport, you will likely be greeted with a hot cup of *mate de coca*, an infusion made from the leaf; it is considered particularly effective against altitude sickness, known as *soroche*.

The effects of the coca leaf were discovered in Europe during the 19th century, when Albert Niemann (a promising PhD student of Friedrich Wöhler, one of the most celebrated chemists of

large tracts of hillside every year to make *íchu* palatable for cows.

The high deserts of southern Peru, such as those on the way to the Colca Canyon, are so dry that not even *íchu* can survive. Instead, green blob-like plants called *yareta* spread along the rocky, lunar surface. This plant's waxy surface and tightly bunched leaves allow it to trap condensation and survive freezing temperatures. It is currently considered an endangered species.

A few trees can be found in Peru's montane valleys. **Eucalyptus,** which was imported to Peru from New Zealand, is used widely by highlanders for firewood and ceiling beams. Eucalyptus is useful but also highly invasive; its rapid spread has greatly reduced the numbers of Peru's most famous highland tree, the

the century) was able to isolate the active constituent of coca, which he baptized as "cocaine." Its stimulating effects were first publicized by Paolo Mantegazza, an Italian doctor, who after experimenting with coca leaves in 1859 wrote, "one starts to become more and more isolated from the exterior world, and one is plunged into a consciousness of blissful pleasure, feeling oneself animated with overabundant life." Angelo Mariani, a Corsican chemist who lived in Paris, saw coca's potential to make serious money, in 1863 making a wine with the coca leaves that he named Vin Mariani, a pleasant-tasting alcoholic brew with a real edge.

The success of the product inspired a number of wine imitations in the United States, including one that was converted into a carbonated soft drink known as Coca-Cola after the temperance movement hit Atlanta, Georgia, in 1885. By 1903 a public outcry over the ill effects of cocaine forced the company to remove cocaine from its beverage. What is not generally known is that Coca-Cola today continues to use flavoring from coca leaves, which have been "decocainized."

Making and taking cocaine today remains a nasty business. Villagers in the impoverished Ene-Apurímac Valley and other areas of Peru grow the plant because they can get as much as US$3 per kilo for the leaves, many times more than they would receive for selling coffee, bananas, or other fruit. Cultivating coca takes a lot out of the soil, and fields therefore have to be changed constantly. The Huallaga Valley, once covered in cloud forest, is nearly denuded and covered with a patchwork of eroding fields.

The process of making cocaine is even worse. The leaves must first be crushed underfoot and soaked in water to remove their essence. This water is then mixed with kerosene and other toxic chemicals and stirred until a white substance floats to the top. This substance, known as *pasta básica* or *bruta*, is further refined to make pure cocaine, known officially as cocaine hydrochloride. About 400 kilograms of coca leaves produces one kilo of cocaine. The villagers who help stir the *pasta básica* can readily be identified by their scarred arms, which are burned pink by the toxic chemicals.

The cocaine industry has also wreaked havoc on Peru's cities. Though cocaine is widely available in Peru and used often by young Peruvians, the real problem lies in the dusty shantytowns, or *pueblos jóvenes*, on the outskirts of Lima. Because cocaine is too expensive, teenagers smoke cheap cigarettes made from the unrefined *pasta básica*, which is different from crack cocaine but equally as powerful. People become addicted immediately to the US$0.30 cigarettes, and, as with crack smokers in the United States, their lives head downhill fast.

Experts say that the collapse of Colombia's Medellin and Calí cartels in the mid-1990s probably boosted Peru's cocaine business by fragmenting the industry and allowing players who were in the shadows to grab new market share. Today, there is a wide number of players, from the Revolutionary Armed Forces of Colombia, or FARC, which began cultivating coca in northern Peru near the Colombian border (and which is also behind a dramatic rise in Peru's cultivation of poppy, used to make opium and heroin), to Mexican and Brazilian cartels. Remnants of the Shining Path, Peru's notorious terrorist group that was crushed in the mid-1990s, are also involved in trafficking in the Apurímac Valley, and have been resurgent in recent years.

queñual, currently also endangered. This scraggly, high-altitude, onion skin-like tree can still be seen in abundance, however, in the Parque Nacional Huascarán, especially on a three-kilometer trail known as María Josefa that starts at the shores of Lake Llanganuco.

Of course the most controversial of Peru's highland plants is coca, chewed and made into tea by highlanders for thousands of years before its refinement into cocaine in the 19th century made it infamous. The plant itself grows abundantly on the eastern slopes of the Andes and in the lowlands of the Amazon, particularly in the the the Ene-Apurímac Valley (east of Ayacucho). The region is the biggest coca-growing valley on earth, and the center of Peru's cocaine production and trafficking. You will come across the gray-green leaves in most highland towns, served as a tea renowned for combating altitude sickness.

ANDEAN FAUNA

The most ubiquitous animals of Peru's Andes are the four species of native camelids, relatives of camels that eat the high-altitude *ichu* grasses and produce wooly coats as protection from the rain and cold. Two of these, the **llama** and **alpaca,** were domesticated thousands of years ago by Peru's highlanders for meat, wool, and transport. Production of alpaca fiber remains high, and the hair is renowned as a superior alternative to wool, because it is water resistant and also hypoallergenic.

Herds of the much smaller and finely haired **vicuña** can be seen in the sparse grasslands above Ayacucho, Arequipa, and Cusco. The fourth camelid, the **guanaco,** is harder to spot because its main range lies south in Chile and Argentina.

Other animals in the Peruvian Andes include **white-tailed deer, foxes, spectacled bears,** and **pumas,** but they remain elusive most of the time. The only animal you are likely to see is the **vizcacha,** which looks like a strange mix between a rabbit and a squirrel.

The most famous bird in the Andes is the **Andean condor,** the world's largest flying bird. Its range extends from the high jungle, including Machu Picchu, all the way to the coast. Mature condors have a black plumage with white upper flight feathers, a fuzzy white neck ruff, a red head, and a hooked beak. Condors can easily be seen in Colca Canyon along with other raptors, including the impressive **mountain caracara,** which has a black body, red face, and brilliant yellow feet. There are also **falcons,** which have a russet belly and can often be seen hovering over grasslands in search of mice or birds.

Water birds can be seen at Lake Titicaca and in the cold, black lakes of the Andean puna. The Andean grasslands are one of the habitats for the **Andean goose** (a huge, rotund bird with a white belly and black back) and a variety of shimmering ducks, including the puna teal and crested duck. There are even flamingos and a few wading birds, such as the red-billed puna ibis. One of the most interesting birds, which can be seen in the river near Machu Picchu and in Colca Canyon, is the **torrent duck.** This amazing swimmer floats freely down white water that even experienced rafters would fear to tackle.

History

Despite its incredible diversity of landscapes and wildlife, the biggest magnet for tourists in Peru remains its rich history of ancient cultures, arguably the most diverse in the Americas.

The first Peruvian states were worshipping at stepped adobe platforms on the coast 5,000 years ago, before the Egyptians were building pyramids at Giza. And as the Roman empire spread across modern-day Europe, Peru's first empire states were spreading across the Andes.

Peru's three large empires—the Chavín, the Huari, and the Inca—spread across Peru

in three stages that historians call "horizons." Like the Aztec empire in Mesoamerica, these cultures spread more through commerce and cultural exchange than through military force.

Following the European arrival in the New World, Peru's history follows the same basic stages as other areas of North and South America. There was first a colonial period, which lasted longer and ended later than that of the United States; a war of independence; and then a period of rapid nation building and industrialization in the 19th and 20th centuries.

ORIGINS OF HUMAN CIVILIZATION

The original settlers in the Americas most likely came from Asia. Human life in Peru, indeed all over the Americas, is a relatively recent event made possible when the last ice age allowed human settlers to cross the Bering land bridge that connected present-day Russia to Alaska between 20,000 and 40,000 years ago. It is also possible that some early migration originated from the Polynesian Islands in the South Pacific.

The first evidence of human civilization in Peru has been dated to as early as 20,000 BC at **Pikimachay Cave** outside of Ayacucho, where arrowheads, animal skeletons, and carbon remains were found. These first human groups began domesticating Andean camelids and *cuys* (guinea pigs) as early as 7000 BC, establishing small hunter-gatherer villages a thousand years later. Potatoes were first cultivated around 6000 BC in the Lake Titicaca region. Around 2900 BC, humans began to plant crops such as manioc, quinoa, lima beans, and cotton at **Caral,** establishing Peru's long-standing agricultural tradition. Caral, some 200 kilometers north of Lima, had a population of more than 3,000. It is Peru's oldest known city and lays claim to the title of oldest city in the Americas.

THE CHAVÍN

Considered the South American counterpart of China's Shang or Mesopotamia's Sumerian civilizations, the Chavín flourished around 900 BC during the First or Early Horizon era (1000 BC-AD 200). The Chavín managed to unite coastal, highland, and eastern lowland societies with a powerful religious ideology.

The Chavín built an elaborate stone temple at Chavín de Huántar, southeast of Huaraz— now a UNESCO World Heritage Site. A complex drainage system was constructed to prevent flooding during the rainy season. The temple was decorated with finely carved stone sculptures and elaborate iconography. These figures depict their worship of a supreme feline deity—the jaguar—as well as other creatures, such as snakes, caimans, and natural spirits.

Despite being known as brilliant and innovative metallurgists who developed refined gold work, as well as builders and strategists, the Chavín's influence began to fade around 300 BC.

MOCHE, NASCA, AND TIAHUANACO

A variety of cultures sprang up to take the place of the Chavín. On the north coast, the Moche (220 BC-AD 600) built the Huaca de la Luna, a stepped adobe pyramid south of present-day Trujillo. Highly militaristic and religious, the Moche spread throughout Peru's northern coast. They are best known for finely crafted metallurgy and ceramics. Moche performed human sacrifices and drank the blood of their enemies.

Living at the same time as the Moche, but on the south coast, the Nasca (100 BC-AD 700) made great advances in irrigation, building an impressive series of aqueducts that are still used today. They began making elegant weavings from cotton and camelid fiber that are considered today the most advanced textiles produced in pre-Columbian America. But of course they are most famous for their complex cosmography, evident in the Nasca Lines, giant etchings in the desert floor.

In the southern Andean region, the Tiahuanaco (AD 200-1000) built an elaborate stone urban and ceremonial center on the southern shores of Lake Titicaca. They also developed a system of raised-bed farming that allowed them to cultivate crops despite the area's freezing temperatures.

THE HUARI

The Huari culture (AD 600-1100) was the first in South America to establish a true empire. They built a sophisticated road network, developed terraced agriculture, and founded the first well-populated cities, notably their capital, Huari, north of Ayacucho. Around AD 650, the Huari spread south toward the Tiahuanaco culture near Lake Titicaca and

Peru Timeline

- **20,000 BC:** First humans arrive in Peru.

- **15,000 BC:** Earliest evidence of human life in Peru: Pikimachay Cave, Ayacucho.

- **7000 BC:** Andean camelids are domesticated.

- **2627 BC:** Sacred city of Caral is built on the coast north of Lima.

- **900-200 BC:** Chavín culture flourishes as the unifier of religious ideology from its ceremonial center in the Marañón basin.

- **900-200 BC:** Paracas emerges in the desert, producing vividly colored textiles.

- **AD 200-600:** Moche, Nasca, and Tiahuanaco flourish as regional civilizations in northern, central, and southern Peru.

- **AD 300:** Moche's Lord of Sipán is buried at Huaca Rajada, northeast of Chiclayo.

- **AD 450:** Moche's Lady of Cao dies at 25 and is buried in El Brujo complex, north of Trujillo.

- **AD 650:** Huari empire starts expanding across most of Peru.

- **AD 900:** Sicán culture builds 20 pyramids at Batan Grande.

- **1200:** Mythical foundation of the Inca empire by Manco Cápac and Mama Ocllo.

- **1400:** Chimú kingdom reaches its maximum expansion.

- **1400:** Inca Pachacútec's 33-year reign begins.

- **1450:** Chimú kingdom is conquered by the Inca empire. Chan Chan and Túcume are invaded.

- **1527-1532:** Huayna Cápac dies. His two sons, Huáscar and Atahualpa, plunge into a civil war.

- **1532:** Francisco Pizarro lands in Tumbes with 168 men, meets Atahualpa in Cajamarca, and takes him prisoner.

- **1533:** Atahualpa is tried and executed. Manco Inca, a puppet leader, is installed. Cusco is invaded and sacked.

- **1535:** Pizarro founds Lima.

- **1536-1537:** Manco Inca rebels and subsequently retreats to Vilcabamba.

- **1538:** Diego de Almagro is executed after rebelling against Pizarro's authority.

- **1541:** Almagro's son murders Pizarro in Lima.

- **1542:** Spain's King Charles I establishes the Viceroyalty of Peru.

- **1542:** Potosí mines reach population peak with 160,000 people.

- **1572:** Túpac Amaru I is captured, tried, and executed.

- **1742:** Juan Santos Atahualpa proclaims himself Inca and rebels in the central jungles near Chanchamayo.

- **1767:** Jesuits are expelled from the Spanish empire.

- **1780-1782:** Túpac Amaru II leads a rebellion against the Spaniards but is captured, tried, and executed.

- **1814:** Revolution breaks out in Cusco.

- **1821:** José de San Martín proclaims Peru's independence.

- **1824:** Battle of Ayacucho. Antonio José de Sucre defeats the Spaniards.

- **1826-1866:** Simón Bolívar leaves Peru. A period of political turbulence starts, with 35 presidents in 40 years.

- **1840:** Peru signs lucrative contract for exporting guano, or bird dung.

- **1849-1874:** Cotton and sugar plantations on Peru's north coast import 100,000 Chinese coolies to replace freed slaves.

- **1879-1883:** War of the Pacific. Peru loses the war against Chile.

- **1911:** Hiram Bingham finds Machu Picchu.

- **1919-1930:** Augusto B. Leguía's 11-year civil dictatorship is marked by strong foreign investment and restriction of civil rights.

- **1927:** Víctor Raúl Haya de la Torre founds the Alianza Popular Revolucionaria Americana (APRA) from political exile in Mexico.

- **1941:** Peru enters a seven-week war over disputed border territories with Ecuador.

- **1955:** Women vote for the first time.
- **1963-1968:** President Fernando Belaúnde Terry begins land reform, heading a very unpopular administration.
- **1968:** Belaúnde is overthrown by socialist-leaning general Juan Velasco Alvarado.
- **1968-1980:** Twelve years of military dictatorship. Velasco nationalizes foreign-owned companies.
- **1970:** A 7.9 earthquake kills 70,000 in Áncash, including 18,000 covered by a landslide in Yungay.
- **1975:** General Francisco Morales Bermúdez, presumably supported by the CIA, overthrows Velasco Alvarado.
- **1980:** Belaúnde is reelected. Sendero Luminoso (Shining Path), a Maoist terrorist organization, launches in Ayacucho a 20-year internal war that plunges Peru into violence and chaos.
- **1982-1983:** El Niño floods devastate northern Peru.
- **1985:** APRA candidate Alan García Pérez is elected president, pushing the country into hyperinflation and a downward economic spiral.
- **1985-1988:** The Accomarca massacre (1985); execution of 200 inmates during prison riots in Lurigancho, El Frontón Island, and Santa Bárbara (1986); and Cayara massacre (1988) mark a period of constant human rights violations under García's administration.
- **1990:** World-renowned novelist Mario Vargas Llosa leads protests against García's intention of nationalizing the Peruvian bank system.
- **1990:** Outsider Alberto Fujimori defeats Vargas Llosa to become president of Peru. He applies a radical economic program tagged the "Fuji-shock."
- **1992:** Fujimori dissolves congress in his "self-coup." Shining Path bombs a building in Lima's middle-class Miraflores district. Abimael Guzmán, Shining Path's leader, is captured.
- **1993:** Peru's economy picks up and becomes the fastest-growing in the world.
- **1996-1997:** The MRTA terrorist group assaults the Japanese ambassador's residence, taking hundreds of hostages and keeping 72 of them for four months. A Peruvian military operation rescues all hostages but one, killing all MRTA members.
- **1998:** El Niño storms ravage the north coast.
- **2000:** Fujimori is reelected president under allegations of electoral fraud. He leaves the country after accusations of extortion, corruption, and arms trafficking. Valentín Paniagua leads the transition government.
- **2001:** Alejandro Toledo is elected president.
- **2003-2004:** Calls for Toledo's resignation heighten as Peru's largest union, the General Confederation of Workers, holds nationwide strikes.
- **2006:** Fujimori, en route to Peru to run for president, is detained and jailed in Chile on charges of human rights violations. Alan García is reelected president, 20 years after his first term.
- **2007:** An 8.0 earthquake hits the Ica region.
- **2009:** After being successfully extradited and taken to trial, Fujimori is sentenced to 25 years imprisonment.
- **2010:** In January, more than 3,000 tourists are stranded for days after a huge mudslide near Machu Picchu.
- **2011:** Ollanta Humala becomes president, narrowly beating Keiko Fujimori, Alberto Fujimori's daughter.
- **2012:** Large protests against the U.S.-owned Minas Conga copper-gold mine in the north result in several deaths and a state of emergency, forcing the company and government to suspend the project.
- **2014:** Peru's once red-hot economy slows considerably due to weaker global demand for copper and other commodities it exports to China and other nations.
- **2016:** Pedro Pablo Kuczynski is elected president, defeating Keiko Fujimori by a slim margin.

Cusco, where they built the huge walled city of **Pikillacta.** The city spreads across 47 hectares of rolling grasslands and contains a maze of walled stone enclosures and elaborate stone aqueducts. The Huari and Tiahuanaco resisted the temptation to go to war and instead existed side by side.

By the time the empire faded around AD 900, the Huari had left an indelible pattern of organization over Peru that would be repeated in larger scale by the Inca.

THE KINGDOMS OF THE LATE HORIZON

Along the coast, the **Chimú** built their mud city, Chan Chan, north of Trujillo and a short distance from the adobe stepped platforms built by the Moche. Chan Chan is the largest city built by Peru's pre-Hispanic cultures, and its walled plazas, passageways, temples, and gardens spread over nearly 20 square kilometers. Over time, the kingdom would spread along the coast of Peru from Chancay, a valley north of Lima, to the present-day border with Ecuador.

As the Chimú were flourishing, other descendants of the Moche culture known as the **Sicán** were building adobe pyramids at Batán Grande, farther north near Chiclayo. Discoveries of royal Sicán tombs there in 1991 revealed a wealth of gold masks, scepters, and ceremonial knives. After a devastating El Niño flood destroyed the center, the Sicán began building even larger pyramids a bit farther north at Túcume. By 1350, the Sicán culture was conquered by the Chimú.

Peru's south coast was dominated by the **Ica-Chincha** kingdom, which spread along Peru's southern desert valleys. This culture developed elaborate aqueducts for bringing water from the mountains under the desert floor.

During this time, other cultures flourished throughout the highlands. The largest of these was the **Chachapoya,** a mysterious federation of city-states that spread across the cloud forests of northeastern Peru. The Chachapoya's most celebrated city is Kuélap,

a stone citadel perched atop a sheer limestone bluff.

THE INCA EMPIRE

There is a tendency to idealize the period of Inca rule, contrasting it with the cruelty and intolerance of the Spanish conquerors. The Inca empire was indeed the pinnacle of pre-Columbian civilization, and its talent for construction was particularly astounding, but the empire was relatively short-lived and punctuated by regular brutal conflicts.

The origins of the Inca empire, referred to in Quechua as the Tahuantinsuyo, or "Four Corners," are obscured by myth. The best-known origin story describes how Inca Manco Cápac and Mama Oclla, children of the sun and moon, arose from Lake Titicaca and searched for a place to found their kingdom. Manco Cápac plunged his golden staff into the ground and named it Q'osqo ("navel of the world"). Historians agree that Manco Cápac was the first Inca leader and began his rule around 1200. For more than two centuries the Inca developed slowly in the Cusco area, until 1438, when the neighboring Chancas tribe threatened to overrun their city. Though Inca Viracocha fled the city, his son Inca Yupanqui beat back the Chancas, took over from his disgraced father, and changed his name to Pachacútec, which means "shaker of the earth." He launched the meteoric rise of the Inca empire, which within a century would stretch for more than 4,000 kilometers from southern Chile to northern Ecuador and include huge chunks of Bolivia and Argentina.

Pachacútec was also responsible for much of the Inca's formidable architecture, including the fortress of Sacsayhuamán above Cusco. Historians also believe he built Machu Picchu, which may have been a *llacta* (administrative center). Buildings in the famous Inca masonry style—blocks weighing tons fitted perfectly together—housed collections of intricately woven textiles, utensils made of precious metals, and musical instruments made of clay, shells, and human bones.

Though the Inca are known for their fine

Pachacútec is widely regarded as the greatest Inca ruler.

is still spoken today by 10 million people in Peru, Bolivia, Ecuador, and Argentina.

However, the Inca also behaved brutally to those who opposed them. After waging a long war against the Chachapoya, the Inca deported half the population to other parts of the empire as part of a forced-labor scheme. In Ecuador, when the Inca met with stiff resistance from the Cara people north of Quito in 1495, tens of thousands were massacred and their bodies dumped into a lake that became known as Yahuarcocha (Lake of Blood).

Pachacútec's son and grandson, Túpac Yupanqui and Huayna Cápac, spent most of their lives abroad, extending the Inca empire to its farthest limits. Huayna Cápac, born in Tomebamba (present-day Cuenca, Ecuador), died in 1527 during a smallpox epidemic that devastated Peru's population and was probably spread by Spaniards who had set foot on the northernmost fringe of the Inca empire during a preliminary trip in 1526.

Huayna Cápac's sudden death, along with that of his eldest son and heir, Ninan Cuyochi, led to a power vacuum. Two other sons, half-brothers Huáscar and Atahualpa, laid claim to the succession. Huáscar lived in Cusco and Atahualpa in Quito. For a couple of years they ruled in tandem, but Huáscar's insistence that Atahualpa swear allegiance to him resulted in civil war. Atahualpa quickly gained the upper hand, because most of his father's armies had been based in the north. The biggest battle occurred near Ambato in Ecuador, where 30,000 soldiers died. Huáscar was driven south, defeated, and imprisoned in 1532. But no sooner had Atahualpa received news of his victory than news of a very different kind reached him: A mysterious band of tall, bearded white men had landed on the coast at Tumbes, frightening locals and making their way inland.

THE SPANISH CONQUEST

Most conquistadores (literally, "conquerors") were low-ranking Spanish noblemen heading to the New World for wealth, fame, and

stonework, they were also exceedingly good administrators, organizing a finely tuned if short-lived empire. Cusco was smaller than other capitals of pre-Hispanic Peru, but the Inca imperial city was at the center of a paved road network that led throughout the empire. Eight meters wide and paved with stone, the highways boasted trees planted for shade and a ditch of fresh water running alongside.

The Inca offered rich economic and cultural benefits to neighboring cultures that submitted peacefully to their rule. When the Ica and Chincha lordships were integrated into the empire, the Inca helped build a vast aqueduct near present-day Chincha that is still used today. Though the Inca changed the names of places they conquered and encouraged spread of their religion and language, they accepted a degree of cultural diversity. Spanish chroniclers such as Pedro Cieza de León were impressed with the variety of languages and native dress in Cusco at the time of the conquest. The Quechua language became widely used throughout the empire and

adventure. Francisco Pizarro, the central figure in the conquest of the Inca, was an illiterate and illegitimate fortune-seeker from Extremadura in southern Spain.

In 1526, while Pizarro was exploring Panama and Colombia, his main pilot, Bartomolé Ruiz, sailed down the Ecuadorian coast on a reconnaissance mission and captured a Manta merchant vessel laden with gold. This news convinced Pizarro that the region contained untold riches. Following several unsuccessful voyages, Pizarro returned to Spain to plead for money and authority. He arrived again in the New World with the title of Governor and Captain-General of Peru. In 1532, he landed in Tumbes in northern Peru with fellow adventurer Diego de Almagro, 180 men, 27 horses, his brothers Gonzalo and Juan Pizarro, and two half-brothers. The Inca initially greeted Pizarro's party with wonder and fear, but rumors of plundering on the fringes of the empire quickly spread, and things turned hostile.

Pizarro and his men rode into the Andes and found Atahualpa and an army of 80,000 Inca soldiers at Cajamarca. The Spaniards invited Atahualpa to a meeting the next day in the square and planned a bold ambush. The ensuing scene on November 15, 1532, would have been fascinating to witness: two leaders meeting in the plaza under the eyes of dozens of Spanish soldiers and thousands of Inca warriors, with tension resonating in the air. Atahualpa, considered a living god by his people and with an army of thousands, made the fatal mistake of underestimating a band of fewer than 200 Spanish. Accounts about the events that followed differ, but most witnesses agree that Atahualpa refused the Spanish chaplain's order to submit to Spain and the Christian god, throwing a Bible down in disgust. At a prearranged signal, Spanish soldiers fired cannons and charged their horses into the heart of the astonished Inca garrison. Within two hours, 7,000 Inca soldiers lay dead, Atahualpa had been captured, and the fate of South America's greatest empire had been sealed.

Among the Europeans, only Pizarro was wounded.

During the nine months of his imprisonment, Atahualpa learned Spanish, chess, and cards while retaining most of his authority. Attendants dressed and fed him, burning everything he touched. Thinking that Pizarro planned to depose him in favor of Huáscar, Atahualpa ordered his captive half-brother killed. When it became clear that his life hung in the balance, Atahualpa offered to buy his freedom. He is said to have reached high on the wall of a room five meters wide by seven meters long, offering to fill it once with gold and twice with silver. The ransom—one of the largest the world has ever known—was assembled and on its way to the capital when Pizarro went back on his word, fearful of the Inca leader's power. Atahualpa was put on trial for polygamy, idolatry, and crimes against the crown and sentenced to be burned at the stake. He reacted with horror at this news because he believed that such a fate would prevent his body from passing into the afterlife. He agreed to be baptized and was garroted on July 26, 1533, in Cajamarca.

In November 1533, Cusco fell to Pizarro and Hernando de Soto, and the Inca empire was all but finished. Important battles remained to be fought: In May 1534, Sebastian de Benalcázar (Pizarro's second-in-command) faced 50,000 Inca warriors under Rumiñahui, a great Inca general who had deserted and burned Quito rather than surrender to the invaders. Benalcázar, aided by Cañari soldiers, defeated him. In 1536, Manco Inca launched a rebellion and laid siege to Cusco with an army of 100,000 soldiers. Against overwhelming odds, the Spaniards routed the Inca from their fortress of Sacsayhuamán during a week of constant fighting. Manco Inca then repelled an army of Spaniards at Ollantaytambo in the Sacred Valley before retreating to Vilcabamba. For the next 35 years, the Inca would use this jungle stronghold to continue their resistance until the last Inca leader, Túpac Amaru, was captured and executed in 1572.

So how did fewer than 200 Spanish soldiers defeat an estimated 500,000 natives? Although the numbers seem unbelievable, they can be explained by a combination of battle tactics, disease, and luck. In the 16th century, Spanish soldiers were among the best in the world, almost invulnerable to attack from the ground when mounted on their fierce warhorses in full battle armor. A dozen mounted soldiers could hold off and even defeat hundreds of Inca foot soldiers. In addition, European diseases, to which the natives had no immunity, killed thousands.

As much as anything, incredible timing sealed the Inca's fate. If the Spanish had arrived a year or two earlier or later, things might have worked out much differently. As it happened, they showed up exactly at the moment of greatest vulnerability; the Inca empire had been split by a civil war and many local tribes were itching to throw off their masters. The conquistadores, especially Pizarro, manipulated the situation brilliantly, installing puppet rulers to pacify the masses and acting with brutal decisiveness.

However, after the defeat of the Inca, their conquerors had little chance to bask in glory and quickly began fighting among themselves. In 1538, Diego de Almagro contested Pizarro's right to govern the new territory of Peru. Almagro was defeated, tried, and sentenced to death in Lima, garroted in the same way as Atahualpa. Francisco Pizarro himself was stabbed to death in his palace in 1541 by the remaining members of a rebel army led by Almagro's son.

The Spanish crown tried to restore order by imposing the New Laws of 1542, aimed at controlling the unruly conquistadores and ending the enslavement of indigenous peoples, already widespread. A new viceroy, Blasco Nuñez, was sent to oversee the budding colonies in 1544, but Gonzalo Pizarro (Francisco's brother) organized resistance and killed Nuñez in the battle of Añaquito near Quito in 1544. Gonzalo Pizarro, in turn, was defeated by royal troops near Cusco in 1548 and beheaded on the field of battle.

THREE CENTURIES OF VICEROYALTY

Spanish Latin America was split into viceroyalties, and the first two were created in Mexico and Peru, with Mexico City and Lima the capitals. The Viceroyalty of Peru extended south into Chile and covered much of the Spanish areas of South America until two new viceroyalties were created in the 18th century: Viceroyalty de la Plata in Argentina and Viceroyalty Nueva Granada in Bogotá.

Cusco became a center of religious art during the viceroyalty but otherwise fell out of the spotlight after the conquest. It may have been the center of the world for the Inca, but it couldn't compete with Lima's port status. In a cynical use of Inca tradition, Viceroy Francisco de Toledo in 1574 legalized the Inca's old labor scheme of *mita* to force huge numbers of indigenous people to work at the Potosí silver mine in present-day Bolivia and the Santa Bárbara mercury mine near Huancavelica. Far from home, thousands perished while working in virtual slavery at these mines. Toledo also established the Inquisition, and terrified natives converted to Christianity for fear of the consequences of refusing, although many fused Christian and shamanic beliefs, an unusual combination that still exists today.

Some indigenous people were forced to relocate to *reducciones,* new settlements that allowed the Spaniards to tax them more efficiently and convert them to Christianity. Rich farmland was divided into *encomiendas* (land grants), and all the native people living on one became slaves to the Spanish owner, known as the *encomendero.* Others were herded into sweatshops *(obrajes),* where they made textiles and other objects for export under prisonlike conditions. Through a combination of harsh working conditions, brutality, and disease, the indigenous population plummeted from over 10 million at the time of the conquest to just 600,000 a century later.

The biggest uprising against Spanish rule in Peru was the 1780-1781 revolt led by Túpac Amaru II, who claimed to be a direct descendant of the last Inca, Túpac Amaru. After a yearlong rebellion, the Spaniards finished him off as they had his ancestor two centuries before—he was garroted in Cusco's main square, and then his body was ripped apart by teams of horses pulling in opposite directions. His entire family was executed with him, and all documents related to his descent were burnt in an attempt to stamp out any remnants of Inca heritage. However, Túpac Amaru II still became a cult hero and rallying figure for future indigenous uprisings.

INDEPENDENCE

After nearly three centuries of Spanish rule, the native-born people of the Peruvian viceroyalty began to itch for independence. News of the American Revolution in 1776 and French Revolution in 1789 filtered to Peru and encouraged a longing for freedom.

Resentment grew among the descendants of Europeans born in Peru, known as *criollos*. They were confined to middle management and resentful of privileges given to Spaniards, who held all the powerful positions in the viceroyalty. Colonial society was rigidly classified into a hierarchy that attempted to make sense of the mixing between races in colonial

Peru. The main categories included *mestizo* (European-indigenous), *mulato* (European-African), *negro* (African), *zambo* (indigenous-African), and *indio* (indigenous).

The revolutionary murmurs became a clamor when Spain suffered defeats in European wars. In 1805, much of the Spanish fleet was destroyed at the Battle of Trafalgar, and in 1808 Napoleon invaded Spain and replaced King Carlos IV with his brother Joseph. Few Latin Americans were happy about pledging allegiance to a French puppet ruler, and independence movements erupted. Peru, the strongest and richest region of Spanish South America, was heavily populated by Spanish forces, and the independence movement took time. By 1820, the last bastion of Spanish control was Peru.

After liberating Chile, Argentine general José de San Martín landed at Pisco, and royalist forces retreated into the mountains, allowing Lima to be taken unopposed. The harshness of the route into the mountains meant that overcoming the Spanish was no easy task. San Martín journeyed to Ecuador to meet with Venezuelan general Simón Bolívar and ceded to him control of the independence struggle in Peru. In 1824, the decisive battle of Ayacucho was won by Bolívar's lieutenant,

a statue of South American liberator Simón Bolívar

Antonio Sucre, despite being outnumbered. Spanish surrender and withdrawal were negotiated, and the last Spanish troops left in January 1826.

Bolívar envisioned a grand union of South American states known as Gran Colombia, modeled on the United States. After serving as Peru's first president for two years, he returned to Bogotá, Colombia, in a last-ditch attempt to hold together the federation, which briefly stretched through Panama, Colombia, Venezuela, Ecuador, and Peru. Bolívar's scheme fell apart, and he died soon afterwards in 1830, bitterly stating on his deathbed that his revolution had "plowed the sea" and calling South America "ungovernable."

Peru plunged into chaos. During the next four decades, more than 35 presidents came and went. A now-familiar political tradition arose: One leader, usually a strong-willed *caudillo* of military background, would seize power with populist rhetoric and grandiose promises, and then he would proceed to distribute power and affluence among his friends and family before being deposed by another *caudillo.*

Amid the chaos, Peru's rising class of merchants found new opportunities to make money besides mining. The biggest business came from bird excrement, or guano, which covered the islands off Peru's coast and was used as an effective fertilizer.

Despite the abundance of natural resources, Peru was devastated by the War of the Pacific against Chile (1879-1883), when Chilean armies sacked Lima. Peru was forced to cede an entire southern province to Chile—Tarapacá—that contained valuable fields of nitrate, used to make fertilizer. After the war, Peru plunged into bankruptcy and had to negotiate with British creditors, who agreed to forgive the debt in exchange for 200 million tons of guano and a 66-year concession over the country's railroads. The British-owned Peruvian Corporation was set up in Arequipa in 1890 and built the current railroads that lead to Arequipa and Cusco.

THE 20TH CENTURY

As foreign investors tightened their grip on Peru's main industries, worker dissent simmered following the Russian Revolution. In 1924, exiled political leader Víctor Raúl Haya de la Torre founded the Alianza Popular Revolucionaria Americana (APRA), a populist workers' party that still exerts tremendous influence over Peruvian politics. When Haya lost the 1931 elections, his supporters accused the government of fraud and attacked a military outpost in Trujillo, killing 10 soldiers. In response the Peruvian military trucked an estimated 1,000 APRA supporters out to the sands of Chan Chan and executed them by mass firing squads.

Peru's economic development in the mid-20th century was hampered by the hacienda system of land ownership inherited from the viceroyalty. The independence movement had passed leadership to the *criollos,* but otherwise Peru's economic structure remained the same—a minority of Peruvians of direct European descent still controlled the bulk of Peru's land and wealth. As Peru moved from an agricultural economy to an industrial one, country folk flocked to Lima in search of a better life and built sprawling shantytowns around the city. Pressure for land reform began to grow.

Fernando Belaúnde, architect and politician, was president of Peru during the 1960s and instituted a few moderate reforms, but he was overthrown in 1968 by General Juan Velasco, who despite being a military man launched a series of radical, left-wing reforms that stunned Peru's white elite and transformed the Peruvian economy. He expropriated nearly all of Peru's haciendas and transferred the land to newly formed worker cooperatives. Velasco kicked out foreign investors and nationalized their fish meal factories, banks, oil companies, and mines. He introduced food subsidies for urban slum dwellers and, in a gesture of recognition of Peru's indigenous people, made Quechua the official second language of Peru.

Velasco's restructuring was so rapid and

ill-planned that nearly all of Peru's major industries plunged to new lows and the country entered a severe economic crisis. In failing health, Velasco was overthrown in 1975, and many historians claim the CIA was behind the coup. His successor, pro-U.S. military leader Francisco Morales Bermúdez, attempted to control the economic chaos, and amid widespread strikes in the late 1970s, APRA politician Haya de la Torre headed a constituent assembly that finally secured full suffrage for all Peruvian citizens and the return to democracy.

TWENTY YEARS OF POLITICAL VIOLENCE

In 1980, Peru's first full democratic election in 12 years coincided with the initial actions of Sendero Luminoso (Shining Path), a terrorist group espousing Maoist ideology. Shining Path was founded in Ayacucho by university professor Abimael Guzmán, later known as "President Gonzalo" by supporters. Shining Path rose alongside the smaller Movimiento Revolucionario Túpac Amaru (MRTA). Both organizations terrorized Peru's countryside over the next decade and began receiving financial support from the cocaine business, which had grown rapidly in the upper Huallaga Valley.

Shining Path established strongholds in Ayacucho, Apurímac, and Huancavelica, but their support and action spread, eventually to Lima. Andean villagers were frequently caught in the crossfire between these terrorist organizations and the Peruvian army. The Shining Path would force the villagers to give them food or supply information, and the army in retaliation would massacre the whole village, or vice versa. The worst massacres of the conflict occurred between 1983 and 1984, the same year that Latin American economies collapsed under a debt crisis and Peru's north was devastated by El Niño rains.

The APRA candidate, Alan García, won the 1985 elections at age 35 because he offered a hopeful future. He promptly shocked the international finance community by announcing that Peru would be making only a small portion of its international debt payments, sparking a two-year spending spree that was followed by Peru's worst economic collapse ever, with hyperinflation so extreme that restaurants were forced to increase their menu prices three times each day. Peru's struggling middle class saw their savings disappear overnight.

The disastrous economic policies of García's administration only added fuel to the guerrillas' cause. The government unsuccessfully sought a military solution to the terrorism, allegedly committing widespread human rights violations. The most important cases include the Accomarca massacre (1985), where 47 peasants were executed by the Peruvian armed forces; the Cayara massacre (1988), in which some 30 were killed and dozens disappeared; and the summary execution of around 200 inmates during prison riots in 1986. An estimated 1,600 forced disappearances took place during García's presidency. In 2003, the Truth and Reconciliation Commission reported that more than 70,000 people were killed during the terrorism years, and 75 percent of them were Quechua highlanders. Half were killed by Shining Path, a third by government forces (police and armed forces), and the rest so far unattributed.

In the late 1980s, Peruvian novelist Mario Vargas Llosa led a series of middle-class protests against García's plan to nationalize Peru's banking system. Vargas Llosa appeared likely to win the 1990 election but was defeated by Alberto Fujimori, a low-profile university rector of Japanese descent who appealed to Peru's mestizo and indigenous voters because he was not part of Lima's elitist white society.

THE FUJIMORI REGIME

Soon after winning the elections, Fujimori reversed his campaign promises and implemented an economic austerity program. His plan aimed to stimulate foreign investment by slashing trade tariffs and simplifying taxes. Fujimori also began privatizing state-owned companies that President Velasco had nationalized in the late 1960s and early 1970s. This program, nicknamed "Fuji-Shock," caused widespread misery among Peru's poor populations as food prices shot through the roof. Fortunately, the program also sparked an economic recovery. Inflation dropped from 7,650 percent in 1990 to 139 percent in 1991.

After struggling to convince Peru's congress to pass legislation in 1992, Fujimori strained international relations with the United States and other countries after he dissolved the congress in his famous *autogolpe,* or "self-coup." That same year, Peru's level of terror reached a high point when Shining Path detonated two car bombs in the heart of Lima's middle-class Miraflores neighborhood, killing 25 people and injuring more than 250.

In September 1992, Fujimori's popularity shot through the roof when the Peruvian military captured both Shining Path leader Abimael Guzmán and the main leaders of the MRTA. This was a watershed moment in Peruvian history, and the country finally began to recover from decades of chaos. The economy picked up and, by 1993, was one of the fastest-growing in the world. Fujimori launched a new constitution and recovered international support by reopening congress.

Having tackled Peru's twin nightmares of terrorism and inflation, Fujimori easily beat former U.N. secretary-general Javier Pérez de Cuéllar in the 1995 elections. The following year, 14 MRTA terrorists led by Néstor Cerpa took hundreds of prominent hostages after storming a cocktail party at Lima's Japanese ambassador's residence. After releasing most of the hostages, the terrorists held 72 prisoners and maintained a tense standoff with the military for four months. As the situation grew desperate, Fujimori authorized Peruvian commandos to tunnel under the embassy and take it by surprise. The operation was an amazing success. One hostage died during the operation—of a heart attack—and one military commando was killed by terrorist fire. Few Peruvians raised objections to the fact that all 14 MRTA members were shot to death—including the ones who had surrendered.

However, at this point Fujimori's popularity began to wane. He ran for an unconstitutional third term in 2000. After alleging vote fraud in the main election, Alejandro Toledo refused to run in the runoff, and the international community threatened sanctions. Fujimori went ahead with the election anyway and was elected president. A huge scandal broke in September of that year, when videos were leaked to the media showing Fujimori's head of intelligence, Vladimiro Montesinos, bribing generals, journalists, politicians, and business executives. The resulting investigation uncovered more than US$40 million in bribes.

Fujimori conveniently resigned from the presidency, via fax, while on a state visit to Japan. Back in Peru, an international warrant for his arrest was issued citing his involvement in paramilitary massacres of left-wing political activists in the early 1990s. In 2005, when Fujimori left Japan to return to Peru and launch a campaign for the presidency, he was arrested in Santiago, Chile, held for six months in jail on charges of corruption and human rights violations, and extradited to Peru. At the end of a 15-month trial, Fujimori was sentenced in April 2009 to 25 years in prison for ordering security forces to kill and kidnap civilians.

Montesinos was also arrested in Venezuela after being on the run for eight months and is in a high-security prison near Lima. About US$250 million in his funds have been recovered from foreign bank accounts. Following Fujimori's departure, congressman Valentín Paniagua became interim president before Toledo was elected in 2001.

RETURN TO DEMOCRACY

Toledo's political inexperience and lack of strong leadership caused his popularity to plunge. Toledo, however, did establish a stable and growing economy. In an amazing development that only South American politics could conjure, Alan García, who presided over disastrous security and economic crises in the

1980s, returned to Peru after years in exile, claimed he'd learned from his mistakes, and won the 2006 election against populist Ollanta Humala, who was inspired if not financially supported by Venezuelan president Hugo Chávez. García's return to the presidency was a result of voting against Humala, a turn of events not many Peruvians were happy with. Nevertheless, García's second presidency was quite successful. He forged trade agreements with Brazil and increased foreign investment. Peru's economy boomed, even in the face of the world economic crisis. However, many voters complained that García shifted from his center-left ideological position to a more neoliberal tack.

In opposition Humala became less radical and narrowly beat Fujimori's daughter Keiko in the 2011 election. The Peruvian stock market plunged following the election of a left-winger, but Humala made several key moderate appointments to his government to soothe market fears. His first year in power was beset with problems, including an ongoing dispute with indigenous groups over mining and an unexpected resurgence of Shining Path in the Apurímac Valley. Initial concerns from the business community that Humala would reverse Peru's economic policies have proved unfounded. Over his five-year term, Humala maintained many of the same investment-friendly policies as his predecessors. Also like his predecessors, his popularity plunged about midway through his term, hurt by weakening economic growth, corruption allegations against his wife, Nadine Heredia, and growing concerns over crime.

Pedro Pablo Kuczynski, an Oxford-educated economist and former World Bank official, won Peru's presidential election in 2016, defeating Keiko Fujimori by a very narrow margin. Kuczynski promised to boost economic growth in order to expand basic services such as running water to Peru's poorest communities.

Government and Economy

GOVERNMENT

After years of political and economic problems, Peru has sustained a strong, growing economy and a relatively stable democracy over the past 15 years.

Fujimori dissolved Peru's bicameral legislative system during his *autogolpe* in April 1992 and launched a new constitution with a single congress with 120 seats. Fujimori's new constitution allowed the president to run for two consecutive terms, a law that was changed after he resigned, and at present presidents cannot run for consecutive terms. The president appoints a council of ministers, with the prime minister at the head. Apart from the president, Peruvian voters also elect two vice presidents. Voting is compulsory between the ages of 18 and 70, and those who do not vote can be fined. Members of the military were not allowed to vote in the past, but now they can.

The weak point of Peru's democracy is its judicial branch, which is rife with corruption. Scandals involving judges who have been bribed to free prisoners or make a favorable ruling are commonplace. The country's top courts include a 16-member supreme court and a constitutional tribunal. Each of Peru's regions also has a superior court that serves as a court of appeals for the lower courts. There is a huge backlog of cases in the Peruvian court system, and temporary courts have been set up.

During the Fujimori government, terrorism suspects were tried in secret military courts in order to protect judges from reprisals. Under such a system, many were sent to jail after unfair trials. Under Toledo's government, some of these suspects received new trials in civilian courts.

ECONOMY

The investment-oriented reforms of the Fujimori years caused Peru to be one of the fastest-growing economies in the world between 1994 and 1997. Much of this growth was easy, however, because in many cases Peru's factories were simply returning to the level of production they had achieved before the chaotic 1980s.

Peru's stock market plummeted in early 1995 because of the "Tequila Effect" caused by Mexico's Zapatista revolution and the collapse of that country's economy. Peru's economy stagnated between 1998 and 2001 because of a variety of other factors, including the El Niño floods of 1998, global financial turmoil, and the collapse of the Fujimori government in 2001.

García maintained investment-friendly policies upon taking office in 2006, and Peru's economy continued to grow. Apart from stagnating in 2009 at the height of the world financial crisis, Peru averaged between 6 and 9 percent growth in GDP between 2005 and 2010. García continued to control the fiscal deficit and inflation fell to just 1 percent (although it rose to more than 4 percent in 2015). GDP per capita stood at US$6,500 in 2015.

Metals still dominate Peruvian exports, among them copper, gold, silver, zinc, lead, and iron. Investments have recently slowed as demand from China declines, hurting metal prices. While Peru's economy remains relatively strong compared to many other Latin American nations, growth in 2015 was slightly less than 3 percent, far lower than the 6 percent annual growth the country had become accustomed to. Fishing is the most important industry after mining. Other key industries include oil and natural gas. Manufacturing produces food, beverages, textiles, machinery, and furniture. Agricultural exports include coffee, cotton, fruit, and vegetables.

Today the Peruvian economy is diversifying, and over half the country's income now comes from services, including banking, retail, and a booming tourism industry. Tourism has grown more quickly than in any other South American country in the past decade, with up to 2.8 million tourists visiting the country each year. Over one million of these visited Machu Picchu in 2014. Hand-in-hand with tourism, Peruvian cookery is a relatively new entrant into world cuisine, and is doing great business worldwide. Lima is home to some of the best restaurants anywhere and is widely considered South America's culinary capital.

People and Culture

Peru's people are as diverse as the country's landscape. Prior to the Spanish conquest, it was only the Inca that united the Andean and coastal regions of Peru under their leadership, and only for a few decades. Before the Inca, Peru was covered by a patchwork of diverse cultures created by the country's extreme geography; coastal valleys were separated by long stretches of barren desert, and canyons and peaks in the Andes led to a high degree of cultural isolation. The jungle region remained impenetrable, with tribes living in isolation for centuries until Jesuit missionaries set up outposts in the 18th century. At least 65 different ethnic groups live in the Peruvian Amazon today.

Peru's cultural mix arguably began during the Inca empire, when the forced-labor scheme, *mita,* was used to move rebellious tribes to other parts of the empire where they would cause less trouble. The Spaniards continued *mita* and moved indigenous peoples long distances to work in different mines. Spanish men quickly took up with local women and a large mestizo population grew. African slaves were imported during the viceroyalty, and large numbers of Asian workers were brought to work in plantations and on the railroad lines from 1850 to 1920. There were also waves of Italian and Palestinian immigrants, and a pocket of German and Austrian colonists established themselves in the jungle at Oxapampa in the Chanchamayo area. As well as immigration from outside Peru, there has been substantial migration within the country from rural to urban areas, especially during the height of Shining Path terrorism in the 1980s. Lima has grown into one of South America's biggest cities, with a population of around eight million. Migration to the jungle region has also increased markedly in recent years, as people have sought to escape the poverty and harsher climate of the Andes, and Iquitos is the biggest city in the world that cannot be reached by road.

DEMOGRAPHICS

Peru's population today is around 29 million and growing at over 1 percent per year, so it will soon top the 30 million mark. Nearly half the people, or 45 percent, are indigenous, 37 percent are mestizo (a mix of white and indigenous), and 15 percent are of European descent. The remaining 3 percent of the population comprises those of African, Japanese, and Chinese descent and also includes some 250,000 Amazon natives divided into 65 ethnic groups. There remains a cultural and economic divide, passed down from colonial times, between the upper class of European descent and the middle and lower classes of mestizos and indigenous people. But Peru's racial dividing lines have, even since the colonial times, been based more on economics than skin color. Marriage certificates from the 18th century, for instance, reveal that affluent mestizos were automatically considered *criollos* because of their wealth. The indigenous people are divided, particularly between generations, between those who proudly hold

onto their heritage and those who adopt a Western form of dress. You will rarely hear Peruvians refer to themselves as mestizo, and note that the word *indio* is considered derogatory, so use either *indigeno* or Quechua.

Over 77 percent of the Peruvian population lives in urban areas, but outside Lima, cities are comparatively small (Arequipa is the country's second-biggest city with a population of 778,000). Peru is still a comparatively poor country but has made huge advances, both in the Fujimori years and during the economic boom of the past decade. Where once the poverty stood at 50 percent, it is now at 31 percent. The current minimum wage is 550 *soles* per month (just over US$200), and infant mortality is 21 per 1,000 births (compared to 6 per 1,000 in the United States). However, nearly 10 percent of the population survives on just US$1 per day, eking out a living in the informal economy.

LANGUAGE

Peru's official language is Spanish, although about four million people in Peru's highland population speak Quechua, the language of the Inca, also known as *runa simi*. Among Quechua speakers, there is a huge range of variations depending where they are located. These mini dialects have grown as a result of the isolating effects of Peru's extreme geography. In the Lake Titicaca area, there is a smaller group of Peruvians who speak Aymara, the language of an ethnic group that spreads into Bolivia. In the Amazon 11 percent of Peru's population is divided into 65 ethnic groups and about 14 linguistic families.

RELIGION

The Spanish conquest spread and, in many cases, enforced Catholicism on Peru, and its legacy is everywhere to be seen: magnificent cathedrals, churches, and a long-lasting, combative relationship. Over 80 percent of the current population consider themselves Catholic. Although that number is far from the actual number of practicing parishioners, it does indicate the connection Peruvians feel toward the religion, more by tradition than by real practice. Festivals like Lima's day of Santa Rosa mean a citywide holiday, and the day of San Blas invites horns and processions in Cusco.

Catholicism, though, is a relatively recent addition to Peru's long list of religions. Peru's first civilization began around 2000 BC, and it, along with the country's other major civilizations, was based on a set of unifying religious beliefs. These beliefs often incorporated nature worship. Deities like the sun, the ocean, the mountains, and mother earth appear in the imagery of several successive cultures. Representations of serpents, felines, and birds also make repeated appearances in pre-Hispanic religious iconography. Serpents symbolize the ground, felines the human life, and birds (often in the form of eagles or condors) the air or gods. The religion of the Chavín culture, which existed 4,000 years ago, incorporated that series of deities. Northern Peru's Moche culture did as well, but, unlike the Chavín, the Moche were clear to distinguish between the spiritual world and the everyday world. The Chimú worshipped the sun, moon, and ocean, and were clear to separate the secular and religious worlds. In its pottery, the southern Nasca culture depicted felines, orcas, anthropomorphized birds, and serpentine creatures. And the Inca gave offerings to the surrounding mountains, the bright sun, and fortifying Pachamama, the mother earth.

As cultures rose and fell, and even when the Spanish conquered the Inca empire, Peru's religions tended to adapt, fluctuate, and blend. The Inca were known for allowing their conquered cultures to continue their own religious practices as long as they also followed Inca religion. When the Spanish arrived and imposed Catholicism, the Inca quietly integrated their imagery. A grand Last Supper painting in Cusco's cathedral shows Jesus eating a guinea pig.

Nearly 500 years after the Spanish conquest, this fusion of religious beliefs continues to define Peru's spiritual and religious customs, and the subject is a draw for many tourists. In areas like Cusco and Lake Titicaca, the traditional mountain cultures continue to use shamans to bless their homes and purify their spirits. Many highlanders use shamans while also going to Catholic Mass, and see no apparent conflict of interest. In turn, travelers contract with shamans to perform offering or cleansing ceremonies. The Sacred Valley is known for its energy centers, and people come from around the world to meditate there. In the jungle, use of hallucinogenic ayahuasca is an essential part of sacred ceremonies.

While there are plenty of followers of ancient beliefs, Peru is also gaining followers of newer religions. Evangelical Christianity is gaining ground, as elsewhere in Latin America, and now practiced by more than 12 percent of the population. Jehovah's Witnesses, Mormons, and Adventist groups have started small but vigilant communities throughout the country. Above all, Peru is a profoundly religious country, and outright atheism is relatively rare and generally frowned upon.

FOOD

Peru not only provides wonderful sights, but wonderful tastes too, and Peruvian cuisine now rivals Mexican as the best in Latin America. Andean Peru gave the humble potato to the world—of which there are 4,000 varieties—and the saying goes "That's more Peruvian than potato." However, Peru also gave us corn, tomatoes, various types of chili peppers, and quinoa, a grain known as the "gold of the Inca" for its antioxidant properties. Before landing in South America, the Spanish had never tasted any of these foods, but they began spreading them with gusto to the Caribbean, Europe, and Asia.

The Spaniards in turn brought olive oil, lime, garlic, and Caribbean sugar to the table as well as better-quality meats in lamb, beef, and pork. Rice was perhaps the most important introduction to Peru. It seems strange to think that rice, the very epitome of Latin

Peru: Origin of the Name

Of South American countries, Peru's name is one of the more unusual. While neighboring country names have relatively obvious derivations—Ecuador from the Equator, Bolivia from Simón Bolívar, Colombia from Columbus—the origin of Peru is more complex.

One theory is that when the Spanish first arrived in South America and asked a native the name of the land he was standing on, he replied "Pelu," apparently an indigenous word for river.

Another suggestion stems from when the Spanish arrived in Panama. They asked the local tribesmen about the land to the south, and they replied that it was called the land of "Biru," after the tribal leader of that territory.

Perhaps the most interesting theory (and this author's preferred version) comes from Gavin Menzies in his book 1421. That theory contends that the word peru translates as "white mist" in Chinese and was used to describe the foggy coastline around Lima by Chinese sailors who visited before the Spanish in the 15th century.

Whichever theory is true, Peru was the name of the viceroyalty given by the Spanish crown to the territory after the conquest of the Inca.

American food, was brought by the Spanish from Asia, and that beans, equally thought of as typically Latin, were spread as a popular dish by African slaves, for whom it was their staple.

In the 19th and 20th centuries, the arrival of Italian, Chinese, and Japanese immigrants made Peruvian cuisine even more complex, giving rise in particular to *chifa*, a mixture of Cantonese and local *criollo* cooking.

Peru's coast is where the food is at its most mouthwatering, but many of the specialties can be found in the Cusco region, in particular the cold seafood soup ceviche (also sometimes spelt *cebiche*), probably Peru's greatest contribution to world cuisine. Chunks of raw fish are marinated in lime juice, spiced with *ají*, and served with sliced red onions, slices of sweet potato, and *choclo* (boiled maize kernels) or *cancha* (roasted maize kernels). Ceviche is also made with shrimp, which are cooked, and clams, which are not. In the Cusco area, ceviche is most commonly made with trout, which is equally delicious. Another great variation is *tiradito*, a fish carpaccio topped with an *ají* and *rocoto* sauce.

The most popular fish on the coast is *corvina* (white sea bass), followed by *dorado* and *lenguado* (sole). Fish is usually offered *frito* (fried), *apanada* (breaded and fried), *al vapor* (steamed), or *a la plancha* (filleted and baked, literally "on the board"). More interesting dishes include *sudado* (steamed), *a la chorillana* (basted with onion, tomato, and white wine), or *a lo macho* (fried seafood with yellow peppers or *ají amarillo*). *Camarones al ajillo* (shrimp in garlic sauce) is also popular. To spice things up, chili is often used in dishes such as *picante de marisco,* a spicy seafood soup. Other shellfish include *cangrejo* (crab), *calamar* (squid), *ostione* (oyster), *choros* (mussels), *conchas negras* (black scallops), and *langosta* (lobster or jumbo shrimp). *Patacones,* small pieces of plantain mashed flat and fried crispy, usually accompany seafood dishes and originally hail from Colombia. Salads accompanying seafood tend to come with a dressing made from lemon juice and salt. Coastal specialties are not confined to seafood. Goat *(cabra)* and duck *(pato)* plus standard meats are common in stews named *seco* or *estofado.*

Lima is where the widest range of cuisine is found. Specialties of the city include *causa limeña* (mashed potatoes with fish), *arroz verde* (rice with coriander), *tacu-tacu* (fried beans with rice), and *lomo saltado* (sautéed beef).

Peru's Andean cuisine stands out for a range of meats, *choclos,* high-altitude grains such as *kiwicha* and quinoa, and a huge variety of more than 200 edible tubers, including potatoes, freeze-dried *chuño* (actually dehydrated potatoes), and tubers like *olluco, oca,* and *camote* (sweet potato). Popular potato dishes include *papa a la huancaina* (potato in spicy cheese sauce) and *ocopa* (peanut sauce). Another popular dish is *ají de gallina,* of French-Peruvian origin. It's shredded chicken cooked in a spicy yellow sauce flavored with cheese, garlic, nuts, and chilis.

A highlight of mountain cooking is *pachamanca,* which means "earth oven" in Quechua and consists of a variety of meats, tubers, corn, beans, and native herbs roasted underground with red-hot rocks. Andean restaurants often serve *trucha,* which is fried mountain trout, and *cuy* (guinea pig), either roasted (in Cusco), stewed (in Huaraz), or fried (in Arequipa).

Soups and broths are widely consumed in the highlands at any time of the day but especially during the early morning. Lamb, beef, and hen, or certain parts of these animals, are all good for making a tasty broth. For the more adventurous, try *cabeza de cordero* (sheepshead broth). For vegetarians a good option is *sopa de quinoa,* made with potatoes and quinoa grains. Be sure to sample *choclo con queso,* which is an ear of steamed corn with a strip of Andean cheese. Gulp it all down with *chicha de jora,* corn beer that can be *fresco* (fresh) or fermented.

Peru's drinks are as famous as the food. Standing out of course is *pisco,* a grape brandy that is combined with lemon, sugar, and egg white to make the famous *pisco sour.* Another traditional drink is homemade *chicha,* which is rather bitter, while the nonalcoholic, purple *chicha morada* made from maize is sweet.

If you want something a little lighter, Peru has some good beers, the best of which is La Cusqueña. Choose between the red, which is a light lager, and the black, which is a sweeter, heavier dark beer.

Peru's numerous fruits make great juices *(jugos)* that can be mixed with milk or yogurt to make a shake *(batido).* It may surprise you to know that in the soda market, the local brand Inca Kola outsells Coca-Cola. This bright yellow drink tastes like something between bubble gum and cream soda. The most useful drink for travelers arriving at high altitudes is the *mate de coca,* made from the coca leaf and renowned for its calming properties. It is tasty and does wonders for altitude sickness. Just don't try to bring any leaves back with you, as customs will likely give you trouble, although sealed teabags are probably acceptable.

Peru is home to the potato, with over 4,000 different varieties.

MUSIC AND DANCE

If you manage to get through a trip to Peru without hearing a version of Simon & Garfunkel's 1970s hit "El Cóndor Pasa" then it will be a miracle. This tune is easily the most famous Peruvian Andean piece of music, played in elevators and hotel lobbies worldwide, but don't hold that against what is a stunningly beautiful song. It was originally composed by Daniel Alomía Robles in 1913 and is the best example of the pre-Columbian genre *huayno,* the most popular dance form in Andean music.

The *huayno* originated in Peru as a combination of traditional rural folk music and popular urban dance music, developing through the colonial period. Andean music sounds different from Western music in part because it relies mainly on the pentatonic scale instead of the diatonic scale. High-pitched vocals are usually accompanied by instruments, including the *quena* (Andean flute), *zampoña* (pan-pipe), *charango* (a small mandolin made from an armadillo shell), *tarka* (a squared flute that produces an eerie sound), and *antara* (single-row panpipe). There is also a huge range of rattles, bells, and drums, such as the *tambor* and *bombo,* which are made from stretched animal skins. Most of these instruments, as excavations prove, have been used at least 5,000 years. In the last five centuries Peru's highlanders have incorporated a range of wind and brass instruments, including clarinets, saxophones, trumpets, euphoniums, and tubas. But the most important European contributions were stringed instruments like the violin, the guitar, and the harp, which was transformed into the Andean harp. This instrument looks like a Western harp with 36 strings but has a half-conical, boat-like base that gives it a rich, deep sound.

In the last few decades *huayno* has turned electronic using synthesizers and electric guitars, which makes it far less endearing to listeners craving a flavor of tradition. The dance form utilizes a distinctive rhythm in which the first beat is stressed, followed by two short beats. The *huayno* is pop music for an audience of millions of listeners across the Andes. Despite constant evolution, its themes remain the pain of love lost and being far from home, reflecting the sufferings of indigenous people from colonial times to the present day.

Fusion of Peruvian music genres has grown apace. In the late 1960s and 1970s, the traditional *huayno* fused with the tropical *cumbia.* As a result, *chicha* was born, the iconic music of highland immigrants living in Lima, having in Chacalón y la Nueva Crema the maximum exponent of this genre. Around the same period of time, hundreds of rock-based bands in the jungle were turning to *cumbia,* either *tropical* or *psicodélica.* Legendary bands such as Juaneco y su Combo and Los Mirlos have been revived in U.S. and European compilations and through local bands in Lima, such as Bareto.

HANDICRAFTS

From the Pisac market in the Sacred Valley to Lima's Miraflores district and the coastal town of Paracas, the depth and variety of handicrafts in Peru is extraordinary. Weavings, knittings, pottery, jewelry, carved gourds—each piece is modern but carries with it a tradition that has existed for centuries.

World-renowned for its textiles, Peru's **weaving** tradition is over 4,000 years old. Using the wool of alpacas, llamas, and the precious vicuñas, the pre-Columbian cultures wove their stories into textiles. Abstract figures, deities, and colors described the lifestyles of these people, who had no written language. In turn, the quality of the textile and the wool reflected one's social status and power. When the Spanish arrived, they introduced sheep's wool and silk into the custom. Now, contemporary weavers have the advantages of machine-spun yarn and even woven fabrics. While those are undeniably used, there are still plenty of traditional weavers who continue to use natural dyes, drop spindles, and handmade looms.

The weaving culture exists primarily in the mountainous regions of Cusco, Huancayo, and around Lake Titicaca. In these areas, women walk through the streets, toting a basket of wool that they are aptly dropping and spinning into yarn. Guided by memory and years of experience, women then dip the wool into dyes and then thread it into a weaving. The start-to-finish process can take anywhere from a month to several months and, consequently, the minimum going price for a cloth is about US$100.

Knitting is another important aspect of Peru's textile tradition. *Chullos* (hats), *mangas* (arm warmers), *polainas* (leggings), *medias* (socks), and *monederos* (change purses) are all typical products of the Quechua and Aymara cultures. As with weaving, the most prominent knitting cultures live in Lake Titicaca's Isla Taquile, Cusco, and Huancavelica. Although customs change between communities, knitting responsibilities are typically divided between men and women. Women spin the yarn and men knit it into clothing, most often hats.

Ceramics have also played an important historical role. Cultures as ancient as the Chavín left behind ceramic remains, and even later cultures like the Moche, Nasca, and Chimú were renowned for their craftsmanship and unique styles. The **Moche** perfected the skill of capturing human features and emotion; the **Chimú** pottery is recognized for its black surface; and **Nasca** ceramics are particularly prized because of their intricate paintings. When the Spanish arrived, they introduced a European form of pottery, which has been particularly influential in the designs of Urubamba-based ceramicist Pablo Seminario. Ceramics are best seen in the areas of Piura, Cusco, and Ayacucho.

Other important handicrafts, like *mates burilados* (carved gourds), jewelry, and even instruments, are best seen in the mountain areas. Again, Cusco, Ayacucho, and Huancayo make excellent bases to begin your exploring. Note that in the tourist markets such as in Pisac and Miraflores, you are likely to find lower-quality, mass-produced wares. If you are in search of the finest quality, look beyond the markets to artisans' workshops, where they will be happy to create custom works, but be prepared to pay more.

LITERATURE

Like the Greeks, the ancient Peruvians had a rich tradition of oral **poetry,** as there were no known writing systems at the time. It consisted of two main poetic forms: *harawis,* a form of lyrical poetry, and *hayllis,* a form of epic poetry. Both forms described the daily

Carved gourds are traditional artisan work in the Peruvian Andes.

life and rituals of the time and were recited by a poet known as the *harawec.*

A variety of 16th-century Spanish chroniclers, most notably **Bernabé Cobo** and **Pedro Cieza de León,** attempted to describe the exotic conditions of the New World through the confining looking glass of the Spanish worldview and lexicon. An entirely different perspective was presented by indigenous writer **Felipe Guamán Poma de Ayala,** whose decision to write the king of Spain, Philip III, blossomed into a 1,179-page letter titled *Nueva Crónica y Buen Gobierno.* The letter was written between 1613 and 1615 but only discovered in the Royal Library of Copenhagen in 1908. Apart from a detailed view of Inca customs, what is most fascinating about this work is the blend of Spanish and Quechua juxtaposed with a series of 400 ink drawings that portray the bloodiest moments of the Spanish conquest, as well as Inca festivities and traditions.

Inca Garcilaso de la Vega (1539-1616) was educated in Cusco as the son of a Spanish conquistador and an Inca princess. He emigrated as a young man to Spain, where he spent the rest of his life writing histories and chronicles of his Inca homeland. His major work, *Comentarios Reales,* written in 1609, is a highly anecdotal and personal view of the Inca empire. Throughout the text Garcilaso employs a variety of rhetorical strategies to ennoble the Inca aristocracy—and in the process, himself—in the eyes of the royal Spanish court. It is the first example of a *mestizo* author from the New World grappling with the complexities of a torn identity.

During the viceroyalty, **theaters** in Lima and Cusco were at the center of the social life of the Peruvian aristocracy. Most of the productions were imported and written by Spain's Golden Age authors, who had no problem being approved by Peru's Catholic censors. Local playwrights were occasionally approved, and their works, though innocuous on the surface, often contain subtle critiques of the viceroyalty's racial and political power structure. Scathing **poetic satire** was

circulated secretly throughout upper-class Peruvian society and reflected the growing tensions as Peru's creole elite strained against the straitjacket of Spanish rule.

Following the 1821 independence, literary Romanticism took root in Peru, evolving in an entirely different direction from its European counterpart. Instead of a preoccupation with personal identity and freedom, Peru's Romantic writers fell into the task of nation-building and describing what it meant to be Peruvian. Some renowned authors of the period were **Carlos Augusto Salaverry** and **José Arnaldo Márquez.** At the same time, *Costumbrismo* developed as a literary or pictorial interpretation of local everyday life, mannerisms, and customs. Peru's best-known writer of this style is **Ricardo Palma** (1833-1919), whose most famous work is a descriptive collection of legends and personality sketches known as *Tradiciones peruanas.* Palma was a man of letters, a former liberal politician, and later the director of the National Library of Peru; he rebuilt the collection after it was sacked by the Chilean army during the War of the Pacific.

Peru's best-known female writer is **Clorinda Matto de Turner** (1852-1909), born in Cusco, who wrote both in Quechua and Spanish. She edited a series of acclaimed literary journals, including *Peru Ilustrado,* and wrote a trilogy of novels, the best known of which is *Aves sin nido (Torn from the Nest),* translated into English in 1904 and republished recently by Oxford Press and the University of Texas Press. Matto de Turner was forced into exile in Argentina after being excommunicated by the Catholic church and having her house burnt down. She died in 1909 and was forgotten for decades, though she is slowly gathering critical acclaim and recognition as one of the pioneers of Latin American feminism.

César Vallejo (1892-1938), poet, writer, and journalist, is considered one of the great poetic innovators of the 20th century. His main works include *Los Heraldos Negros* (1918), the revolutionary *Trilce* (1922), and

Poemas Humanos (published posthumously in 1939). Always a step ahead of the literary currents, each of Vallejo's books was distinct from the others and, in its own sense, revolutionary. Born in Santiago de Chuco in Peru's northern highlands, he moved to Paris in the 1920s, where he spent the rest of his life immersed in the vanguard movement and the rise of international communism. His complete poetry has been published in English by the University of California Press.

The growing industrialization of Peru in the 20th century and the continued oppression of the indigenous population gave birth to a new genre of socially conscious literature known as *indigenismo*. José María Arguedas (1911-1969) was born to a white family but was raised by a Quechuan-speaking family in Andahuaylas, in Peru's southern Andes. He ended up in Lima, where he was educated at the prestigious University of San Marcos. His works of social realism portray the oppression of indigenous communities and helped inspire the liberation theologies that continue to cause conflict in Peru's Catholic church. Two of his most famous novels, *Yawar Fiesta* and *Los Ríos Profundos* (Deep Rivers), are in English and have been published by the University of Texas Press.

Ciro Alegría (1909-1967) was a mestizo born in the Marañón Valley of northern Peru whose lyrical novels, like those of Arguedas, portray the suffering of Peru's Andean peoples. His best-known works are *La Serpiente de Oro (The Golden Serpent)* and *El Mundo Es Ancho y Ajeno (Broad and Alien Is the World)*, which became widely known outside Peru in the mid-20th century and were translated into several languages.

Mario Vargas Llosa (born 1936) is one of Latin America's most significant novelists and essayists, and one of the leading authors of his generation. Some critics consider him to have had a larger international impact and worldwide audience than any other writer of the "Latin American Boom" of the 1960s. Latin America's boom writers dropped the regionalist, folkloric themes of their predecessors and experimented wildly with form and content. Nearly all of Vargos Llosa's novels, including his world-acclaimed *Conversación en la Catedral (Conversation in the Cathedral)*, *La guerra del fin del mundo (The War of the End of the World)*, and *La fiesta del chivo (The Feast of the Goat)*, have been translated into English and make an excellent introduction for those wishing to explore Peruvian literature. Once a supporter of Castro and communism during his youth, Vargas Llosa led a middle- and upper-class revolt against President Alan García Pérez in the late 1980s and then ran for president in 1990. After being defeated by Alberto Fujimori, Vargas Llosa went to Spain. Nowadays he lives for part of the year back in Lima's Barranco neighborhood and is actively involved in Peruvian politics and social issues. A prolific writer and columnist in newspapers around the world, Vargas Llosa is a die-hard defender of neoliberalism and unquestionably a seeker of freedom through his writing.

Alfredo Bryce Echenique (born 1939) is Peru's other best-known novelist. He has produced a dozen novels and numerous collections of short stories. After spending much of his life in Europe, he now resides in Peru.

Several middle-aged and young Peruvians are making waves on the international literary scene. Alonso Cueto and Santiago Roncagliolo both won international prizes for their 2006 novels, *The Blue Hour* and *Red April,* respectively. The works deal with Peru's history of terrorism and war. More recently, Daniel Alarcón (born 1977), a promising Peruvian-born writer raised in the United States, has published *War by Candlelight* and *Lost City Radio,* his debut novel. For Spanish speakers, Alarcón has a worthwhile podcast with excellent journalism called Radio Ambulante (www.radio-ambulante.org).

SPORTS

Peruvians go wild about *fútbol,* or soccer, which is the main social activity in small towns across Peru. Matches, such as a *clásico* between Alianza Lima and Universitario de Deportes ("La U"), fill stadiums throughout the year in major cities across Peru. The country will often come to a standstill during key matches at both club and national levels. However, the national team has had a hard time of late and has fallen far since its golden era in the 1970s, when it performed well in several World Cups. Peru has not qualified for the World Cup since 1982, a sore point considering the recent success of other South American nations, including neighboring Ecuador. However, on a club level there have been some successes. Cienciano, an underfunded team from Cusco, made world news when it defeated huge, internationally acclaimed teams such as River Plate in Argentina and Santos of Brazil—Pele's old team. In December 2003 Cienciano became the first Peruvian team ever to win the coveted Copa Sudamericana.

Essentials

Getting There

The most common way to arrive to Peru is by plane, and all international flights arrive in Peru's capital, Lima. Because of flight patterns, most visitors either spend a night in Lima upon arrival or spend a day in Lima upon departure, or both. Flights from most U.S. destinations arrive at night, and you need to wait until the following morning to connect to Cusco. The exception is flights from Los Angeles, which arrive in the morning. If you are flying from other South American cities, many of these flights also arrive in the morning, so connections to Cusco are easier.

AIR

Because Peru lies in the same time zone as the East Coast of the United States and Canada, North American travelers feel no jet lag after arriving in Peru. Depending on where you are flying from in North America, the flight can be anywhere from 6 to 10 hours. The cheapest tickets to Lima in high season start around US$600-700 from Miami through American, but US$650-750 is more common.

Most Europeans find it cheaper to travel to Peru via flights with stopovers in the United States or the Caribbean, though there are direct flights from Madrid and Amsterdam. The cheapest flights from major European cities start around US$1,000. Travelers from Asia, Africa, New Zealand, and Australia will also need to make at least one layover en route to Lima.

The most expensive times to fly to Peru are the Christmas vacations and the high tourist months from June to August. Prices begin to drop around May and September and are at their lowest during the shoulder seasons from October to December and January to April.

Demand for flights to Cusco is so high that the government has recently approved construction of a separate **Cusco-Chinchero airport** at the small town of Chinchero northwest of Cusco. The airport, at a cost of more than $460 million, will provide easier access to the Sacred Valley and Machu Picchu. It will accommodate larger aircraft than the small airport in Cusco and will also be an international airport, enabling tourists to bypass Lima completely. This is good for tourists, but not so good for Lima's tourism industry. There is considerable opposition to the project among environmentalists, who argue that the huge volume of tourism traffic is already having a detrimental effect on the region. The airport is in its early planning stages and is not expected to open before 2019.

Lima Airport

All overseas flights from Europe and North America arrive in Lima at **Aeropuerto Internacional Jorge Chávez** (Jorge Chávez International Airport, tel. 01/517-3500 24-hour flight info, www.lap.com.pe). From here flights continue on to Cusco and other cities. Most planes from North America arrive at night, and flights to Cusco begin from about 5am onward. Some travelers wait in the airport for connecting flights, while the majority head to Miraflores, San Isidro, Barranco, or even Lima's historic center, where there is a good selection of hotels.

If you'd rather stay in the airport area overnight, the **Costa del Sol-Ramada** (Av. Elmer Faucett s/n, Aeropuerto Internacional Jorge Chávez, tel. 01/711-2000, www.costadelsol-peru.com, US$275 s/d with buffet breakfast included) has a good restaurant and sushi bar and plenty of facilities. The hotel is actually within the airport compound.

On the return, most flights from Cusco arrive here midday and leave for the United States at night—meaning many visitors have at least a half day in Lima. Some stay in the airport, while others make a whistle-stop tour of Lima's historic center (taxi US$15-20 one-way, 45 minutes to 1 hour).

Jorge Chávez has come a long way and is a modern airport with a range of services, including banks, money exchange booths, ATMs, a post office, stores, a café, two food courts, duty-free shops, and a rent-a-cell service. There is the **Sumaq VIP Lounge** for international arrivals. If you want to store your luggage, go to **Left Luggage** (tel. 01/517-3217, at the side of Domestic Arrivals, US$1.50 per piece of luggage per hour, or US$9 per piece of luggage per 24 hours). If you need Wi-Fi, try the Starbucks on the second floor. There is Wi-Fi after you go through security at a cost of about $10 for two hours.

Pushy taxi drivers will be waiting for you outside the airport. The best thing to do is contract a taxi through **Taxi Green** (tel. 01/484-4001), a private company that has stands just outside luggage claim. Have your destination address written down. Taxi prices from the airport to the center should be around US$15, to Miraflores about US$18. You may be able to get a cheaper taxi if you negotiate with a driver in the airport parking lot, but be sure to know where you are going, and always ask for identification. Hard-core budget travelers will walk outside the gate of the airport and save a few dollars by taking a taxi, *combi,* or *colectivo* on the street. Be very careful with your luggage if you do this!

There is a US$9 tax on all domestic flights leaving Lima and a US$31 tax on all departing international flights, but these are usually included in the price of your ticket. On your way home, arrive at the airport 2-3 hours in advance for international flights and 1-2 hours for domestic flights.

Aeropuerto Internacional Alejandro Velasco Astete in Cusco has flights arriving from Santa Cruz and La Paz, Bolivia, with **Aerosur** (www.aerosur.com). **Aeropuerto Internacional Rodríguez Ballón** in Arequipa has flights from Arica, Chile, with **Sky Airline** (www.skyairline.cl).

Cheap Fares

The best way to get a cheap fare to Peru is to travel outside the high season months of June through August. Within Peru's three-month high season, it will be difficult to find a discount fare to Peru and onward to Cusco and other main destinations.

The easiest way to start a search for airfare is to use an airfare price comparison website like **Kayak** (www.kayak.com), which compiles the best prices from hundreds of sources, including online travel engines like Travelocity, Expedia, CheapTickets, and Orbitz. Other options include **Mobissimo** (www.mobissimo.com) and **BookingBuddy** (www.bookingbuddy.com).

Students and teachers can buy discounted airfare from **STA Travel** (www.sta.com). This web page links to STA representatives in nearly 75 countries and has a search engine for cheap fares. Students under 26 can purchase a US$25 student ISIC card that entitles them to trip insurance, student airfares, and a range of discounts for everything from bus fare to museum admission. Student discounts are very common in Peru—get this card if at all possible.

From North America

Direct flights from Miami are available, on a daily basis, through **LAN** (www.lan.com) and **American Airlines** (www.aa.com). **United Airlines** (www.unitedairlines.com) has regular flights from New York, Newark, and Houston. Airlines with flights from Miami with one layover to Lima include **Avianca** (www.avianca.com), with a stop in Bogotá, Colombia; and **Copa** (www.copaair.com), with a stop in Panama City, Panama.

From Fort Lauderdale direct flights are available on **Spirit Airlines** (www.spiritair. com), from Los Angeles and New York on LAN, from Dallas-Fort Worth on American, and from Atlanta through **Delta** (www.delta.com).

From Toronto, **Air Canada** (www.aircanada.com) offers direct flights to Lima.

Recommended U.S. agencies that deal with a number of consolidators include **World Class Travel** (U.S. tel. 800/771-3100, www.peruperu.com), **eXito Latin American Travel Specialists** (U.S. tel. 800/665-4053, www.exitotravel.com), and **Big Sky Travel** (U.S. tel. 800/284-9809, www.bigsky-travel.com).

From Mexico, Central America, and the Caribbean

Direct flights from Mexico City are available through **Aeromexico** (www.aeromexico.com). Taca, Copa, Avianca, and other airlines operate a range of direct and layover Lima flights from Cancún, Mexico; Santo Domingo, Dominican Republic; La Havana, Cuba; Panama City, Panama; San José, Costa Rica; and San Salvador, El Salvador.

From Europe

Direct flights to Lima from Europe are from Amsterdam through **KLM** (www.klm.com), from Paris through **Air France** (www.airfrance.com), and from Madrid though LAN, **Iberia** (www.iberia.com), and **Air Europa** (www.aireuropa.com). Carriers that make one stopover in the United States en route to Lima also include LAN, American, Delta, and United.

In the United Kingdom, good consolidators include **North-South Travel** (U.K. tel. 0124/560-8291, www.northsouthtravel.co.uk), which gives part of its proceeds to an international development trust it has set up. Others include **Travel Bag** (U.K. tel. 0800/804-8911, www.travelbag.co.uk) and **Quest Travel** (U.K. tel. 0871/423-0135, www.questtravel.com). **Flight Centre International** (U.K. tel. 0870/499-0040, www.flightcentre.co.uk) is good for tickets between the United Kingdom and the United States only. A leading South America specialist in the United Kingdom is **Journey Latin America** (U.K. tel. 020/3432-9264, www.journeylatinamerica.co.uk).

From France, good consolidators include **Last Minute** (France tel. 0899/78-5000, www.fr.lastminute.com), **Nouvelles Frontiéres** (France tel. 0825/00-0747, www.nouvelles-frontieres.fr), and **Voyageurs de Monde** (France tel. 0892/23-5656, www.vdm.com).

From Germany, a good option is **Last Minute** (Germany tel. 01805/77-7257, www.de.lastminute.com) or **Just Travel** (Germany tel. 089/747-3330, www.justtravel.de). In the Netherlands, try **Airfair** (Netherlands tel. 0900/771-7717, www.airfair.nl). In Spain, there is **Barcelo Viajes** (Spain tel. 902/116-226, www.barceloviajes.com).

From Asia, Africa, and the Pacific

From Asia there are no direct flights at this time to Lima. All flights from Hong Kong, Tokyo, and other Asian cities go via the United States. Good Asian consolidators include **Japan's No 1 Travel** (Japan tel. 03/3200-8977, www.no1-travel.com), Hong Kong's **Four Seas Tours** (Hong Kong tel. 2200-7777, www.fourseastravel.com), and India's **STIC Travels** (India tel. 79/2642-3518, www.stictravel.com).

From New Zealand and Australia, flights usually have stopovers in Los Angeles or Miami, or in Santiago or Buenos Aires, before heading to Lima. A good agency for flights to the United States is **Flight Centre International** (Australia tel. 133-133, www.flightcentre.com.au).

From Africa, travelers to Lima head to Europe first, though **South African Airways** (South Africa tel. 0861/359-722, www.fly-saa.com) has a flight from Johannesburg to São Paolo, Brazil. A good African agency is **Rennies Travel** (South Africa tel. 0861/100-155, www.renniestravel.com).

Within South America

More than a dozen South American cities have daily flights through **LAN** and **Avianca** to and from Lima, the regional hub for both airlines. LAN and Avianca fly from/to Guayaquil and Quito in Ecuador; Bogotá,

Cali, and Medellín in Colombia; Caracas in Venezuela; La Paz and Santa Cruz in Bolivia; Montevideo in Uruguay; Santiago in Chile; Buenos Aires in Argentina; and São Paulo and Rio de Janeiro in Brazil. **Aerolineas Argentinas** (www.aerolineas.com) flies from Buenos Aires. **Sky Airline** (www.skyairline.cl) flies from Santiago to Lima.

BUS

It is possible to reach Peru by international bus service from the surrounding countries of Paraguay, Uruguay, Ecuador, Bolivia, Chile, Brazil, and Argentina. The major buses that run these routes can be quite comfortable, with reclining seats, movies, and meals. The longest international bus trips leave from Lima. Some major neighboring cities from which buses travel to Lima are: Guayaquil in Ecuador, Santa Cruz in Bolivia, Asunción in Paraguay, Córdoba and Buenos Aires in Argentina, Montevideo in Uruguay, São Paulo and Rio de Janeiro in Brazil, and Santiago in Chile. Buses leave frequently from/to La Paz, Bolivia, for the five-hour direct journey to/from Puno and on to Cusco. The main international bus companies are **Cruz del Sur** (Lima tel. 01/311-5050, www.cruzdelsur.com.pe), **Ormeño** (Lima tel. 01/472-1710, www.grupo-ormeno.com.pe), **Caracol** (tel. 01/431-1400, www.perucaracol.com), and **El Rápido** (Lima tel. 01/425-1066, www.elrapidoint.com.ar).

Getting Around

Peru's diverse landscape includes long stretches of desert, high Andean passes, and endless tracts of swampy jungle. Not surprisingly, Peru can be a complicated country to navigate. Nearly all of Peru's major jungle destinations require a flight unless you want to try a cargo boat or endure one, two, or even three days riding in a bumpy bus. Train service is limited, except in the Cusco area, and generally restricted to comparatively expensive tourist services, but new highways have made traveling by bus much faster and more comfortable than it was a decade ago.

AIR

If you are on a tight schedule and want to see a range of places, flying is the best way to go. In Peru, a round-trip fare can be less expensive than one-way, but that depends on the season and the airline. The best way to buy tickets or reconfirm them is through the airline's local office or website, where you can buy tickets online for almost all domestic flights. Finding tickets around Christmas, Easter, and the national holiday of Fiestas Patrias in the last weekend of July is expensive and difficult.

The major Peru airlines are **LAN** (www.lan.com), **Star Perú** (www.starperu.com), **Peruvian Airlines** (www.peruvianairlines.pe), and **LC Peru** (www.lcperu.pe). Of these, LAN tends to be the most expensive and the others slightly cheaper. Keep your eyes out for regular promotions. Last-minute flights tend to be more expensive.

BUS

Because most Peruvians travel by bus, the country has an incredible network of frequent, high-quality buses—much better, in fact, than in the United States or Europe. You will be safer if you avoid the dirt-cheap bus companies that pick up passengers along the way. Some of these buses have been adapted (stretched) to the point where they are structurally unsound.

Bus companies in Peru have a confusing variety of labels for their deluxe services, which include Imperial, Royal Class, Cruzero, Ejecutivo, Especial, and Dorado. The absolute best services, comparable to traveling business class on an airplane, are Cruz del Sur's Cruzero or Cruzero Suite class and Movil's better service 180° Bus-Cama class, which unfortunately only serves Huaraz. Deluxe bus service means nonstop (only for driver shifts), more legroom, reclining seats, onboard food and beverage service, videos, safer drivers, and clean bathrooms.

Reputable bus companies in Lima are **Cruz del Sur** (tel. 01/311-5050, www.cruzdelsur.com.pe), **Ormeño** (tel. 01/472-1710, www.grupo-ormeno.com.pe), **Movil Tours** (tel. 01/332-9000, www.moviltours.com.pe), and **Oltursa** (tel. 01/225-4499, www.oltursa.com.pe).

Bus travel is easier in cities like Arequipa, Puno, and Cusco, where all the bus companies are consolidated in a main bus station, which is usually known as the *terminal terrestre*. Travelers can arrive there, shop around, and usually be on a bus in an hour or two. In other cities, such as Lima, each bus company has its own bus terminal, some even with VIP lounges, and travelers can save time by buying a ticket through an agency or at a Wong or Metro supermarket through **Teleticket.**

Luggage theft can still be a problem for bus travelers, especially for those who travel on the cheap bus lines. Always keep your hand on your luggage at a bus station, and do not underestimate how skilled some thieves are. Once on the bus, the luggage that is checked underneath is usually safe because passengers can only retrieve bags with a ticket. The big problem is carry-on luggage. Place it on a rack where you can see it, but never do this if it contains valuables. Some people bring oversized locks to chain their luggage to a rack, but thieves will just razor through your bag and take what they want. The most important thing is to keep your valuables where you can see them, ideally about your person but out of sight. If you have an expensive camera, sleeping on the bus is just asking for trouble. There is something to be said for avoiding night buses completely, as they are the riskiest.

Assaults on night buses are also still a problem in Peru, especially on less expensive buses. Highway bandits either hold the bus up by force or sometimes board as normal passengers and hijack it en route. Passengers are not hurt, but are shaken down for their money and passports. Though some companies use a camcorder to film all passengers getting on board, no company can eliminate the risk entirely. Accidents are another risk of traveling at night, especially on mountain roads. If possible, travel during the day.

TRAIN

The decade-long monopoly enjoyed by Belmond-owned **PeruRail** (www.perurail.com) has finally broken up. The newest entrant into the market to provide train service from Cusco to Machu Picchu is **Inca Rail** (www.incarail.com). PeruRail also operates trains from Cusco to Puno.

During high season, it is best to reserve tickets online ahead of time to travel to Machu Picchu. Buying tickets once you arrive in Cusco is a hassle, but many of Cusco's nicer hotels will purchase them for their guests.

COMBI **AND** *COLECTIVO*

The cheapest way to move around a major city like Lima, Cusco, Iquitos, Trujillo, Arequipa, or Chiclayo is by public transportation. There are buses, *combis* (imported Asian vans that dart along the roads), and *colectivos* (station wagons with room for five passengers). The buses are cheap but slow, while *combis* are a bit faster but tend to be cramped, and *colectivos* are the fastest of all.

Bus fares usually hover around US$0.40-0.60; *colectivos* are about twice that, but fares go up on weekends and evenings. You can tell where buses and *combis* are going by the sticker on the front windshield, *not* by what is painted on the side. Before you take public transportation, ask a local for specific directions to where you are going. It can be a fun, inexpensive way to travel around. To get off a bus or *colectivo* simply say *"baja"* ("getting off") or *"esquina"* ("at the corner"). Fares are collected during the ride or right before you get off, by the *cobrador* or the person who also shouts out the route or destination the bus or *combi* is leading to, practically hanging out the bus door. *Combis* and *colectivos* are a particularly convenient way to shuttle between the towns in the Sacred Valley.

TAXI

The fastest (but not overly expensive) way to get around Peru's cities is via taxi or *motocar,* the three-wheeled canopied bikes that buzz around cities and towns, including Pisac and Ollantaytambo (although you won't find them in Cusco or Lima). The typical fare for in-city travel is US$0.40-1 for a *motocar* and US$2-5 for a taxi.

Assaults on taxi passengers can be a problem in Cusco, Lima, and Peru's other tourist hot spots. The best way to avoid this is to have your hostel call for a taxi or to flag down only registered taxis on the street. Avoid young, suspicious-looking drivers and beat-up cars with tinted windows and broken door handles. If you must flag down a cab on the street, then never take an unmarked cab and always look for the driver ID on the dashboard before entering. When traveling, sit on the backseat diagonally opposite the driver.

Bargaining is an essential skill for anyone taking a taxi, because taxis in Peru do not use meters. Find out from your hotel or restaurant approximately what the fare should be and stand somewhere where your taxi driver can pull over without holding up traffic. Always negotiate the fare before getting in the car. A typical bargaining conversation would start with you asking *"¿Cuánto cuesta a Barranco?"* (or wherever you're going); the taxi driver replies, *"Ocho soles."* You bargain with, *"No, seis pues,"* and so on. You get the picture. If you can't get the fare you want, wave the driver on and wait for the next taxi. Have in mind that rates can rise during rush hours and the evenings.

Private drivers can also be hired for the hour or day, or for a long-distance trip. The fee can often start at US$7 per hour and go up to US$60-70 for all day. Ask at your hotel for recommended drivers.

RENTING A CAR OR MOTORCYCLE

Renting a car does not usually make sense cost-wise in Peru because taking taxis or hiring a private car can be cheaper. Also, gas is expensive (about US$5-6 per gallon, depending on the grade), and distances between cities are considerable. Your best bet is to get to your destination and then rent a car to get around.

The phone book of any major Peruvian city is filled with rental car options, which are usually around US$70 per day once you

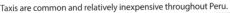

Taxis are common and relatively inexpensive throughout Peru.

factor in extra mileage, insurance, and other hidden costs. Four-wheel-drive cars are usually US$100-120 per day. Major rental companies include **Hertz** (www.inkasrac.com), **Avis** (www.avisperu.com), and **Budget** (www.budgetperu.com). All these companies have offices in Aeropuerto Internacional Jorge Chávez, Lima, Arequipa, and Cusco. Smaller companies operate in many other cities. To rent a car, drivers usually need to be at least 18 years of age, have a driver's license from their country, and have a credit card.

BIKE

Biking is a great way to explore Peru's back roads and get to know local people along the way. Many of Peru's adventure agencies, especially those that offer rafting trips, rent **mountain bikes** starting at US$15-20 per day, though quality varies tremendously and the bikes are generally meant for local use only. Adventure agencies in Lima, Arequipa, Huaraz, Cusco, and Puno offer multiday bike expeditions with tents, a support vehicle, and a cook. These trips follow fabulous single-track routes up and over the mountains, with mind-boggling descents on the other side.

Dozens of cyclists pass through Peru each year as part of their epic Alaska-Patagonia pilgrimage. Those who want to start their tour from Peru will have to box their bike up and fly it with them, as good bicycles are extremely expensive in Peru. Some airlines provide a box in which your bike will fit once you take the handlebars off. If your bike is or looks new, smear mud on it so you can get through customs without having to pay duty taxes. Most people use mountain bikes to travel on dirt roads, often with slicks for road and highway travel.

When planning your route, keep in mind that the Pan-American Highway (Carretera Panamericana) is a dangerous bike route because buses pass at high speeds and the shoulder is cluttered with debris. The same applies for major routes into the mountains, including the Cañon de Pato near Huaraz. The best trips are on remote back roads, which are invariably spectacular and much safer. Keep in mind altitude, weather extremes, drinking water, and the complete lack of repair parts outside of major cities.

A good source of information is the Adventure Cycling Association in the United States (www.adventurecycling.org). One of Peru's best-known bikers, **Omar Zarzar Casis** (www.aventurarse.com), has written a book in Spanish, called *Por los Camino de Perú en Bicicleta,* describing 10 of Peru's most beautiful mountain-bike circuits. It is available in many Peruvian bookstores.

HITCHHIKING

People in Peru are not afraid to flag down whatever transport happens to pass by, and drivers usually charge them a bit of money for gas. Instead of sticking a thumb up, Peruvians in the countryside swish a handkerchief up and down in front of them to attract drivers' attention. Hitchhiking is fairly safe on country roads where there are no other options. When near cities or large highways, though, always take buses. If you hitchhike, always do it with a companion, and make sure your driver is sober before getting in. Women traveling without male companions should avoid hitchhiking completely.

TOURS

Organized tour groups are a good idea for travelers wary of traveling on their own or who long for a hassle-free, action-packed tour. Excellent (though often expensive) agencies operate in Peru and offer anything from general tours with a bit of soft adventure to well-tailored adventures for trekkers, climbers, bird-watchers, or spiritual seekers.

With the right company, tours can be safe and enlightening, and a great way to make new friends. Common complaints include a lack of flexibility on meals and lodging options, a go-go schedule that allows no time for relaxation, and a large up-front payment.

Before booking, read the fine print and ask a lot of questions. Find out what hotels you are staying in and then check them with this guide and on online forums. Look for hidden expenses such as airport transfers, meals, and single rooms if you are traveling alone. Find out who your guide will be and what his or her experience and language skills are. Ask about the size of the group, the average age of the other passengers, and the cancellation policy. Get everything in writing and add up the costs of doing the trip independently using this guide. Peru is a relatively inexpensive place to travel in, and you may be able to do it cheaper on your own. Remember that tour companies exist to make a profit, so you always pay extra for the service and convenience.

Day-Tour Operators
Because of all the public transport in Peru, independent travelers can usually find their way even to the country's most remote sites, if they don't mind waiting around for an hour or two, walking, and sometimes hitchhiking.

No one likes to be in a large group of tourists, but taking a day tour is the fastest, easiest, and sometimes cheapest way to see a given area's sights, like taking a group taxi. In most cities, tour agencies are clustered together on the main square or along a principal street. Before paying, confirm how good your guide's English is and get tour details confirmed in writing, including sites visited, how many people maximum will be in the group, and whether the cost includes lunch and admission fees. If your guide does a good job, give him or her a reasonable tip (US$10-25 for a day tour).

Package Tours
Package tours typically include airfare, hotels, and some meals—but you choose what to do and where to eat. Many Peru-bound airlines offer package tours, including **American Airlines Vacations** (tel. 800/321-2121, www.aavacations.com), **Delta Vacations** (tel. 800/654-6559, www.deltavacations.com), and **United Airlines Vacations** (tel. 800/301-3800, www.vacations.united.com). The web page of the **United States Tour Operators Association** (www.ustoa.com) has a search engine to find package tours and specialty tour operators.

Resort hotels in Ica, Tarapoto, Puno, Cusco, Máncora, and Cajamarca often promote specials for Lima weekenders on their web pages. These all-inclusive packages can be an excellent value for foreign travelers because they are very competitively priced, taking into account the limited resources of most locals.

Overland Journeys
Many companies in the United States and the United Kingdom offer overland backpacking trips for large groups. You and 39 others hop on a retrofitted Mercedes bus for a one- or two-month tour that could begin in Santiago, Chile, or São Paolo and end in Lima, visiting Cusco, Machu Picchu, and all the other sites along the way. These companies strike bargains with hotels ahead of time and take care of all food, lodging, and transport.

The trips move like an army, camping on beaches and in the mountains, ticking off major sites with incredible efficiency. With a two-month trip costing around US$3,000, these trips are about as good of a value as you are likely to find. A pair of budget-minded travelers could, however, do the same trip for the same cost or a little less. Last-minute web specials often offer 25 percent discounts on these trips.

The best agencies to look at are **Dragoman Overland** (www.dragoman.com) and **South American Safaris** (www.southamericansafaris.com). A final highly recommended option is Australia-based **Tucan Travel** (www.tucantravel.com), which offers a range of trips, including language schools and custom packages for independent travelers.

International Tour Agencies
Peru has a huge range of good tour operators with overseas agents, who can work with you regardless of what country you are calling from. The operators in Peru will be the ones you meet when you arrive there. The local operators are listed throughout this book. Contacting these operators directly can

sometimes be cheaper, though they are officially supposed to offer the same price to you as their agent overseas does. Many of the agencies listed will organize a tour for as few as two people, with options for trip extensions. In the Cusco area, for instance, tour operators generally offer trip extensions to Lake Titicaca or the jungle.

Adventure tourism is growing fast in Peru, and new tour operators appear every year. To keep abreast of the latest operators, watch the classified ads sections of adventure magazines such as *Outside* and *National Geographic Adventure* or online resources such as www.andeantravelweb.com.

World Class Travel Services (U.S. tel. 800/771-3100, www.peruperu.com) is a leading seller of consolidated tickets and arranges professional, organized tours. It works with the best operators in Peru, such as **Amazonas Explorer** and **InkaNatura.** World Class offers tours all over Peru, including a US$750 four-day package that includes all but a few meals for visiting Cusco, Sacred Valley, and Machu Picchu. World Class owner Bob Todd personally inspects all the hotels to which he sends clients and is willing to work with groups as small as two people.

CULTURE AND SOFT ADVENTURE

The Seattle-based nonprofit travel organization **Crooked Trails** (U.S. tel. 206/383-9828, www.crookedtrails.com) offers excellent travel programs, culturally sensitive and with exciting off-the-beaten-path destinations around Peru for families, schools, universities, and any type of group. There are at least 10 different packages, such as The Andes and the Sacred Valley, a 15-day tour including Cusco and Machu Picchu, along with homestays with villagers and their families in Vicos (Cordillera Blanca) or Chinchero (Cusco). La Gran Ruta Inca is a seven-day trek on one of the Inca highway's best-preserved segments southeast of the Cordillera Blanca.

Far Horizons Archaeological & Cultural Trips (U.S. tel. 800/552-4575, www.farhorizons.com), a California-based agency, is the right choice for those with a passion for archaeology. Tours hit all of Peru's major ruins and are guided by an American university professor. Along the way, guests attend lectures by Peru's most noted archaeologists, including Walter Alva, who excavated the Lord of Sipán tombs. Their tours often include a complete tour of the north coast, Chavín ruins in the Cordillera Blanca, Cusco, Machu Picchu, and Lima's main museums.

Nature Expeditions International (U.S. tel. 800/869-0639, www.naturexp.com) has been in business for more than three decades and runs a range of upscale trips throughout Peru. Its 12-day Peru Discovery trip passes through Lima, Arequipa, and the whole Cusco area and includes stays in top-notch hotels like the Hotel Libertador in Cusco and the Machu Picchu Pueblo Hotel. It works with groups of just two people and can arrange lectures on a range of topics, from natural healing to Peruvian cuisine.

For a more luxurious trip, **Abercrombie & Kent** (U.S. tel. 800/554-7016, www.abercrombiekent.com) pampers its travelers with small groups, the top hotels of the country, and luxury train travel. The trips are expensive, but there are occasional discounts available on the company's website.

Seattle-based **Wildland Adventures** (U.S. tel. 800/345-4453, www.wildland.com) is renowned worldwide for its diverse international trips. In Peru alone, it offers 16 distinct trips that cover the three major geographic zones: coast, mountains, and jungle. In addition to the more traditional Inca Trail and Cordillera Blanca treks, the company also offers trips designed especially for families. On a trip like the lodge-based Andes & Amazon Odyssey, kids and their parents visit and interact with local schools and markets.

ADVENTURE AND NATURE TOUR OPERATORS IN NORTH AMERICA

The top choice for treks anywhere in Peru is **Andean Treks** (U.S. tel. 800/683-8148, www.andeantreks.com). It is affiliated with the highly recommended Peruvian Andean Treks in Cusco, and its treks range from a six-day/five-night Inca Trail trek (US$870), to a Salcantay trip (US$1,145), to an 18-day Vilcabamba expedition (prices vary). The company has been around since the 1970s and has been a leader in taking care of the environment and porters—it's probably the only agency in Peru that pays retirement to its porters!

Adventure Specialists (U.S. tel. 719/783-2076, www.adventurespecialists. org) is based out of a spectacular ranch in Westcliffe, Colorado, and has operated quality educational and creative adventure programs in Peru since 1971. Founder and co-owner Gary Ziegler, a fellow of the Royal Geographical Society and Explorers Club, is a true adventurer, archaeologist, and noted Inca expert. His expeditions have rediscovered and surveyed the important Inca sites Corihuayrachina, Cota Coca, and Llaqtapata. The company specializes in archaeology-focused horse trips around Cusco, but Ziegler and his crew can custom-design nearly any adventure you are looking for.

Adventure Life International (U.S. tel. 406/541-2677 or 800/344-6118, www.adventure-life.com) is a company based in Missoula, Montana, that is a good bet for budget-minded trekkers. Its 10-day Machu Picchu Pilgrimage includes Cusco, Machu Picchu, and a well-run Inca Trail trek for US$2,395. It also offers affordable trips to the Tambopata Research Center. It uses three-star, family-run hostels and local guides, and gives independent travelers flexibility on where they eat. Maximum group size is 12, though it often sends off groups as small as two people.

South Winds (U.S. tel. 800/377-9463, www.southwindadventures.com) is based in Littleton, Colorado, and offers a range of eco-adventures from the jungle to the high Andes. It comes highly recommended from people who have done the trips and from *Condé Nast Traveler* magazine.

The Miami-based **Tropical Nature Travel** (U.S. tel. 877/827-8350, www.

tropicalnaturetravel.com) works with a variety of conservation organizations across Latin American to plan jungle trips. In Peru it works with InkaNatura, the owner of some of Peru's best jungle lodges. Choices range from the Manu Wildlife Center and Cock of the Rock Lodge in the Manu area to the Sandoval Lake and Heath River lodges around Puerto Maldonado.

GAP Adventures (U.S./Canada tel. 800/708-7761, www.gapadventures.com) stands for Great Adventure People and is one of Canada's leading tour outfits. It is a good choice for independent-minded travelers who prefer small groups. Groups stay in locally owned hotels, and GAP is known for socially responsible tourism that includes a good deal of interaction with local communities.

One of the best international climbing agencies in Peru is Seattle-based **Alpine Ascents** (U.S. tel. 206/378-1927, www.alpine-ascents.com). The company's Peru guide, José Luis Peralvo, splits his time between Everest, his home in Ecuador, and Peru and has been guiding the world's toughest peaks for about two decades. Alpine Ascents is extremely responsible about acclimatization and small rope teams.

For esoteric tours and ayahuasca sessions, check out **El Tigre Journeys** (U.S. tel. 303/449-5479, www.biopark.org). This for-profit company has been in business since 1997 and is associated with the nonprofit **International Biopark Foundation** in Tucson, Arizona. It leads ayahuasca ceremonies in the Amazon, spirit journeys, and solstice celebrations throughout the year.

ADVENTURE AND NATURE TOUR OPERATORS IN THE UNITED KINGDOM

Based in Edinburgh, Scotland, **Andean Trails** (U.K. tel. 0131/467-7086, www.andeantrails.co.uk) was cofounded in 1999 by a former South American adventure guide. The company leads interesting, small-group mountain-bike and trekking adventures throughout Peru.

Journey Latin America (U.K. tel. 020/8747-8315, www.journeylatinamerica. co.uk) is the United Kingdom's largest operator of specialty tours and has been in business for more than 25 years. It does rafting, kayaking, trekking, and cultural tours that can either be escorted groups or tailored for two people. It also sets up homestays and language classes.

Exodus (U.K. tel. 0870/950-0039 or 844/227-9087, www.exodustravels.com) is one of the United Kingdom's larger adventure tour operators, with more than 25 years of experience and trips in countless countries. Its 28 Peru trips often include visits to Bolivia or Ecuador.

World Challenge Expeditions (U.K. tel. 01/494-853-579, www.world-challenge.co.uk) is a London-based adventure company for student groups in Peru. Its coordinator in Peru, Richard Cunyus, is a full-time resident, takes great care of the students, and tracks down excellent adventures, such as trekking in the Cordillera Huayhuash or paddling a dugout in the Reserva Nacional Pacaya Samiria. The company also works with many students from the United States.

ADVENTURE AND NATURE TOUR OPERATORS IN AUSTRALIA

World Expeditions (Australia tel. 1300/720-000, www.worldexpeditions. com.au) is Australia's leader in adventure tours and treks to Peru. It works with Tambo Tours, a small and reputable trekking outfit in Cusco. In Peru, trips include treks through the Lake Titicaca grasslands, forays into Colca Canyon, and longer trips that take in Peru, Bolivia, and the Amazon jungle. It has representatives in the United Kingdom (enquiries@worldexpeditions. co.uk), the United States (contactus@worldexpeditions.com), and Canada (info@worldexpeditions.ca).

Visas and Officialdom

VISAS AND PASSPORTS

At present, citizens of the United States, Canada, United Kingdom, South Africa, New Zealand, and Australia do not require visas to enter Peru, nor do residents of any other European or Latin American country. When visitors enter the country, they can get anything from 30 to 180 days stamped into both a passport and an embarkation card that travelers must keep until they exit the country. If you require more than 30 days, be ready to support your argument by explaining your travel plans and showing your return ticket.

Extensions can be arranged at Peru's immigration offices in Lima, Arequipa, Cusco, Iquitos, Puno, and Trujillo for US$21. There are also immigration offices on the border checkpoints with Chile, Bolivia (Desaguadero and Yunguyo), and Ecuador, though at this point it is easier just to leave the country, stay the night, and reenter on a fresh visa.

Always make photocopies of your passport and your return ticket and store them in a separate place. Carry your passport in a money belt underneath your clothing, or leave it in a security box at your hotel. If your passport is lost or stolen, your only recourse is to head to your embassy in Lima. If you have lost or had your passport stolen before, it may take up to a week for your embassy to run an international check on your identity.

EMBASSIES AND CONSULATES
Peruvian Embassies and Consulates Abroad

If you are applying for a work visa or other type of special visa for Peru in the United States, contact the consular section of the Peruvian embassy (tel. 202/833-9860, www.embassyofperu.org), located in **Washington D.C.** Additionally, there are consulates in Atlanta, Boston, Chicago, Dallas, Denver, Hartford, Honolulu, Houston, Los Angeles, Miami, New Orleans, New York, Paterson, Phoenix, Sacramento, Salt Lake City, San Francisco, San Juan, Seattle, St. Louis, and Tulsa.

The Peruvian embassy in Canada is in Ottawa (tel. 613/233-2721, www.embassyofperu.ca), with consulates in Calgary, Montreal, Toronto, Vancouver, and Winnipeg. In the United Kingdom the embassy and consular section are both in London (tel. 020/7235-1917, www.peruembassy-uk.com). In South Africa, the Peruvian embassy and consulate are in Pretoria (tel. 27/12-440-1030, embaperu6@telkomsa.net).

In Australia the embassy is in Barton, Canberra (tel. 612/6273-7351, www.embaperu.org.au), with consulate offices in Brisbane, Melbourne, and Sydney. In New Zealand the embassy is in Wellington (tel. 64/4-499-8087, embassy.peru@xtra.co.nz), and there are two honorary consulates in Auckland and Christchurch. There is a complete list of Peruvian embassies and consulates around the world at http://pe.embassyinformation.com.

Foreign Embassies in Peru

Many foreign travelers are surprised by how little help their own embassy will provide during an emergency or a tight situation abroad. If you have been robbed and have no money, expect no help from your embassy, apart from replacing your passport. The same applies if you have broken Peruvian law, even by doing something that would be legal in your own country. Go ahead and contact your embassy in an emergency, but don't wait for them to call back.

These embassies are all in Lima: United States (Av. La Encalada, Block 17, Surco, tel. 01/618-2000, http://lima.usembassy.gov, 8am-5pm Mon.-Fri.), Australia (Av. Victor Andres Belaunde 147, Vía Principal 155, Torre Real Tres, Of. 1301, San Isidro, tel. 01/221-4996, www.embassy.gov.au/peru, 9am-5pm Mon.-Fri.), Canada (Libertad 130, Miraflores, tel. 01/319-3200, www.canadainternational.gc.ca/

peru-perou, 8am-11am and 2pm-4pm Mon.-Fri.), United Kingdom (Av. Larco 1301, 22nd Fl., Miraflores, tel. 01/617-3000, https://www.gov.uk/government/world/peru, 8am-1pm Mon.-Fri.), and South Africa (tel. 422/2280, www.dfa.gov.za/foreign/sa_abroad/sap.htm, 9am-1pm Mon.-Fri.).

If you find yourself in trouble, your best hope for finding a lawyer, good doctor, or a bit of moral support may not be with your embassy, but with the South American Explorers Club (SAE) (www.saexplorers.org), which has offices in Cusco (Pardo 847, tel. 084/24-5484, cuscoclub@saexplorers.org, 9:30am-5pm Mon.-Fri., 10am-1pm Sat.) and Lima (Enrique Palacios 956, Miraflores, tel. 01/444-2150, limaclub@saexplorers.org, 9:30am-5pm Mon.-Fri., 9:30am-1pm Sat.).

TAXES

Foreign travelers are required to pay a US$31 exit tax before boarding an international flight and US$9 for all domestic flights, but these are usually included in the price when you book.

Foreigners no longer have to pay a 19 percent value-added tax, commonly known as IGV or *impuesto general a las ventas*, on rooms or meals purchased at hotels. When you check into a hotel, the receptionist will usually photocopy your passport or at least note down the details. Check your bill upon leaving.

Foreigners still have to pay the 19 percent IGV at upscale restaurants that are not affiliated with hotels. These restaurants often tack on a 10 percent service charge as well. Be sure to check if you have been charged for service because no further tip should be necessary.

CUSTOMS

Peru's customs office *(aduana)* is notorious for being strict with travelers coming back from Miami with loads of imported goodies. That is why you will see a line of Limeños nervously waiting to pass through the stoplight at the Peruvian customs checkpoint. If you get the unlucky red light, you should know the rules. Travelers are allowed to bring three liters of alcohol and 20 packs of cigarettes into Peru duty-free. You can also bring in US$300 worth of gifts, but not to trade or sell.

On your way home, it is illegal to leave Peru with genuine archaeological artifacts, historic art, or animal products from endangered species. If you're caught you will surely be arrested and prosecuted. Your home country will not let you bring in coca leaves but rarely do they hassle you about coca teabags.

Note that drug trafficking is a huge problem in Peru, so don't be surprised to be stopped at Cusco or Lima airport to have your luggage meticulously searched by the police (from personal experience, travel writers are not exempt from this either!). Many young foreigners are caught carrying drugs. Needless to say, never accept anything from anybody, and check your luggage thoroughly before traveling. Peruvian police do not mess about, and you will be staring at 15 years in horrendous conditions.

BORDER CROSSINGS

Peru has around 10 official border crossings with Chile, Ecuador, Brazil, and Colombia. They are open year-round and are not usually a hassle as long as one's passport and tourist card are in order.

POLICE

Peruvian police officers are incredibly helpful and, for the most part, honest. Always carry your passport with you or a photocopy of it if you decide to leave your passport where you are staying. Other means of identification are pretty much worthless, unless you're renting a car and need to show your international driver's license. If you are stopped on the street, the only thing police are allowed to do is check your Peruvian visa or passport. If police hassle you for a bribe for whatever reason, politely refuse and offer to go to the police station, or just act like you don't understand. Police will usually just give up and let you go.

Police corruption is much less common now in Peru than it was a decade ago. If you have an encounter with a crooked cop, get the officer's name and badge number and call Peru's 24-hour, English-speaking **tourist police hotline** (tel. 01/574-8000).

Peru has set up tourist police offices in Arequipa, Ayacucho, Cajamarca, Chiclayo, Cusco, Huancayo, Huaraz, Ica, Iquitos, Lima, Nasca, Puno, Tacna, and Trujillo. In Lima, the emergency number for the police is **tel. 105**, but English-speaking operators are usually not available. Your best bet is to call the 24-hour hotline.

Conduct and Customs

ETIQUETTE

Peruvians are in general more relaxed than North Americans, a trait reflected in a lax attitude toward time and an ability to smile through the frequent frustrations that punctuate life in Peru.

Latin Americans are also much more physical in day-to-day interactions than their northern neighbors. Men give a firm handshake to other men both when arriving and leaving; women give one peck on the cheek when being introduced to another woman, and usually to another man (although men should wait for the woman to offer the kiss).

Highlanders are more reserved, and a handshake is more common.

Verbal greetings are also essential; Peruvians invariably exchange a *buenos días* (good morning), a *buenas tardes* (good afternoon), or a *buenas noches* (good evening). It's normal to begin any conversation with these greetings, and even complete strangers will greet each other in this way, unprompted. *"Hola"* ("Hello") is often followed by *"Como está?"* ("How are you?") in informal situations, even if you don't know the person. In more formal situations, *"con mucho gusto"* means "pleased to meet you." If you see someone eating, it's polite to say *"Buen provecho"* ("Enjoy your meal"). This use of physical and verbal greetings is all part of the Latin American preoccupation with appearances. It is frowned upon to be rude in public, and foreigners sometimes acquire a reputation for being unfriendly and cold if they don't use greetings properly.

The title *señora* is reserved for older or married women with children and can be quite insulting if addressed to a younger girl. *Señorita* is for younger, usually unmarried women. *Señor* is used to address men, and *don* or *doña* is used for elder men or women as a sign of respect. *Caballero* (gentleman) is another respectful greeting for a man, often used by service personnel.

Peruvians typically dress nicely and conservatively, especially when dealing with official business or entering a church. Women in these cases should consider wearing pants or a skirt that is longer than knee length, and men should avoid shorts and casual T-shirts. Despite that, fashion in Lima and Amazon towns is more relaxed. You are likely to see men in shorts and women in shorts or short skirts. You should feel comfortable doing the same. Away from Lima or the jungle, shorts can be worn when participating in an athletic activity that requires them: trekking, beach volleyball, or even running. Foreigners will call less attention to themselves if they wear generally inconspicuous clothing, and women in particular should avoid wearing very revealing clothes apart from on the beach.

HOSPITALITY

Peruvians love to be hospitable, and this is particularly gratifying for visitors. Don't be surprised if you are quickly invited to functions and parties, and you shouldn't feel like you're putting them to any trouble. On the contrary, they will be delighted to host you and will probably be disappointed if you decline. Any get-together often expands into a full-blown party, celebrated long and hard into the night. Note that if a Peruvian uses the word *invitar* (invite), this usually means that

he/she will pay. Equally, if you invite someone, you will be expected to pay. This is particularly true across the genders; men are expected to pay for women. If your hosts want to pay for you, it's best to let them and then return the favor on another occasion. You could offer to split the bill, but refusing to let them pay for you could cause offense.

CULTURE

Family is still the center of Peruvian society. Extended families often live in neighboring houses, and young cousins can be raised together as if they were brothers and sisters, especially in rural areas and small cities and towns. It is perfectly normal to remain living with parents in your 20s and even 30s. Women travelers over the age of 20 might be asked whether or not they are married or have children.

Many Peruvians seem to not be bothered with high noise levels, a cultural difference that most Western foreigners find grating. Shops will blare merengue, *tecnocumbia*, and other Latin pop music to the point where conversation becomes impossible but commerce goes on as usual. Radios tend to be turned up at the first sign of morning light, and workmen start hammering at dawn, so sleeping in is often out of the question. Ear plugs can be handy under these circumstances.

Most Peruvians are also used to crowded spaces and don't mind sitting close to one another on buses and *colectivos*. While at the bank, they will stand just inches away from one another even though there is plenty of space around. In the highlands, houses tend to be small, often with many family members sleeping in the same room. Women travelers often think that men are pressing in on them, when actually they just have a different sense of space.

Peruvians also have a very different relationship toward time, taking things relaxed and slow without the hectic attitude of Westerners. If you agree to meet somebody at noon, expect to wait at least 15-30 minutes. You will inevitably sit in a restaurant longer than anticipated, waiting for your food, then your bill, and then waiting some more for your change. You are never going to change this, so just sit back, bring a book, be patient, and smile.

Another important aspect of Peruvian culture is a fierce sense of patriotism. This can be good and bad. On the positive side, Peruvians are proud to show off their country to foreigners, and it is important to them that visitors feel welcome, enjoy their stay, and encourage others to come to Peru. On the downside, Peruvian nationalism can be overbearing at times. Most Peruvians are educated to believe that all the countries surrounding them stole their territory, and they consider that large chunks of Ecuador, Bolivia, and Chile should be Peruvian. It's best to avoid the topic of territorial disputes, as it is often a sore point.

GENDER AND SEXUALITY

Machismo is very much a part of Peruvian culture. Men tend to be the traditional heads of the household, and women manage the home and raise the children. However, Latin American women have begun to assert themselves and claim new freedoms in work and daily life.

The challenges women face are clear: Female beauty is overwhelmingly emphasized, and women are expected to spend a lot of time on their appearance. Women also receive lower salaries than men and none at all for housework, and male dominance runs through society from top to bottom. Women find themselves in a split position—both elevated on a platform as the saintly wife/mother figure, and looked down upon and protected as the "weaker sex." Most daughters are expected to live with their parents until marriage. However, things are changing in Lima.

Machismo manifests itself in ways ranging from subtle to blatant. Men will often direct dinner conversation only toward other men. (Women can handle this situation by directing conversation at both the men and women at the table.) Whistles and catcalls are seen as harmless, but men find themselves feeling they have to prove their manhood in their posturing, driving, and womanizing. Add in the Latino preoccupation with appearances and it's no surprise that there is enormous hypocrisy when it comes to sexuality. Men boast about their sexual conquests, and there is a notable lack of shame about cheating on a partner. Many women, on the other hand, feel compelled to maintain an illusion of virginity, and it's no surprise that clandestine "motels," usually in seedier areas of towns, are common meeting points for lovers.

PANHANDLING

Whether or not to give money to those asking for it on the street is a personal decision. The hardest to turn down are the street kids with rosy, dirt-covered cheeks and an outstretched hand. In the countryside, children will frequently ask for money in exchange for having their picture taken. Remember that when you give them money, you are encouraging the practice in the future. Also, know that parents often have their children working as teams to collect money in the street. Instead of money, the best-prepared travelers give pens, notebooks, food, or other useful items.

Travel Tips

WHAT TO PACK

Travel light and have a carefree vacation—drop-off laundry is common in Peru, so bring five days' **clothing** and put it all in a medium-sized backpack. For the warmer weather of the Sacred Valley and Machu Picchu, bring light, fast-drying clothing that protects your arms and legs from sun and insects. Protect yourself from the sun with a wide-brimmed hat, bandanas, sunscreen, and sunglasses. For the colder weather of Cusco, or the Inca Trail, add a lightweight rain jacket, fleece jacket, and silk-weight long underwear.

Miscellaneous items include a Leatherman-style folding knife, small roll of duct tape for repairs, mending kit, hand sanitizer, headlamp with extra batteries, camera, voltage adapter, water bottle, roll of toilet paper (Peru's public bathrooms are always out), binoculars, pocket English-Spanish dictionary, book, journal, and a tiny calculator for confirming money exchanges. Don't forget your **medical kit** with standard medicines, insect repellent, and water purification tablets.

Paperwork should include valid passport, plane ticket, student card if you have one (preferably ISIC as this is the only one accepted for discounts), a yellow vaccinations card, travelers checks, credit card, and a copy of your travel insurance details. Email yourself numbers for travelers checks, passport, and credit cards in case these things get stolen. Photocopies of the first few pages of your passport and your plane ticket are also a good idea.

ACCOMMODATIONS

Choosing the right place to stay is key to having a relaxed, enjoyable trip to Peru. The quality of lodging ranges dramatically in most Peruvian cities and often has no correlation whatsoever with price. If you plan well, you should usually be able to find a safe and quiet room, with a charming environment and a helpful staff.

Because where you stay makes a huge difference in the quality of your experience, it is recommended to make advance reservations by email—especially in hot spots like Lima, Arequipa, Huaraz, Cusco, and Puno, and especially during the busy months of May-September. Rates can increase as much as 50 percent during local festivals or national holidays such as the July 28 Fiestas Patrias weekend.

Walk-in travelers often get better rates than those who make reservations over email, but those with a reservation often get the corner room with a view, the quieter space off the street, or the room with a writing desk—especially if you ask for it in advance.

Lodging rates can be negotiated at budget hotels. That said, most hotels except for the top-end ones will probably have a low-season rate posted October-April, considerably lower than the usual rate posted year-round. But this depends on the city and can vary month to month.

Before you pay for a room, ask to see one or two rooms to get a sense of the quality standard at the hotel. Look carefully at how safe a hotel is, especially what neighborhood it is in, and avoid lodging around discos, bars, bus stations, or other places nearby that might make your room noisy at night. Check the mattress, inspect the bathrooms carefully, and turn on the hot water to make sure it exists. If you are in a cold area, like Puno or Cusco, ask if the hotel provides electric heaters. If you are in a jungle city, ask if there are fans. If you are planning to make calls from your room, ask if there is direct-dial service that allows the use of phone cards—otherwise you will have to wait for the receptionist to make your call at a hefty rate that can be as much as US$0.50 per minute for local calls.

Budget Hotels

The cheaper establishments are called *hospedajes* or *hostales*. There are government rules that define the difference between both and a hotel. Key things to look for with a budget place are the quality of the beds, perks like shared kitchen or free Internet (or, increasingly nowadays, Wi-Fi), the cleanliness of the bathroom, and how the water is heated. A few hotels use water heaters with a limited supply of hot water. A few others use electric showerheads, which heat water with an electrical current like that of a toaster oven. Often the device needs to be turned on at the showerhead or via a circuit breaker in the bathroom. The whole concept is unnerving, but the devices are generally safe. The problem is they often make the water only lukewarm, which is not great if you are in dire need of a hot shower in a cold city. Fortunately, the majority of hostels have switched to gas water heaters.

Midrange Hotels

This category of lodging is the most varied in Peru—if you are lucky, you can find a charming, comfortable hotel with clean, well-equipped rooms, a terrace or lounge area, and helpful staff, but if you're unlucky you'll end up with a budget-level room in a charmless building. Midrange hotels are usually a safe bet for private bathrooms with hot water, security, phones, Wi-Fi, and cable TV.

High-End Hotels

Nearly all major Peruvian cities have high-end hotels with the full range of international creature comforts, including swimming pools, Wi-Fi Internet, spring mattresses, alarm clocks, refrigerators, loads of hot water, bathtubs, and direct-dial phones. The fancier establishments often have kitchenettes, slippers, bathrobes, and complimentary toiletries. Suites are more expensive but much more luxurious. Because most of these hotels are used by businesspeople and high-end tour operators, quality is usually very good. These hotels invariably charge a 19 percent value-added tax, which by law must be refunded to travelers.

DINING

Many travelers are very impressed by the quality of cuisine in Peru, which could easily claim to be the best, most interesting, and most varied food in Latin America. However, note that sanitation can be a problem in cheaper restaurants frequented by backpackers. Many travelers return with fond memories of the exquisite and surprising range of flavors, while others return with their stomachs crawling with bacteria or parasites. Choose where you eat carefully and work from the recommendations in this guide or from fellow travelers. Peruvians often recommend *huariques,* or hole-in-the-wall restaurants that work well for their hardy stomachs but not necessarily for yours.

Service at Peruvian restaurants is broken down into various steps, which include receiving the menu, ordering, waiting for food, waiting for the bill, and then waiting for change. If you are eating lunch, you can order from the *menú del día,* the fixed menu of the day, usually a two-course meal with a drink and occasionally a simple dessert. À la carte items are more expensive than the *menú*. If you get good service it is encouraged to leave around 10 percent of the bill as a gratuity.

Many travelers choose to make their own breakfasts by buying yogurt, cereal, and some fruit.

EMPLOYMENT

Jobs teaching English in Peru are easy to find and can often be arranged in-country without a work visa (which doesn't mean you will be legal). You should first scan expatriate bulletin boards in Lima, where language schools often advertise jobs for around US$8 per hour.

International organizations that help find teaching positions include **Amerispan** (www.amerispan.com) and **TEFL** (www.tefl.com). These organizations are also worth contacting: **International Schools Services** (U.S. tel. 609/452-0990, www.iss.edu), **Británico** (Lima tel. 01/447-1192, www.britanico.edu.

pe), **Teaching Abroad in the U.K.** (www. teaching-abroad.co.uk), and **i-to-i** (www.i-to-i.com). Wherever you work, make sure you get a contract in writing.

Good ESL job websites include **Dave's ESL Café** (www.eslcafe.com) and **ESL Employment** (www.eslemployment.com).

Other paid employment can be found through the **International Jobs Center** (www.internationaljobs.org). This organization collects information on current international job openings with governments, government contractors, United Nations agencies, private voluntary organizations, and student exchange organizations. Membership, including posting your credentials in its database and access to profiles of major employers, is US$26 for six weeks.

For tips on living in Peru see **Living in Peru** (www.peruthisweek.com) or **Expat Peru** (www.expatperu.com); both webpages have resourceful information for expatriates, with everything from apartments to tips on how to deal with cultural differences.

VOLUNTEERING

There are hundreds of volunteer opportunities in Peru, involving art and culture, community development, disability and addiction services, ecotourism and the environment, education, health care, and services for children and women. Although these organizations do not pay salaries, they often provide food or accommodation in exchange for your time.

The most common complaints with volunteer work are that the organization is disorganized, there is not enough meaningful work, and that organizations are exploiting eager beavers for their own bottom line. For that reason, do research and try to speak with people who have worked with the organization in the past.

One source for volunteer information in Peru is **South American Explorers Club** (Lima office: Enrique Palacios 956, Miraflores, tel. 01/445-3306, www.saexplorers.com, 9:30am-5pm Mon.-Fri., 9:30am-1pm Sat.; Cusco office: Pardo 847, tel. 084/24-5484,

cuscoclub@saexplorers.org, www.saexplorers.org, 9:30am-5pm Mon.-Fri., 9:30am-1pm Sat.). If you're a member, you can even access the volunteer database online. If you're not, you can send an email or buy a phone card and talk to someone in person. Another organization in Lima that hooks up volunteers with organizations is **Trabajo Voluntario** (www.trabajovoluntario.org). A good global resource for finding volunteer organizations is www.idealist.org.

There are many Spanish-language schools that combine teaching with volunteering. If you take morning language lessons, the school will often set you up with volunteer work for a minimal administration fee.

There are also many Peru-based volunteer organizations. Check out **Lucho Hurtado**'s programs in Huancayo (www.incasdelperu.org); the organization **Center for Social Well Being** (www.socialwellbeing.org), in Carhuaz in the Cordillera Blanca; and **Awamaki** in Ollantaytambo (www.awamaki.org).

Crooked Trails (U.S. tel. 206/383-9828, www.crookedtrails.com) is a nonprofit, community-based travel organization with excellent three- to four-week volunteer travel programs in communities located in countries such as Peru, Ecuador, Guatemala, India, Nepal, Thailand, Bhutan, and Kenya, creating true cultural exchange bonds that make positive contributions to host countries and achieving lasting effects on their travelers.

Cross-Cultural Solutions Peru (U.S. tel. 800/330-4777, U.K. tel. 01237/66-6392, www.crossculturalsolutions.org) runs highly professional volunteer programs mainly for students from the United Kingdom and the United States in Lima, Trujillo, and Ayacucho. In Lima, the company works in Villa El Salvador, the shantytown that was a Nobel Peace Prize nominee for its community organization. The program is quite expensive but recommended for its professional staff. Costs are US$2,489 for two weeks, with every additional week costing US$272.

World Leadership School (U.S. tel. 303/679-3412, www.worldleadershipschool. com) helps middle and high schools in the United States create global programs with schools in Peru. During the three- to four-week programs, volunteers focus on a single global issue, such as climate change, education, or public health. Volunteers understand and develop competence with each issue by working on solutions at the community level. The programs include a leadership curriculum and mentorship from local leaders, who share their perspective and wisdom.

ProWorld (U.S. tel. 877/429-6753, U.K. tel. 870/750-7202, www.proworldsc.org) has locations in Peru, Belize, and Mexico. In Peru, ProWorld is based out of Urubamba, where, since 2000, it has built schools, irrigation systems, and bridges; replanted forests; helped develop sustainable industries like agro-tourism; and sent volunteers to work with countless local nonprofits. It has programs ranging from two weeks to a semester in length, and it offers academic credit. Prices begin at US$1,795 for two weeks.

World Youth International (www. worldyouth.com.au) organizes volunteer programs in Cusco, such as the Clínica San Juan de Dios, which is a well-organized resident program for children with disabilities.

Kiya Survivors (U.K. tel. 01273/72-1092, www.kiyasurvivors.org) works with special-needs children, abandoned women, and young single mothers. It is run by British citizen Suzy Butler out of Cusco and offers volunteer placements of 2-6 months. A standard six-month placement includes in-country tours, accommodations, and a tax-deductible donation to the organization.

The highly recommended nonprofit **Mundo Azul** (Lima tel. 01/447-5190, www. mundoazul.org/english) is dedicated to conserving natural biodiversity, and its volunteers play a firsthand role in helping that mission happen. The two-week to monthlong volunteer programs take participants to the ocean to research dolphin populations or dive into open water to collect marine species. (Only experienced divers can apply for the latter option.) A rainforest trip to Manu involves researching tapirs, macaws, and giant river otters.

Ania (Lima tel. 01/628-7948, http:// aniaorg.pe/en) is an innovative nonprofit founded by Peruvian Joaquín Leguía in 1995. The nonprofit has focused mainly on helping children across Peru, and the world, connect with their love for nature through a creative, grassroots effort that includes Ania, a cartoon character, and a series of Tierra de Niños natural areas. These "Children's Lands" are owned, designed, and maintained by children and range from only a few square meters to a giant nature reserve near Puerto Maldonado. Leguía, who has been awarded the prestigious Ashoka fellowship, plans to begin working with volunteers, so check for available placements.

OPPORTUNITIES FOR STUDY

Peru has a variety of great Spanish-language programs in Lima, Huaraz, Cusco, Urubamba, Arequipa, Huancayo, and Puerto Maldonado. These programs offer either private instruction for US$7-15 per hour or much cheaper group classes that last between a week and a month. Many of these programs will also set up homestays, hikes, classes, and other activities. The schools vary in quality, so we recommend asking the school for email addresses of former students in order to contact them. Many of the schools also engage in volunteer projects, which is a great way to immerse yourself in a Spanish-speaking situation. When choosing a school, think carefully about what situation will provide the most immersion. We recommend a homestay where you will not be able to speak English and a city where there are few foreigners.

Council on International Educational Exchange (www.ciee.org) organizes study-abroad programs and has links to a variety of programs.

BSES Expeditions (U.K. tel. 0207/591-3141, www.bses.org.uk) runs annual science expeditions for British teenagers, though Americans also sign up. The trips usually include science "base camps" in unusual areas of Peru, along with trekking, rafting, and other adventure activities.

WOMEN TRAVELING ALONE

Machismo is alive and well in Peru, so women traveling in Peru should know what to expect. Many Latin men assume that a woman traveling on her own, especially a blonde, must be promiscuous. So you have to set the record straight. At some level, there is the larger issue that some men feel threatened by women who travel abroad, study, work, and are generally independent, because it conflicts with their perceptions of how women should be.

How you interact with men makes a huge difference. Speak with men you do not know in public places only. Treat them neutrally and avoid intimate conversation and behaviors, like friendly touches that might be misinterpreted. Wear modest clothing. A fake wedding ring or a reference to a nonexistent husband or boyfriend may help, but it can also result in the reply *"no soy celoso"* ("I'm not jealous").

Peruvian men, and often teenagers, will ingratiate themselves with a group of female gringas and tag along for hours, even if they are completely ignored. The best way to deal with this is by telling them early on that you want to be alone: *"quiero estar sola, por favor."* The next step would be a loud and clear request to be left alone: *"déjeme, por favor."* The final step would be to ask passersby for help *"por favor, ayúdeme."* The bad side of machismo is harassment, but the flip side is protection.

Be especially careful at night. Choose a hotel in a safe, well-lit part of town. Take care when flagging down a taxi and do not walk around alone at night, especially in tourist towns like Cusco. Walk with confidence and purpose, even if you do not know where you are going. Women who look lost are inevitably approached by strangers. Peruvian women ignore catcalls, aggressive come-ons, and flirtatious lines called *piropos,* which are almost a form of poetry among men. You should do the same.

Do not walk alone in out-of-the-way places in the countryside. There have been reports of women who have been assaulted while walking alone on popular travelers' routes. Trek or hike in the daylight and with at least one other person. If you are robbed, surrender your purse rather than risk physical harm. Mace, whistles, alarms, and self-defense skills are effective tools that are likely to catch most assailants off-guard.

GAY AND LESBIAN TRAVELERS

Machismo extends to attitudes toward gay people, and homophobia is pervasive here. Gay travelers need to bear in mind that being open about their sexuality can lead to anything from embarrassment to religious rants or even violence. However, there is a burgeoning community, and Lima has the biggest gay scene in the country, although it's smaller than in other South American capitals. There are various well-hidden and exclusively gay bars, restaurants, and clubs in cities like Lima, and a few in Iquitos and Cusco—though none cater exclusively to lesbians.

The only way to find about gay and lesbian establishments is online. The concept of gay rights is still relatively new in Peru, so gay and lesbian travelers are advised to be discreet and exercise caution. A good online resource is **Gay Peru** (www.gayperu.com), a great site on gay travel, including gay-oriented package tours, although it is in Spanish only.

Those interested in learning about gay rights in Peru should check the website (in Spanish) of the **Movimiento Homosexual de Lima** (www.mhol.org.pe), one of the oldest gay movements in Peru.

The San Francisco-based **Now Voyager** (www.nowvoyager.com) is a worldwide gay-owned, gay-operated full-service travel agency, as is **Purple Roofs** (www.purpleroofs. com). The **International Gay and Lesbian Travel Association** (www.iglta.org) has an extensive directory of travel agents, tour operators, and accommodations that are gay- and lesbian-friendly. **Above Beyond Tours** (www.abovebeyondtours.com) is a California-based gay travel specialist offering independent and group travel packages.

ACCESSIBILITY

Facilities for people with disabilities are improving in Peru but are far from adequate. Most bathrooms are impossible to enter in a wheelchair. Hotel stairways are usually narrow and steep, and ramps are few and far between. Peru's sidewalks are hard to navigate with a wheelchair because they are frequently narrow, potholed, and lack ramps. Cars usually do not respect pedestrians, so cross streets with extreme caution.

The exceptions are airports and high-end hotels. Peruvian hotel chains such as **Libertador** (www.libertador.com.pe) and **Casa Andina** (www.casa-andina.com) stand out for providing accessible rooms in hotels in Trujillo, Lima, Cusco, the Sacred Valley, the Colca Canyon, Arequipa, and Nasca.

PromPeru, the government tourism commission, has launched a major accessibility campaign and now claims that more than a hundred tourist facilities in Aguas Calientes, Cusco, Iquitos, Lima, and Trujillo have been approved for travelers with disabilities. PromPeru lists these wheelchair-accessible places on its website (www.promperu.gob. pe). Other resources for disabled travelers include **Access-Able Travel Source** (www.access-able.com) and **Society for Accessible Travel and Hospitality** (U.S. tel. 212/447-7284, www.sath.org).

SENIORS

Many organized tours of Peru cater to senior travelers. The major airlines offer discounts for seniors, as do international chain hotels, but other than that, senior discounts in Peru are nonexistent. For visiting the jungle, Amazon cruise boats are an excellent option for people with limited walking abilities.

Good senior agencies include **SAGA Holidays** (www.saga.co.uk), which offers all-inclusive tours and cruises for those 50 and older. **Road Scholar** (U.S. tel. 800/454-5768, www.roadscholar.org) arranges study programs for people 55 and over in countries worldwide, including Peru.

TRAVELING WITH CHILDREN

Traveling with kids through Peru can be enjoyable, but careful planning is essential. Kids tend to attract lots of attention from passersby and can cause interesting cultural interactions. By traveling through Peru, children learn a great deal and gain an understanding of how different life can be for people across the world.

Experts suggest that children should be involved in the early stages of a trip in order to get the most out of it. Children's books and movies that deal with the history of the Inca and the Spaniards will help your kids better relate to the ruins they will see later on. Parents should explain to children what they will encounter, prep them for the day's activities, and then hear from them how it went afterwards.

Keeping your children healthy means taking precautions. Make sure your children get the right vaccinations, and watch what they eat while they are in Peru, because the major threat to their health is dehydration caused by diarrhea. Bacterial infection can be prevented by washing children's hands frequently with soap or using hand sanitizer.

For very young children, don't bother bringing your own baby food, as it is cheaper in the country. You will have a hard time, however, finding specialty items like sugar-free foods, which should be brought from home. Outside of Peru's major cities, there is not much selection in supermarkets, so stock up while you can. Always carry a good supply of snacks and bottled water with you, as there can be long stretches where nothing to eat or drink is available.

Pack your **medical kit** with everything you will need for basic first aid: bandages and gauze pads, antibacterial ointment, thermometer, children's mosquito repellent (vitamin B acts as a natural mosquito repellent), envelopes of hydrating salts, and strong sunscreen. Items like Children's Tylenol *(paracetamol infantil)* can easily be found in the local pharmacies, though quality varies. Medical services are very good in Lima and often quite good in the countryside, where city-trained, English-speaking medical students perform residency. Medical care is so cheap in Peru that parents should never hesitate about seeing a doctor. Bring photocopies of your children's medical records.

Your embassy may be of some help, but the best place to contact for advice or help is probably the **South American Explorers Club** (Enrique Palacios 956, Miraflores, tel. 01/445-3306, www.saexplorers.com, 9:30am-5pm Mon.-Fri., 9:30am-1pm Sat.).

Think carefully about your travel arrangements. Kids are likely to enjoy a sensory-rich environment like the Amazon jungle much more than back-to-back tours of archaeological ruins. Buses generally allow children to travel for free until 5 years old and/or if they sit on your lap, but choose flights over long bus rides that could make kids crabby. Choose family-oriented hotels that offer playgrounds and lots of space for children to run around unsupervised. If you ask for a room with three beds you generally won't have to pay extra. If you have toddlers, avoid hotels with pools, because they are rarely fenced off. Children's rates for anything from movies to museums are common and, even if they are not official, can often be negotiated.

Because parents are often distracted by their children, families can be prime targets for thieves in public spaces like bus stations and markets. Even if you have taught your children to be extra careful about traffic at home, you will have to teach them a whole new level of awareness in Peru. Time moves slower in Peru, and families spend a lot of time waiting for buses, tours, or meals. Be prepared with coloring books and other activities. Above all, know that you simply cannot cover as much ground with children, and hikes and sightseeing tours need to be shorter—otherwise the kids may get tired and grouchy.

Health and Safety

It pays to think ahead about your health before traveling to Peru. With the right vaccinations, a little bit of education, and a lot of common sense, the worst that happens to most visitors is a bit of traveler's diarrhea.

Things get more complicated if you decide to visit the jungle, because Peru, like parts of Africa and Asia, lies in the tropical zone. Travelers who visit the Amazon should be vaccinated against yellow fever and take full precautions against mosquitoes. Consider taking malarial medicine to be safe, although most visitors to Peru don't bother because the disease is far rarer than in Africa.

VACCINATIONS

Vaccination recommendations can be obtained from the **Centers for Disease Control (CDC)** (U.S. tel. 877/394-8747, www.cdc.gov/travel), which recommends the following vaccinations for Peru: **hepatitis A** and **typhoid. Yellow fever** is recommended for people traveling into the jungle below 2,300 meters. **Rabies** is recommended if you are going to be trekking through areas where the disease is endemic. **Hepatitis B** is recommended if you might be exposed to blood (for instance, health-care workers), plan on staying for more than six months, or may have sex with a local. Travelers should also

Packing a Medical Kit

Having a small medical kit will come in handy over and over again in Peru, especially in remote areas. Here's a checklist of what should be included:

- Ace bandage
- acetaminophen (Tylenol—bring lots)
- antacid tablets (Tums)
- antibacterial ointment (Neosporin)
- antihistamine (Benadryl)
- bandages, gauze pads, and cloth tape
- butterfly bandages or superglue (for sealing gashes)
- CPR shield (if you are CPR-certified)
- decongestant spray (Afrin)
- diarrhea medication (Imodium)
- fungus cream (Tinactin)
- hydrocortisone cream for bug bites
- ibuprofen (Advil—bring lots)
- insect spray for clothing (permethrin)
- insect repellent (12-35 percent DEET or above)
- latex gloves

be vaccinated against **measles** and **chicken pox** (those who have had these diseases are already immune) and have had a **tetanus/ diphtheria** shot within the last 10 years.

Unless you are coming from a region in the Americas or Africa where yellow fever is a problem, you are not required by Peruvian law to have any vaccinations before entering the country. The yellow immunizations pamphlet, which doctors tell you to guard so carefully, is rarely checked, but you should carry it with your passport. The shots can be quite expensive, in the United States at least, and many of the shots require second or even third visits. Hepatitis A, for instance, requires a booster shot 6-18 months after the initial shot, which most people get after returning from Peru. Hepatitis B is generally received in three doses, and there are new vaccines now

that combine both hep A and hep B in a series of three shots. Rabies is also given in three shots, though both yellow fever and typhoid are single shots.

Most vaccinations do not take effect for at least two weeks, so schedule your shots well in advance. If you are taking multishot vaccinations such as hep B, you will need to receive your first shot five weeks before departing, even under the most accelerated schedule. Getting shots in Peru is easy and a lot cheaper than in the United States, but you will not be protected for the first 2-4 weeks.

TRAVELER'S DIARRHEA

Traveler's diarrhea pulls down even the stoutest of Peru travelers eventually and can be very unpleasant. It can be caused by parasites or viruses, but most often it is caused by bacteria

- Moleskin, both thin and foam

- motion-sickness medication (Dramamine)

- packages of rehydration salts

- Pepto-Bismol (liquid is better)

- scissors or knife

- syringe and needles

- thermometer

- tweezers

- water purification tablets

Your doctor might suggest the following: Advil for pain (no more than 2,000 milligrams per day), Tylenol for fevers over 101.5°F (38.6°C), and Pepto-Bismol for stomach upset and diarrhea.

The following antibiotics can be prescribed by your doctor before traveling as well: Keflex (cephalexin) works for systemic infections, like when a cut causes your foot to swell; Zithromax or erythromycin for respiratory infections; and ciprofloxacin for gastrointestinal issues—though it is better to consult a local doctor before taking any of these medicines. Acetazaolamide, commonly known as Diamox, is effective for altitude sickness.

Travelers should also put in their medical kit their brief medical history, including recent allergies and illnesses. If you take prescription drugs, include written instructions for how you take them and the doctor's prescription as well, just in case you get stopped in customs.

The medical kit only works at the level of the person who is using it. If you can't take a first-aid course, a backcountry wilderness guide like that published by Wilderness Medicine Institute (www.nols.edu/wmi) will come in handy. Nearly all these medicines, including the antibiotics, can be bought in a pharmacy in Peru without a prescription—either generic or high-quality brands.

carried in food or water. Plenty of other diseases in Peru are spread this way, including cholera, hepatitis A, and typhoid. Nothing is more important for you health-wise than thinking carefully about everything you eat and drink.

Drink only bottled water or water that has been previously boiled. Instead of buying an endless succession of plastic bottles, which will end up in a landfill, travel with a few reusable hard plastic bottles and ask your hotel to fill them with boiling water every morning. Refilling bottles is especially easy at hotels that have water tanks, or *bidones,* of purified water. Order drinks without ice unless you can be assured it is bagged ice or made with previously boiled water. Wipe the edges of cans and bottles before drinking or carry straws.

Avoid street vendors and buffets served under the hot sun. Instead, choose restaurants that come well recommended for taking precautions for foreigners. If the kitchen looks clean and the restaurant is full, it is probably all right. Before and after you eat, wash your hands with soap where available. Carry an antibacterial hand sanitizer as a backup.

The safest foods in restaurants are those that are served piping hot. Soups, well-cooked vegetables, rice, and pastas are usually fine. Eat salads and raw vegetables with extreme caution because they are either unwashed or rinsed with water from the faucet. Better yet, if you have the facilities to cook your own meals, prepare your own salads with food disinfectants for sale in most Peruvian supermarkets.

An exception to the no-raw-foods rule is ceviche, which is raw fish marinated in bacteria-killing lime juice. As long as you are in a reputable restaurant, ceviche is a safe bet.

Market foods that are safe include all fruits and vegetables that can be peeled, like bananas, oranges, avocados, and apples. Many local fruits are okay as well, including *chirimoya,* tuna (the prickly cactus fruit), and *granadilla.* Dangerous items include everything that hangs close to the ground and could have become infected with feces in irrigation water. These include strawberries, mushrooms, lettuce, and tomatoes. There are plenty of safe things to buy in the market that, when combined with other safe items like bread and packaged cheese, make for a great lunch.

Pork and shellfish are the biggest culprits when it comes to food poisoning, and if you're not careful, you could get seriously ill. You generally are safe in good-quality restaurants, although bear in mind that shellfish in the Cusco area has traveled a long distance and so is best avoided in all but the highest-class places.

If you do get sick, it is essential to keep hydrated. Buy hydration packs or simply make your own with water, salt, and sugar (it tastes bad but it is essential). Eat simple food such as rice and bread. If the symptoms are accompanied by a fever or do not subside after two days, then you probably have a more serious infection and should see a doctor. Luckily there are plenty of specialist antibiotics for parasites, amoeba, and bacteria, but you may need to do some tests to check exactly what is the cause of your sickness.

ALTITUDE SICKNESS

Cusco sits at 3,400 meters, and your main health concern should be altitude sickness. You will know if you're suffering from this illness very soon after your arrival. Symptoms include shortness of breath, quickened heartbeats, fatigue, loss of appetite, headaches, and nausea. There is no way to prevent it, but you can minimize the effect by avoiding heavy exercise until you get acclimatized and by

drinking plenty of water and liquids in general. Also avoid alcohol.

Many travelers carry acetazolamide, commonly known as Diamox, usually prescribed by a doctor in doses of 125-250 milligrams, taken during the morning and evening with meals. However, these medications are not for everybody and can cause drowsiness. In Cusco, coca leaf tea *(mate de coca),* taken in plentiful amounts, is the best remedy for *soroche,* the Quechua word for altitude sickness. And it works. A 100-milligram dose of the Chinese herb ginkgo biloba, taken twice a day, seems to work efficiently too.

If you feel sick, it's good to know that all hospitals and clinics in Cusco have bottled oxygen. If you happen to be in a five-star hotel chain like Monasterio, Libertador, or Casa Andina Private Collection, they will provide oxygen in the rooms upon request. The best cure for altitude sickness is to ascend slowly. Flying directly to Cusco from Lima and staying overnight is best avoided. Go down in altitude to the Sacred Valley, which is below 3,000 meters, and return to Cusco after a few days. Bear in mind that altitude sickness, if not taken care of appropriately, can develop into **high-altitude pulmonary edema,** with acute chest pain, coughs, and fluid buildup in the lungs, or **high-altitude cerebral edema,** involving severe headaches coupled with bizarre changes of personality. In both cases, these illnesses can lead to death if not treated immediately and adequately.

Hospital Regional (Av. de la Cultura, tel. 084/24-3240) and the **Hospital Lorena** (Plazoleta Belén 1358, Santiago district, tel. 084/22-1581) are the main health centers in Cusco. A bit more expensive, but faster and more reliable, is **Clínica Pardo** (Av. de la Cultura 710, tel. 084/24-0387). In an emergency situation try going to the hospital with a local if you're not fluent in Spanish.

DOGS AND RABIES

There are lots of wild (or at least surly) dogs in Peru, as trekkers in places like the Cordillera Huayhuash soon find out. If you are planning to spend a lot of time trekking in Peru, you should consult with your doctor about getting a rabies vaccine.

There are lots of things you can do to avoid being bitten by a dog. As cute or as hungry as a dog may look, be careful about petting a dog in Peru unless you know the owner. Many street dogs have been mistreated and have highly unpredictable behavior.

If you are walking into an area with dogs, collect a few stones. All Peruvian dogs are acutely aware of how much a well-aimed stone can hurt, and they will usually scatter even if you pretend to pick up a stone, or pretend to throw one. This is by far the best way to stop a dog, or a pack of them, from bothering you.

If you do get bitten, wash the wound with soap and water and rinse it with alcohol or iodine. If possible, test the animal for rabies. Regardless, always seek medical attention because rabies is a fatal disease. If there is any doubt about whether the animal was rabid, you should receive rabies shots immediately.

Rabies is also carried by bats and some monkeys. If you are bitten by either of these, seek medical attention immediately.

HYPOTHERMIA

Peru's snow-covered mountains, highlands, and even cloud forests have plenty of cold, rainy days, conditions in which hypothermia is most likely to occur. Watch yourself and those around you for early signs of hypothermia, which include shivering, crankiness, exhaustion, clammy skin, and loss of fine coordination. In more advanced hypothermia the person stumbles, slurs his or her speech, acts irrationally, and eventually becomes unconscious, a state doctors refer to as the "metabolic ice box."

The key to preventing hypothermia is being prepared for the elements, and that starts with clothing. When you go for a hike, pack plenty of different layers in a plastic bag. Remember that cotton is great for evaporating sweat and cooling down on a hot day, but actually works against you in wet, cold weather. Artificial

fibers like fleece or polypropylene work when wet because they wick water away from your body. Wool is another good choice because it insulates even when wet. And a waterproof poncho or a Gore-Tex jacket will help keep you dry. Having a lot of food and water is also important, and in demanding conditions you and everyone you are with should be fueling up constantly.

The key to avoiding hypothermia is catching it early. If you or someone in your group is shivering or having a hard time zipping up a jacket, take action immediately. In mild hypothermia, the body is still trying to warm itself, and all you have to do is support that process. Feed the person water and a variety of foods, from fast-burning chocolate to bread and cheese. Have them do vigorous exercises like squatting and standing over and over, or swinging their arms around like a windmill. If the person remains cold, set up a tent and put him or her in a sleeping bag with hot-water bottles. Monitor the person carefully until body temperature returns to normal. A person who was on the edge of hypothermia one day is more susceptible the next, so allow for at least a day or two of rest and recuperation.

SEXUALLY TRANSMITTED DISEASES

HIV/AIDS is a worldwide health problem that is spreading in Peru, along with **hepatitis B** and other sexually transmitted diseases. The United Nations officially classifies Peru's AIDS epidemic as low-level and estimated in 2005 that there were between 89,000 and 93,000 people in Peru living with HIV/AIDS. About 74 percent of the adults were men. The number of infected women and children is rising.

Despite state-promoted campaigns that have increased the concept of safe sex in the public's mind in Peru, many men still refuse to use condoms. Travelers should take full precautions before engaging in sex, beginning with the use of condoms.

MEDICAL CARE IN PERU

Peru's health-care system is quite good considering the fact that many Peruvians live in poverty. Even small villages usually have a medical post, or *posta médica,* which is often staffed with a university-trained medical student completing his or her residency. Midsize cities like Huaraz have a range of health options, including a few government hospitals and a few private clinics. In general, the clinics provide more personalized, high-tech service, but plenty of state hospitals offer in general better health care than what you could ever get in the United States. A country doctor in Peru is probably going to identify your particular stomach ailment faster than a specialist in the United States, simply because the Peruvian doctor has seen your condition many times before.

For serious medical problems or accidents, we recommend that people travel to Lima. The best hospitals are there, and insurance companies abroad are often able to handle payments directly with them (elsewhere the patient is expected to shell out the cash and hopefully be reimbursed later).

Nearly all international medical policies will cover a speedy evacuation to your country if necessary, which is one of the main reasons for getting insurance in the first place. A good resource for advice in medical situations is the **South American Explorers Club** in Lima (Enrique Palacios 956, Miraflores, tel. 01/445-3306, www.saexplorers.org).

MEDICAL TRAVEL INSURANCE

Most medical insurance will not cover you while traveling abroad, so most Peru travelers buy overseas medical insurance. Go with a reputable insurance company, or you will have trouble collecting claims. Nearly all Peru hospitals will make you pay up front, and then it's up to you to submit your claim.

Some U.S.-based companies that have been recommended by travelers include **Medex Assistance** (tel. 800/732-5309, www.medexassist.com), **Travel Assistance International** (tel. 800/237-2828, www.travelassistance.com), **Health Care Global** by Wallach and Company Inc. (tel. 800/237-6615, www.wallach.com), and **International Medical Group** (tel. 800/628-4664, www.imglobal.com). Students can get insurance through the **STA** (tel. 800/226-8624, www.statravel.com).

Some companies sell additional riders to cover high-risk sports such as mountain climbing with a rope, paragliding, and bungee jumping. One good company is **Specialty Risk International** (tel. 800/335-0611, www.specialtyrisk.com), which insures for as little as three months. Membership with the **American Alpine Club** (tel. 303/384-0111, www.americanalpineclub.org) is open to anyone who has climbed in the last two years and includes rescue and evacuation for mountain climbers around the world.

PRESCRIPTION DRUGS

Generic medicines are easy to buy in Peru and are much cheaper than in the United States or Europe, though quality might not always be the same. Travelers used to stock up their medical kit in Peru, but nowadays there are more restrictions with prescribed medicine, especially if you want to purchase it in big pharmacies, hospitals, or clinics. Specific birth control or allergy pills can be hard to find in Peru, unless you go to a private clinic pharmacy.

Though it's tempting due to the ease of access to medications over the counter at the pharmacy, avoid self-medicating. Visiting a Peruvian doctor is inexpensive compared to U.S. and European rates. They are the world's leading experts on bacteria and parasite conditions specific to Peru, anyway, so it's worth it. You can waste a lot of time and money (and negatively affect your health) by taking ciprofloxacin, for instance, when another medicine would have been better.

ILLEGAL DRUGS

According to the present Peruvian Criminal Code, the use and possession of drugs for personal consumption is not punished if the quantities are under the amounts stipulated by law (Art. 299: 2 grams of cocaine, 7 grams of marijuana). The problem is that almost no travelers and even very few police know this, and the police will probably still take you to the *comisaría* and charge you until a judge defines the amounts you carry. So to keep it safe, it is highly recommended not to take drugs while in Peru.

The penalties for smuggling out drugs are very strict for cocaine, which is common and of very high purity in Peru, and not as cut with all kinds of dangerous chemicals as in the United States and Europe. There is no bail for drug trafficking cases, and the legal process can drag on for up to two years. Your embassy will most likely decline to get involved.

Peru is well known for confidence scams that involve drugs. A typical one generally targets men and can start with a random meeting in the street with an attractive young woman. After conversation and moving to a bar or discotheque the woman will offer up some drugs. Suddenly and unexpectedly, police appear from nowhere and the attractive girl disappears.

What follows is extortion in exchange for not being arrested. The so-called "police" will explain that you could spend the next five years or more in jail unless you give them money. If you don't react, they will take you to the police station. If you decide to offer them money, the police will drive you to a series of ATMs in order to take as much money as possible from your accounts. Several hours later, and after having your bank account cleaned out, you will probably be dropped off in some remote area of Lima. The worst part is that the perpetrators probably are not even real police.

CRIME

Peru is generally a safe country, so travelers should not feel paranoid. But as in any other place in the world, follow commonsense rules and realize that thieves target travelers because they have cash and valuable electronics on them. You will be easy prey for thieves only if you are distracted.

Be alert and organized and watch your valuables at all times. Your money and passport should be carried under your clothes in a pouch or locked in a safety box at your hotel. Keep a constant eye on your luggage in bus stations. When in markets, place your backpack in front of you so that it cannot be slit open. When in restaurants or buses, keep your purse or bag close to you.

Make yourself less of a target. Do not wear jewelry or fancy watches, and keep your camera in a beat-up hip bag that is unlikely to draw attention. Be alert when in crowded places like markets or bus stations, where pickpockets abound. Go only to nightspots that have been recommended. Walk with a sense of purpose, like you belong exactly where you are. When withdrawing money from an ATM, be with a friend or have a taxi waiting.

Experienced travelers can sense a scam or theft right before it happens, and nine times out of ten it involves momentary distraction or misplaced trust. If someone spits on you, latch onto your camera instead of cleaning yourself. If someone falls in the street in front of you or drops something, move away quickly. If an old man asks for your help in reading a lottery ticket, say no. If a stranger motions you over or offers a piece of candy, keep going. Be distrusting of people you do not know.

At nightspots, do not accept alcohol from strangers, as it might be laced with a sleeping drug. Do not do drugs. If you have been drinking, take a taxi home instead of walking.

Be careful when taking taxis and when changing money. When riding to Aeropuerto Internacional Jorge Chávez in Lima, lock your luggage in the trunk and hold onto your valuables. When traffic becomes heavy on Avenida La Marina, teams of delinquents often break windows and snatch bags before speeding away on a motorcycle.

Information and Services

MONEY

Thanks to ATMs, getting cash all over Peru is about as simple, easy, and cheap as it is in your own country. U.S. banks usually charge a US$3 fee per transaction, but the benefits of using bank cards outweigh the risk of carrying loads of cash. Banks usually charge hefty commissions for cashing travelers checks, but a modest supply is nice to have along in case your bank cards are stolen (check with your bank before you go to find out if it is even possible to replace your bank cards overseas). Credit cards are useful, and it's increasingly common to use them to purchase almost everything in big cities. Throughout the country Visa cards are easiest to use in restaurants and hotels, but also ask if establishments accept MasterCard or American Express. If your bank cards get stolen and you spend all your travelers checks, you can always get a cash withdrawal off your credit card. Bottom line: Rely on your ATM card and bring some travelers checks and a credit card or two.

Peruvian Money

The official Peruvian currency is the *nuevo sol* (S/.), which has depreciated strongly against the U.S. dollar, much like other emerging market currencies. The *sol* has gone from almost 2.50 per US$1 to 3.40 per US$1 in late 2015. A daily, official rate is updated on the central bank's website (www.bcrp.gob.pe). Peruvian bills come in denominations of 10, 20, 50, 100, and 200 *soles*. Note that ATMs routinely dispense 100-*sol* bills, which can cause serious problems when making small purchases. When exchanging money, try to get plenty of 10s and 20s. The *sol* is divided into 100 smaller units, called *céntimos*, which come in coins of 1, 5, 10, 20, and 50 *céntimos*. There are also heavier coins for 1, 2, and 5 *soles*. Beware that 2- and 5-*sol* coins look very much alike, the only difference being the size (5-*sol* coins are slightly bigger), so take care not to confuse them. Currency calculations with today's rate can be made with online currency converters such as XE.com (www.xe.com). Exchange rates are commonly listed on signs in front of banks and exchange houses and are also posted in daily newspapers.

Changing Money

The U.S. dollar, despite being the most common foreign currency to exchange, is far from being the strongest. Nowadays, it is fairly easy to exchange euros in most Peruvian towns, but other currencies can only be exchanged in big cities.

Inspect your dollar bills carefully before leaving your country and treat them with care. Note that people in Peru are paranoid about counterfeit money, and even the smallest tear in a Peruvian or dollar bill may lead to it being rejected, so take care of your bills. In the best case, you might be able to cash a tattered bill on the street for a lower rate, but regardless, US$50 and US$100 bills are difficult to exchange. There are a few banks and money exchange houses in almost all big airports in Peru. Generally speaking, most Peruvians exchange their dollars at exchange houses, called *casas de cambio,* because they give a slightly higher rate than banks. These are usually clustered around the Plaza de Armas or main commercial streets in every city and town. In major cities, representatives of these *casas de cambio* will even come to your hotel to exchange money, depending on the amount.

In major cities, there are also money changers on the street who wear colored vests and an ID card. These people are generally safe and honest, though they will sometimes take advantage of you if you don't know the daily exchange rate. Never change money with unlicensed money changers, who will sometimes have rigged calculators. Whenever you change

Avoiding Counterfeit Money

Counterfeit money prevails in Peru. It includes both U.S. bills and Peruvian bills and coins. No counterfeit euros have been detected so far. Peruvians can recognize counterfeit *nuevos soles* quite easily, either in bills—mostly 100- and 50-*sol* notes, but also the 2- and 5-*sol* coins, which are very similar in design but a bit different in diameter. Getting money from an ATM or a bank reduces the risk but not totally. You will know when you have been scammed with a fake note. Depending on the value, it might be easier or harder to pass it on.

Here are a few tips for avoiding counterfeit bills:

- **Feel and scratch the paper.** Counterfeit bills are usually smooth and glossy, while real bills are crisp and coarse and have a low reflective surface. For U.S. dollar bills, many Peruvians scratch the neck area of the person pictured on the bill. The lapel should have a bumpy quality, unless it is an old bill. Hold both ends and snap the bill—it should have a strong feel.

- **Reject old bills.** This includes ones that are faded, tattered, ripped, or taped, especially if they are U.S. notes. You will never get rid of these bills unless you trade them on the street at a lesser rate. Banks will not change them, unless they are Peruvian notes. Counterfeit bills are made of inferior paper and often rip.

- **Hold the bill up to a light.** In both Peruvian and American bills there should be watermarks and thin ribbons that only show up when put against a light source. In the new U.S. $10 and $20 bills, the watermark is a smaller, though fuzzy, replica of the person pictured on the bill. These bills also have thin lines that run across the bill and say "US TEN" or "US TWENTY."

- **With Peruvian bills, look for reflective ink.** When you tilt a Peruvian bill from side to side, the ink on the number denomination should change color, like a heliogram. So far, Peruvian counterfeiters have been unable to reproduce this ink.

money on the street, check the amount with your own calculator.

When you change money, check each bill carefully to see that it is not counterfeit. Hand back all bills that have slight rips, have been repaired with tape, or have other imperfections. Insist on cash in 20- and 50-*soles* bills. Unless you are at a supermarket or a restaurant, the 100-*soles* bills are hard to change, and you will end up waiting as someone runs across the street to find change for you.

Money Machines

ATMs, known as *cajeros automáticos,* are now commonplace in tourist towns, even small ones. The most secure ATMs are in glass rooms that you unlock by swiping your card at the door. Most ATMs accept cards with Visa/Plus or MasterCard/Cirrus logos. Banco de Crédito and Global Net are the only machines that accept American Express cards. Interbank (available in most big cities in Peru) is the only bank with special ATMs

that deliver coins. ATMs deliver the cash you requested first and then will give your card back. If you forget to pull it out, it will be eaten by the machine and be quite difficult to get back. Thieves sometimes wait for people to take cash out of their ATM and then follow them, sometimes on a motorcycle, to a secluded spot. For this reason, use ATMs during the day.

Banks and Wire Transfers

Banks are generally open 9am-5pm Monday-Friday, mornings only on Saturday, and are closed on Sunday. Banks are useful for cashing travelers checks, receiving wire transfers, and getting cash advances on credit cards (Visa works best, but MasterCard and American Express are also accepted). Bank commissions for all these transactions vary US$20-30, so it is worth shopping around.

A cheaper option for wire transfers is often **Western Union,** which has offices in many Peruvian cities. Call the person you want to wire money to you and give them an address and phone number where Western Union can contact you. Once your money has arrived, you just go to the Western Union office with your passport to pick it up.

Travelers Checks

American Express is the most widely accepted travelers check and can easily be exchanged in banks. From the United States these checks can be ordered over the phone by calling toll-free 800/721-9768. The best place to change travelers checks in Peru is at **Banco de Crédito,** also known as BCP, which often charges no fee at all. The other banks charge a 2.5 percent commission or a flat fee that can be as much as US$10. *Casas de cambio* charge even higher fees.

Remember to record the numbers of your travelers checks and keep them in a separate place. Some travelers email these numbers to themselves so that they are always available when needed. If you end up not using your travelers checks, they can always be converted into cash back home for their face value.

If your American Express travelers checks get stolen, you can call the company collect either in Peru at 0800/51-531 or in the United States at 801/964-6665. You can also go online to www.americanexpress.com to find the nearest office. American Express maintains representatives in Peru in Chiclayo, Trujillo, Lima, and Arequipa. In Lima its representative is Viajes Falabella, which has a half-dozen offices in the city, including in Miraflores (Larco 747, tel. 01/444-4239, 9am-6pm Sun.-Fri.).

Credit Cards

In recent times the use of credit cards has expanded to almost all big cities in Peru for even the smallest purchases. Be sure you ask, though. Not all cards are accepted everywhere. By far, the best cards to have in Peru are Visa or MasterCard, though Diners Club and to a lesser extent American Express are increasingly accepted. Apart from their in-country toll-free numbers, most credit cards list a number you can call collect from overseas. Carry this number in a safe place or email it to yourself so that you have it in an emergency.

For Visa cards, you can also look online at www.visa.com or call collect in the United States to 410/902-8022. For MasterCard, see www.mastercard.com or call its collect, 24-hour emergency number in the United States at 636/722-7111. For American Express, see

Change money at banks or at currency exchange stores.

www.americanexpress.com or call the company in the United States at 336/393-1111. To contact Diners Club (www.dinersclub.com) while in Peru call 01/615-1111.

Bargaining

Bargaining is common practice in Peru, especially at markets and shops, and to a minor extent in mid-budget hotels. Bargaining can be fun, but don't go overboard. Have a good sense of what an item should cost beforehand. Ask them how much it costs *("¿Cuánto cuesta?")* and then offer 20 percent less, depending on how outlandish the asking price is. Usually vendors and shoppers meet somewhere in the middle. Some people bargain ruthlessly and pretend to walk out the door to get the best deal. On the other hand, a smile, humor, and some friendly conversation can work better.

Remember that the extra dollar you are arguing about most likely means a lot more to the vendor than it does to you. If you have a reasonable price, accept it graciously. There is nothing worse than seeing a gringo bargaining a campesino into the ground over a pair of woven mittens. We might go and have a coffee with the money we save, while the vendor might use it to buy shoes for his daughter!

Discounts

Student discounts are ubiquitous in Peru, so get an ISIC card (International Student Identity Card) if you can, and flash it wherever you go. If you are in Peru for a week or two it is usually possible to make up the money you spent on that South American Explorers Club membership just in the discounts you are entitled to at hotels, restaurants, and agencies—the hardest part is remembering to ask for it before you pay. The SAE Clubs in Lima and Cusco have lists of establishments that accept their discounts.

Tipping

Tipping is a great way for foreign travelers to get money to the people who need it the most—the guides, waiters, hotel staff, drivers, porters, burro drivers, and other frontline workers of the tourism industry. Though not required, even the smallest tip is immensely appreciated. It's also a good way of letting people know they are doing a great job. Tipping is an ethic that varies from person to person.

In restaurants a tip of 10 percent is ideal but not enforced. Try to give the tip to the waiter personally, especially when the table is outdoors or you pay with a credit card. It is not necessary to tip taxi drivers in Peru, but you should give a few *soles* to anyone who helps you carry your bags, including hotel staff or an airport shuttle driver. Assuming you were pleased with their service, you should tip guides, porters, and mule drivers at least one day's wage for every week worked. If they did a great job, tip more. Tipping in U.S. dollars or other foreign currency is not necessarily a good deal for these people, especially if they live away from big cities where they can't exchange the money. Tip in local currency. Note that in top-end restaurants a service charge is usually included, so tipping is unnecessary.

MAPS AND TOURIST INFORMATION
Maps

You can buy a range of maps in Arequipa, Cusco, and Huaraz, but the best maps are to be found in Lima. South American Explorers Club in Lima and Cusco sells the leading country maps, plus a good selection of military topographic maps. To find topographic maps for remote areas you will have to make a trip down to Lima's Instituto Geográfico Nacional (tel. 01/475-3030, www.ign.gob.pe).

Good bookstores generally sell the better national maps, and we especially liked the maps in the back of the *Inca Guide to Peru* and the *Lima 2000* series (scale 1:2,200,00). Many hotels and Iperú offices give out free city maps. A good online map store is www.omnimap.com.

Tourist Offices

The Peruvian government has set up tourist offices—known as Iperú—in most major cities, including Tumbes, Chiclayo, Trujillo,

Chachapoyas, Iquitos, Huaraz, Lima, Ayacucho, Cusco, Arequipa, Puno, and Tacna. They receive questions and have a website in English, French, German, Portuguese, Italian, and Spanish (tel. 01/574-8000, www.peru. travel). They can give you brochures, maps, and basic info.

The Iperú office is also the place to go if you want to file a complaint or need to solve a problem. These can include a bus company not taking responsibility for lost luggage, a tour company that did not deliver what it promised, or an independent guide who is not honest. In an emergency, you should contact the police and also call Iperú's 24-hour hotline (tel. 01/574-8000).

FILM AND PHOTOGRAPHY

Peru is a very photogenic country, and don't be surprised if you shoot twice as much as you were expecting. Note, however, that in Peru, photographing soldiers or military installations is against the law.

Digital Cameras

Memory cards and other accessories are increasingly available in Lima and other large Peruvian cities. Shops that sell cameras and other electronic equipment will usually take a full memory card and burn it onto a compact disc for about US$5—but that requires the toggle cable that comes with your camera. Bring a few large-capacity cards, an extra battery, and maybe a pen or thumb drive for extra backup. Unless you have your own laptop, there will be long stretches away from the large towns when you will not be able to download.

Film Processing

When it comes to conventional cameras, nearly every Peruvian city has a photo-processing lab, which is usually affiliated with Kodak. Quality varies, however, and if you are looking for highly professional quality, wait until you return home or get to a big city like Lima, Trujillo, Cusco, Arequipa, or Puno.

Ask permission before taking photos of local people.

Developing black-and-white or slide film is limited to big cities too.

Photo Tips

The main issue for photography on the coast and in the highlands is the intense sunlight. The ideal times to photograph are in the warm-color hours of early morning or late afternoon. Use filters that knock down UV radiation and increase saturation of colors. In the jungle, the main problem is lack of light, so a higher ASA is recommended whether using conventional or digital cameras. If you want to take pictures of wildlife, you will have to bring a hefty zoom and have a lot of time to wait for the shots to materialize. A good source of information on travel photography is **Tribal Eye Images** (www.tribaleye.co.uk). The author offers free tips on choosing equipment and film, general techniques and composition, photographing people, and selling your work.

Photographing Locals

Before you take a picture of people, take the

Peru's Area Codes

Abancay: 83
Aguas Calientes: 84
Arequipa: 54
Ayacucho: 66
Cajamarca: 76
Chachapoyas: 41
Chiclayo: 74
Chincha: 56
Cusco: 84
Huancayo: 64
Huánuco: 62
Huaraz: 43
Ica: 56
Iquitos: 65
Lima: 01
Máncora: 73
Nasca: 56
Piura: 73
Pucallpa: 61
Puerto Maldonado: 82
Puno: 51
Tacna: 52
Tarapoto: 42
Trujillo: 44
Tumbes: 72

time to meet them and establish a relationship. Then ask permission to take their photo.

The most compliant subjects are market vendors, especially those from whom you have just bought something. Children in the highlands will ask for money in order to have their picture taken. Adults will even ask if you will be making business selling their portraits.

COMMUNICATIONS AND MEDIA
Mail

Peru's national post office service is **Serpost** (www.serpost.com.pe), and there is an office in nearly every village, or at the very least a *buzón* or mailbox. Postal service in Peru is fairly reliable and surprisingly expensive. Postcards and letters cost US$2-4 to the United States and Europe, and more if you want them certified. Letters sent from Peru take around two weeks to arrive in the United States, but less time if sent from Lima. If you know Spanish, check for a complete list of post offices by region and province on Serpost's website under Red de Oficinas. To ship packages out of Peru use **DHL, FedEx**, or another courier service.

If you become a member of South American Explorers Club, you can receive personal mail at its offices in Lima or Cusco. You can also receive mail at your respective embassy in Lima.

Telephone Calls

International rates continue to drop, both from overseas into Peru and from Peru overseas. Of course, the cheapest option for calling Peru is **Skype** (www.skype.com), and most Peruvians have a Skype account. Even if they don't you can charge your Skype account with money and, via a service called "Skype Out," use Skype to call a Peruvian land line or cell phone. Calling cards, which can be purchased online, also make calling Peru incredibly cheap. **Alosmart** (www.alosmart.com) has a search engine for finding the best card depending on the type of calls you are going to make.

If you would like someone from home to be able to reach you, you should consider renting or buying a **cell phone.** In the baggage claim area of the airport, there are cell phone agents who rent phones from Peru's major carriers: Telefónica, Claro, and Nextel. Claro gets the widest service. Buying a cell phone will cost you a minimum of US$30. If you take your cell phone from home with you and it is unlocked, you can buy instead just the sim card for about US$5-10 and have a local number. A new phone comes with a standard number of minutes. Once you expend these minutes, you will need to buy a recharge card, which comes in denominations of US$3.50, US$7, or US$11. You can also charge your phone minutes online. These cards allow users to call both nationally and internationally—receiving calls is free once you have the phone.

Most towns have public phones on the main square and usually an office of

Telefónica, Peru's main phone company. The phones are coin-operated, but most people buy telephone cards.

The most popular prepaid card is called 147 and can be bought in denominations of US$3-30 at most pharmacies and supermarkets, and from the Telefónica offices themselves. Also available are HolaPerú cards for international calls. In either case, dialing the United States is more or less about US$0.80 per minute, and a local call, with 147, is about US$0.15 per minute. Surcharges are applied to all calls made from pay phones, so use your hotel phone or walk into any small store in Peru with the green-and-blue phone symbol above it.

All major **international phone cards** can be used in Peru, as long as you know the access code: AT&T is 0800-5000, TRT is 0800-50030, and Sprint is 0800-50020. Worldlink has no direct access in Peru.

The cheapest way to make long-distance calls from Peru, however, is via the **net-to-phone** systems available at many Internet places for as low as US$0.17 per minute calling to the United States or Europe. There can be a lag when calling with most of these services, though Internet cafés that have cable service are usually crystal clear—often even better than a phone!

All long-distance calls in Peru are preceded by a 0 and the area code of that particular region, or department, of Peru. For instance, for calling Cusco all numbers are preceded by 084 (these preceding numbers are listed whenever a number is listed in this guide). All home phones in Lima have seven-digit numbers, and numbers are six digits in other towns and cities in the rest of the country. All cell phones have nine-digit numbers in all of Peru.

Peru's country code is **51,** and each of the 23 regions in Peru has a different code. Cusco, for instance, is 84. So dialing a Cusco number from the United States would be 011 (used for all international calls) + 51 (country code) + 84 (city code) and then the number. All cities in Peru have two-digit city codes when dialing

from overseas, except Lima. When calling Lima from the United States, dial 011-51-1 and then the number. When dialing Lima from within Peru, however, you must first dial 01.

To place a direct international phone call from Peru, dial 00 + country code + city code + number. The country code for Argentina is 54, Australia is 61, Canada is 1, Chile is 56, Denmark is 45, France is 33, Germany is 49, Netherlands is 31, Israel is 972, Japan is 81, New Zealand is 64, Norway is 47, Spain is 34, Switzerland is 41, the United Kingdom is 44, and the United States is 1. So for calling the United Kingdom from Peru, callers should dial 0044 before any number, and for the United States 001.

Collect calls are possible from many Telefónica offices, or you can dial the international operator (108) for assistance. The correct way to ask for a collect call is: *"Quisiera hacer una llamada de cobro revertido, por favor."*

The following codes can be called for help: directory assistance 103, emergency assistance in Lima 105, international operator assistance 108, national operator assistance 109, fire 116, and urgent medical assistance 117. The chance of finding an English-speaking operator at these numbers is slim. However, Iperú maintains a 24-hour English-speaking operator at Aeropuerto Internacional Jorge Chávez in Lima for emergencies (tel. 01/574-8000).

Fax

Sending a fax from Peru to another country is expensive, ranging US$2-9 per page to the United States or Europe. Instead of a fax, scan your document and send it as an email attachment. Fax machines are available at most hotels, photocopy stores, and Telefónica offices.

Internet Access

Using a computer is by far the cheapest and most convenient way to communicate in Peru. Internet cafés are everywhere and are popping up even in tiny towns. Using the Internet is cheap (US$0.40-0.70 per hour), and often you can also make cheap net-to-phone overseas calls through **Skype.**

There is a lot that goes into choosing an Internet café, however. First off, make sure it is a high-speed connection, which in Peru is generally referred to as "speedy." Some speedy connections, however, are much faster than others. If your email takes more than a minute or two to open up, we suggest you head elsewhere. Another huge factor is noise, especially with Internet places that cater to schoolkids, who show up each afternoon and shout and scream and wrestle with each other over who gets to use what machine.

Besides speedy, which is a DSL line, Lima and the bigger cities now have faster connections with cable modems and—most important—crystal-clear, dirt-cheap international calls. Sometimes a remote jungle town can have a satellite Internet center, which is also amazingly fast.

Nowadays most upscale and midrange hotels will have free Wi-Fi access for guests traveling with laptops. In Lima and other touristy cities like Cusco, Arequipa, Trujillo, Puno, or Huaraz, you will find cafés with free Wi-Fi access.

Printed and Online News

Publications in Spanish are headed by *El Comercio* (http://elcomercio.pe), the largest and oldest standard daily newspaper with major credibility in Peru. It has a variety of supplements and magazines with good information on cultural activities and performing arts, including *Somos,* a weekly magazine published every Saturday. Among a dozen tabloids, two are worth checking out: *Perú21* (http://peru21.pe), with a moderate center political standing, and *La República* (http://larepublica.pe), traditionally left-oriented.

Caretas (www.caretas.com.pe) is a weekly magazine that has been around for more than half a century, founded by the Gibson/Zileri family. It is published every Thursday and contains a good deal of local political content,

as well as sections devoted to art, humorous essays, interesting letters to the editor, jokes, crossword puzzles, and great photographs.

DedoMedio (www.dedomedio.com), with its rude name ("middle finger") and slogan *"la verdad aunque te duela"* (the truth even if it hurts you), is a brilliant monthly publication full of satire, highly acidic content, great caricatures, and very good articles about almost any topic you can think of, including politics, art, and music.

Some useful news websites in English include **Living in Peru** (www.peruthisweek.com), which also has classified ads and vast information on cultural activities, tourism, and gastronomy, among other subjects. One of the oldest English-language newspapers in South America, **The Andean Air Mail & Peruvian Times** (www.peruviantimes.com), resurfaced some years ago in the Internet, offering feature articles, op-ed columns, and good overall coverage of what is going on in Peru. The **Expat Peru Network** (www.expat-peru.com) also offers local news coverage—actually linked to *The Peruvian Times*—but focuses more on service information, such as legal aspects and traveling to Peru. It offers several discussion forums by topic.

WEIGHTS AND MEASURES

Peru uses the metric system for everything except gallons of gasoline.

Electricity

The electrical system of Peru is 220 volts and 60 cycles. If you absentmindedly plug in a 110-volt appliance from the United States into a 220-volt Peruvian outlet, you will start a small fire. All high-end hotel chains (Casa Andina Private Collection and Libertador, for example) have additional outlets of 110 volts.

You can use 110-volt appliances in Peru with a converter, which can be quite heavy. You can buy one in an electronics shop, though they are cheaper in Peru. Make sure you get the right type, as a hair dryer needs a more robust converter than, say, a digital camera battery charger.

Voltage surges are common in Peru, so it is also a good idea to bring a surge protector from home that can be plugged between your appliance and the converter. Most laptops and digital cameras these days can take either 110 or 220 volts, so check on this before you buy a converter.

TIME ZONES

Peru is in the same time zone as New York, Miami, Bogotá, and Quito. Peru does not use daylight saving time, meaning that its time remains constant throughout the year. The entire country is in the same time zone (GMT -5:00).

Resources

Glossary

abra: high pass

aguaymanto: an Inca fruit, also known as *capulí,* from which delicious jams, desserts, and other delicacies are made

ají: any chili pepper; yellow peppers are *ají amarillo*

ají de gallina: creamy chicken stew with yellow chili served over boiled potatoes, garnished with hard-boiled eggs and black olives

aluvión: mudslide

anticuchos: grilled beef heart brochettes served with an assortment of spicy sauces

arroz con pato: duck with rice, originally from the north coast but now found everywhere

café (con leche): coffee (with milk)

camarones: freshwater prawns/crawfish

camote: sweet potato

cancha: roasted corn kernels, a popular snack to nibble with beer, usually served with ceviche

canela: cinnamon

cañón: canyon

causa: cold mashed potatoes mixed with yellow chili peppers and a dash of lime juice, layered with chicken, tuna fish, shrimp, or veggies mixed with mayonnaise, avocado, and diced onions

cerveza: beer; also *chela*

ceviche: the trademark of Peruvian cuisine: fish, shrimp, scallops, or squid, or a mixture of all four, marinated in lime juice and chili peppers for five minutes; traditionally served with corn, sweet potatoes, and onions; also *cebiche*

chacana: a sacred symbol, also known as the Andean Cross, with varied and complex links to Inca cosmology; a common motif at Inca temples and other sacred sites

chancho/cerdo: pig/pork

chela: slang word for beer

chicha or *chicha de jora:* drink made from different kinds of fermented corn or peanuts, quinoa, or fruit

chicha morada: sweet, refreshing drink made from boiled purple corn and fruit, mixed with clove and cinnamon and served chilled with a dash of lime juice

chicharrón: deep-fried pork, chicken, or fish

chifa: Peruvian-Chinese food/Chinese restaurant

chilcano: a refreshing drink made with pisco, ginger ale, lime juice, and a dash of Angostura bitters

chilcano de pescado: a fish broth good for hangovers

chirimoya: a sweet and pulpy, juicy white fruit with a mushy texture and a bitter dark green skin

choclo: fresh Andean corn

choclo con queso: steaming-hot corn on the cob with slices of cheese and *ají* sauce

chupe: Quechua word for a highly concentrated soup with beef, fish, or seafood with potatoes, corn, vegetables, and sometimes milk

cocha: Quechua word for lake

conchitas negras: black scallop delicacy common in northern Peru

cordillera: mountain range

crocante de lúcuma: a meringue dessert made with a fruit called *lúcuma culantro:* cilantro/coriander

cuy: guinea pig; stewed, fried, or spit-roasted

granadilla: sweet, pulpy passion fruit with a hard shell

guanabana: indescribably delicious jungle fruit

guayaba: guava

huaca: in Quechua, *huaca* is a sacred object that is revered, such as a rock

huacatay: black mint

humita: fresh corn tamale that can be either sweet or salty

Inca Kola: a unique and quite sweet Peruvian pop/soda originally made out of lemongrass

juanes: tamale stuffed with chicken and rice

jugo: juice

kiwicha: purple-flowered grain high in protein, which is folded into breads, cookies, and soups

lago: lake

laguna: lagoon

langostino: river or sea shrimp

limón: key lime or just lime

lomo saltado: popular and inexpensive dish of stir-fried beef loin, with strips of *ají amarillo,* onions, tomatoes, and french fries, served with rice

lúcuma: a small fruit recognizable by its dark peach color and smoky flavor; a popular ice cream, yogurt, and milk shake flavor

manzanilla: chamomile or chamomile tea

maracuyá: passion fruit, served as a juice, in a pisco sour, or in cheesecake

masato: alcoholic drink made from fermented *yuca* or manioc

mate de coca: coca leaf tea

mazamorra morada: pudding-like dessert made from purple corn

mirador: lookout point

nevado: mountain

ocopa: a spicy peanut-based sauce, served over boiled potatoes and garnished with hard-boiled eggs and black olives

pachamanca: the utmost Andean meal, made up of beef, pork, alpaca, *cuy,* and chicken cooked together with potatoes, sweet potatoes, and lima beans inside heated stones in a hole in the ground, covered with herbs

paiche: Amazon fish; the largest freshwater fish in the world

palmito: ribbons of palm heart that look like pasta when served

palta: avocado

Panamericana or Carretera Panamericana: Panamerican Highway

papa: potato; Andean tuber originally from Peru and generic name for more than 3,000 different types of potatoes

papa a la huancaina: cold appetizer of potatoes in a spicy light cheese sauce with *ají amarillo*

papa rellena: fried oblong of mashed potatoes stuffed with meat, onions, olives, boiled eggs, and raisins

pescado: fish

pirañas: small, vicious, sharp-fanged fish found in oxbow lakes and rivers

pisco: grape brandy; distilled spirit

pisco sour: cocktail with made three parts pisco, two parts lime juice, and one part simple syrup, mixed with ice, a bit of egg white, and a dash of Angostura bitters

plátano frito: fried bananas

playa: beach

pollo: chicken

pomelo: grapefruit; also *toronja*

pongo: river gorge that is often dangerous in high water

puna: high plains, often grasslands

quebrada: narrow valley, ravine

quinoa: a round golden-brown grain, rich in protein

quipu: a system of knotted, multicolored cords that the Inca used to keep records and transmit data, such as weather forecasts, crop production, and accounting

río: river

rocoto: a red, bell pepper-shaped chili consumed in Arequipa

rocoto relleno: red bell pepper stuffed with meat and spices

sachatomate: a red fruit, also known as a *tamarillo,* that has an egg shape, an inside like a tomato, and a sweet, tangy taste

seco de cabrito: roasted goat marinated with *chicha,* served with beans and rice

s/n: abbreviation for *sin numero* (without number); refers to addresses with no street number

tacu tacu: bean and rice patty, fried in a pan and topped with a fried egg, beef or fish stew, or any other kind of garnish

tiradito: sashimi-like fish cuts with a chili sauce on top

toronja: grapefruit; also *pomelo*

tumbo: banana passion fruit

tuna: prickly pear from desert cactus

valle: valley

volcán: volcano

wayrana: a three-sided Inca building with the fourth side left open for ventilation

yuca: cassava root

Spanish Phrasebook

Spanish commonly uses 30 letters—the familiar English 26, plus four straightforward additions: ch, ll, ñ, and rr, which are consonants.

PRONUNCIATION

Spanish pronunciation rules are straightforward and easy to learn because—in contrast to English—they don't change. Spanish vowels generally sound softer than in English. (*Note:* The capitalized syllables below receive stronger accents.)

Vowels

a like ah, as in "hah": *agua* AH-gooah (water), *pan* PAHN (bread), and *casa* CAH-sah (house)

e like ay, as in "may": *mesa* MAY-sah (table), *tela* TAY-lah (cloth), and *de* DAY (of, from)

i like ee, as in "need": *diez* dee-AYZ (ten), *comida* ko-MEE-dah (meal), and *fin* FEEN (end)

o like oh, as in "go": *peso* PAY-soh (weight), *ocho* OH-choh (eight), and *poco* POH-koh (a bit)

u like oo, as in "cool": *uno* OO-noh (one), *cuarto* KOOAHR-toh (room), and *usted* oos-TAYD (you); when it follows a "q" the u is silent; when it follows an "h" or has an umlaut, it's pronounced like "w"

Consonants

b, d, f, k, l, m, n, p, q, s, t, v, w, x, y, z, ch pronounced almost as in English; h occurs, but is silent—not pronounced at all

c like k as in "keep": *cuarto* KOOAR-toh (room), Tepic tay-PEEK (capital of Nayarit state); when it precedes "e" or "i," pronounce c like s, as in "sit": *cerveza* sayr-VAY-sah (beer), *encima* ayn-SEE-mah (atop)

g like g as in "gift" when it precedes "a," "o," "u," or a consonant: *gato* GAH-toh (cat), *hago* AH-goh (I do, make); otherwise, pronounce g like h as in "hat": *giro* HEE-roh (money order), *gente* HAYN-tay (people)

j like h, as in "has": *Jueves* HOOAY-vays (Thursday), *mejor* may-HOR (better)

ll like y, as in "yes": *toalla* toh-AH-yah (towel), *ellos* AY-yohs (they, them)

ñ like ny, as in "canyon": *año* AH-nyo (year), *señor* SAY-nyor (Mr., sir)

r is lightly trilled, with tongue at the roof of your mouth like a very light English d, as in "ready": *pero* PAY-doh (but), *tres* TDAYS (three), *cuatro* KOOAH-tdoh (four)

rr like a Spanish r, but with much more emphasis and trill. Let your tongue flap. Practice with *burro* (donkey), *carretera* (highway), and Carrillo (proper name), then really let go with *ferrocarril* (railroad)

Note: The single small but common exception to all of the above is the pronunciation of Spanish **y** when it's being used as the Spanish word for "and," as in *Ron y Kathy*. In such case, pronounce it like the English ee, as in "keep": Ron "ee" Kathy (Ron and Kathy).

Accent

The rule for accent, the relative stress given to syllables within a given word, is straightforward. If a word ends in a vowel, an n, or an s, accent the next-to-last syllable; if not, accent the last syllable.

Pronounce *gracias* GRAH-seeahs (thank you), *orden* OHR-dayn (order), and *carretera* kah-ray-TAY-rah (highway) with stress on the next-to-last syllable.

Otherwise, accent the last syllable: *venir* vay-NEER (to come), *ferrocarril* fay-roh-cah-REEL (railroad), and *edad* ay-DAHD (age).

Exceptions to the accent rule are always marked with an accent sign: (á, é, í, ó, or ú), such as *teléfono* tay-LAY-foh-noh (telephone), *jabón* hah-BON (soap), and *rápido* RAH-pee-doh (rapid).

BASIC AND COURTEOUS EXPRESSIONS

Most Spanish-speaking people consider formalities important. Whenever approaching anyone for information or some other reason, do not forget the appropriate salutation—good morning, good evening, etc. Standing alone, the greeting *hola* (hello) can sound brusque.

Hello. *Hola.*
Good morning. *Buenos días.*
Good afternoon. *Buenas tardes.*
Good evening. *Buenas noches.*
How are you? *¿Cómo está usted?*
Very well, thank you. *Muy bien, gracias.*
Okay; good. *Bien.*
Not okay; bad. *Mal or feo.*
So-so. *Más o menos.*
And you? *¿Y usted?*
Thank you. *Gracias.*
Thank you very much. *Muchas gracias.*
You're very kind. *Muy amable.*
You're welcome. *De nada.*
Goodbye. *Adios.*
See you later. *Hasta luego.*
please *por favor*
yes *sí*
no *no*
I don't know. *No sé.*
Just a moment, please. *Momentito, por favor.*

Excuse me, please (when you're trying to get attention). *Disculpe or Con permiso.*
Excuse me (when you've made a boo-boo). *Lo siento.*
Pleased to meet you. *Mucho gusto.*
How do you say . . . in Spanish? *¿Cómo se dice . . . en español?*
What is your name? *¿Cómo se llama usted?*
Do you speak English? *¿Habla usted inglés?*
Is English spoken here? (Does anyone here speak English?) *¿Se habla inglés?*
I don't speak Spanish well. *No hablo bien el español.*
I don't understand. *No entiendo.*
My name is . . . *Me llamo . . .*
Would you like . . . *¿Quisiera usted . . .*
Let's go to . . . *Vamos a . . .*

TERMS OF ADDRESS

When in doubt, use the formal *usted* (you) as a form of address.

I *yo*
you (formal) *usted*
you (familiar) *tu*
he/him *él*
she/her *ella*
we/us *nosotros*
you (plural) *ustedes*
they/them *ellos* (all males or mixed gender); *ellas* (all females)
Mr., sir *señor*
Mrs., madam *señora*
miss, young lady *señorita*
wife *esposa*
husband *esposo*
friend *amigo* (male); *amiga* (female)
sweetheart *novio* (male); *novia* (female)
son; daughter *hijo; hija*
brother; sister *hermano; hermana*
father; mother *padre; madre*
grandfather; grandmother *abuelo; abuela*

TRANSPORTATION

Where is . . . ? *¿Dónde está . . . ?*
How far is it to . . . ? *¿A cuánto está . . . ?*
from . . . to . . . *de . . . a . . .*
How many blocks? *¿Cuántas cuadras?*
Where (Which) is the way
 to . . . ? *¿Dónde está el camino a . . . ?*
the bus station *la terminal de autobuses*
the bus stop *la parada de autobuses*
Where is this bus going? *¿Adónde va
 este autobús?*
the taxi stand *la parada de taxis*
the train station *la estación de ferrocarril*
the boat *el barco*
the launch *lancha; tiburonera*
the dock *el muelle*
the airport *el aeropuerto*
I'd like a ticket to . . . *Quisiera un boleto
 a . . .*
first (second) class *primera (segunda)
 clase*
round-trip *ida y vuelta*
reservation *reservación*
baggage *equipaje*
Stop here, please. *Pare aquí, por favor.*
the entrance *la entrada*
the exit *la salida*
the ticket office *la oficina de boletos*
(very) near; far *(muy) cerca; lejos*
to; toward *a*
by; through *por*
from *de*
the right *la derecha*
the left *la izquierda*
straight ahead *derecho; directo*
in front *en frente*
beside *al lado*
behind *atrás*
the corner *la esquina*
the stoplight *la semáforo*
a turn *una vuelta*
right here *aquí*
somewhere around here *por acá*
right there *allí*
somewhere around there *por allá*
road *el camino*
street; boulevard *calle; bulevar*
block *la cuadra*

highway *carretera*
kilometer *kilómetro*
bridge; toll *puente; cuota*
address *dirección*
north; south *norte; sur*
east; west *oriente (este); poniente (oeste)*

ACCOMMODATIONS

hotel *hotel*
Is there a room? *¿Hay cuarto?*
May I (may we) see it? *¿Puedo
 (podemos) verlo?*
What is the rate? *¿Cuál es el precio?*
Is that your best rate? *¿Es su mejor
 precio?*
Is there something cheaper? *¿Hay algo
 más económico?*
a single room *un cuarto sencillo*
a double room *un cuarto doble*
double bed *cama matrimonial*
twin beds *camas gemelas*
with private bath *con baño*
hot water *agua caliente*
shower *ducha*
towels *toallas*
soap *jabón*
toilet paper *papel higiénico*
blanket *frazada; manta*
sheets *sábanas*
air-conditioned *aire acondicionado*
fan *abanico; ventilador*
key *llave*
manager *gerente*

FOOD

I'm hungry *Tengo hambre.*
I'm thirsty. *Tengo sed.*
menu *carta; menú*
order *orden*
glass *vaso*
fork *tenedor*
knife *cuchillo*
spoon *cuchara*
napkin *servilleta*
soft drink *refresco*
coffee *café*
tea *té*
drinking water *agua pura; agua potable*

bottled carbonated water *agua mineral*

bottled uncarbonated water *agua sin gas*

beer *cerveza*

wine *vino*

milk *leche*

juice *jugo*

cream *crema*

sugar *azúcar*

cheese *queso*

snack *antojo; botana*

breakfast *desayuno*

lunch *almuerzo*

daily lunch special *comida corrida* (or *el menú del día* depending on region)

dinner *comida* (often eaten in late afternoon); *cena* (a late-night snack)

the check *la cuenta*

eggs *huevos*

bread *pan*

salad *ensalada*

fruit *fruta*

mango *mango*

watermelon *sandía*

papaya *papaya*

banana *plátano*

apple *manzana*

orange *naranja*

lime *limón*

fish *pescado*

shellfish *mariscos*

shrimp *camarones*

meat (without) *(sin) carne*

chicken *pollo*

pork *puerco*

beef; steak *res; bistec*

bacon; ham *tocino; jamón*

fried *frito*

roasted *asada*

barbecue; barbecued *barbacoa; al carbón*

SHOPPING

money *dinero*

money-exchange bureau *casa de cambio*

I would like to exchange traveler's checks. *Quisiera cambiar cheques de viajero.*

What is the exchange rate? *¿Cuál es el tipo de cambio?*

How much is the commission? *¿Cuánto cuesta la comisión?*

Do you accept credit cards? *¿Aceptan tarjetas de crédito?*

money order *giro*

How much does it cost? *¿Cuánto cuesta?*

What is your final price? *¿Cuál es su último precio?*

expensive *caro*

cheap *barato; económico*

more *más*

less *menos*

a little *un poco*

too much *demasiado*

HEALTH

Help me please. *Ayúdeme por favor.*

I am ill. *Estoy enfermo.*

Call a doctor. *Llame un doctor.*

Take me to . . . *Lléveme a . . .*

hospital *hospital; sanatorio*

drugstore *farmacia*

pain *dolor*

fever *fiebre*

headache *dolor de cabeza*

stomachache *dolor de estómago*

burn *quemadura*

cramp *calambre*

nausea *náusea*

vomiting *vomitar*

medicine *medicina*

antibiotic *antibiótico*

pill; tablet *pastilla*

aspirin *aspirina*

ointment; cream *pomada; crema*

bandage *venda*

cotton *algodón*

sanitary napkins use brand name, e. g., Kotex

birth control pills *pastillas anticonceptivas*

contraceptive foam *espuma anticonceptiva*

condoms *preservativos; condones*

toothbrush *cepilla dental*

dental floss *hilo dental*

toothpaste *crema dental*

dentist *dentista*

toothache *dolor de muelas*

POST OFFICE AND COMMUNICATIONS

long-distance telephone *teléfono larga distancia*

I would like to call . . . *Quisiera llamar a . . .*

collect *por cobrar*

station to station *a quien contesta*

person to person *persona a persona*

credit card *tarjeta de crédito*

post office *correo*

general delivery *lista de correo*

letter *carta*

stamp *estampilla, timbre*

postcard *tarjeta*

aerogram *aerograma*

airmail *correo aereo*

registered *registrado*

money order *giro*

package; box *paquete; caja*

string; tape *cuerda; cinta*

AT THE BORDER

border *frontera*

customs *aduana*

immigration *migración*

tourist card *tarjeta de turista*

inspection *inspección; revisión*

passport *pasaporte*

profession *profesión*

marital status *estado civil*

single *soltero*

married; divorced *casado; divorciado*

widowed *viudado*

insurance *seguros*

title *título*

driver's license *licencia de manejar*

AT THE GAS STATION

gas station *gasolinera*

gasoline *gasolina*

unleaded *sin plomo*

full, please *lleno, por favor*

tire *llanta*

tire repair shop *vulcanizadora*

air *aire*

water *agua*

oil (change) *aceite (cambio)*

grease *grasa*

My . . . doesn't work. *Mi . . . no sirve.*

battery *batería*

radiator *radiador*

alternator *alternador*

generator *generador*

tow truck *grúa*

repair shop *taller mecánico*

tune-up *afinación*

auto parts store *refaccionería*

VERBS

Verbs are the key to getting along in Spanish. They employ mostly predictable forms and come in three classes, which end in *ar, er,* and *ir,* respectively:

to buy *comprar*

I buy, you (he, she, it) buys *compro, compra*

we buy, you (they) buy *compramos, compran*

to eat *comer*

I eat, you (he, she, it) eats *como, come*

we eat, you (they) eat *comemos, comen*

to climb *subir*

I climb, you (he, she, it) climbs *subo, sube*

we climb, you (they) climb *subimos, suben*

Here are more (with irregularities indicated):

to do or make *hacer* (regular except for *hago,* I do or make) to go ir (very irregular: *voy, va, vamos, van*)

to go (walk) *andar*

to love *amar*

to work *trabajar*

to want *desear, querer*

to need *necesitar*

to read *leer*

to write *escribir*

to repair *reparar*

to stop *parar*

to get off (the bus) *bajar*

to arrive *llegar*

to stay (remain) *quedar*

to stay (lodge) *hospedar*

to leave *salir* (regular except for *salgo*, I leave)

to look at *mirar*

to look for *buscar*

to give *dar* (regular except for *doy*, I give)

to carry *llevar*

to have *tener* (irregular but important: *tengo, tiene, tenemos, tienen*)

to come *venir* (similarly irregular: *vengo, viene, venimos, vienen*)

Spanish has two forms of "to be":

to be *estar* (regular except for *estoy*, I am)

to be *ser* (very irregular: *soy, es, somos, son*)

Use *estar* when speaking of location or a temporary state of being: "I am at home." *"Estoy en casa."* "I'm sick." *"Estoy enfermo."* Use *ser* for a permanent state of being: "I am a doctor." *"Soy doctora."*

NUMBERS

zero *cero*

one *uno*

two *dos*

three *tres*

four *cuatro*

five *cinco*

six *seis*

seven *siete*

eight *ocho*

nine *nueve*

10 *diez*

11 *once*

12 *doce*

13 *trece*

14 *catorce*

15 *quince*

16 *dieciseis*

17 *diecisiete*

18 *dieciocho*

19 *diecinueve*

20 *veinte*

21 *veinte y uno* or *veintiuno*

30 *treinta*

40 *cuarenta*

50 *cincuenta*

60 *sesenta*

70 *setenta*

80 *ochenta*

90 *noventa*

100 *ciento*

101 *ciento y uno* or *cientiuno*

200 *doscientos*

500 *quinientos*

1,000 *mil*

10,000 *diez mil*

100,000 *cien mil*

1,000,000 *millón*

one-half *medio*

one-third *un tercio*

one-fourth *un cuarto*

TIME

What time is it? ¿Qué hora es?

It's one o'clock. *Es la una.*

It's three in the afternoon. *Son las tres de la tarde.*

It's 4am. *Son las cuatro de la mañana.*

six-thirty *seis y media*

a quarter till eleven *un cuarto para las once*

a quarter past five *las cinco y cuarto*

an hour *una hora*

DAYS AND MONTHS

Monday *lunes*

Tuesday *martes*

Wednesday *miércoles*

Thursday *jueves*	June *junio*
Friday *viernes*	July *julio*
Saturday *sábado*	August *agosto*
Sunday *domingo*	September *septiembre*
today *hoy*	October *octubre*
tomorrow *mañana*	November *noviembre*
yesterday *ayer*	December *diciembre*
January *enero*	a week *una semana*
February *febrero*	a month *un mes*
March *marzo*	after *después*
April *abril*	before *antes*
May *mayo*	

Suggested Reading

HISTORY

Burger, Richard. *Chavín and the Origins of Andean Civilization.* Thames and Hudson: London, 1995. A groundbreaking investigation of the Chavín culture, which spread across Peru's highlands 2,000 years before the Inca.

Hemming, John. *Conquest of the Incas.* New York: Harcourt Brace & Company, 1970. This is a masterpiece of both prose and history, in which famed Peru historian John Hemming lays out a gripping, blow-by-blow account of the Spanish conquest of Peru. Hemming, who was only 35 when *Conquest* was published, has written nearly a dozen books about Inca architecture and the native people of the Amazon.

Heyerdahl, Thor, and Daniel Sandweiss. *The Quest for Peru's Forgotten City.* London: Thames and Hudson, 1995. Norwegian explorer Thor Heyerdahl was most famous for piloting the *Kon-Tiki* balsa-wood raft from Callao, Peru, to the Polynesian Islands in 1947. From 1988 until he died in 2002, Heyerdahl's obsession with early ocean travel focused on the inhabitants of Túcume, a complex of 26 pyramids north of present-day Trujillo that was built by the Sicán culture around AD 1050. This remains the best work on Túcume.

Kirkpatrick, Sidney. *Lords of Sipán: A True Story of Pre-Inca Tombs, Archaeology, and Crime.* New York: William Morrow, 1992. Shortly after grave robbers unearthed a royal tomb of the Sipán culture near present-day Trujillo, Sidney Kirkpatrick documented the underworld of artifact smugglers and their Hollywood clients. At the center of this real-life drama is Peruvian archaeologist Walter Alva, who struggles against an entire town as he fights to preserve his country's heritage.

MacQuarrie, Kim. *The Last Days of the Incas.* New York: Simon & Schuster, 2007. Peru travelers with time to read just one book should read *The Last Days of the Incas,* written by an Emmy Award-winning author and filmmaker with years of life experience in Peru. MacQuarrie has produced what is, beyond a doubt, the most readable, fast-moving, and factual account of Peru's Spanish conquest. He describes the conquest and its aftermath in detail and integrates both 16th-century Spanish chronicles and recent historical research. Unlike the more scholarly *Conquest of the Incas,* by

John Hemming, *The Last Days* does not end with the collapse of the Inca empire—the final chapters are devoted to 20th-century explorers such as Hiram Bingham, who was credited with rediscovering Machu Picchu, and Gene Savoy, who discovered the real "lost city" of the Inca—Vilcabamba.

Mosley, Michael. *The Incas and Their Ancestors*. London: Thames and Hudson, 1993. This masterly work is still the best general introduction to the history of Peru's early cultures, including the Nasca, Moche, Huari, and Tiahuanaco.

Muscutt, Keith. *Warriors of the Clouds: A Lost Civilization in the Upper Amazon of Peru*. Albuquerque: University of New Mexico, 1998. This book provides a good overview of what archaeologists know of the Chachapoya, a cantankerous cloud-forest empire that was never dominated by the Inca. The book is replete with beautiful images of ruins in the remote cloud forest of northeastern Peru.

Protzen, Jean-Pierre. *Inka Architecture and Construction at Ollantaytambo*. Oxford: Oxford University Press, 1993. Jean-Pierre Protzen spent years at the Inca site of Ollantaytambo in order to understand its historical significance and construction. This hard-to-find book is the best single work on Ollantaytambo, the most important Inca ruin next to Machu Picchu.

Savoy, Gene. *Antisuyo: The Search for the Lost Cities of the Amazon*. New York: Simon & Schuster, 1970. Gene Savoy, who is second only to Hiram Bingham in his knack for sniffing out lost cities, describes in somewhat stilted prose his search for Espíritu Pampa, the last stronghold of the Inca.

Starn, Orin, Carlos Iván Degregori, and Rob Kirk, eds. *The Peru Reader*. Durham, NC: Duke University Press, 1995. This is a great paperback to bring on the airplane or a long train ride, stuffed with an endlessly entertaining and eclectic collection of short stories, anthropological essays, translated chronicles, and a bit of poetry.

Von Hagen, Adriana, and Craig Morris. *The Cities of the Ancient Andes*. Thames and Hudson: London, 1998. Writer Adriana von Hagen, daughter of the renowned German-born Peruvianist Victor von Hagen, and a curator of New York's America Museum of Natural History teamed up for this highly recommended introduction to Peru's major archaeological sites. This is the most concise and accessible history of Peru's ancient cultures, written around the centers and cities they left behind.

CHRONICLES

Cieza de León, Pedro. *The Discovery and Conquest of Peru: The New World Encounter*. Durham, NC: Duke University Press, 1999. Pedro Cieza de León arrived in Peru in 1547 as a wide-eyed 27-year-old, and he proceeded to explore every nook and cranny, describing everything as he went. He is the first Spaniard to describe Spanish mistreatment of Peru's natives. His reliable voice paints the Spanish-Inca encounter in simple and clear language.

Garcilaso de la Vega, Inca, and Harold Livermore, translator. *Royal Commentaries of the Inca and General History of Peru*. Austin: University of Texas Press, 1966. Inca Garcilaso was the son of a conquistador and an Inca princess who moved to Spain in his youth and spent the rest of his life documenting the myths, culture, and history of the Inca. Though criticized for historical inaccuracies and exaggeration, Inca Garcilaso's 1,000-page *Royal Commentaries* contains subtitles that make this work easy to thumb through.

Poma de Ayala, Felipe Guamán. *Nueva Crónica y Buen Gobierno*. This magnificent 16th-century manuscript has become the New World's best-known indigenous chronicle since it was discovered in the Royal Library of Copenhagen in 1908. It is a 1,200-page history of the Spanish conquest, told from the Andean point of view in an eclectic mixture of Quechua and Spanish. Its harangues against Spanish injustice are complemented by 400 drawings made by Poma de Ayala. Parts of this text, which was intended as a letter to Spanish king Philip III, have been translated into English and are published on the Internet at www.kb.dk/permalink/2006/poma/info/en/frontpage.htm.

LITERATURE

Alarcón, Daniel. *War by Candlelight: Stories.* New York: Harper Perennial, 2006. Born in Peru and raised in Birmingham, Alabama, Alarcón returned to Peru on a Fulbright scholarship. He wrote a series of short stories that evoke the sorrows and beauty of a ravaged land with a precision and steadiness that stand in inverse proportion to the magnitude of the losses he so powerfully dramatizes. Floods and earthquakes destroy what little equilibrium remains in a relentlessly violent world in which the authorities and the rebels are equally vicious and corrupt.

Alegria, Ciro. *Broad and Alien Is the World.* Chester Spring, PA: Dufour Editions. This award-winning lyric novel (*El Mundo Es Ancho y Ajeno,* 1941) was written by a celebrated Peruvian novelist who spent his career documenting the oppression of Peru's indigenous peoples. Look also for Alegria's other classic, *The Golden Serpent* (*La Serpiente de Oro*). The Spanish versions of these works are available in most bookstores in Peru.

Bryce Echenique, Alfredo. *A World for Julius.* Madison: University of Wisconsin Press, 2004. Bryce Echenique explores Peruvian society while describing a world of illusion created for little Julius, who eventually will have to fit perfectly in this society.

A true masterpiece from one of Peru's top novelists.

Vargas Llosa, Mario. *Aunt Julia and the Scriptwriter.* New York: Penguin, 1995. This autobiographical tale of taboo mixes radio scripts with the steamy romance that a young radio writer carries on with his aunt—this is Vargas Llosa with Julia Urquidi, who became his first wife. This was one of Vargas Llosa's first novels revealing a glimpse into highbrow Lima society.

Vargas Llosa, Mario. *Captain Pantoja and the Secret Service.* New York: Harper Collins, 1978. This is the funny and ludicrous story of a faithful soldier, Pantaleón Pantoja, and his mission to begin a top-secret prostitution service for Peru's military in Iquitos, Peru. His problem is that he is too successful.

Vargas Llosa, Mario. *Conversation in the Cathedral.* New York: Harper Perennial, 2005. This is one of Vargas Llosa's masterworks. *Conversation in the Cathedral* takes place in 1950s Peru during the dictatorship of Manuel A. Odría. Over beers and a sea of freely spoken words, the conversation flows between Santiago and Ambrosio, who talk of their tormented lives and of the overall degradation and frustration that has slowly taken over their city. Through a complicated web of secrets and historical references, Vargas Llosa analyzes the mental and moral mechanisms that govern power and the people behind it. It is a groundbreaking novel that tackles identity as well as the role of a citizen and how a lack of personal freedom can forever scar people and a nation.

Vargas Llosa, Mario. *The Green House.* New York: Harper Perennial, 2005. Vargas Llosa's classic early novel takes place in a Peruvian town, between desert and jungle, where Don Anselmo, a stranger in a black coat, builds a brothel, bringing together the innocent and the corrupt: Bonificia, a young indigenous girl saved by the nuns, who becomes a prostitute; Father García, struggling for the church; and four best friends drawn to both excitement and escape.

TRAVEL AND EXPLORATION

Bingham, Hiram. *Phoenix: Lost City of the Incas.* Edited by Hugh Thomson. London: Phoenix Press, 2003. Bingham's classic description of how he discovered Machu Picchu lends historical detail to Peru's standout attraction and also explains why Bingham went on to become the leading inspiration for movie character Indiana Jones.

Kane, Joe. *Running the Amazon.* New York: Vintage, 1990. Starting from a glacier at 17,000 feet, Joe Kane and a team of adventurers attempted the never-before-done feat of navigating the entire length of the Amazon River from source to mouth. The story begins as an accurate description of life in Peru's highlands and ends with the difficulties of managing personalities in a modern-day expedition.

Lee, Vincent. *Sixpac Manco: Travels Among the Incas.* This self-published book is a must-read for Vilcabamba explorers and is available at the South American Explorers Club in Lima. It is out of print, but used copies can be found at Amazon.com or other Internet sites that sell used books. The book comes with highly accurate maps of the area around Espíritu Pampa and has an amusing, shoot-from-the-hip adventurer's attitude.

Mathiessen, Peter. *At Play in the Fields of the Lord.* New York: Vintage, 1991. Set in a malarial jungle outpost, this Mathiessen classic depicts the clash of development and indigenous peoples in the Amazon jungle. It was made into a motion picture as well.

Muller, Karin. *Along the Inca Road, A Woman's Journey into an Ancient Empire.* Washington, D.C.: National Geographic, 2000.

The author traces her 3,000-mile journey along Inca roads in Ecuador, Peru, Bolivia, and Chile. Along the way she shares her insights about modern exploration and Inca history.

Schneebaum, Tobias. *Keep the River on Your Right.* New York: Grove Press: 1998. In 1955, New York intellectual Tobias Schneebaum spent eight years living with the Akarama tribe in the remote Madre de Dios jungle. His book describes his participation in homosexual and cannibalistic rituals and became an immediate jungle classic when it was published in 1969.

Shah, Tahir. *Trail of Feathers: In Search of the Birdmen of Peru.* London: Orion Publishing, 2002. A 16th-century mention of Inca who "flew like birds" over the jungle leads one journalist on a quest to unlock the secret of Peru's so-called birdmen. His journey takes him to Machu Picchu, the Nasca Lines, and finally into the Amazon itself.

Thomson, Hugh. *The White Rock, An Exploration of the Inca Heartland.* New York: Overlook Press, 2001. British documentary filmmaker Hugh Thomson returns to Vilcabamba, where he explored in his early 20s, to weave a recollection of his travels together with an alluring blend of Spanish chronicles and Inca history. It contains vivid, sometimes scathing, depictions of local personalities and makes for a fast, exciting way to read up for a Peru trip.

TRAVEL GUIDES

Frost, Peter. *Exploring Cusco,* 5th ed. Lima: Nuevas Imágenes, 1999. This book continues to be one of the best-written, most readable historical and archaeological approaches to the Cusco area, written by long-time Cusco resident Peter Frost.

Wust, Walter, et al. *Inca Guide to Peru.* Lima: Peisa, 2003. This excellent highway guide, sponsored by Mitsubishi, contains the country's best road maps and detailed descriptions of all the driving routes. There is also some historical and cultural information on each of Peru's main destinations, though little information on hotels and restaurants. This company has also published *Guia Inca de Playas,* which runs down all the remote camping and surfing spots along Peru's coast from Tumbes to Tacna. These books are for sale in Ripley department stores and most Lima bookstores.

Zarzar, Omar. *Por los Caminos de Peru en Bicicleta.* Lima: Editor SA, 2001. This is a guide to Peru's best mountain-biking routes. Though written in Spanish, the maps and itineraries are useful even for non-Spanish speakers.

BIRDING

Clements, James, and Noam Shany. *A Field Guide to the Birds of Peru.* Temecula, CA: Ibis Publishing Company, 2001. Though much criticized by bird-watchers for its faulty pictures of certain birds, this US$60 tome catalogs nearly 1,800 birds known to reside in, or migrate to, Peru. This is the best alternative for birders unable to afford *Birds of Peru.*

Krabbe, Nils, and John Fjeldsa. *Birds of the High Andes.* Copenhagen: Denmark Zoological Museum of the University of Copenhagen, 1990. Birders consider this a must-have masterpiece. It includes all the birds you are likely to encounter in the temperate and alpine zones of Peru.

Schulenberg, Thomas, Douglas Stotz, Daniel Lane, and John O'Neill. *Birds of Peru (Princeton Field Guides).* Sanibel Island, FL: Ralph Curtis Books, 2007. This long-awaited bible of Peru birding is coveted by every professional bird guide in Peru. It represents a huge step forward and was a colossal undertaking, as reflected by its beautiful color renderings of birds and its high price tag.

Valqui, Thomas. *Where to Watch Birds in Peru.* 1st ed. Peru, 2004. This comprehensive self-published guide to birding in Peru explains not only what birds you'll see where, but how to get there and where you might stay along the way. This is an excellent resource, and there's nothing else like it on the market. The book is now out of print, but you may be able to find a used copy.

Walker, Barry, and Jon Fjeldsa, illustrations. *Field Guide to the Birds of Machu Picchu.* Lima: Peruvian National Trust for Parks and Protected Areas, 2005. This portable guide, written by Cusco's foremost bird expert and owner of Manu Expeditions, is available in Cusco. It has 31 superb color plates and descriptions of 420 species.

PHOTOGRAPHY

Milligan, Max. *Realm of the Incas.* New York: Universe Publishing, 2001. English photographer Max Milligan spent years trekking to the remote corners of Peru to capture images that range from the sacred snows of Nevado Ausangate to the torpid meanderings of the Río Manu.

Weintraub, Adam L. *Vista Andina. A Photographic Perspective on Contemporary Life in the Andes.* PhotoExperience.net, 2010. Seattle-based photographer Adam Weintraub explores Cusco and its surroundings through his lens, attempting a journalistic and zealous look into the intimate world of the city's inhabitants.

FOOD

Acurio, Gastón. *Peru: Una Aventura Culinaria.* Lima: Quebecor World Peru, 2002. This large-format photo book written in Spanish profiles Peru's array of foods in chapters titled Water, Land, and Air. It includes a range of recipes and profiles of Peru's leading chefs and is available in Lima bookshops.

Custer, Tony. *The Art of Peruvian Cuisine.* Lima: Cimino Publishing Group, 2003. This book has high-quality photos and an excellent selection of Peruvian recipes in both Spanish and English.

Morales, Edmund. *The Guinea Pig: Healing, Food, and Ritual in the Andes.* Tucson: University of Arizona Press, 1995. This is the first major study, with good pictures, of how Andean highlanders not only eat guinea pig but also use it for medicinal and religious purposes.

PromPeru. *Perú Mucho Gusto.* Lima: Comisión de Promoción del Peru, 2006. This Spanish-English book is a glamorous large-format cookbook. Starting with the history of the country's cooking, the book gives a general overview of Peru's traditional cooking. The last chapter is dedicated to the creative chefs who will lead Peru's cooking into the future. Available in Lima bookstores.

SPIRITUAL AND ESOTERIC

Milla, Carlos. *Genesis de la Cultura Andina.* 3rd ed. Lima: Fondo Editorial C. A. P., 1983. If you can read Spanish, this book presents esoteric theories based on many of Peru's ancient ceremonial centers. Milla's 2003 book, *Ayni: Semiotica Andina de los Espacios Sagrados,* focuses on astrology.

Villoldo, Alberto, and Erik Jendresen. *The Four Winds: A Shaman's Odyssey into the Amazon.* New York: Harper Collins, 1991. Even Peru's shamans respect this work, which documents the author's spiritual initiation into Amazon rituals.

WEAVING

Heckman, Andrea. *Woven Stories: Andean Textiles and Rituals.* Albuquerque: University of New Mexico Press, 2003. A series of ethnographic essays on Andean life and weaving by a researcher with two decades in the field.

Pollard Rowe, Anne, and John Cohen. *Hidden Threads of Peru: Q'ero Textiles.* London: Merrell Publishers, 2002. In vibrant pictures and concise prose, this book documents the extraordinary weavings of Q'ero, a remote town in south Peru where the authors have been researching for nearly four decades.

CHILDREN

Hergé, *The Adventures of Tintin: Prisoners of the Sun,* 1949. In this Hergé classic, a sequel to *The Seven Crystal Balls,* Tintin, Captain Haddock, and Milou catch a steamer to Peru to rescue a kidnapped professor. The adventure leads them through the Andes and the Amazon, which are depicted in fascinating detail and through the romanticized lens of the mid-20th century.

Internet Resources

TRAVEL INFORMATION

Andean Travel Web
www.andeantravelweb.com
This is the best of several Peru-based websites that evaluate hotels, restaurants, and agencies.

Expat Peru
www.expatperu.com
A very useful directory for expats.

Living in Peru
www.peruthisweek.com
A directory of resources for foreigners living and traveling in Peru.

Peru Links
www.perulinks.com
This huge website of links lists tons of hard-to-find Peru websites, including gay and

lesbian clubs, alternative medicine, chat rooms, and more.

Peru Travel
www.peru.travel
The Peruvian Tourist Office's comprehensive website.

South American Explorers
www.saexplorers.org
This web page for the South American Explorers Club has books for sale, information on insurance providers, an online bulletin board, and interesting links.

GOVERNMENT RESOURCES

U.S. Department of State Peru country profile
http://travel.state.gov/
Click on "Peru" in the country menu.

U.S. Embassy in Peru
http://lima.usembassy.gov
Useful for immigration information and emergency contacts.

Presidency of Peru
www.presidencia.gob.pe
The latest news and views from Peru's government.

LANGUAGE

SpanishDICT.com
www.spanishdict.com
Online Spanish dictionary.

Study Spanish
www.studyspanish.com
Free, award-winning online tutorial.

NEWS AND MEDIA

Miami Herald
http://www.miamiherald.com/news/nation-world/world/americas/
The best English-language daily coverage of Latin America.

The Peruvian Times
www.peruviantimes.com
Lima's oldest English-language publishing house is the best for getting news as well as a directory of expat and international organizations.

South America Daily
www.southamericadaily.com
Compilation of latest news stories from media across the continent.

Weather.com
www.weather.com
Five-day and ten-day forecasts throughout Ecuador.

FLIGHT INFORMATION

Lima Airport
www.lap.com.pe
This is the home page of the Jorge Chávez International Airport in Lima.

Tráfico
www.traficoperu.com
This agency newsletter is an updated list of all international and domestic flights in Peru.

OTHER USEFUL WEBSITES

Culture of the Andes
www.andes.org
A labor of love from Peru fanatics Russ and Ada Gibbons, this site focusing on Andean culture includes short stories, jokes, music, songs in Quechua, poetry, and riddles.

Peru Surf Guides
www.perusurfguides.com
Peru's most popular website for surfing and ocean conditions along the coast.

Index

NOP

QR

S

List of Maps

Photo Credits

Also Available

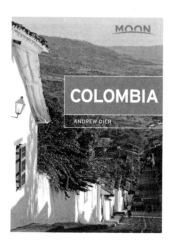

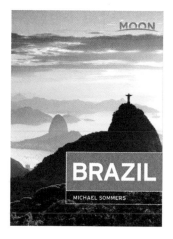

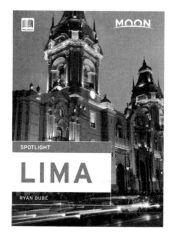